AND KEEP MOVING ON

GREAT CAMPAIGNS OF THE CIVIL WAR

SERIES EDITORS

Anne J. Bailey
Georgia College &
State University

Brooks D. Simpson
Arizona State University

MARK GRIMSLEY

And Keep Moving On

The Virginia Campaign, May–June 1864

University of Nebraska Press
Lincoln and London

© 2002 by the University of Nebraska Press
All rights reserved
Manufactured in the United States of America
⊗
Library of Congress Cataloging-in-Publication Data
Grimsley, Mark.
And keep moving on : the Virginia campaign,
May–June 1864 / Mark Grimsley.
p. cm.—(Great campaigns of the Civil War)
Includes bibliographical references (p.) and index.
ISBN 0-8032-2162-2 (cloth : alk. paper)
ISBN 0-8032-7119-0 (paper : alk. paper)
1. Virginia—History—Civil War, 1861–1865—Campaigns.
2. United States—History—Civil War,
1861–1865—Campaigns.   I. Title.   II. Series.
E476.5 .G75 2002
973.7'455—dc21
2002005683

For Allan R. Millett

Semper Fidelis

Contents

Illustrations

Maps

Series Editors' Introduction

Americans remain fascinated by the Civil War. Movies, television, and video—even computer software—have augmented the ever-expanding list of books on the war. Although it stands to reason that a large portion of recent work concentrates on military aspects of the conflict, historians have expanded our scope of inquiry to include civilians, especially women; the destruction of slavery and the evolving understanding of what freedom meant to millions of former slaves; and an even greater emphasis on the experiences of the common soldier on both sides. Other studies have demonstrated the interrelationships of war, politics, and policy and how civilians' concerns back home influenced both soldiers and politicians. Although one cannot fully comprehend this central event in American history without understanding that military operations were fundamental in determining the course and outcome of the war, it is time for students of battles and campaigns to incorporate nonmilitary themes in their accounts. The most pressing challenge facing Civil War scholarship today is the integration of various perspectives and emphases into a new narrative that explains not only what happened, why, and how but also why it mattered.

The series Great Campaigns of the Civil War offers readers concise syntheses of the major campaigns of the war, reflecting the findings of recent scholarship. The series points to new ways of viewing military campaigns by looking beyond the battlefield and the headquarters tent to the wider political and social context within which these campaigns unfolded; it also shows how campaigns and battles left their imprint on many Americans, from presidents and generals down to privates and civilians. The ends and means of waging war reflect larger political objectives and priorities as well as social values. Historians may continue to debate among themselves as to which of these campaigns constituted true turning points, but each of the campaigns treated in this series contributed to shaping the course of the conflict, opening opportunities, and eliminating alternatives.

The Overland campaign of 1864 pitted the two leading generals of the war in a six-week struggle across central Virginia. Ulysses S. Grant came east with an impressive string of military triumphs to his credit; nevertheless, he sensed the whispers circulating around the headquarters of the Army of the Potomac that he had yet to meet Robert E. Lee, whose victories in Virginia served as proof of his extraordinary abilities. Observers speculated that this clash of titans would decide the outcome of the war. Yet, as Mark Grimsley so ably explains, some six weeks of relentless combat resulted in Grant laying siege to Petersburg and the Confederate capital at Richmond. The human cost had been horrendous: The various campaigns claimed some one hundred thousand men as casualties, and many other soldiers were exhausted by the continual grinding. Moreover, Grant's other Virginia offensives had come to grief, due in large part to the bungling of subordinates who owed their jobs to their political influence. It had not been the campaign Grant had envisioned, but it was one he was prepared to fight, as was Lee. The Confederate commander confided to a subordinate that if Grant's men commenced siege operations, it would be only a matter of time before they would claim victory. But in an election year, time was precious indeed, and it looked to many voters in the North as if the two major field armies were stalemated. Grant would have to look elsewhere if his overall grand strategic plan was to succeed; at best he had come close to nullifying Lee's ability to wrest the initiative away as he had done so often in the past.

Grimsley's assessment of the performances of Grant and Lee is sure to provoke discussion. Equally rewarding is his treatment of the impact of this new style of war on the officers and men of both armies. Conscripts and bounty hunters were no replacement for the veterans of three years of war, a good number of whom were counting the days until they could go home and crossing their fingers that they would survive that long. Both the Army of the Potomac and the Army of Northern Virginia gave as good as it got during those six weeks of spring, and neither was ever quite the same again.

Preface

"The art of war," maintained Lt. Gen. Ulysses S. Grant, "is simple enough. Find out where your enemy is. Get at him as soon as you can. Strike at him as hard as you can and as often as you can, and keep moving on."[1] By the spring of 1864, Grant had demonstrated that philosophy in a series of campaigns that marked him as the North's preeminent commander. In gratitude, and with the expectation that he would win the war, President Abraham Lincoln placed him in charge of all Union forces. Of his own accord, Grant soon placed himself with the Army of the Potomac, the nation's largest, most famous, and arguably least successful fighting force.

The hard luck that plagued this army stemmed primarily from the skill and élan of its opponent, the Army of Northern Virginia, led by Gen. Robert E. Lee. Although destined to be depicted as very different commanders—Grant the bludgeoner, Lee the master of maneuver—in reality the two commanders were almost identical in style. The art of war, as Grant expressed it, fit Lee's approach as well as it did his own. Both men believed in seizing the initiative and attacking fast and hard. They were unafraid to mix things up. They could improvise. They would keep moving on. And above all, they would not concede defeat if they could possibly help it.

Grant's presence with the Army of the Potomac, and Lee's command of the Army of Northern Virginia, ensured that the spring campaign of 1864 would pit the Civil War's two most successful generals against one another in a duel that became legendary almost before it began. And because both men were such fierce champions of the offensive, the resulting encounter saw the most savage, sustained fighting of the entire war.

Indeed, the conflict had previously seen nothing like it. Apart from sieges, Civil War armies had hitherto been in direct contact for only brief periods. The titanic struggle at Gettysburg, for example, took three days; the misnamed Seven Days' battles lasted about six, with a one-day break in contact. By contrast, when the Army of the Potomac crossed the Rapidan River on May 4, 1864, it began a continuous monthlong grapple with the Army of Northern Virginia.

The fighting was not restricted to a duel between Grant and Lee, either. In order to maximize his chance of success, Grant put into motion virtually every Union soldier in the eastern theater. As a result, the struggle between the main armies—eventually dubbed the Overland campaign—was only part of a larger offensive that included major expeditions in western and southeastern Virginia as well as numerous impromptu raids aimed at the Confederate transportation infrastructure. Grant and Lee not only had to take these maneuvers into account; they often supervised them as well. It is therefore better to think, as they did themselves, in terms of a single, massive Virginia campaign of spring 1864.

Grant confronted Lee with four subsidiary offensives in addition to the Army of the Potomac's main advance: two in southwestern Virginia against Confederate saltworks, lead mines, and railroads; a third in the Shenandoah Valley under Maj. Gen. Franz Sigel; and a fourth in the James River estuary under Maj. Gen. Benjamin F. Butler. Grant intended these lesser offensives to divert strength from Lee's army and, if possible, to achieve significant results on their own. He had particularly high expectations of Butler, believing that Butler could threaten Richmond, interdict Confederate communications with the Deep South, and help place Lee at a ruinous disadvantage. But by shifting their outnumbered forces adroitly, the Confederates thwarted Grant's offensive at every turn, defeating Sigel and Butler and administering sharp checks to the Army of the Potomac in the battles of the Wilderness, Spotsylvania, the North Anna, and Cold Harbor.

The outcome of the campaign depends on one's point of view. Then and later, some have argued that Lee outgeneraled Grant, forcing him to accept the ten-month stalemate in the Richmond-Petersburg trenches. Others have maintained that Grant won because he kept up the pressure. Although Lee parried his adversary's thrusts, the one thing he could not do was to force Grant to relinquish the initiative. After each reversal, the Union general in chief simply revised his plans and pressed onward. Indecisive in itself, the Virginia campaign nevertheless became an archetype of Federal strategy during the war's final year: to make the enemy's armies the main focus of attack; to gain success through maneuver if possible, by attrition if not; to attack the Confederate supply system; to use the North's advantage in manpower and matériel to maximum advantage; and above all else, to maintain continual pressure against the Confederacy. In doing so, the logic runs, Grant doomed Lee to eventual defeat at Appomattox.

But whatever else it may be, the story of the Virginia campaign is also about the demise of two great armies. At the outset, in May 1864, the Confederate Army of Northern Virginia and the Union Army of the Potomac still had much the same command structure and esprit de corps as in the days of Antietam, Chancellorsville, and Gettysburg. By its close, Lee's army had lost a third of its senior leadership, about thirty-three thousand of its best troops, and most of its offensive capability. The same could be said of Meade's army—or Grant's army, as the press insisted on calling it. Over fifty-five thousand Federals were killed, wounded, or captured in the forty days of the campaign. Thousands more left the army because their enlistments had expired. Losses in the officer corps were just as heavy as among the Confederates. The remaining commanders noted that their troops were no longer as responsive as they had once been. They attacked sluggishly, tentatively. Sometimes they refused to attack at all. In short, both armies emerged from the campaign as shadows of their former selves.

In that sense, the campaign is unique in U.S. history—an American Golgotha with more in common with Verdun than Belleau Wood, Normandy, even Iwo Jima or the Chosin Reservoir. For that reason, simply to record the casualty figures seems inadequate, even a bit obscene, as if one were using human bone and gristle as a score card to measure which side was up or down. Thus, this book devotes an entire chapter to the human suffering generated by the Virginia campaign and its impact on the two home fronts as well as the troops themselves.

Even so, it does not present the action primarily from the viewpoint of the common soldiers who fought it. On the contrary, its focus remains on the senior command: Grant, Lee, Meade, their corps commanders, and key subordinates such as P. G. T. Beauregard, Benjamin F. Butler, Franz Sigel, and John C. Breckinridge. This approach would not have appealed to Leo Tolstoy, who was giving life to his majestic *War and Peace* even as the Armies of the Potomac and Northern Virginia grappled in the Wilderness.

To emphasize the role played by military commanders, Tolstoy maintained, is all wrong. On the contrary, in words that anticipated the sociocultural historians of our own day, he argued that to study the laws of history, one must entirely change the subject under observation, away from elites (who only seem to be in control) and toward "the common, infinitesimally small elements that influence the masses." Napoleon, Tolstoy insisted, did not win the battle of Borodino, but merely "played his part as the representative of authority.... He did nothing to hinder the progress of the battle; he inclined to the most reasonable opinions, created no confusion, did not contradict himself, lose his head, or flee the battlefield, but, with his sound judgment and great military experience, calmly and competently performed his role of appearing to be in command."[2] Much the same could be said of Grant, who whittled on a stick while the Union army battled in the Wilderness, or of Lee, who passively remained at his headquarters while his troops fought the battle of Cold Harbor. What Tolstoy overlooked, however, was that these men initiate the battle and give meaning to the outcome (Grant sending the Army of the Potomac south after the two-day fight in the Wilderness being perhaps the classic example). Indeed, making sense of any campaign without reference to the perspectives of those in charge of it is hard. In that respect, the commanders create the narrative. Moreover, Tolstoy was unfair to senior commanders even as regards their role in the fighting, for the senior leadership often chooses when and where to send in additional troops and, occasionally, inspires the troops by their personal presence on the field (the "Lee to the rear" episodes in the Wilderness and at Spotsylvania are classic examples of that).

I have dissented from Tolstoy in a third respect as well. Unlike the great novelist, who viewed military commanders somewhat as pompous marionettes, I have evaluated the principal leaders as sympathetically as possible, always bearing in mind that they were intelligent men who operated under extraordinary conditions and pressures. True, to write is to judge, and ultimately I have made judgments that are sometimes harsh, but I have encountered few historical actors—even such perennial goats as Ben Butler—for whom I could not muster at least some respect.

Finally, I have been impressed by the way in which this campaign—like Napoleon's Russian campaign, where Tolstoy set his novel—quickly became, in part, a mythical campaign, a duel between Grant the butcher and Lee the fox. The concluding chapter shows how interpretations of the campaign that began while it was still under way metamorphosed into interpretations that served various postwar agendas, but particularly those of the Lost Cause. Indeed, the Overland campaign remains, more than any other, the *locus classicus* of the Southern myth that the Confederacy was defeated not by insufficient valor, poor strategy, or internal strains but rather by the stronger battalions. The Confederates ended the campaign in the certain belief that they had won a solid triumph over their Yankee assailants, with the prospect of independence still bright. Memory changed that. As one prominent Confederate officer summarized the outcome in retrospect, "However bold we might be, however desperately we might fight, we were sure in the end to be worn out. It was only a question of a few months, more or less."[3]

Acknowledgments

This is primarily a work of synthesis. As such, my foremost thanks are due to the authors of the specialized studies on which it is based. They are noted in the section on "Further Reading," but one historian, Gordon C. Rhea, merits special mention. His multivolume study of the Overland campaign, though still incomplete, is already an extraordinary resource, and when finished will stand as a model of how to write Civil War operational history.

Thanks are also due to numerous archives for their courtesy in providing access to manuscript sources and illustrations. These include the U.S. Army Military History Institute, Carlisle Barracks, Pennsylvania; National Archives and Library of Congress, Washington; Valentine Museum, Richmond, Virginia; and Virginia Military Institute Archives, Lexington. And I appreciate the fine efforts of my cartographer, Chris Brest, who translated a raft of sketches into the excellent maps that grace this book.

If plentiful maps are indispensable to the study of military operations, there is no substitute for seeing the terrain over which the armies moved and fought. I benefited substantially from multiple visits to the campaign's many battlefields, most of which are preserved within the Fredericksburg and Spotsylvania National Military Park and Richmond National Battlefield Park. The New Market Battlefield Park is worthy of note, while the recently established North Anna Battlefield Park permits access to perhaps the best preserved expanse of Civil War field fortifications in the country.

Knowledgeable friends accompanied me on many of these forays, among them Noel Harrison of the National Park Service; Col. William

Odom, U.S. Army; and Prof. Matthew Oyos of Radford University. I'm grateful for both their insights and the general pleasure of their company.

Thanks to a combination of initial hubris, bouts with ill health, and unexpected professional demands, this book took years longer to complete than originally planned. I'm grateful to both Daniel J. J. Ross, former director of the University of Nebraska Press, and the series editors, Anne J. Bailey and Brooks D. Simpson. Their patience and understanding have been extraordinary.

Three anonymous readers for the press made valuable suggestions that greatly helped the final product. So did two readers who, over the years, have repeatedly extended me the gift of their time, effort, and judgment. Timothy S. Hartley of Vandalia, Ohio, appraised the book's first draft, telling me what worked and what didn't. And Prof. Peter Maslowski of the University of Nebraska at Lincoln read the penultimate draft with his unique combination of cheerful encouragement and ruthless criticism, particularly in matters of style.

Finally, this book is dedicated to Allan R. Millett, Colonel, USMC (Ret.), as well as the Raymond Mason Professor of Military History at the Ohio State University. For over twenty years, Allan has been, successively, my undergraduate instructor, graduate adviser, and colleague. He is one of a handful of scholars whose vision and energy made military history a viable academic discipline, yet one that unabashedly retains its engagement with both the national security community and the general reader. Allan's breadth of knowledge, incisive mind, extensive scholarship, and professional leadership—to say nothing of the dozens of doctoral students he has produced over the years—make him an example impossible to emulate. He is sui generis, the most omnicompetent person I have ever met.

AND KEEP MOVING ON

CHAPTER ONE

Campaign Plans and Politics

Spring had come, but barely, the day a train carrying Lt. Gen. Ulysses S. Grant wheezed into Culpeper Court House, Virginia. Once a thriving market town fifty miles southwest of Washington DC, Culpeper had become the locus of the Army of the Potomac's winter encampment, a vast domain of smoke, guns, and mud-stained soldiers. A chill afternoon downpour washed away the last of the winter snow. It was March 25, 1864. The war was edging into its fourth year.[1]

Grant emerged from the train without fanfare, looking more like a headquarters clerk than the general in chief of the Union armies. He cultivated a phlegmatic air, low-key, not austere but immensely reserved. Lt. Col. Theodore Lyman, a Harvard-educated staff officer who saw him around this time, described the famous general as having "somewhat the air of a Yankee schoolmaster, buttoned in a military coat." He was quiet, even taciturn, but beneath the calm exterior Lyman glimpsed a vein of iron. "[Grant] habitually wears an expression as if he had determined to drive his head through a brick wall, and was about to do it. I have much confidence in him."[2]

Lyman's faith stemmed from more than Grant's appearance. By 1864 he was the North's preeminent general, having captured two Confederate armies (at Fort Donelson and Vicksburg), repelled a third (Shiloh), and driven a fourth in full retreat from a formidable defensive position (Chattanooga). But the way in which Grant seemed not to notice his own success, his simple attention to business, only added to his mystique. At Chattanooga, for example, the Union army had been besieged by a Confederate army entrenched on the mountains overlooking the city. The troops inside the town had been virtually cut off from the outside world, and they were hungry and demoralized. Everything seemed to change when Grant showed up. "We began to see things move," one veteran recalled. "We felt everything came from a plan. He came into the army quietly, no splendor, no airs, no staff. He used to go about alone. He began the campaign the moment he reached the field."[3]

Within weeks, Grant had organized the counterpunch that broke the Confederate army's grip on Chattanooga and sent it reeling into Georgia. For that, President Abraham Lincoln decided to place him in charge of all the Union armies, with the revived rank of lieutenant general, a grade previously held only by George Washington.[4]

Grant was not quite forty-two years old when he became general in chief. He replaced forty-nine-year-old Henry Wager Halleck, who had assumed the post in July 1862 after presiding over a notable string of Union victories in the western theater. Halleck was not sorry to relinquish the job. As general in chief, he had adopted the principle that he ought not give field commanders specific instructions. Only the general on the spot, he believed, could know the true situation and make fully informed decisions. For that reason he usually stopped short of giving direct orders, much to Lincoln's dismay. On one occasion, when Halleck refused to tell a subordinate what specific course to take, the president erupted, "If in such a difficulty as this you do not help, you fail me precisely in the point for which I sought your assistance." Halleck refused to bend and instead offered to resign in light of the "very important difference of opinion" that divided them. Lincoln grudgingly withdrew his complaint, but thereafter regarded Halleck as merely "a first-rate clerk."[5]

After Grant took over, Halleck stayed on as army chief of staff—a position which, wisecracked one general, was "very much like a fellow marrying a woman with the understanding that he should not *sleep* with her." But Halleck did not mind. He continued to function much as he had done previously, coordinating the vast military-administrative responsibilities of the War Department and Army Headquarters.[6]

Grant, unlike his predecessor, had few qualms about giving subordinates precise direction. Indeed, his conception for the coming campaign of 1864 depended upon an activist command style. He intended for all the Union's field forces to begin offensive operations at the same time and in accordance with a common plan. This was a sharp departure from earlier practice, when most field commanders selected objectives and timetables themselves. In a famous simile, Grant said that previously Union armies had acted "like a balky team, no two ever pulling together," thus enabling the Confederates to shift their own forces from one threatened point to another. The result had largely negated the Federal advantage in numbers.[7]

The new general in chief also observed that a great many Northern troops were passively defending one or another strategic point. It struck him as a needless waste of manpower: They could shield these points as effectively by advancing as by standing still. And by moving forward, they would put additional pressure on the Confederates and divert strength away from the main Union armies. When Grant explained the new policy to Lincoln, the president acted impressed. "Oh! yes, I see that," he exclaimed in his homespun way. "As we say out West, if a man can't skin he must hold a leg while somebody else does." In fact, as those intimate with the president well knew, Lincoln had been fruitlessly pushing such a policy for years.[8]

Grant planned for two offensives in the western theater: the first from Chattanooga into northern Georgia, to be led by his friend and confidant, Maj. Gen. William T. Sherman; the second against Mobile, Alabama, led by Maj. Gen. Nathaniel P. Banks. Sherman would launch the combined armies of the Tennessee, Cumberland, and Ohio—over one hundred thousand men in all—against fewer than sixty thousand Confederates of Gen. Joseph E. Johnston's Army of Tennessee. Although Sherman would head generally for the Southern industrial and rail city of Atlanta, his specific objective, Grant stipulated, was Johnston's army. Sherman was to "break it up," then inflict all possible damage upon Confederate war resources in the region.[9]

Grant had less confidence in Banks, a politician-turned-general of only limited combat ability. But Banks's expedition against Mobile would at least oblige the rebels to detach troops to oppose him and, if successful, would seal off one of the Confederacy's two remaining ports (the other being Wilmington, North Carolina). Unfortunately, Banks was already involved in what Grant regarded as a peripheral foray up the Red River valley in northern Louisiana: on the wrong side of the Mississippi River and in the wrong direction. But the project was too far advanced, and the political influences behind it too great, for Grant to cancel it. The best he could do was to urge Banks to wrap up the Red River operation as fast as possible and attend to the Mobile expedition.

That left the eastern theater, the graveyard of Union military reputations. There, one Northern offensive after another had come to grief, a circumstance made doubly unfortunate because the eastern theater contained both national capitals—Washington on the Potomac, Richmond a hundred miles south—and therefore received a disproportionate amount of public scrutiny. The political and even diplomatic effects of Northern defeats in the east were thus greatly amplified.

Much of the poor Union showing could be attributed to the top Confederate general in the theater, Robert E. Lee, whose fame as a military genius was worldwide, and to the tough veterans of the Army of Northern Virginia. But geography also played a substantial role. By the winter of 1864, every news-literate person in America was familiar with the topography of the eastern theater. For all practical purposes, it consisted of a relatively narrow corridor of Virginia between the Chesapeake Bay and the Allegheny Mountains (although Confederate offensives had twice expanded it briefly into Maryland and southern Pennsylvania). The proximity of sea and mountains greatly reduced maneuvering room. Just as bad, the rivers of Virginia ran generally west to east, presenting numerous barriers to north-south movement. In the western theater, where Grant had made his reputation, geography favored the Union. In Virginia it did not.

It did not, that is, with one glaring exception. The Union enjoyed a formidable edge in sea power. It could transport and supply troops almost anywhere on the Southern coast, and the eastern fringe of Virginia was bathed by navigable water. That raised the possibility of landing somewhere on the coast, bypassing the network of barrier rivers or even converting them into highways of invasion, as Maj. Gen. George McClellan had done in his 1862 Peninsula campaign. Indeed, in January 1864 Grant had urged the abandonment of the traditional overland approach against Lee's army. The thing to do, he wrote Halleck—then still general in chief—was to march sixty thousand troops from Suffolk, Virginia, into North Carolina, there to strike the railroads that linked Virginia with the lower South.

Such a move, he argued, would virtually compel Lee to evacuate the state. It would allow the Federals to subsist in part from the countryside (as Grant had done in several western campaigns), and might well cause thousands of North Carolina troops to desert in light of this direct threat to their homes. Moreover, it would force the enemy to fight on less familiar ground and would for all practical purposes interdict the city of Wilmington, the most important seaport still in Confederate hands. Then too, the warmer Carolinas weather would permit an offensive to begin several weeks before one in northern Virginia.[10]

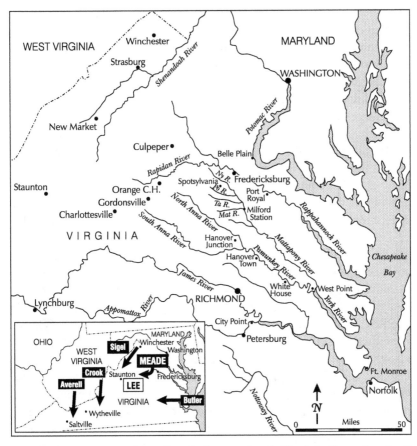

1. The Virginia Theater. *Inset*: Grant's Concept for the Virginia Campaign, April 30, 1864

Halleck disagreed. Most of the required sixty thousand men would have to come from the Army of the Potomac, and to weaken that army to such a degree would be like offering Lee a license to run amok. As for Grant's notion that the North Carolina operation would compel Lee to move his army out of Virginia, Halleck considered it rot: "I do not think so. Uncover Washington and the Potomac River, and all the forces which Lee can collect will be moved north, and the popular sentiment will compel the Government to bring back the army in North Carolina to defend Washington, Baltimore, Harrisburg, and Philadelphia." The crucial thing, the only thing, was to eliminate Lee's army. It was the best army the Confederacy possessed, and Lee was its ablest general. "We cannot take Richmond . . . and we cannot operate advantageously on any point from the Atlantic coast, until we destroy or disperse that army, and the nearer to Washington we can fight it, the better for us. . . . If we cannot defeat him here with our combined force, we cannot hope to do so elsewhere with a divided army."[11]

Although it sounded a bit like pique—the carping of a lame duck general in chief—Halleck in fact was giving Grant the situation as the Lincoln administration understood it. Halleck's letter formed Grant's introduction to the great political sensitivity of the Virginia theater and also the immense wariness and respect with which the Lincoln administration regarded Lee. Moreover, Halleck was almost certainly correct about Lee's likely response to the Suffolk expedition. Lee had already demonstrated on at least three occasions that given the slightest opening he would strike north, and though Halleck could not have known it, in the winter of 1864 Lee toyed with the idea of yet another northward raid. A sizeable detachment from Meade's army would have been all the encouragement he needed. And just as Halleck told Grant, every one of Lee's previous offensives had provoked panic in the North. In short, while it might or might not be possible to destroy Lee's army in battle, keeping him on the defensive was politically vital.[12]

Grant did not argue further. From then on he accepted that the Army of the Potomac would strike Lee head-on. But such a direct offensive did not rule out the possibility of a subsidiary thrust that might accomplish on a smaller scale what Grant originally expected from the Suffolk expedition. It so happened that southeastern Virginia already contained about 21,500 Union troops. Known officially as the Department of Virginia and North Carolina, this force defended Norfolk, Portsmouth, and several other locations in the Hampton Roads area, including Fort Monroe.

Hitherto little had been expected from this department in the way of offensive action, but Grant perceived that by marching westward along the south bank of the James River, its field force could threaten Richmond, complicate Lee's effort to defend the Confederate capital, and still shield the Hampton Roads region. Accordingly, Grant issued orders for the department to be reinforced by ten thousand troops from the X Corps, then lying idle along the South Carolina coast.[13]

At the end of March, Grant went to Fort Monroe to visit the department commander, forty-three-year-old Maj. Gen. Benjamin F. Butler. Butler was a political general, a Massachusetts lawyer and congressman who had gained quite a reputation early in the war. In May 1861 he electrified the nation by providing refuge to fugitive slaves at a time when official Union policy still upheld slavery. A Confederate officer brashly showed up to reclaim them, basing his demand on the Fugitive Slave Act of 1850, no less. Although this was an awkward situation, given the Lincoln administration's elaborate denials of any intent to disrupt the South's "peculiar institution," the wily Butler had no trouble concocting a rebuff. He would not return the fugitives, Butler smoothly informed the officer; they had recently been used to construct rebel fortifications. Therefore, he was entitled to hold them as "contraband of war." Abolitionists sang Butler's name, and even conservative Northerners relished his elegant legal justification. A year later Butler served as commandant of occupied New Orleans. There he maintained a basically mild regime but outraged Southerners by cracking down hard on the more vocal secessionists. For that, he was known throughout the South as "Beast" Butler.[14]

Butler's flamboyant war career did not extend to actual combat. He had never before led troops in the field, and there was no reason to suppose he would be good at it—but equally no reason to suppose he would not. Plenty of erstwhile lawyers, politicians, and county sheriffs had proven able commanders. Besides, upon meeting Butler, Grant discovered that the Massachusetts man had conceived an offensive scheme against Richmond that much resembled his own. Indeed, it was actually better because it called for an initial seaborne movement up the James River estuary and thus obviated the need for a slower overland march. The main point of debarkation would be Bermuda Hundred, a peninsula formed by the confluence of the James and Appomattox Rivers. Just beyond it lay one of the main railroads linking Richmond with Petersburg and thence with the rest of the Confederacy. Richmond itself was only sixteen miles north of the peninsula. Petersburg, an important rail center in its own right, lay just eight miles to the south. Once installed at Bermuda Hundred, Butler could threaten either of these cities, perhaps seize one of them outright. Even if that proved impossible, his presence would require an energetic response from the Confederate government and doubtless divert reinforcements for Lee's army.[15]

Grant liked the proposal and adopted it. The final plan called for landings not only at Bermuda Hundred but also at City Point, a village at the mouth of the Appomattox River from which a short railroad ran the few miles to Petersburg. And it would be more than a simple diversionary thrust. Grant thought it possible that the Army of the Potomac would be unable to destroy Lee's army along the Rapidan River but would instead gradually shove it back into the Richmond entrenchments. In that event, the Army of the Potomac would link up with Butler's force and the two armies together would operate against Lee and Richmond. In the meantime, Butler was to operate principally against Richmond, hugging the south bank of the James River as he advanced.[16]

Grant next had to consider how to get at the Army of Northern Virginia, which lay just beyond the Rapidan River about fifteen miles southwest of Culpeper Court House and which in three years of war had become the Confederacy's de facto northern border. Lee's army occupied a string of encampments between Gordonsville and Orange Court House, with strong detachments posted to cover the Rapidan fords. From these positions, Lee guarded the strategic railroad junction at Gordonsville and lay on the flank of any Union thrust directly south toward Richmond. He also enjoyed easy access to the Shenandoah Valley, a region from which he drew substantial foodstuffs and whose geography offered a protected route by which he could raid northward, as he had done the previous summer during the Gettysburg campaign.

The Army of the Potomac had three potential ways to get at Lee. The first, a headlong assault upon the Rapidan River strongpoints, Grant rejected as obviously suicidal. He toyed with the idea of moving around Lee's left (western) flank, which would cut Lee off from any possibility of threatening the North, but concluded that it would be too difficult to keep such a movement adequately supplied. Finally he decided that the best course would be to cross the Rapidan River east of (below) Lee's position. An advance by that route would be easier to supply. It would also be easier to link up with Butler should the need arise.

Grant left the details of this movement to the Army of the Potomac's commander, Maj. Gen. George G. Meade, a forty-eight-year-old Penn-

sylvanian of patrician manner, volatile temperament, and cautious strategic instincts. Keeping Meade in charge of the army was to some degree an
act of faith. Compared with the Union's other main field commands, his
was a hard-luck outfit. In almost three years of war, the Potomac Army
had lost each of its major battles except two—Antietam and Gettysburg—
and those were marred by a perceived failure to vigorously follow up
success. Meade's three predecessors had been removed from command.
Meade himself was under fire from critics who charged that he had wanted
to retreat from Gettysburg and that his subordinates had won the battle
almost in spite of him.[17]

Such slanders were cruel as well as false. Still, the fact remained that in
the eight months since Gettysburg, Meade had been unable to bring Lee
to battle. Indeed, on one occasion his army had been forced to fall back
almost to Washington. Well aware of his questionable reputation, Meade
volunteered to step down from command of the Army of the Potomac if
Grant thought another general could better do the job. Although Grant
in fact *was* thinking of replacing Meade, this gesture of self-abnegation
impressed him. "It is men who wait to be selected," he believed, "and
not those who seek, from whom we may always expect the most efficient
service." Thus, Meade stayed in command, and while Grant planned to
accompany the Army of the Potomac during the spring campaign, he
intended to leave its day-to-day management in Meade's hands.[18]

To Meade's chief of staff, Brig. Gen. Andrew A. Humphreys, went the
job of devising a plan to turn Lee's right flank. The chief obstacle was
a dense tangle of second-growth woodland that covered about seventy
square miles of northern Spotsylvania County and that the Union army
would encounter as soon as it crossed the Rapidan. It was called the
Wilderness, and Federal forces knew it well from previous campaigns.
In May 1863 it had been the scene of one of the Union army's most
humiliating defeats, the battle of Chancellorsville. Launching a second
offensive in the region the following November, the Federals had needed
almost thirty hours just to traverse the Wilderness, thereby permitting
Lee to occupy a strong position along Mine Run at its western fringe—a
position so strong, in fact, that the whole operation had to be called off.[19]

Humphreys had a healthy respect for this gloomy region. The dense
forest of the Wilderness was bad enough, he would later explain, but beneath it lay "nearly impenetrable undergrowth, which it was very difficult
for even small bodies of men to move in." Except along the few main roads
and in the rare open ground, artillery could find neither room to deploy

nor clear fields of fire, rendering it almost useless. The problems did not end there: "An enemy remaining on the defensive awaiting attack where this undergrowth existed, would be unseen, while the troops advancing to attack would make their presence known, and thus the tangled growth would serve in some measure as an intrenchment, at least for the first and most destructive fire." Moreover, in such difficult country the Army of the Potomac's numerical superiority would count for less.[20]

Humphreys's plan therefore called for the Army of the Potomac to race through the Wilderness as fast as possible, to avoid having to fight in such forbidding terrain. Since Lee would probably take up the Mine Run line, as he had done the previous November, the idea was to swing so widely that the Union column would reach the stream's headwaters, where its defensive potential would be nil. Ideally, the movement would be completed in one breathless day—long before Lee, boiling up from his encampments around Orange Court House, got close enough to interfere. With the Mine Run line thus rendered untenable, Lee would be obliged to retreat, or, if he chose to fight, would have to do so in open country.[21]

Meade liked the plan. So did Grant, who, as commander of all Union armies, could do much to help it succeed. Forcing Lee to fall back or fight in open country was good. The rebel general's life could be made yet more miserable if Union forces lying idle in West Virginia were dispatched against key economic targets in southwestern Virginia: the Virginia and Tennessee Railroad, the lead mines of Wytheville, and the salt works of Saltville. Thus Grant organized yet a third eastern offensive, this one to be made by Maj. Gen. Franz Sigel's Department of West Virginia.

Actually this "offensive" was more like a set of coordinated raids. Grant gave instructions for two columns to advance from Charleston against the Virginia and Tennessee Railroad, partly to break up the railroad and partly to destroy the Confederate lead mines and salt works. Since the raiders might return by way of the Shenandoah Valley, he instructed the thirty-nine-year-old Sigel to march up the valley to meet them. All told, these three expeditions would involve fewer than twenty thousand men, but at a minimum they would prevent Confederate forces in southwest Virginia from reinforcing Lee. "[I]f Sigel can't skin himself," Grant wrote Sherman, borrowing Lincoln's metaphor, "he can hold a leg while some one else skins."[22]

To be sure, Grant believed that Sigel's expeditions would amount to little. Like Butler, Sigel was a political general, accorded high rank mainly because he was the darling of the German-American community.

Unlike Butler, Sigel had experience with combat command, but it was mostly wretched. The Union high command regarded him with disdain. Halleck wrote that it seemed "little better than murder" to give important commands to men like Sigel—and for that matter, Butler or Banks—"and yet it seems impossible to prevent it." The reason tells much about the political climate in which the spring campaign would be waged.[23]

Eighteen sixty-four was a presidential election year, only the second time Americans would choose their leader in wartime—the first had been during the War of 1812—and the outcome was universally seen as crucial. If Lincoln lost, he would be succeeded by a Democrat, certainly a candidate opposed to emancipation and possibly opposed to continuing the war at all. And Lincoln's defeat was quite conceivable. He was under fire on a variety of charges. The war had dragged on too long because of his mismanagement. His emancipation policy had converted a war for the Union into an unconstitutional and hellish plot to free the slaves. His administration had abused its authority through political arrests, the suspension of habeas corpus, and military conscription. He had intransigently refused all negotiations with the South and thus had scuttled any chance to reach a political accommodation. Under such circumstances, Lincoln needed all the reelection support he could get. He certainly could not afford to expend political capital by alienating the friends of powerful men like Banks, Butler, and Sigel.

The point was especially acute in the case of Butler. He was an odd-looking man. Theodore Lyman described him as "the strangest sight on a horse you ever saw," with his "stout shapeless body, his very squinting eyes, and a set of legs and arms that looked as if made for somebody else and hastily glued to him by mistake." But this Rabelaisian nightmare was also an energetic, canny, no-holds-barred political operator—"Woe to those who stand up against him in the way of diplomacy!"—and famed as one of the toughest "war in earnest" men in the Union. Butler was not the only one to regard his overstuffed body as presidential timber; others did as well. The last thing Lincoln needed was to free Butler to interfere with his reelection plans or, worse, run for his party's nomination. Since Butler desperately craved a field command and held the proper rank—he was in fact the third senior general in the Union army—Grant would have to oblige him. The politics of war required it.[24]

If Grant had to take into account that it was a Northern election year, so too did the Confederates. Recognizing that Lincoln was its most implacable foe, the rebel government had strong reason to prevent his reelection in any way it could. The most potent method, plainly, was military success. "Every bullet we can send . . . is the best ballot that can be deposited against his [Lincoln's] election," opined the *Augusta (Georgia) Constitutionalist* in January 1864. The most bothersome Confederate success would be a victory gained on the offensive, and at least one Southern general proposed to mount such an offensive for explicitly political ends. In March 1864, Lt. Gen. James Longstreet urged a campaign to seize the border state of Kentucky "as a political move." The North would be "greatly demoralized and disheartened" by such a campaign, Northern recruitment would diminish, and Lincoln's political fortunes would become dire. "Lincoln's re-election seems to depend upon the results of our efforts during the present year. If he is reelected, the war must continue, and I see no way of defeating his re-election except by military success."[25]

Longstreet's plan received a full hearing at the highest levels: Longstreet, Lee, President Davis, and senior military adviser Gen. Braxton Bragg all met in Richmond on March 10 to discuss it. In the end they rejected it—but only because of practical obstacles, not flaws in its political logic. Lee too believed that the coming military campaign would be crucial and that the Confederates must grasp any opportunity to seize the offensive, frustrate the enemy's plans, "and compel him to conform his movements to our own." He hoped that Gen. Joseph Johnston, commander of the Army of Tennessee in northern Georgia, might find such an opening. And he looked tirelessly for one in Virginia.[26]

Yet the Confederates had their own political troubles. Defeats at Vicksburg, Chattanooga, and (to a lesser degree) Gettysburg had badly shaken Southern morale. The sacrifices required to sustain the war were wearing heavily on Confederate society. Although founded on states' rights and limited national government, driven by the demands of war the Confederate States of America had dramatically expanded its centralized authority. Many people resented and resisted this, and sometimes local political pressures adversely affected Lee's army.

There was, for instance, the matter of independent companies. The Confederate government still permitted individuals to organize units for local service; it had proven politically impossible to curtail the practice. Given the choice between service far away or service near their communities, many men found the latter option attractive—so attractive, indeed, that they did not let prior assignment to the Army of Northern Virginia debar them from skipping home to enlist in one of these local units.

Although technically such men were away without leave, extracting them from such units once they joined was next to impossible. Political friends within the community invariably blocked efforts to reclaim them.[27]

Similarly, large numbers of Confederate troops simply left military service altogether. While many men absent without leave were merely abusing a furlough or taking "French leave," a growing number were deserters. A New York cavalryman wrote home in January 1864, "Deserters are coming over from the enemy nearly every day. Some 20 or 30 came to the brigade headquarters one day last week." Many complained that the Confederacy was asking more of them than they could endure. Wryly, the New Yorker observed, "We try and not discourage them in that idea."[28]

The desertions reflected the Confederacy's internal tensions. Despite later myths about a solid South contending against northern tyranny, many white southerners resented the Confederate government quite as much as they resented the Yankees. Thus, when deserters came home, their communities tended to help them. Even when provost marshals arrested citizens who were blatantly harboring deserters, local courts often compelled their release. Under such conditions, Lee dispatched parties to recover deserters with great reluctance. One regiment he sent, months before, to North Carolina on such duties had yet to return. "These detachments weaken the army, and I have only resorted to them when in despair of otherwise mitigating the evil."[29]

The extent of the "evil" was appalling. In April, Lee informed President Jefferson Davis that the returns for the previous month showed that almost 5,500 men—10 percent of the army—were away without leave, although only 322 were officially classified as having deserted (the practice in most regiments was to downplay absenteeism as long as possible). Lee's solution was to shoot deserters when caught, and he urged the president to grant clemency sparingly. Shows of mercy, he argued, simply encouraged more men to leave the army. Executions were the only effective deterrent, "and which I am sure will be found to be truly merciful in the end."[30]

Lee's troubles did not end there. His correspondence during the winter of 1863–64 was one long lament about the dearth of supplies. In part the lack of sufficient food and forage owed to mismanagement by Lt. Col. Lucius Northrop, the Confederacy's notoriously incompetent commissary general, who blandly urged Lee to make up deficiencies through impressment. But Lee believed the policy of impressing goods only exacerbated the problem. "Wholesale impressments will give us present relief, but I fear it will injure our future supplies," for it would encourage farmers to hide their crops or worse, fail to plant them at all. "Already I hear of land in Virginia lying idle from this cause."[31]

If the lack of supplies hurt Lee's army and desertion diverted strength from it in dribs and drabs, the clamor for local defense threatened to divert strength by whole brigades. Although based in northern Virginia, Lee had to concern himself with a much larger region extending westward into the Appalachian Mountains and southward as far as South Carolina. Within this expanse, over twenty thousand Confederate troops guarded railroads and key points such as Richmond, Petersburg, and Wilmington. Lee preferred to think of the area as one from which he could draw reinforcements—it was his settled opinion that to try to protect everything was to protect nothing—but in fact the region frequently operated as a drain on his own army.

For example, Maj. Gen. George E. Pickett's division (of Gettysburg fame) was now more or less on permanent loan to southside Virginia. Lee tried to make the best of it. In January 1864, aware that pressures were mounting to attack the Federal enclaves in coastal North Carolina, the Virginian voluntarily detached an additional brigade for the purpose. Eventually that brigade, under Brig. Gen. Robert F. Hoke, played a significant role in the recapture of Plymouth, North Carolina. But the outcome proved the danger of such detachments: Hoke's brigade did not return before the spring campaign opened.[32]

Also absent were two divisions under Longstreet, Lee's "Old War Horse," dispatched to northern Georgia during an emergency in September 1864 and now wintering in east Tennessee after an unsuccessful bid to recapture Knoxville. (His presence in the region had prompted Longstreet to suggest an expedition into Kentucky.) Pickett's division and the two detached with Longstreet together constituted Lee's entire First Corps, containing fully a third of his infantry. Without it, he was helpless to make any aggressive move of his own. He could only await Grant's spring offensive.

In the meantime, Lee tried to gauge Federal intentions. For this he relied on a loosely structured but extensive network of spies, scouts, and operatives, many of them handled through his cavalry chief, Maj. Gen. J. E. B. Stuart, while others reported through the Richmond provost marshal or directly to Maj. Charles S. Venable, an officer on Lee's personal staff. Although Venable and a second staff officer, Maj. Walter H. Taylor, probably assessed some of the reports that came in, Lee had no formal chief of intelligence. In effect he held that job himself.[33] Although his sources were unsophisticated—mostly scouting reports, civilian gossip, and Northern newspapers—he still deduced a great deal. From the *Washington Chronicle* of April 4, for example, he learned that Maj. Gen. William F. Smith had been ordered "to the command of the troops around Fort Monroe." Since Smith was a West Pointer who had held high commands elsewhere, this nugget of information told Lee that "operations are contemplated from that quarter, which they [the Union high command] do not wish to trust to General Butler," a political general. From a scout in Culpeper he discovered that while many Union troops had been arriving by railroad, "the troops on disembarking from the cars separate into squads and move off to the different camps, and do not march in a body"—which meant that they were soldiers returning from furlough, not fresh reinforcements.[34]

Through careful evaluation of dozens of such reports—paying greater attention to those which indicated a sound military purpose, discarding those which seemed unlikely or lacked confirmation—Lee almost perfectly divined Grant's plan for the Virginia campaign. On April 30 he informed Davis, "Everything indicates a concentrated attack on this front [the Rapidan]." He also predicted that troops in Sigel's department would strike toward the Virginia and Tennessee Railroad or Staunton. He picked up as well on Butler's advance, erring only in supposing that it would be merely "a strong demonstration made north or south of the James River," not a full-scale offensive.[35]

Despite his impressive success overall, Lee's deductions failed him in one important respect. On the eve of the campaign he estimated the Army of the Potomac's strength at only seventy-five thousand men. In fact, Meade's army already numbered over one hundred thousand and would shortly be joined by the IX Corps (sixteen thousand men) under Maj. Gen. Ambrose E. Burnside. (Lee had correctly located the IX Corps in Annapolis, Maryland, but thought it was probably awaiting sea transport for North Carolina.) The Confederate chieftain thus underestimated the force he confronted by some 36 percent. And even when Longstreet returned from east Tennessee, the Army of Northern Virginia would have barely sixty-four thousand with which to oppose the main Federal thrust, to say nothing of Butler's and Sigel's offensives.[36]

Yet numbers did not tell the whole story. If they had, Lee, who had always fought outnumbered, would have been beaten long before. When, before the Seven Days' battles in 1862, one of his generals complained that the enemy's long-range guns made defeat mathematically certain, Lee told him to stop it: "[I]f you go to ciphering we are whipped beforehand." He won the Seven Days while outnumbered five to four. Since then he had bested the Army of the Potomac against much greater odds: three to two at Second Manassas, two to one at Fredericksburg, two-and-a-half to one at Chancellorsville.[37]

Whenever possible Lee took the offensive, whatever the odds, and he accepted a defensive posture with reluctance. To some extent, his distaste for the defensive reflected conventional military wisdom—"The logical end to defensive warfare," opined the great Napoleon, "is surrender." But it also reflected Lee's conviction that the Confederacy was at a significant military disadvantage and as a result had to take chances. "He knew oftentimes that he was playing a very bold game," wrote a man who discussed Lee's campaigns with him after the war, "but it was the only *possible* one."[38]

Lee's penchant for the offensive may also have reflected his earlier Mexican War experience. There, a small American army repeatedly beat a larger but less aggressive Mexican army. This hinted strongly that moral or psychological factors mattered more in battle than numbers or firepower. Lee's Civil War experiences seemed to confirm as much. Although he never destroyed or even severely damaged the much larger Union armies confronting him, he repeatedly defeated them by defeating the enemy commander. His aggressive tactics first threw the enemy commander on the defensive, then pummeled him so fiercely that his adversary retreated, not because he had no choice but rather because psychologically he *believed* he had no choice. This sounds like hocus pocus until one considers the terrible weight of command—the responsibility for the life or death of thousands—which is a far heavier burden than anything most human beings ever endure. A man who could fail to doubt himself in such circumstances was rare. Lee specialized in squeezing those doubts to the breaking point.[39]

The instrument by which he did so, the Army of Northern Virginia, consisted of three infantry corps and a cavalry corps. It had possessed such a structure for nearly a year. Longstreet, of course, led the First Corps, composed of two divisions totaling about ten thousand men. Lt. Gen. Richard S. Ewell led the Second (three divisions, 17,229 men), and Lt. Gen. Ambrose Powell Hill led the Third (three divisions, 22,344 men). Longstreet was generally considered the most consistently competent of the three: slow to get into a fight, perhaps, but tough and unflappable once he did. A. P. Hill was fiery but erratic. On his good days, he was perhaps the army's best combat commander, but he was often sick and out of sorts (a modern biographer suggests that he probably suffered from chronic prostatitis). Dick Ewell was the most questionable of the three. Able enough when given precise instructions, he seemed unwilling to make prompt, independent judgments—Lee characterized the problem as "a want of decision."[40]

Commanding the cavalry corps (two small divisions, 7,932 men) was Maj. Gen. J. E. B. Stuart. Aside from Lee and the dead hero Stonewall Jackson, Stuart was the most famous man in the Army of Northern Virginia. The other senior commanders might be important names to news-literate Southerners, but Stuart was a celebrity, a self-created cavalier whose public reputation actually ran counter to his real values and gifts. With a banjo player on his staff and a penchant for flirting with young females, Stuart had an image as a rakehell. In fact, he was a happily married man and devoutly religious. Similarly, he was generally known as a raider (on three occasions his cavalry rode completely around the Union army), but Lee valued him most for his ability to gather and sift tactical intelligence.[41]

The Army of the Potomac also possessed three infantry corps and a cavalry corps. The Union corps commanders were oddly similar in quality to their Confederate counterparts. Longstreet's opposite number was Maj. Gen. John Sedgwick—"Uncle John" to all who knew him. Sedgwick led the VI Corps (three divisions, 24,048 men). Like Longstreet, he was the senior corps commander; again like him, he had a reputation for being dependable more than brilliant. Nearest in resemblance to A. P. Hill was Maj. Gen. Winfield Scott Hancock, whose II Corps contained four divisions and 26,681 men. Like Hill, Hancock led the largest corps in his army; like Hill, he possessed dash. And he too suffered from chronic health problems—in his case, a wound received at Gettysburg that never properly healed.

Although no one knew it at the time, Maj. Gen. Gouverneur Kemble Warren was a bit like Ewell in his inability to adjust to the demands of corps command. Ewell had problems exercising the independent judgment his position required. Warren had a corresponding problem with the delegation of responsibility. During the upcoming campaign, Grant would notice that Warren habitually took his three V Corps divisions (24,125 men) into action one at a time, so that he could personally supervise the deployment of each.

Stuart's opposite number was Maj. Gen. Philip H. Sheridan, who commanded the Cavalry Corps (three divisions, 15,825 men). Coarse and bullet-headed, Sheridan was never accused of being a romantic, but, like Stuart, the Union cavalry leader had a taste for raiding and mounted combat, as well as savage, aggressive instincts. The key difference between the two was that whereas Stuart led cavalry throughout his military service, Sheridan until recently commanded infantry. And Sheridan differed from the other corps commanders in one other respect: His previous Civil War experience was entirely in the western theater. Grant brought him east expressly to lead the Army of the Potomac's cavalry. Indeed, Sheridan would function far more as Grant's subordinate than Meade's.[42]

Separate from the Army of the Potomac but destined to operate alongside it was the IX Corps (four divisions, 19,250 men) under Maj. Gen. Ambrose E. Burnside. Arriving in northern Virginia late in April, Burnside's corps took a position guarding the railroad that supplied Meade's army around Culpeper. Logically it ought to have been under Meade's direct control, but Burnside was senior to Meade in rank and had in fact once commanded the Army of the Potomac. To avoid any awkwardness, he therefore reported directly to Grant (though before the campaign ended, this cumbersome arrangement would be abandoned).[43]

Without exception, the nine Union and Confederate corps commanders were graduates of the U.S. Military Academy at West Point—as were Grant, Lee, and Meade. Except for Grant and Burnside (who left the service in 1854 and 1853, respectively), all had served in the Regular Army continuously until the outbreak of the Civil War. As such they exemplified the budding professionalism of the antebellum American officer corps. The prewar army gave them scant preparation for the commands they now held—six of the nine corps were larger than the entire United States Army in 1861, and the rest were not far behind—but it did provide them with a solid understanding of army administration, discipline, and values. It also gave them a sense of officership as a distinct professional calling, and while many of them had political patrons who supported their careers, they tended to avoid partisan politics. In those respects they were a different breed from the generals who conducted previous American wars. Indeed, their corporate identity was exceptionally tight: all were well acquainted with one another, if not personally then by reputation. And along with other West Pointers, they set the standard for command. Within these two armies, no non–West Pointer attained high rank without the approval of the West Point graduates.

On active campaign, the corps commanders were the generals principally responsible for maneuvering the armies prior to battle and for deploying their fighting power for combat. The battles themselves were directed largely by division commanders. The Union army (including the IX Corps) contained nineteen division commanders and senior artillery chiefs (in their responsibilities the rough equivalent of division commanders). Of these, ten were West Pointers. Another three had extensive prewar Regular Army experience, while two more had been active in the militia. The remaining four had no military experience before 1861. Their median age was thirty-nine. The oldest, Brig. Gen. James W. Wadsworth of the V Corps, was fifty-six; the youngest, Brig. Gen. James H. Wilson, was twenty-six.[44]

The Army of Northern Virginia's command makeup was similar. Ten of the fourteen division commanders and senior artillery chiefs were West Point graduates. Two more were alumni of the Virginia Military Institute, which offered equivalent military education, while another officer had been directly commissioned into the prewar army. One general had been a lawyer and legislator before 1861 but had seen a year of volunteer service in the Mexican War. Only one man possessed no military experience prior to 1861. Here again, the median age was thirty-nine. The oldest of the group, Brig. Gen. William Nelson Pendleton, was fifty-four; the youngest, Maj. Gen. Fitzhugh Lee, was twenty-eight.[45]

The basic fighting unit of Civil War armies was the brigade, and the officers who most directly handled tactical operations were the brigade commanders. Unlike division commanders, they usually accompanied their men into combat. At this level, in both armies, the number of officers without prewar military experience was much higher. Fifty officers held brigade commands or their artillery equivalents in the Army of the Potomac. Of the thirty-three for whom biographical information is available, fourteen were West Pointers, two served in the Mexican War, and three served in the U.S. Army or Navy. Eleven (33 percent) had no previous military experience; three served in the militia.

Of the forty-one men who led brigades (or their artillery equivalents) in the Army of Northern Virginia, sixteen had attended West Point or VMI, while five had fought in the Mexican War and four had served in the U.S. Army or Marine Corps. But twelve—almost 30 percent—had no prior military experience of any kind, and two more had served only in the militia. Their median age was thirty-five.

By 1864, nearly all brigade commanders, whether Union or Confederate, had extensive combat experience. And at this level no clear demarcation existed between professionally trained and citizen soldiers. Both had their share of brilliant and merely adequate commanders (plus a few outright clunkers). It is possible that the citizen soldiers were somewhat weaker on tactical nuances. Then again, it was Dick Ewell, a West Pointer, who confessed that in his prewar service on the western plains, "I learned all about commanding fifty United States dragoons and forgot everything else."[46]

In any case, the hard reality was that at every level, from corps command on down, the field officers on both sides learned their functions on the job. They had a general's uniform and a captain's military education. If good soldiers died because of it, it could not be helped. A story told about Robert E. Lee illustrates the basic problem.

During one of the battles of the 1864 campaign, an amateur brigade commander, supposedly Brig. Gen. Ambrose R. Wright, botched an assignment so badly that his corps commander, A. P. Hill, indignantly went to Lee and sputtered that he would place Wright before a court of inquiry. Lee quietly vetoed the idea. "These men are not an army," he told Hill. "They are soldiers protecting their country. General Wright is not a soldier; he's a lawyer." Many stratagems that might be possible with a trained army were impossible with his own, Lee explained, not because the troops were not up to it—"they have fought magnificently"—but because their generals lacked expertise. "Sometimes I would like to mask troops and then deploy them," Lee said, "but if I were to give the proper order, the general officers would not understand it; so I have to make the best of what I have and lose much time in making dispositions." The fact that the generals were often favorite sons of their native states complicated matters further: "If you humiliated General Wright, the people of Georgia would not understand." Besides, Lee asked, who would replace Wright? Civil War armies were far too large to be properly officered with the limited cadre of professional officers. The use of gallant if sometimes inept citizen generals was unavoidable. "You'll have to do what I do," Lee concluded. "When a man makes a mistake, I call him to my tent, talk to him, and use the authority of my position to make him do the right thing the next time."[47]

With a command pool even more heavily based on citizen commanders, General Meade could have made a similar speech. But unlike Lee, he would have mentioned one further problem, namely, that the quality of his soldiers was more uneven than Lee's. True, the Army of Northern Virginia received its share of unseasoned conscripts—perhaps two or three thousand during the winter of 1864—but most of its troops were veterans, and the new soldiers who did arrive were placed in older regiments where they rapidly learned the ropes by observing seasoned officers and men. In the Army of the Potomac, however, most of the green troops belonged to new regiments with a scant leavening of veteran soldiers. One Union artillery colonel estimated that as many as a third of Meade's troops lacked significant military experience.[48]

Worse, the quality of the new men was suspect, chiefly because of flawed Union manpower policies. The North's armies had originally contained volunteers who freely enlisted from patriotism, love of adventure, or community pressure. But by early 1863 the flow of volunteers had diminished and the federal government passed the Enrollment Act, a military draft. Designed less to secure conscripts directly than to threaten conscription if Northern states did not send more volunteers, the Enrollment Act spurred state governments and local communities to offer substantial bounties—cash payments of up to $1,000—to men willing to enlist. While this increased the flow of volunteers, it also created the "bounty jumper," a con artist who enlisted, took his bounty, and deserted at the first opportunity. Even those who remained gambled, stole, malingered, and disgusted the volunteers. Bounty men had to be watched like hawks to keep them in the army. They could not be trusted to perform any job that required them to work unsupervised. Sentry or outpost duty was unthinkable. "If those fellows are trusted on picket," wrote a Massachusetts soldier, "the army will soon be in hell." All in all, most veterans considered the bounty men a curse, not a source of additional fighting strength.[49]

If the veterans really disliked the bounty men—or anything else about army life, for that matter—they could leave, because for many of them their enlistments were about to expire. These were the remaining "boys of '61"—the original volunteers who sprang to arms in the months after the firing on Fort Sumter and somehow escaped death or mutilation in the dozens of battles since. They enlisted for three years in the spring and summer of 1861. Accordingly, their terms of service would end during the spring and summer of 1864. In theory the Federal government might have compelled them to stay, but politically this was impossible. Instead it could only offer bounties and furloughs as enticements to reenlist. Ultimately, some twenty-seven thousand Army of the Potomac soldiers extended their enlistments. But thousands more declined, and since their terms of service were due to expire *during* the upcoming campaign, many of them were less willing to run the risks they might have assumed earlier. Nobody wanted to get shot just weeks before he could go home for good.[50]

Between conscripts, bounty men, and short-timers, then, the Army of the Potomac was a less potent instrument than it had been even six months previously. One soldier, dismissing "worthless bounty jumpers and such trash" and discounting the raw recruits as mere "pigeons for Lee's veterans to shoot at," concluded that at most Meade would have about sixty-five thousand experienced troops in the coming campaign. Adding the six thousand veterans in Burnside's IX Corps, that gave the Federals just a shade over seventy thousand seasoned troops to throw at Lee's army—a number that included thousands of men whose enlistments were about to expire.[51]

The Army of Northern Virginia had weaknesses, too. Desertion, already chronic, was a growing problem, and the conscripts who joined the Confederate ranks were little better than those augmenting the Army of the Potomac. "A good many conscripts were sent us from South Carolina during the winter," noted a soldier from the Palmetto State. "These, however, were no great addition to the brigade. Some of them, certainly, made excellent soldiers; but between discharges then or subsequently, their ill health or aversion to duty, we made little out of the majority of them."[52]

Still, excepting its numerical disadvantage, the Army of Northern Virginia was in better shape than its Union counterpart. Because the Confederate government simply required its veterans to reenlist, the men knew they were going nowhere until the war was over. And unlike their opposite numbers in the hard-luck Army of the Potomac, they had the esprit that comes from a tradition of victory. One Army of Northern Virginia soldier recalled that on the eve of the 1864 campaign, it literally did not occur to him that defeat was a possibility.[53]

Nevertheless, most observers characterized the Potomac Army's morale and material condition as excellent. Its quartermaster, Brig. Gen. Rufus Ingalls, believed that probably no army in history "was in better condition in every respect." The troops had abundant clothing, good equipment, plentiful rations, and an efficient logistical system from which the North's economic bounty flowed in a continual stream. The supply train supporting the initial movement alone comprised a staggering 4,300 wagons. Moreover, an entire fleet of ships was ready to resupply the army, when necessary, via the great tidal estuaries.[54]

Then too, most Union soldiers had faith in the army's top leadership. They knew their corps commanders possessed courage and skill, and they had the same impression of Grant. Yet the men had few illusions about the coming campaign. "I have great confidence in our army & leaders," ran a typical comment. "But the road to Richmond is long & tough."[55]

CHAPTER TWO

The Wilderness

Signs of the coming offensive were abundant. By mid-April the sutlers—merchants who supplied soldiers with pies, stationery, and other goods—had been ejected from the Union camp. Civilian passes were impossible to come by. The number of trains arriving at the army's principal depot, Brandy Station, increased, as did the bustle in the various regiments. Lee's informants kept him continually apprised of the activity across the Rapidan River, and by April 28 he reported to President Davis that the enemy had apparently completed his preparations. Indeed, he seemed slightly surprised that Grant was not yet on the move.[1]

One thing was certain: An offensive *was* coming, and Lee needed every man he could get. Longstreet and two of his wayward divisions had recently returned to the army, but the third division, Pickett's, had not, nor had the brigades of Brig. Gens. Robert Hoke and R. D. Johnston. Lee had urged their return for weeks, arguing that "every preparation should be made to meet the approaching storm, which will apparently burst on Virginia," but the Davis administration had balked. Pickett and Hoke were required for operations in North Carolina, it maintained, and Johnston's brigade was covering a key railroad chokepoint at Hanover Junction. On the eve of the campaign, these troops had yet to arrive. And, of course, a major feature of Grant's campaign plan was to make sure they never would.[2]

Shortly after midnight on May 4, Meade's divisions filed onto the roads that slanted down to the Rapidan River. Sheridan's cavalry moved out first, drove the Confederate pickets from the crossing points, and splashed across black water into enemy country. Next came the engineers, who manhandled five pontoon bridges into position, then stepped aside for the rest of the army to cross. Around 6 A.M. the lead units of Warren's V Corps appeared at Germanna Ford, uppermost of the three crossing points, followed by Sedgwick's VI Corps. The II Corps, under Hancock, crossed four miles downstream at Ely's Ford, while a massive wagon train—3,476 wagons and 591 ambulances, drawn by more than twenty-four thousand mules and horses—forded the Rapidan at an intervening crossing called Culpeper Mine Ford. Behind the wagons trailed a herd of cattle to be slaughtered as needed to provide the men with fresh meat.[3]

By launching the offensive at night, Meade hoped to get a few hours' jump on Lee, but the Confederates maintained a signal station on Clark Mountain, ten miles south of Culpeper, and in the predawn darkness the signalmen spotted marching Federals, plainly silhouetted against distant campfires. At first it was impossible to tell if they were headed toward the left or right flank of Lee's army, but by morning the signalmen could report: "From present indications, everything seems to be moving to the right on Germanna Ford and Ely's Ford roads, leaving cavalry in our front."[4]

Lee put his army on the road promptly. He had already alerted Ewell's Second Corps to be ready to move at daybreak. Now he instructed Ewell to leave a small rear guard and hustle the rest of his corps eastward along the Orange Turnpike, a macadamized road that led from Orange Court House to Fredericksburg, passing through the Wilderness. Similarly, he ordered A. P. Hill to march with two divisions east along the Orange Plank Road, which paralleled the Turnpike a mile or so to the south, leaving Hill's third division to watch the Rapidan fords north of Orange Court House. Lee himself rode at the head of Hill's column.[5]

The Confederate general also sent word to Longstreet. Initially he instructed his senior lieutenant to fall in behind Hill's corps as it marched toward the Wilderness, but Longstreet argued that it would be better to have his two divisions take a more southerly route. True, it would require a trek down narrow back roads, but the suggested route would cut the distance to the battlefield and minimize traffic congestion. Lee approved the change. By early afternoon the entire Confederate army was in motion, marching to meet the enemy along three parallel routes: Ewell on the Turnpike, Hill on the Plank Road, and Longstreet by a succession of back roads farther south.[6]

Stuart's cavalry, meanwhile, trotted up major highways and narrow country lanes, converging on the Union army from east, south, and west, its mission less to delay the Federals than to gain information about their dispositions. The Union cavalry, for its part, effectively screened the advance and kept Confederate gleanings to a minimum, though surprisingly they made little effort to gain intelligence about Confederate movements.

In those early hours, neither side had much feel for the other's location or intentions. Lee knew for sure only that "those people," as he habitually called the Federals, had crossed the Rapidan at Germanna and Ely's Fords. He did not yet know their destination. Certainly they could not simply head straight for Richmond, because a march of more than ten miles in that direction would expose their supply line to ruinous interdiction. More likely, the Federals would either turn east to Fredericksburg to establish a new supply line using the Rappahannock River, or else swing west to confront his own army as fast as possible.

Lee, in turn, had three possible responses. The first two were defensive. He could return to the formidable Mine Run line, which would be a good place to fight if Meade came west. He could also fall back to the North Anna River, which offered an advantageous position if Meade changed his base to Fredericksburg. But both alternatives yielded the initiative to the enemy, something Lee rarely did if he could avoid it. He therefore selected an aggressive option that offered him a chance to gain as much influence as possible over the combat that must come. He would try to strike the Union army while it was still in the Wilderness. There, the dense woodlands and undergrowth would offset the Union numerical advantage in infantry and nullify its substantial edge in artillery. There too, he might be able to catch the enemy forces in a mistake that he could exploit to advantage. Accordingly, Lee intended to get his infantry within easy striking distance of the Federal army, then attack or defend as the situation might require.

Aggressiveness was one thing, foolish aggressiveness quite another. Lee made no fetish of the offensive. He knew that until all three of his infantry corps reached the battlefield, it would be unwise to bring on a fight whose result would be final. He therefore instructed Ewell and Hill to make contact with the enemy but avoid a general engagement. The preliminary objective would be to disrupt the Army of the Potomac's offensive plans and, if possible, discover an opening for a counterstroke. The counterstroke itself would have to wait until Longstreet's arrival.[7]

Twenty miles away at Germanna Ford, Meade and Grant watched the VI Corps veterans stride across the Rapidan. Each commander had his own perspective on the situation. The movement across the Rapidan

River was the first step in bringing Lee to battle. In Meade's view, Lee's most likely responses were to stand at Mine Run or retreat to the North Anna. If Lee indeed chose to reoccupy the former position, the planned flanking movement by Hancock's II Corps offered the best chance of defeating him. If, on the other hand, Lee headed toward the North Anna, the Federal scheme could readily be modified to accommodate that.

Meade gave scant consideration to the possibility that Lee would come east of the Mine Run position, probably because from his perspective it was the weakest of Lee's options. If Lee did so, he would be forsaking a defensive position (whose strength Meade knew all too well) in favor of battle on equal terms. That would have made no sense. In most of his engagements, Meade had been the attacker. He knew firsthand the power of the defense. At Antietam his division had formed part of a corps-level attack that had simply dented the rebel line at harrowing cost. At Fredericksburg, his division had broken through the Confederate line briefly but was compelled to retreat for lack of support. As an army commander at Gettysburg, he had won his first and only victory on the defensive. Thus, the thing Meade feared most in the coming campaign was the prospect of attacking the enemy on ground that the enemy had chosen.

Grant had just the opposite instinct. Each of his bad moments had occurred on the defensive, as at Shiloh, or when difficult terrain made it hard for him to close with the enemy, as during the frustrating early months of the Vicksburg campaign. But on the offensive Grant had never suffered a serious reverse. Attacks at Fort Donelson, Port Gibson, Champion Hill, and Chattanooga had all succeeded. Even the failed May assaults on Vicksburg had been merely chapters in the saga of his greatest victory. In the battles to come, the divergent outlooks of these two Union commanders, Grant and Meade, would have consequences more than once.

All that day the two armies marched, each certain that a collision was imminent but equally aware that a battle on May 4 was unlikely. By midafternoon Meade halted his infantry squarely in the middle of the Wilderness. He wanted to give his massive supply train time to catch up. Besides, his men had been marching for fifteen hours. They needed a rest. The V and VI Corps halted between the Germanna Ford and a forlorn place called Wilderness Tavern where the Orange Turnpike and Germanna Plank Road converged. The II Corps bivouacked three miles east at Chancellorsville, where the rival armies had clashed almost exactly one year earlier. Disconcertingly, Hancock's soldiers found numerous bleached skeletons in the surrounding fields and woods.[8]

The Confederate Second and Third Corps reached their assigned stopping points around dusk: Ewell at Locust Grove just east of Mine Run, Hill at a dusty hamlet called New Verdiersville. The Army of Northern Virginia had closed to within four miles of its opponent. But Lee was still missing more than a third of his infantry. The Third Corps division of Maj. Gen. Richard H. Anderson remained near Clark Mountain, guarding the Rapidan ford in that area lest the enemy make a movement against Lee's left rear. And Longstreet, who did not receive instructions to march until 1 P.M. (and moved out only at 4 P.M.), was still some twenty miles away, at Brock's Bridge on the North Anna headwaters.[9]

That evening Lee pitched his headquarters tent in a grove beside a New Verdiersville residence and waited for intelligence reports. The first to arrive from Stuart's cavalry were disappointing: They gave no clear picture of the enemy's intentions. The Union army might be turning west to engage him, but with equal plausibility it might be en route to Fredericksburg. In the absence of firm information, Lee opted to be aggressive. At 8 P.M. his adjutant, Lt. Col. Walter H. Taylor, wrote Ewell of Lee's intentions: "He wishes you to be ready to move on early in the morning. If the enemy moves down the river, he wishes to push on after him. If he comes this way, we will take our old line"—meaning the Mine Run position that had defied Meade's army in November. "The general's desire," Taylor concluded, "is to bring [the enemy] to battle as soon now as possible."[10]

The evening's correspondence also included a dispatch from President Jefferson Davis. Irritatingly, it told Lee to expect a delay before units on detached duty returned, including the powerful division of Maj. Gen. George E. Pickett, which constituted a third of Longstreet's corps. These troops were being held in anticipation of a Union movement on the Peninsula and in hopes of recapturing New Berne, North Carolina. It was an old and tiresome thing, this itch to dissipate military strength instead of concentrating it. Lee had scant patience with such thinking. "It is only by the concentration of our troops that we can hope to win any decisive advantage," he believed, and now he set about, tactfully, to put the president straight.[11]

He had already wired the president that Meade had crossed the Rapidan. Lee began, "Whether with the intention of attacking, or moving towards Fredericksburg, I am not able to say. But it is apparent that the long threatened effort to take Richmond has begun, and that the enemy has collected all his available force to accomplish it." Butler's army on the Peninsula had not advanced as yet, but it would surely do so in concert with Meade, and one could safely assume it was as strong as the enemy could make it.

"Under these circumstances," Lee continued, "I regret that there is to be any further delay in concentrating our own troops." While he appreciated the advantages of retaking New Berne, "they will not compensate us for a disaster in Va. or Georgia." The true solution lay in defeating the enemy's main armies. Do that, Lee argued, and the country now occupied by the enemy could be more easily recovered—if indeed the beaten enemy did not relinquish it of his own accord. Lee threw in the usual blandishments about Davis's superior information and wisdom, but his central point was plain: "It seems to me that the great efforts of the enemy here and in Georgia have begun, and that the necessity of our concentration at both points is immediate and imperative."[12]

As the night deepened, further intelligence arrived at headquarters, most of it more helpful than the ambiguous early reports. Scouts from the cavalry division of Maj. Gen. Fitzhugh Lee (a nephew of the army commander) had infiltrated to Chancellorsville and discovered that the enemy infantry was turning west toward Orange Court House, not east toward Fredericksburg. Stuart passed along that information, along with an adroit bit of deduction. Some of his horsemen had observed enemy cavalry riding along the Orange Plank Road just west of the hamlet of Parker's Store, only to see the cavalcade halt, pause for a moment, then retire rapidly to the east. Queried by the Confederates, a local citizen told them he knew the reason for the sudden withdrawal. He had seen a Union courier gallop up to "General Wilson"—that would be James Harrison Wilson, one of Sheridan's three division commanders—and tell him that "he was too far from the rest of [his] command, which could not get farther than the church to-night." Since only a few churches dotted that sparsely populated region, Stuart had little trouble deciding that the one in question must be Wilderness Church, at the junction of the Orange Turnpike and Plank Roads, not quite two miles west of Chancellorsville.[13]

Stuart's dispatch, time stamped 11:15 P.M., must have reached Lee hours after midnight. He probably learned of it only at 3 A.M., his customary waking hour on active campaign. But whenever he learned of the report, it surely increased his confidence in the course he had set for his army. The Union army was deep in the lonely forest of the Wilderness—

terrain the Confederates knew intimately and the Federals hardly knew at all, where the woodlands would lame the formidable Union artillery and dilute the enemy's superior numbers. In short, Lee believed that Grant had made a mistake. Now he would pay for it, as Meade's predecessor, "Fighting Joe" Hooker, had paid in the same place exactly a year before. Lee would pin Meade in the Wilderness with Ewell and Hill, then strike hard and cunningly when Longstreet came up. As dawn bloomed on May 5 and the scent of breakfast wafted through the air, staff officers found the commanding general buoyant, even high-spirited.[14]

The men of Ewell's Second Corps were up at dawn as well, cajoled from bedrolls to resume their places in the long column. By 5 A.M. they were swinging along down the Orange Turnpike, route step, muskets at all angles, bantering the way soldiers always did on the march. Ewell was feeling as jovially combative as Lee. Asked by a young officer if he would mind divulging his orders, Ewell chirped, "No, sir; none at all—just the orders I like—to go right down the [Turnpike] and strike the enemy wherever I find him."[15]

He found the enemy just three miles east. To be precise, his skirmishers did, and a brief pop-pop-popping erupted as they traded shots with the enemy picket line. Ewell dispatched an aide with word of the contact and of his intention to push through the picket line until he found the enemy in force. Not so fast, Lee told the aide. A. P. Hill was lagging behind a bit, and Longstreet was still many miles away. If he wished, General Ewell was free to send forward a strong, supported skirmish line to locate the enemy and ascertain his strength, but he was not to get his troops "entangled so as to be unable to disengage them, in case the enemy were in force."[16]

The aide galloped back to the Turnpike and discovered that his commander had deployed the Second Corps' lead division, under Maj. Gen. Edward "Allegheny Ed" Johnson (so-called because of his early service in the Allegheny Mountains) in a defensive posture at the western fringe of a large uncultivated field. Called Saunders' Field after the farm family who owned it, it straddled the Turnpike and offered one of the few extensive clearings in the Wilderness region. A good rifle shot from one end to the other, it gave Johnson's troops an enviable field of fire. When he received the aide's report, Ewell ordered his remaining divisions into position as well. Maj. Gen. Robert E. Rodes's division extended Johnson's line to the south. That of Maj. Gen. Jubal A. Early remained in reserve.[17]

No sooner did they halt than Ewell's infantrymen spontaneously threw up breastworks to protect themselves. Such field fortifications were no

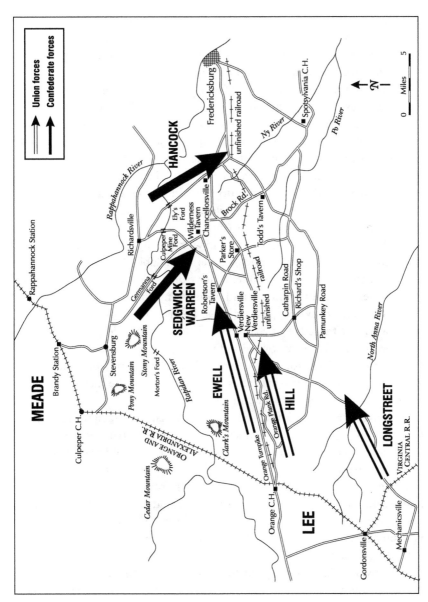

2. The Wilderness: Movement to Contact, May 4, 1864

novelty: prewar doctrine prescribed them, and entrenchments had dotted any number of battlefields from Big Bethel (June 1861) onward. But for the first two years of the war, fieldworks had been used almost exclusively to defend fixed points, as with Lee's June 1862 use of entrenchments to hold Richmond with a reduced force while he marched with most of his army to assume the offensive during the Seven Days. Only gradually did Civil War armies develop the habit of erecting field fortifications for the express purpose of protecting troops on active campaign. Lee had ordered his army to entrench after Fredericksburg and during the early stages of the Chancellorsville campaign; the Union army entrenched at both Chancellorsville and Gettysburg; and during the autumn maneuvers of 1863 Lee made extensive use of fieldworks to protect the reduced force at his disposal, especially at Mine Run.[18]

Such entrenchments typically began with the digging of rifle pits, with some troops wielding picks and shovels if available, bayonets, tin cups, and mess pans if not. Meanwhile, other troops went off to collect fence rails, stones, or fallen branches and, time permitting, would supplement these with tree trunks toppled by axes. Postwar photographs of Ewell's breastworks at the edge of Saunders' Field display rifle pits about two feet deep covered in front by palisades of logs some five feet high. These last were neatly laid atop each other, chinked with mud, and reinforced at intervals by traverses—palisades perpendicular to the main work and intended to reduce the risk of enfilade fire.

Although scarcely unknown before the Overland campaign, such field-works would become its hallmark (the same was true of Sherman's campaign in Georgia), and troops on both sides would spontaneously construct them at every opportunity. Fighting largely on the defensive, the Confederates derived the greatest benefit from these entrenchments, and within two weeks Theodore Lyman would be writing his parents about how quickly the rebels could erect them: "Within one hour, there is a shelter against bullets, high enough to cover a man kneeling, and extending often a mile or two. When our line advances, there is the line of the enemy, nothing showing but the bayonets, and the battle-flags stuck on top of the work. It is a rule that when the Rebels halt, the first day gives them a good rifle-pit; the second, an infantry parapet with artillery in position; and the third a parapet in front and entrenched batteries behind. Sometimes they put this three days' work into the first twenty-four hours." On May 5, Ewell's men were clearly attempting to compress three days' labor into one.[19]

Meanwhile, word of the Confederate presence flew up the chain of command to Meade, who with his staff had just reached the Wilderness Tavern, where the Turnpike met the Germanna Plank Road. The first dispatch implied that rebel force must be small. Succeeding reports gave much the same impression. Nevertheless, Meade suspended the planned movement for the day—which would have completed the Army of the Potomac's circuit through the Wilderness—and gave orders to attack. Just why he jettisoned his original, carefully devised scheme is unclear. It may be that he ordered the halt simply to get a better sense of what the Confederate presence to the west might mean. But apparently he reasoned that if Lee had placed any part of his army east of the formidable Mine Run barrier, it would be a good idea to "punish him." Grant concurred. The whole point of the campaign was the destruction of the Army of Northern Virginia. If the opportunity arose to pitch into a part of Lee's army, Meade should do so at once, "without giving time for disposition."[20]

Although neither Grant nor Meade initially gave much thought to the matter, the odds of punishing Lee would have been much enhanced had they possessed a better grasp of the Confederate army's overall dispositions. This was precisely the information Meade expected Sheridan's cavalry to glean. The orders issued on the eve of the campaign called for Sheridan's three cavalry divisions to screen the army's movements and protect its massive wagon train. One of these, under Brig. Gen. James H. Wilson, was to send strong reconnaissance parties down the Orange Turnpike, Orange Plank Road, and Catharpin and Pamunkey Roads, "until they feel the enemy." If properly carried out, these orders would have located the corps of Ewell and A. P. Hill on the evening of May 4 and given the Union high command a much better picture of Lee's intentions. Instead Wilson merely picketed each of these roads in succession, from north to south, retrieving his vedettes as the infantry came up on the assumption that they would send out scouting parties of their own. By the morning of May 5, Wilson had most of his division on or near the Catharpin Road—the one avenue then devoid of approaching rebel infantry. He would spend most of the day in a spirited but irrelevant duel with Confederate cavalry in the region.[21]

The balance of Sheridan's cavalry, meanwhile, was supposed to screen the army's trains and its southeastern perimeter, but instead gathered itself for a foray against Maj. Gen. Fitzhugh Lee's cavalry division, believed to be at Hamilton's Crossing near Fredericksburg. Thanks to the late arrival of one of his divisions, Sheridan's offensive never came off. This was just as well, considering that Fitz Lee had long since departed Hamilton's Crossing, but it was additional testimony to Sheridan's casual attitude toward the mission Meade had given him.[22]

The Union troops near Saunders' Field belonged to the V Corps under Maj. Gen. Gouverneur Kemble Warren, one of the Potomac Army's rising stars. At Gettysburg his quick thinking and prompt action had helped save the Union army, and Grant regarded him as the best man to replace Meade should a change in command become necessary. When Meade personally told him to attack toward Saunders' Field, Warren began at once to comply. The division nearest the enemy—three brigades under Brig. Gen. Charles Griffin—would strike directly west. A second division under Brig. Gen. John C. Robinson would remain in reserve, save for one brigade that would reinforce Griffin. The V Corps' remaining divisions, under Brig. Gens. James S. Wadsworth and Samuel W. Crawford, had already advanced well beyond the Orange Turnpike along a narrow country lane that angled southwest toward Parker's Store on the Orange Plank Road. Their advanced position was a bit problematic. Instead of having them backtrack, Warren concluded, it would be better to send them west as well, cross-country, to support Griffin's left.

That meant marching straight into the Wilderness. The men of Wadsworth's division soon discovered that moving a line of battle through its bramble-choked thickets was every bit as bad as it was cracked up to be. They struggled through mean jumbles of jack pines, chinquapins, and oak trees, few of them thicker than a man's arm, across a forest floor carpeted with dry leaves, infested with briars, and riddled with vines. "A wild and formidable thicket," wrote one soldier, "so dense that even at noonday the sun's light barely penetrated it." Another man characterized it as "jungle. . . . The undergrowth was rank and heavy; the trees, averaging three to five inches in diameter, grew abundantly . . . and these trees, thus thickly massed, were often still further bound together by long creeping vines not larger than one's finger, and running their winding length, at varying heights, through thirty, forty, fifty, or more in length."[23]

Daniel M. Holt, a surgeon in the 121st New York, thought it "the raggedest hole I about ever saw. . . . Swampy, hilly, bushes thick as dog's hair, grape vines, rotten logs and fallen trees, make up this pretty picture. A fine place to fight in surely: a perfect quag mire." This country seemed to hate every man who dared walk through it. It was less a patch of vegetation than a force of nature. It took four mortal hours for Wadsworth's troops to reach a position on Griffin's left, though that destination was barely a mile from the road on which they started.[24]

Crawford's division, for its part, did not even attempt to obey Warren's order. Halted on an open knoll at the Chewning farm, a mile to the southwest, General Crawford saw additional Confederate infantry advancing along the Orange Plank Road not far away. (Although Crawford could not know it, this was the vanguard of A. P. Hill's Third Corps.) Under the circumstances the Union division commander did not dare leave his present position. A mile east of the Confederates lay a key intersection where Plank Road crossed Brock Road, the region's only north-south highway. Hancock's II Corps was already well south of that junction, which meant that if the rebels continued their advance unchecked, they would soon cut Hancock off from the rest of the Union army.

Indeed, as the day grew warm, generals all over the Army of the Potomac became increasingly aware that Lee was neither falling back to the North Anna nor preparing a defensive line at Mine Run, as had been earlier supposed. Instead he was making straight for the Union army, boldly and in strength. Fresh reports confirmed the advance of Hill's corps. Others placed Confederate cavalry north of the Orange Turnpike, in position to interdict the Rapidan River crossings. Although Meade still wanted to attack, he belatedly realized that his own forces were badly strung out. Even as he prepared an offensive, he gave orders to contract his extended units and fill in the gaps between them. Most important, he sent a VI Corps division, led by Brig. Gen. George W. Getty, to occupy the critical Brock Road intersection.[25]

Warren, meanwhile, made two unhappy discoveries. First, Crawford was refusing to budge from the Chewning farm, arguing that the ground he held was crucial and that, if reinforced, he could smash Hill's advancing column. Second, the Confederate line on Orange Turnpike extended well to the north, so that if Griffin attacked without support from that direction, his right flank would be ruinously exposed. Warren handled the first problem by insisting, ever more shrilly, that Crawford must comply with the order to hook up with Wadsworth's division and support Griffin's attack. Meade dealt with the second by arranging for a VI Corps division under Brig. Gen. Horatio G. Wright to cover Griffin's right flank.[26]

Noon came, however, and Wright had not arrived. Wadsworth was up, but only tenuously connected to Griffin's left. In such circumstances Griffin did not want to attack. The Confederate trenches across Saunders' Field were already strong. The regular crash of falling trees gave assurance that the rebels were strengthening them even more. Warren also thought it better to wait. Meade, however, insisted that the attack be made at once. And so, despite misgivings, the divisions of Griffin and Wadsworth began their advance.

In theory, the nine brigades involved in the assault moved forward in line of battle, each regiment in two dressed ranks, each soldier keeping "touch of elbows" with the man on either side. In reality, the dense Wilderness thickets cruelly mocked these linear tactics. In no time at all, orderly formations dissolved into desperate groups of Union soldiers, scrambling forward as best they could as vines and roots tripped them and branches slapped them in the face. A participant reported that, by the time Griffin's division reached the eastern edge of Saunders' Field— barely a thousand yards from its starting point—"all semblance of a line of battle was gone and there were gaps everywhere between regiments and brigades." They had scarcely yet come under fire.[27]

Brigadiers moved from one unit to another and tried to restore an orderly battle line. This accomplished, the two divisions charged. It was 1 P.M. At Saunders' Field, a brisk flurry of skirmish fire greeted the arrival of Griffin's division. It exploded into full volleys as the Federals moved into the open. South of the field, the dense forest reduced visibility to almost nothing. The Federals advancing in that sector were thereby spared an immediate volley, but had to contend with trees, vines, and undergrowth that tore their battle lines to shreds. One captain had to break a trail for his company to follow, single-file, behind him.[28]

In such conditions many units lost their way. The brigade on the extreme left of Wadsworth's line drifted northwest, so that when it struck the Confederate line it presented its left flank and suffered ruinously as a result. Near the center of the Union line, the vaunted Iron Brigade, one of the army's toughest units, lost contact with the units on either side, got hit by a sudden Confederate counterattack, and, for the first time in its career, broke for the rear in panic. Still another brigade floundered into a swamp—"that champion mud hole of mud holes," one man described it—and lost all cohesion. Within forty minutes, Wadsworth's division was in such disarray that it no longer functioned as an organized force.[29]

Things were just as bad at the northern fringe of Griffin's division, where it transpired that the Confederate line was actually longer than that of the Federals. The rightmost Union brigade was thus exposed to a vicious cross fire. Only in Saunders' Field itself did the attack make head- way. Supported by two cannon that unlimbered on the Turnpike halfway

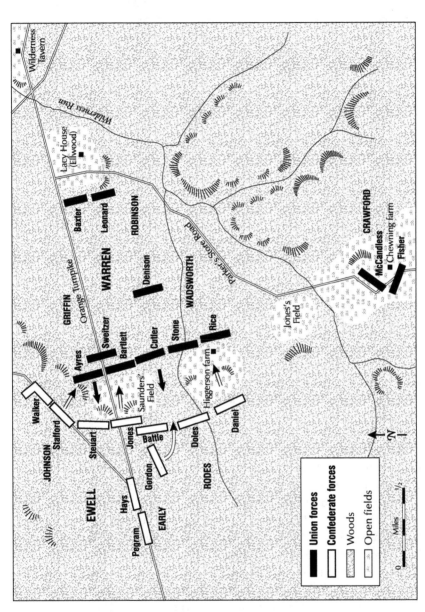

3. Warren's Attack, 1 P.M., May 5, 1864

across the field, the brigade of Brig. Gen. Joseph J. Bartlett swept over Ewell's breastworks, routed a brigade of Virginians, and triumphantly pursued the rebels far down the Orange Turnpike, only to realize that it was advancing alone, because the brigades on either side had failed to break through. Having just cut their way through the rebel line, Bartlett's men had no choice but to turn and cut their way out again.[30]

Behind them, a pall of yellowish-white smoke bloomed at the far end of Saunders' Field. Part of the Confederate earthworks had been ignited by the blaze of musketry. A high wind rapidly spread the flames. Parched from lack of rain, the Wilderness was ready to burn. The veterans had expected this, and it terrified them. "I am willing to take my chances of getting killed," said one man, "but I dread to have a leg broken and then to be burned slowly; and these woods will surely be burned if we fight here." Now that dread became reality for hundreds of men who lay bleeding in the woodlands. Those who could do so hobbled to safety. Those who could not cried out for help from uninjured comrades.[31]

Soon the flames reached prostrate forms in the woodlands, perhaps dead, perhaps still living, and touched off the rounds in their cartridge boxes. A soldier who heard the sound of this recalled it as an incongruously cheerful pop-pop-pop, but the wounds inflicted were hideous. The prospect of such an end was more than most men could bear. "I saw many wounded soldiers in the Wilderness who hung on to their rifles, and whose intention was clearly stamped on their pallid faces," remembered Pvt. Frank Wilkeson. "I saw one man, both of whose legs were broken, lying on the ground with his cocked rifle by his side and his ramrod in his hand, and his eyes set on the front. I knew he meant to kill himself in case of fire—knew it as surely as though I could read his thoughts."[32]

By 2:30 P.M. the attack had plainly failed. The survivors stumbled back to safety and set up a defense. The division commander, Griffin, was furious. Stern and flushed, he stormed to Meade's headquarters, still near the Wilderness Tavern, and accosted the commanding general himself. His men had driven Ewell three-quarters of a mile, Griffin raged, but Wadsworth had been forced back and Wright's VI Corps division had never arrived, thereby exposing both his flanks and compelling him to retreat. He implied that Wright had been culpably negligent and, from what one could make of his harangue, seemed equally critical of Gouverneur Warren. Grant and his staff were nearby and heard the whole thing. After Griffin stalked back to his division, Grant's chief of staff pronounced his language mutinous. Grant agreed. Getting the culprit's name slightly garbled, he inquired of Meade, "Who is this General *Gregg?* You ought to arrest him!" With uncharacteristic calm, Meade responded, "It's Griffin, not Gregg, and it's only his way of talking." Then, strangely, he reached over and gently buttoned Grant's coat for him.[33]

As the fight on the Turnpike dwindled in intensity, a second battle was brewing about three miles south, as A. P. Hill advanced along the Orange Plank Road, Maj. Gen. Henry "Harry" Heth's division in the lead, Maj. Gen. Cadmus M. Wilcox's trailing behind.

During the morning hours, a regiment of Union cavalry repeatedly sparred with the Confederates and withdrew, intent less on delaying the rebel advance than keeping tabs on it. Preceded by skirmishers, Heth's men swept through threadbare Parker's Store and onward into that vast thicket of mean little scrub pines. As the day reached full warmth, they reached the neglected farm of a widow named Catherine Tapp. From this point onward the cavalry did not withdraw so readily. Its feud with Heth's vanguard grew more intense, and finally Heth reinforced the skirmish line to brigade strength in order to bull his way forward. That helped, but as the sun neared its zenith, Heth's skirmishers encountered a tremendous blast of musketry. The Federals had finally dug in their heels.

It was not Union cavalry who barred the way, but infantry, men of Getty's VI Corps division, here in response to Meade's order to seize the intersection of Brock Road and Orange Plank Road. Their arrival was dramatic. Riding at the head of his division a few rods short of that objective, Getty sent a staff officer to scout ahead. Within minutes the officer returned, shouting that the Confederates were about to seize the intersection. Getty put spurs to his horse and led his staff right into the center of the crossroads. "We must hold this point at any risk," he told them. "Our men will be up soon."[34]

His men indeed appeared in minutes, hustling along at the double-quick. The lead regiment intentionally overshot the intersection, then, at a shouted command, stepped from column into line of battle and fired the full volley that brought Hill's advance to a sudden halt. Its colonel threw out skirmishers who shouldered forward through the undergrowth, driving back their rebel counterparts and gathering a few prisoners. Along the way they passed crumpled gray-clad bodies, some within thirty yards of the intersection.[35]

By this time the Tapp farmyard, a mile to the west, had attracted several Confederate generals: A. P. Hill, Jeb Stuart, Brig. Gen. William N. Pendleton, the army's artillery chief, and Lee himself. Ringed by couriers

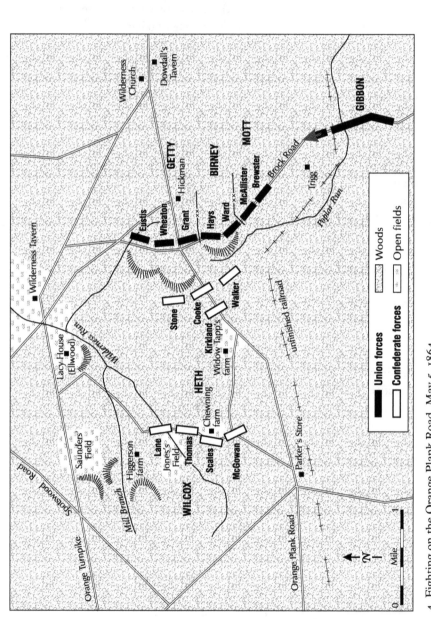

4. Fighting on the Orange Plank Road, May 5, 1864

and staff officers, they sat in the shade and reviewed the situation. Lee was in generally good spirits but concerned that the march of Ewell and Hill had carried them too far apart. Originally almost side by side, the divergence in the roadbeds of the Orange Turnpike and Orange Plank Road had sent the two corps slanting off at angles to each other, so that they were now separated by nearly three miles. Worse, Hill's corps was not only three miles south of Ewell but also as many miles east, because he had been able to advance farther before encountering the enemy. True, it had been crucial to make solid contact with the enemy in order to deny him room to maneuver. But, with that achieved, it was now important for the Second and Third Corps to make solid contact with each other.

As if to underscore the fact, a line of Union skirmishers emerged from the woods north of the Tapp house. Hill froze; Stuart stood up and stared; Lee strode toward the Plank Road, shouting for his adjutant as he went. Then, sensibly, the startled commanders found their horses and galloped to safety. Equally startled, the Federals faded back into the woods, pursued by a squad of rebel infantry.[36]

Fortunately for Lee, the interlopers belonged to Crawford's division, still near the Chewning farm about a half mile distant. That division was belatedly falling back in response to Warren's order that they join Griffin's attack on the Orange Turnpike; the skirmishers retreated with them. No further threat materialized from that direction. Nevertheless, Lee sent Wilcox's division up the narrow lane that led from Parker's Store past the Chewning farm and thence to the Orange Turnpike. Somewhere along the way, he knew, they would encounter the right flank of Ewell's corps.

An hour passed, then two, and the Federals at the Brock Road intersection did little save entrench. Always offensive-minded, Lee began to wonder what a little aggressiveness might yield. He sent a staff officer to ask Heth if he could capture the Brock Road intersection without bringing on a general engagement. The enemy, Heth replied, were holding the Brock Road with a strong force. He could determine whether the intersection could be seized only by attacking with his whole division, and he could not tell ahead of time if this would result in a general engagement. "I am ready to attack if he says attack," Heth emphasized—but Lee would have to make the call.[37]

In the end, it was not Lee who made the call but Meade. For much of the morning and early afternoon he had fired off a succession of dispatches to Hancock, ordering him first to cease his march, then to countermarch, and finally—in three separate missives—to add Getty's division to his command, place his divisions alongside it, and attack. The shrillness conveyed by this fusillade of messages stemmed from Meade's desire to relieve enemy pressure on Warren's front and his misperception of the location of Hancock's corps. Evidently the army commander believed the corps was within easy march of the Brock Road crossing. True, Hancock and his staff had ridden to the intersection by 1 P.M., but the II Corps infantrymen were spread out over six miles of narrow dirt roads. The first two divisions did not begin to arrive for another hour; the remaining divisions arrived hours after that. Patiently, Hancock tried to obey Meade's instructions while waiting long enough to put sufficient strength behind his attack. But shortly before 4 P.M., a staff officer from army headquarters gave Getty a direct order, straight from Meade himself: Attack at once.[38]

Some commanders—Warren, for instance—would have disobeyed the order. Hancock had nearly completed his arrangements for the assault, and it made sense for several divisions to strike rather than for one to go it alone. But Getty prided himself on always obeying a superior. If instructed to march his division across the Atlantic Ocean, he said, he would at least put his men in salt water up to their necks before reporting the order impracticable. That spirit had earlier led him to plant his own person in the Brock intersection as a proxy for his division. Now it made him launch an attack he knew to be ill-advised.[39]

Six thousand men, arrayed in three brigades, stepped over their breastworks and marched into the woodlands. Briars scraped exposed skin. Vines clutched at ankles. Like their V Corps comrades on the Turnpike, Getty's men found it impossible to maintain a line of battle amid the tangle of trees and underbrush that tore formations into mere clots of men. And while everyone knew the enemy was near, few had any idea of the Confederates' exact position. Their education came in the form of a massed volley fired at only seventy-five yards.

That initial volley—always the most dangerous, because its cartridges were the most carefully loaded and the muskets most carefully aimed— cut down dozens of men. A second volley followed the first, then another, then another. A Vermont soldier wrote that the rebels "poured their bullets into us so fast that we had to lie down to load and fire." Had they fired a little lower, he added, they would have annihilated the whole line: "They nearly did it as it was."[40]

Getty's men could see nothing to fire at in return. The best they could do, remembered Col. Lewis A. Grant, was aim "at the wall of fire and smoke in our front." He noted that the distance separating between the two sides was so short that ordinarily the Federals could have timed the enemy volleys and launched a bayonet charge between them, overrunning the Confederates before they could reload. But in the Wilderness that was impossible; a battle line could pick its way forward with difficulty even when completely unopposed. "Anything like a dash upon the enemy was simply out of the question."[41]

So Getty's division stood there and took it, making no progress but not giving an inch, either, while Hancock feverishly completed arrangements for his own attack. The first of his divisions, an understrength two-brigade affair led by Brig. Gen. Gershom Mott, went forward fifteen minutes after Getty. Mott's troops had an even rougher time, if such a thing were possible. A sudden "double volley" crashed through the woodlands, paralyzing all but the bravest men with fear. Those who continued to advance received a second staggering volley that killed or wounded many men and compelled those still on their feet to withdraw. Abruptly the division dissolved: "Regiment after regiment, like a rolling wave, fell back," wrote Robert McAllister, one of Mott's brigade commanders, "and all efforts to rally them short of the breastworks were in vain." The ferocious rebel fire played a role in the collapse, McAllister acknowledged, but so did the fact that many of the troops were short-timers whose enlistments were about to expire.[42]

The next Union division to enter the fight was that of Maj. Gen. David Birney. It did so one brigade at a time, since Birney's assignment was to support Getty's division rather than attack outright. Like their predecessors, Birney's men took heavy casualties, among them Brig. Gen. Alexander Hays, who had helped to repel Pickett's Charge ten months previously. The struggle was epic, like nothing anyone had experienced in three years of war. "Usually," wrote Getty's chief of staff, "when infantry meets infantry the clash is brief. Here neither side would give way, and the steady firing rolled and crackled from end to end of the contending lines, as if it would never cease."[43]

Across the brief stretch of smoldering woodland, Heth's Confederates kept up the musketry, pouring it on, as an unbroken hour of battle stretched into two and faces grew black with powder and smoke. For them the fight was every bit as desperate as it was for their adversaries. Heth, with 6,500 men in line, reckoned the enemy's strength at twenty-five thousand—a good estimate, for Hancock's already had seventeen thousand in the divisions of Getty, Mott, and Birney, with two more divisions moving up into position. If the II Corps commander could ever mass them for one hard concerted push, Heth's line would crack.[44]

Lee knew that Heth needed help, and at 5 P.M. he recalled Wilcox's division. When Wilcox got the message, he was at the Chewning farm, having tied in with Ewell's corps less than an hour before. Now he came pounding back, his two rear brigades—those closest to the Orange Plank Road—already en route to Heth after receiving direct orders from Lee.

Wilcox rode ahead, found Heth not far behind the battle line, and discovered that Heth had already fed his lead brigade into the fight. "I gave him my views," Heth wrote, "which were briefly that, having successfully resisted all of the enemy's attacks up to the present time, I thought that we should now, in our turn, attack." Wilcox concurred: in the Army of Northern Virginia's aggressive military culture, meeting attack with counterattack was almost reflexive.[45]

So Wilcox's brigades counterattacked, one by one, as they reached the field. Unable to see anything of the battle line for the trees and smoke, Wilcox deployed them partly by earshot ("where the firing was heaviest, there my brigades would be ordered"), and partly on the advice of Heth, who, being first on the scene, presumably had the surest grip on the situation. The first brigade, five South Carolina regiments under Samuel McGowan, piled through the center of Heth's line, keening the rebel yell. This was a mistake: "We should have charged without uttering a word until within a few yards of the Federal line," noted a lieutenant. "As it was, we drew upon ourselves a terrific volley of musketry."[46]

The heavy Union fire slowed the McGowan's counterattack. So did the saplings and undergrowth. So did the appalling realization that Heth's troops, now behind McGowan's men, were firing *through* their formation in a misguided attempt to assist. Although the South Carolinians managed to overrun one of four cannon posted on the Orange Plank Road, they soon had to relinquish it and withdraw. Other brigades from Wilcox's division had similar experiences. All in all, Heth regretted having advised Wilcox to counterattack. "I should have left well enough alone."[47]

Nevertheless, the counterattack yielded one important benefit. It put the Federals in a defensive frame of mind, even as Hancock pumped his last two divisions into the fight. The Federal thrust struck a powerful blow to the reeling Confederates, but the thoughts of the Union field officers were less on achieving a breakthrough than on sheer survival. Lyman, sent to Hancock's front to report on the situation, reflected the prevailing sentiment in a dispatch to army headquarters: "We barely hold our own;

on the right the pressure is heavy. General Hancock thinks he can hold the plank and Brock roads, in front of which he is, but he can't advance." A postscript added, "Fresh troops would be most advisable."[48]

Fresh troops were already coming, though not to the Brock Road sector. Union signalmen had earlier witnessed an unidentified Confederate column marching south from the Chewning farm to the Orange Plank Road. Unaware of the troops' identity—they were Wilcox's men, rushing to the support of Heth—Grant assumed the column must represent a detachment from Ewell's corps. Accordingly, he advised Meade to renew the attack along the Orange Turnpike in the belief that this sector was now more weakly defended than before. At the same time, he suggested that Wadsworth's division strike the left flank of the Confederates defending the Plank Road.[49]

Already in reserve near the Lacy House on the Orange Turnpike, Wadsworth's division was only a mile northwest of A. P. Hill's left flank. But that mile consisted of roadless thickets, steep ravines, and a marshy branch of Wilderness Run. Wadsworth set off gamely enough—embarrassed by his division's poor performance earlier in the day, he was anxious to redeem its reputation—but the dense vegetation slowed his advance. Worse, one of his brigades collided with rebel pickets, panicked, and broke, delaying the operation for precious minutes while officers retrieved them and restored the line. But at 7 P.M. the first of Wadsworth's troops stumbled into the Plank Road battle area: tentatively, unsure of their situation, but perfectly positioned to wreck Hill's corps if they remained and were reinforced. The only Confederate unit at hand was a 150-man Alabama battalion detailed to guard Union prisoners. In desperation, Lee ordered the Alabamians to attack. They did so, yelling all the way, shaking the Union troops so badly that they faded back into the woods.[50]

Wadsworth's abortive foray was the last major development in the three-hour engagement along the Orange Plank Road. As night descended, Hancock suspended his attacks and ordered his men to entrench. Hill's Confederates had even more reason to entrench. They were outnumbered and needed to be regrouped into proper formations. But the men were exhausted, and Lee thought it more prudent to let them rest. After all, Longstreet's First Corps would be up before daybreak to relieve them. And so the day's action flickered out, with the rival forces, in some places, within a stone's throw of each other.[51]

Lee had reason to be pleased with the day's fighting. He had stopped the Union advance and forced it to fight in the Wilderness. His troops had repulsed every attack made upon them and had done so without bringing on a general engagement. Even during the first day's fighting, Lee had been spoiling to take the offensive. Twice he had urged Ewell to see if there was a way by which to interpose his corps between the Union army and the Rapidan crossings. There was not. But Longstreet's First Corps was expected to arrive by midnight. Once it was up, Lee could counterattack and defeat this latest Union offensive.

Grant and Meade should have been disgruntled. The Army of the Potomac had been slow to respond on this first day, Warren's attack had been a frustrating failure, Wright's division, when it reached the battlefield at 3 P.M., had accomplished nothing, and Hancock alone had made progress. Grant, however, did not see it that way. He told his staff that because neither Burnside's corps nor Longstreet's corps had yet been engaged, and the troops of both armies had spent most of the day struggling through thickets and fighting for position, the day's battle had "not been much of a test of strength." He continued, "I feel pretty well satisfied with the result of the engagement, for it is evident that Lee attempted by a bold movement to strike this army in flank before it could be put into line of battle and be prepared to fight to advantage; but in this he has failed."[52]

Although Grant overestimated Lee's intentions on May 5, both he and Meade accurately believed that A. P. Hill's two divisions on the Orange Plank Road had suffered severely and would be vulnerable to a renewed assault. Accordingly, they made plans to launch a concerted attack on Hill at 4:30 A.M. The V and VI Corps would pin down Ewell's corps in the Turnpike sector. The II Corps, reinforced by the divisions of Getty and Wadsworth, would strike west along the Orange Plank Road. Burnside's IX Corps, meanwhile, would move into the gap between the Turnpike and the Plank Road and attack Hill's left flank and rear.[53]

It was a good plan, complicated slightly by the fact that Burnside reported to Grant, not Meade, thanks to the IX Corps' independent status. That arrangement had made some sense while the corps guarded the Orange and Alexandria Railroad. But now that Burnside's men had crossed the Rapidan and were maneuvering in the bowels of the Army of the Potomac, it was awkward. Worse, Burnside had presided over the Army of the Potomac's humiliating defeat at Fredericksburg in December 1862. Many had reservations about him. At least one officer openly doubted that Burnside would reach his assigned jump-off point on time. Meade seems to have been sufficiently concerned to ask Grant to postpone the attack until 6 A.M. Grant grudgingly gave him an extra thirty minutes, but no more. If the attack were delayed for even a few minutes after 6 A.M., he feared, Lee might take the initiative.[54]

As it happened, Lee attacked first anyway. During the night he ordered Ewell to assault the Federal works at dawn, probably with the idea of diverting Union attention from Hill's beleaguered divisions along the Orange Plank Road. Ewell dutifully charged at 4:45 A.M. "Uncle John" Sedgwick, preparing his own 5 A.M. attack, wisecracked that Ewell's watch must be a quarter-hour fast. Although the Confederate thrust made little headway, it proved an unintentional spoiling attack. Sedgwick fended off Ewell's first assaults, then launched a brief two-brigade foray that got nowhere. Most of the VI Corps, in fact, remained on the defensive. Farther south, the V Corps never left its trenches, for Warren declined to attack until Sedgwick's entire force went forward. Learning of the delay, Meade tried to insist. Warren, having seen the damage to his corps when it had attacked the previous day without support, just as stubbornly refused. The morning wore into afternoon, the V and VI Corps sputtered fitfully, but in the end, nothing like a major Union thrust along the Orange Turnpike ever occurred.[55]

Hancock, on the other hand, attacked just as ordered. Punctually at 5 A.M. he attacked with five divisions: three of his own and one each from the army's other two corps. The early morning sunlight filtered through the woodlands and glinted off the infantrymen's muskets and the upraised swords of their officers. It made a memorable sight, but one only the Federals could see: the thick vegetation completely obscured the Confederates' view. A Union soldier doubted it mattered. From the crunch of boots in dry leaves, "they could very well guess at what course to direct their fire."[56]

Unfortunately for the troops of Heth and Wilcox—hungry, thirsty, and fought out from the day before—they were in no condition to receive an attack. The Confederate lines, noted A. P. Hill's chief of staff, "were like a worm fence, at every angle." Third Corps generals would argue for years over who was to blame for this state of affairs, but as Hancock's assault loomed out of the forest—"moving on our front, rear, and right," one brigadier recalled—many rebel soldiers drew a commonsense conclusion. After firing a volley or two, they abandoned their positions and headed west. One Confederate called the rout "disgraceful," but another rejected such talk: "There was no panic and no great haste; the men seemed to fall back from the deliberate conviction that it was impossible to hold the ground, and, of course, foolish to attempt it. It was mortifying, but it was only what every veteran has experienced."[57]

Only two out of eight Confederate brigades held their ground even temporarily. The others broke to the rear. Within minutes, hundreds of gray-clad infantrymen were streaming past the Tapp house and the tents of Lee's headquarters, pitched in the yard. Sixteen cannon were posted just east of the house, but their gunners had to wait until the infantry got out of the way before they could open fire. Once that occurred, they sent a salvo of canister scything across the clearing, then another, desperately, to keep the Federals at bay. But without strong infantry support, such an expedient could scarcely hold for more than a few minutes. The Federals would surely work their way around and pick off the gunners.

Lee saw the fugitives and rode down to the Plank Road, utterly beside himself, not at all the cool Southern gentleman of legend. He spoke "rather roughly" to the fleeing soldiers and to one brigadier exploded: "My God! General McGowan, is this splendid brigade of yours running like a flock of geese?" McGowan objected that the men simply needed a place to regroup. That was cold comfort. With Longstreet not up and thousands of Federal troops piling in, a place to regroup might well not exist.[58]

Hancock, trailing behind his advancing divisions, was as elated as Lee was appalled. Spying one of Meade's staff officers, he boomed happily, "We are driving them, sir; tell General Meade we are driving them most beautifully. Birney has gone in," he concluded, referring to the commander of his Third Division, "and he is cleaning them out be-au-ti-fully." The staff officer had some bad news: Burnside had only one division in position and was not yet ready to attack. "I knew it," Hancock fumed. "Just what I expected. If he would attack now, we would smash A. P. Hill all to pieces."[59]

Burnside indeed was late, and the staff officer's report was overly sanguine: Not a single IX Corps division was in place to attack. Having bivouacked just south of Germanna Ford the previous night, Burnside's men had resumed their march at 2 A.M. but were still stumbling forward down the road to Parker's Store. At 6:30 A.M., with the sound of musketry sputtering to the south, Burnside halted the column so the men could get some breakfast. It sounds completely irresponsible until one recalls that his corps had marched forty miles in thirty-six hours, with an average of four hours' sleep. Soldiers could not be driven so hard and still be expected to fight.[60]

Or perhaps they could. While Burnside's men boiled their morning coffee, Longstreet's men appeared, tramping up the Orange Plank Road. They had been on the road since 3 A.M.—had, indeed, been marching for thirty-five of the last forty hours—but they arrived on the field jaunty, confident, and filled with jibes for Hill's fleeing men. Longstreet calmly arrayed his corps for action. Ordinarily he liked to gather his full strength before striking a blow, but plainly there was no time for that. He would pump each brigade into the fight as soon as it arrived.

It was not easily done. Like everyone else, Longstreet's men had to contend with the Wilderness thickets. They also had to cope with the soldiers from Hill's corps who were still heading west. In later years Longstreet's chief of staff recalled of his corps: "I have always thought that in its entire splendid history the simple act of forming line in that dense undergrowth, under heavy fire and with the Third Corps men pushing to the rear through the ranks, was perhaps its greatest performance for steadiness and inflexible courage and discipline."[61]

As the first of Longstreet's brigades advanced past him, Lee rode up to its commanding general, John Gregg. "General, what brigade is this?" he inquired. The Texas brigade, he was told. "I am glad to see it," Lee said. "When you go in there," he continued, indicating the battle up ahead, "I wish you to give those men the cold steel—they will stand and fight all day, and never move unless you charge them." He told Gregg to tell his troops specifically that he would be watching them. "Attention Texas Brigade," Gregg shouted above the sound of the fighting. "The eyes of General Lee are upon you. Forward. March."

Nobody who witnessed the scene ever forgot it. As the brigade moved forward, Lee roared, "Texans always move them!" and the Texas brigade responded with a yell and a storm of emotion that brought tears to men's eyes. Lee attempted to follow the troops into action, but they would have none of it. An army commander had no place at the front, and any man on horseback, as Lee was, was bound to get shot. "Go back, General Lee. Go back!" they screamed, and when he showed no signs of withdrawing, they slowed their step. "We won't go forward unless you come back." Several men grabbed at the bridle of Lee's horse, Traveller, and the Texas brigade commander personally pleaded with Lee to go to the rear. Finally he agreed, and the 800 Texans went forward without him. Fewer than 250 returned unharmed.[62]

Longstreet presently counterattacked with both his divisions. Disordered by their early success, Hancock's men could not withstand this

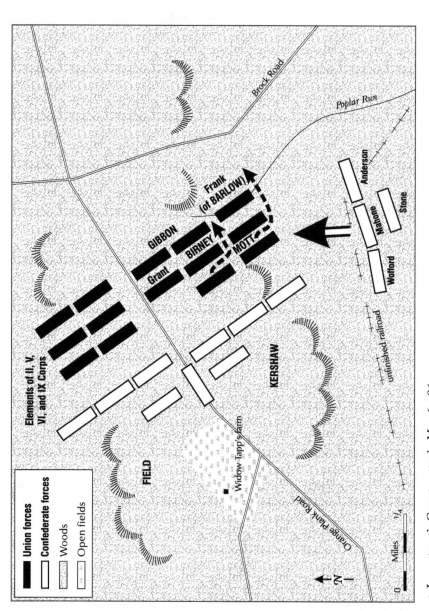

Elements of II, V, VI, and IX Corps

Union forces
Confederate forces
Woods
Open fields

GIBBON

Grant

BIRNEY

MOTT

Frank (of BARLOW)

Anderson

Mahone

Stone

Wofford

KERSHAW

FIELD

Widow Tapp's farm

Brock Road

Poplar Run

unfinished railroad

Orange Plank Road

N

Miles
0 ¼

5. Longstreet's Counterattack, May 6, 1864

assault by fresh troops. They fell back about halfway to their original position, halted and kept up a desultory fire. Barely two hours after his attack had begun, Hancock saw his glittering early morning triumph turning into stalemate, if not outright defeat. "They are pressing us on the road a good deal," he notified Meade at 7:10 A.M. "If more force were here now I could use it; but I don't know whether I can get it in time or not. I am filling up the [cartridge] boxes of the men who are returning, and re-establishing my lines."[63]

Worse, only two of Longstreet's divisions had been identified. That left the third, Pickett's division, unaccounted for, as well as that of Richard H. Anderson, the third division of A. P. Hill's corps. Wary from long experience, the Federals looked anxiously toward their exposed left flank. Sure enough, reports began to arrive about an unidentified Confederate force in the vicinity of Todd's Tavern, on the Brock Road four miles south of Hancock's entrenchments. The story was moonshine—Pickett's division was many miles away near Richmond, while Anderson was forging up the Orange Plank Road—but it led Hancock to hold back the better part of two divisions, just in case.

The morning wore on. Burnside's IX Corps began to appear, but instead of striking together, one of its three divisions was kept in reserve by army headquarters and later parceled out to reinforce the troops already engaged. The remaining two continued down the Parker's Store road, only to be shelled by Confederate artillery and harassed by a lone Confederate brigade with instructions to fill the gap between Ewell and A. P. Hill. At 8 A.M., Meade reassured Hancock that "two of Burnside's divisions have advanced nearly to Parker's Store. . . . They ought to be engaged now and will relieve you." In fact, the IX Corps was stalled in front of the Chewning farm. Burnside and a covey of staff officers gazed at the high ground held by the Confederates and wondered what to do. No one liked the idea of taking the hill by assault, but no one could think of a better way to resume the march. For over an hour Burnside's advance remained at a standstill.[64]

Lee, meanwhile, pondered how to turn the situation to advantage. Having staved off disaster, he could now return to his original plan to seize the initiative and launch a major strike of his own. Richard H. Anderson's division had reached the field. Although it belonged to Hill's corps, Lee assigned it temporarily to Longstreet, the general who led his freshest troops and, quite probably, the one he most trusted in the current situation. The army commander also sent his chief engineer, Maj. Gen.

Martin L. Smith, to explore the local topography. Around 10 A.M. Smith
returned, found Longstreet, and reported that he had found an unfinished
railroad grade, just south of the Plank Road, that offered an unguarded
route to the Union left flank. Longstreet summoned his chief of staff,
a trim, serious twenty-six-year-old named G. Moxley Sorrel. "Colonel,"
Longstreet told him, "there is a fine chance of a great attack on our right."
He waved an arm to the south. "If you will quickly get into those woods,
some brigades will be found much scattered from the fight. Collect them
and take charge." Hit the enemy hard, Longstreet continued, but not until
you have everything ready. He would be listening for Sorrel's opening
gunfire. When he heard it, he would order the troops astride the Plank
Road to attack as well.[65]

Within an hour, Sorrel had organized an ad hoc division composed of
four brigades and sent them hustling down the railroad bed. He guided
them into position and quite likely led them into action as well. His attack
struck the Federals not on the Brock Road, where Hancock was expecting
an attack, but on the left flank of the Union assault force about midway
between the Brock Road and the Tapp farm. The Confederates caught
the Northerners facing west, almost perpendicular to their direction of
attack, and although the Federals tried to wheel to meet their threat, they
could not do so in time. Two Union brigades on the extreme left broke
to the rear. Their collapse, in turn, exposed the brigades closer to the
Plank Road, who also ran. Fatigue as well as surprise played a role in the
debacle. "There was no chance for us when the left gave away but to run
or be taken prisoner. . . . I was shamelessly demoralized," confessed one
Vermonter. "I didn't know where my regiment had gone to, and to be
candid about it, I didn't care. I was tired almost to death, and as hungry
as a wolf. . . . My patriotism was well nigh used up, and so was I, till I had
some refreshments."[66]

From imminent triumph five hours earlier, Hancock now passed
abruptly to ignominious defeat. Longstreet's flank attack, he said ruefully,
"rolled me up like a wet blanket." Simultaneously, the rest of Longstreet's
corps attacked from the front, completing the victory. Hancock's men fled
toward the crucial Brock Road intersection. Some ran panic-stricken, but
most, after clearing the battle area, dropped to a sullen, deliberate walk.
"They were not running, nor pale, nor scared, nor had they thrown away
their guns," Theodore Lyman recalled. "They had fought all they meant
to fight for the present, and there was an end of it!" Trying to rally these
wayward men, Lyman got a vivid glimpse of where a staff officer figures in

the infantryman's esteem: "I drew my sword and rode in among them. . . . I would get one squad to stop, but, as I turned to another, the first would quietly walk off."[67]

The troops kept going until they reached the line of earthworks at the Brock Road intersection. Hancock rode along the line and told the men to get down and hold the works at all hazards. In response, many complained that they could not find their units. "Never mind that now," Hancock said, "but hold these works." Meanwhile, color bearers planted their colors on the fieldworks and called out the names of their regiments. It took time—perhaps thirty minutes or more—but finally the troops were reorganized.[68]

They received an unexpected reprieve. Longstreet, attempting to organize yet another attack, rode with a large party of officers down the Orange Plank Road. In the smoke and confusion of the Wilderness, soldiers from the Twelfth Virginia, who had just taken part in Sorrel's assault, mistook the cavalcade for Federals. They opened fire. The fusillade killed a brigade commander (Micah Jenkins), a staff officer, and a courier. It also wounded Longstreet in the neck.

As the corps commander reeled in the saddle and blood drenched his face and torso, horrified staff members thought he would surely die. He held on, however, and a surgeon who examined the wound cautiously pronounced it "not necessarily fatal." Nevertheless, the man whom Lee called his War Horse was out of action, for months if not forever. At Lee's direction, the planned attack was delayed, then abandoned. No one save Longstreet knew the location of all his brigades, and it would take time for a new commander to take charge and get a grasp of the situation.[69]

Not until after 4 P.M. did Lee resume the offensive, this time with a frontal assault against Hancock's earthworks in hopes that an aggressive lunge at troops already battered by defeat would complete their ruin. The gamble failed. At one or two places, charging Confederates managed to clamber over the earthworks and into the Federal position, but Union infantry and massed artillery soon compelled them to retreat. "This attack ought *never, never* to have been made," fumed Longstreet's chief artillerist. "It was sending a boy on a man's errand. It was wasting good soldiers whom we could not spare."[70]

After this abortive stroke against the Brock Road intersection, the battle of the Wilderness was nearly at an end. A Union attack scheduled for 6 P.M. was cancelled when Hancock, who was supposed to have made it, reported that his troops were too disorganized and low on ammunition after beating back Lee's assault. The Confederates made one final offensive stab when, at sunset, three brigades under Brig. Gen. John B. Gordon struck the northern end of Sedgwick's line.

The flank attack evolved over the course of the day from orders that Lee had given Ewell for May 6. These instructed him to cut the Federals off from Germanna Plank Road if it could be done "without too great a sacrifice." The brigade on the left flank belonged to Gordon, and any such attack would involve him heavily. Gordon had earlier fought in the Saunders' Field area—it was his counterattack which had routed the Iron Brigade—but after midnight on May 6 his brigade was shifted to the extreme left, next to the brigade of John Pegram. Gordon sent out scouts. They reported that the Union line ended opposite Pegram; there was nobody on Gordon's front. And from the First North Carolina Cavalry, patrolling beyond Ewell's left flank, Gordon got the impression that Germanna Ford was unprotected.[71]

Intrigued but not yet convinced, Gordon sent out a second wave of scouts to verify the information. They confirmed that the Union right flank was indeed "in the air," unprotected by any obstacle or defensive measure and so inviting attack. Gordon then crept forward to reconnoiter in person, accompanied by a cavalryman from the First North Carolina. "We were soon in ear-shot of an unsuppressed and merry clatter of voices," he wrote. "A few feet nearer, and through a narrow vista, I was shown the end of General Grant's temporary breastworks. There was no line guarding the flank. As far as my eye could reach, the Union soldiers were seated on the margin of their rifle-pits, taking their breakfast. Small fires were burning over which they were boiling their coffee, while their guns leaned against the works in their immediate front."[72]

Having seen for himself that the information checked out, Gordon set about persuading Ewell to adopt his plan. His operational concept was to start a kind of avalanche. He would flank the northernmost Federal brigade and set off a chain reaction. While the unsuspecting Federals drank their coffee, Gordon's troops would slip behind a screen of thick underbrush and form squarely on Sedgwick's flank, reaching a point far beyond that flank so as to capture his routed men as they broke to the rear. Then, when Gordon's brigade rushed from its ambush position, a simultaneous demonstration would be made along Ewell's entire line. As each of Sedgwick's brigades gave way under Gordon's assault, the Confederate brigade whose front was cleared by the Federal rout would swing into the column of attack on the flank, "thus swelling at each step of our advance the numbers, power, and momentum of the Confederate forces as they swept down the line of works and extended another brigade's length to the unprotected Union rear."[73]

Gordon sent an aide to find Maj. Gen. Jubal A. Early, his division commander, to brief him on the opportunity and the plan. The aide chanced upon Ewell and began briefing him instead. Ewell received the proposal noncommittally at first—one of Ewell's staff officers judged him actually in favor of it—but soon Early rode up and strongly opposed the plan. He marshaled his objections in the crisp, incisive style of the prosecutor he once had been. Gordon's brigade was too weak to do the job. The most recent intelligence reports placed Burnside's corps behind Sedgwick; thus a Confederate flank attack was liable to have its own flank turned. There had also been reports of a Union force north of Gordon's position and west of the Germanna Plank Road; these might slip into Gordon's rear. A serious military reversal at this juncture would be disastrous. Gordon then tried in person to sell the plan. But Ewell, impressed by Early's objections, told him there would be no flank attack, at least until the situation became clearer.[74]

Early's objections disappeared as the day went on. First, at 1 P.M. Robert D. Johnston's brigade arrived from Taylorsville, where it had been guarding the Hanover Junction sector. Placed to the left of Gordon's brigade, it extended Confederate flank even farther. Then the Federal threat west of the Germanna Plank Road disappeared, and by afternoon Burnside was confirmed to be on Longstreet's front and thus far removed from Sedgwick's sector. Around sunset, Gordon received the go-ahead for his attack.

Gordon had three brigades with him now: his own, Johnston's, and a third brigade under Col. John S. Hoffman. Numbering perhaps four thousand men in all—about the same strength as Sorrel's flanking column earlier in the day—the force filed quietly into a field that Gordon had discovered during his morning reconnaissance. It offered a good place to deploy into line of battle. Officers gave the necessary commands in whispers. The men struggled to keep their rifles and equipment from clattering.

In front of them lay two Union brigades under Truman Seymour and Alexander Shaler. These troops had borne much of the burden of Sedgwick's tentative attacks on the Confederate line that morning. They were tired and disheartened by the loss of so many comrades in two days of fighting. Some had just finished a burial detail. Others were

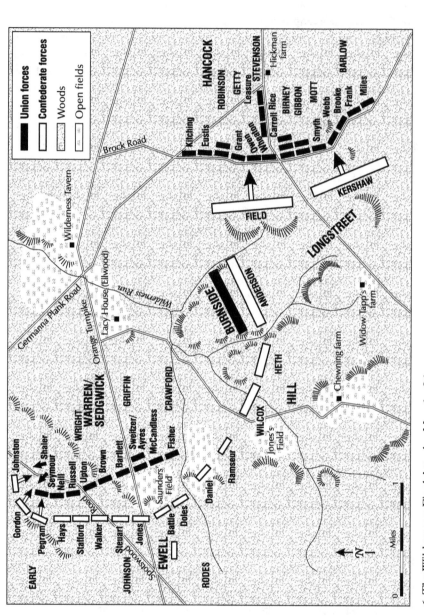

6. The Wilderness: Final Attacks, May 6, 1864

huddled around cooking fires. They had a skirmish line out front. From that direction came an occasional gust of musketry and a steady trickle of wounded men. Some of the wounded voiced ominous forecasts of imminent danger. Nobody paid much attention; wounded men often talked like that.

Abruptly the woodlands reverberated with the crash of gunfire and the unearthly rebel yell. The skirmishers came streaking through the bivouac and disappeared into the thickets to the rear. Hard on their heels were hundreds of Confederates, who vaulted the breastworks and plunged onward with a blood-curdling "Ki-yi, Ki-yi," as a New York surgeon recalled it. Shaler's brigade, on the extreme right of the Union line, was nearly shattered by the surprise assault. A few units in Seymour's brigade scrambled into line of battle but soon realized the futility of making a stand in their exposed position. Soon the men of both brigades were in headlong retreat.[75]

Shaler and Seymour were not present with their men when the attack took place. They were back at Sedgwick's headquarters on the Spotswood Road, making their reports. The crash of gunfire to the north sent them to their horses, and they spurred off to see what had occurred. Each saw that a complete rout was in progress, and each did what he could to stanch it. "Halt! For God's sake, boys, rally!" Sedgwick shouted. Then he recalled that a corps commander's job was to mobilize reinforcements, and he rode off to get them. Shaler halted on a wagon track that offered an obvious rally point. "For God's sake, men, make a stand on this road, if you think anything of the Army of the Potomac, make a stand on this road!" The brigadier's words had little effect. Within minutes, rebel soldiers held their muskets on him and he was taken prisoner. So, it turned out, was Seymour.[76]

It was a dramatic Confederate triumph, but almost devoid of real impact. Gordon's brigade did most of the damage. Neither Johnston nor Hoffman hit the enemy squarely. It was just too difficult to maintain an accurate orientation in the dense woods and deepening twilight. Meanwhile, Sedgwick mobilized his corps to shore up the threatened flank. One brigade went directly to the imperiled sector, while others extended Sedgwick's left to the Germanna Ford. Gordon, trying to capitalize on the initial success, made a second attack around 10 P.M. It got nowhere. For the rest of his life he blamed Early and Ewell for not letting him attack sooner. "Had it been made at an early hour in the day instead of at sundown," Gordon believed, "the 6th of May would have ended in the crushing defeat of General Grant's army."[77]

It would have done no such thing. A three-brigade attack was simply too weak for such exalted results, and besides, the twilight actually assisted the assault by concealing the approach, heightening the surprise, and obscuring Confederate numbers. An attack early in the day might well have achieved less success, even outright failure. But for some Northerners, harried after a day of unpleasant surprises, Gordon's attack seemed the crowning blow. One general rushed to Grant and told him that "this is a crisis that cannot be looked upon too seriously. I know Lee's methods well by past experience; he will throw his whole army between us and the Rapidan, and cut us off completely from our communications." Normally phlegmatic, Grant snapped, "Oh, I am heartily tired of hearing about what Lee is going to do. Some of you always seem to think he is suddenly going to turn a double somersault, and land in our rear and on both of our flanks at the same time. Go back to your command, and try to think what we are going to do ourselves, instead of what Lee is going to do."[78]

The next morning Grant reappraised the situation. The ferocity of the clash in the Wilderness was worse than anything in his experience, even the awful fight at Shiloh two years before. He was surprised the Confederates still remained on the field, and he told a subordinate that Joseph Johnston, the top Confederate commander in the western theater, "would have retreated after two days of such punishment." But he saw the battle as a draw—"we can claim no victory over the enemy, neither have they gained a single advantage"—and the question was whether to renew the fight or go somewhere else. The former option was unattractive. With Lee solidly posted behind earthworks, a fresh attack promised little but carnage. That left the second option. Grant quickly made up his mind to disengage the army and send it slanting off to the southeast, around Lee's flank. At 6:30 A.M. he wrote new orders for Meade: "Make all preparations for a night march to take position at Spotsylvania Court House."[79]

That day Theodore Lyman saw Grant under a pine tree, puffing on a briarwood pipe. "To-night," Grant predicted, "Lee will be retreating south." Like many in the Army of the Potomac, Lyman believed Grant still underestimated their adversary. "Ah! General," he imagined himself responding, "Robert Lee is not Pemberton [Grant's opponent at Vicksburg]; he will retreat south, but only far enough to get across your path, and then he will retreat no more." Lyman composed that fancied exchange in a letter to his parents dated May 18, after he knew the outcome of Grant's next movement. But it accurately reflected the rueful faith that most Potomac soldiers reposed in General Lee.[80]Yet these same troops were also starting to learn something about Grant. That night, as Hancock's corps awaited orders to move out, the men had no idea of their destination. In previous years after a slugfest like the Wilderness, they had always retreated. They were unsure that this time it would be any different. Then they spotted Grant. He jingled by with his staff along the Brock Road, past Hancock's earthworks, and everyone saw it: *Grant was riding south.* Instantly, every man was on his feet, cheering at the top of his lungs. Some set pine knots aflame to light the commander's path. The fitful light danced on the faces of the bearded, dusty men, in the heart of the dark forest. It was like a Nordic legend come to life. Everyone was deeply impressed except Grant, who considered the demonstration "most unfortunate" because it might give away the army's movement. He sent his officers around to shush the men, but the cheers did not finally subside until the general in chief was out of sight.[81]

CHAPTER THREE

"Grant Is Beating His Head against a Wall"

Grant need not have silenced the soldiers who hailed him in the dank thickets of the Wilderness. Lee already suspected the Army of the Potomac was heading for Spotsylvania Court House. He reached that conclusion in his usual methodical way. Unlike the panicky Union general who accosted Grant on the night of May 6, Lee did not believe his adversary could perform double somersaults. As far as he could see, Grant had exactly four options. He could retire across the Rapidan and abandon the campaign. He could renew the battle for a third day. He could resume his march toward Richmond by going to Fredericksburg and turning south along the Richmond Stage Road. Or he could move against Richmond by the most direct route, which would carry his army through Spotsylvania.

As the sun climbed over the smoldering Wilderness on May 7, it became obvious that Grant did not intend to launch a new attack. Nor did Lee. Instead, recalled one veteran, the two armies faced each other behind earthworks, "panting like two dogs after a hard fight." Nevertheless they probed, skirmished, tried to gauge their adversary's position and intentions. Near the Rapidan River, Confederate patrols discovered that the road to Germanna Ford was no longer defended. (Grant had given orders for the pontoon bridges there to be taken up and sent east to Ely's Ford, where they could assist in the evacuation of the Union wounded. Since it was no longer necessary to protect Germanna Ford, Sedgwick pulled back his northern flank slightly to better defensive ground.) From this information, Lee concluded that the Federals must be about to change to a new supply line, probably via the Potomac River and Fredericksburg, else they would not have abandoned their best route back to the winter encampment at Culpeper. Logically, that meant Grant was not going to retreat. Since he had not attacked, either, the only conclusion was that he was going to move: either east to Fredericksburg or south to Spotsylvania.[1]

Of the two possibilities, a lunge toward Spotsylvania was the most dangerous. The village itself was of no consequence; it was merely the seat of Spotsylvania County. What mattered was its road network. There the Brock Road intersected with a second road from Fredericksburg and two others that connected with the main Richmond highway. Spotsylvania lay barely ten miles south of the Wilderness battlefield, and the Federals were closer to it than Lee. If Grant got there first, he would be squarely between Lee's army and Richmond. Lee would then have to retreat fast or attack in open country where superior Union numbers and artillery would weigh heavily against him. Precisely because it was the most dangerous thing Grant could do, Lee gambled that Grant would do it. By 2 P.M. on the seventh he told his adjutant to direct Jeb Stuart to gain a thorough knowledge of the roads leading to Spotsylvania. "The enemy now and then advance and feel our lines," Taylor informed the cavalry chief, "and the general thinks there is nothing to indicate an intention on his part to retire, but rather that appearances would indicate an intention to move toward Spotsylvania Court-House. . . . General Ewell reports that they [the enemy] have abandoned the Germanna road, and the general thinks they may move toward Fredericksburg or Spotsylvania Court-House and must open some new way of communication."[2]

Putting Stuart's cavalry into action was insufficient. Lee had to ready his infantry corps as well. The most important of these was Longstreet's corps, still on the Orange Plank Road but manning earthworks that extended south of it for more than a mile. As the corps closest to Spotsylvania, it was the obvious choice to lead the march. There were two problems, however. First, with the experienced Longstreet badly wounded, it had a new commander, Richard H. Anderson, a division commander in the Third Corps but at least an officer with previous service in the First Corps. Anderson had good people skills, and he had been Moxley Sorrel's recommendation when Lee pumped Longstreet's chief of staff for candidates. But Anderson's combat record was mixed, and it remained to be seen whether a merely competent division commander could handle the expanded responsibilities of a corps, particularly with the prospect of an urgent night march directly ahead.

The second problem was the absence of a direct route to Spotsylvania from Anderson's current position. As matters stood, his divisions would have to countermarch to Parker's Store, some three miles to the rear, before they could turn south. Given the fact that the Union army had a straight shot down the Brock Road, that was unacceptable. Accordingly, Lee directed his chief of artillery, Brig. Gen. William Nelson Pendleton, to construct a military road leading directly to the Catharpin Road, four miles south. With so little time available, Pendleton did not build much of a road. Barely a track through the Wilderness, it was plagued with roots and tree stumps. Anderson's artillery could never use it—they would have to swing around via Parker's Store—but the infantry could manage.

Lee personally gave Anderson his instructions. Withdraw your corps as soon as it is dark enough to hide the movement from the enemy, Lee said. "When you have done this, march the troops a little way to the rear and let them have some sleep. At 3 o'clock punctually, march towards Spotsylvania Court-House. I have reason to believe that the enemy is withdrawing his forces from our front and will strike us next at that point. I wish you to be there to meet him, and in order to do so, you must be in motion by 3 o'clock in the morning."[3]

In the event, Anderson had his troops under way as early as 10 P.M. He expected to march them only a mile or two before halting for the night, but the surrounding woodlands still burned from fires touched off during the battle. They were also full of corpses, already rotting in the heat. Even after the column reached unburned country, Anderson could find no suitable area large enough to hold his two divisions. And so the First Corps stayed on the road, plowing onward through the night, the men becoming steadily more exhausted as the hours lengthened.[4]

Eastward a few miles, the Federal situation was equally nightmarish. Meade got his troops on the road around 8:30 P.M. Warren's V Corps marched down the Brock Road; Sedgwick took a route that carried his corps through Chancellorsville; Burnside and Hancock functioned as the rear guard. The army made terrible time. Delayed by ambulances crammed with wounded, the VI Corps got almost nowhere. Warren tried to forge ahead, but his soldiers were backed up for miles. "The road . . . was literally jammed with troops moving one step at a time," Col. Charles S. Wainwright noted in his journal. The problem, he eventually discovered, was "a couple of hundred yards of wet road, over which the water ran an inch deep, and where the men were picking their way one at a time." He could not understand it. Yes, every officer and enlisted man in the army was weary and, yes, the night was dark. But the very fact that the army was making a night march "was enough to tell every man that we wanted to reach some place without Lee's knowing it; and one would

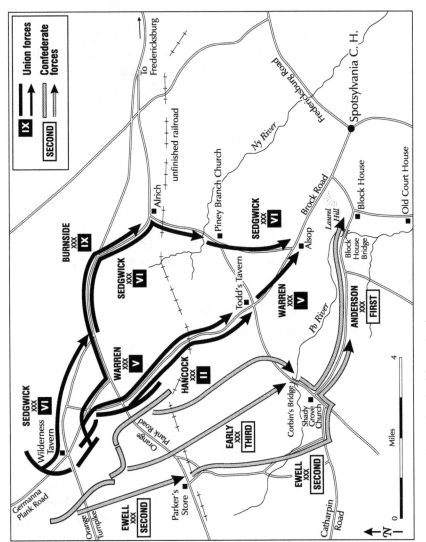

7. Movement to Spotsylvania, May 7–8, 1864

think that a desire for their own safety would spur them all up to do it, so as to avoid a fight." The Army of the Potomac's provost marshal, Brig. Gen. Marsena Patrick, declared the march one of the most disgraceful he ever witnessed. And its commander, George Gordon Meade, grew steadily more exasperated.[5]

Meade's breaking point came when he reached Todd's Tavern, a tired wooden building at the junction of the Brock and Catharpin Roads. There he discovered two cavalry divisions, inert, horses tethered and troopers asleep in the tavern yard and surrounding fields. Cavalrymen weren't supposed to be anywhere near this location, for Meade had ordered Sheridan to cover the army's movement and every trooper was supposed to be patrolling the roads. But Sheridan patently failed to carry out his orders. Meade interrogated the two division commanders, Brig. Gen. David McMurtrie Gregg and Brig. Gen. Wesley Merritt. Neither man knew anything about a night march to Spotsylvania, nor had they received instructions from Sheridan. They were at Todd's Tavern only because their outfits had fought a stiff engagement with Jeb Stuart's horsemen earlier in the day. The dead from the battle, in fact, still lay where they fell.

Sheridan, as far as Meade was concerned, had been nothing but trouble since he had taken over the Army of the Potomac's Cavalry Corps. No sooner had the fiery young man—he was barely thirty-three—arrived in April than he had come barging into Meade's office demanding that the cavalry perform less picket duty. Meade did his best to accommodate him, only to see Sheridan turn in a marginal performance during the Wilderness fight. The Ohioan spent much of the battle sparring with Jeb Stuart in meaningless but evidently soul-satisfying cavalry actions. A breathless dispatch to Meade characterized the just-concluded Todd's Tavern clash as "sharp and hotly contested," and added, "Our cavalry behaved splendidly." But the stark fact was that Sheridan failed in his primary mission to screen the army. On May 4, Lee had been able to close with the Army of the Potomac before anyone knew it. Meade fought on May 5 in ignorance of Confederate strength and dispositions. And because Sheridan had failed to get past Stuart and obtain a reliable picture of Confederate dispositions, Hancock on May 6 needed to leave many of his best troops on Brock Road to guard against a possible flank attack from that direction.[6]

Nothing could be done about Sheridan at one o'clock in the morning, however, so Meade put his good engineer's mind to work crafting instructions for Gregg and Merritt. He knew that, to reach Spotsylvania, both armies must traverse the Po River, a minor stream that nevertheless could be crossed only at a few bridges. Meade dispatched the cavalrymen to block the two spans that Lee's army would have to use if it marched on Spotsylvania. Gregg received orders to ride to Corbin's Bridge, where the Catharpin Road crossed the Po. Merritt's instructions required him, in part, to picket the Block House Bridge. The move to the Block House would carry Merritt's cavalry through Spotsylvania. "It is of the utmost importance that not the slightest delay occur in your opening the Brock road beyond Spotsylvania Court-House," Meade stressed to Merritt, "as an infantry corps is now on its way to occupy that place."[7]

While Gregg and Merritt went off to ready their divisions, Meade wrote one final message, this one to Sheridan. "I find Generals Gregg and Torbert [*sic*] without orders. They are in the way of the infantry and there is no time to refer to you. I have given them the inclosed orders, which you can modify to-day after the infantry corps are in position." That accomplished, the army commander lay down to grab what sleep he could.[8]

No more sleep awaited the troopers of Gregg and Merritt. They hauled themselves from bedrolls and saddled their horses. It took an hour or more for the two divisions to ready themselves and mount up, but by 3 A.M. they were on the road, with Gregg's men riding west along the Catharpin Road and Merritt leading his men south down the Brock Road. Gregg encountered little trouble, but Merritt traveled barely two miles before his men encountered fallen trees, an obvious roadblock. Troopers stumbled forward on foot to remove the trees, only to receive an angry fusillade from dismounted rebel cavalry: Fitzhugh Lee's division, it turned out, backed by artillery. A brisk firefight got under way. Merritt pumped more and more of his troops forward, until by daylight he had his entire division in action. But the Confederates refused to draw off, and finally Merritt threw in the towel. At 6 A.M. he requested infantry support.[9]

The nearest infantry belonged to Brig. Gen. John C. Robinson's division of Warren's corps, which was about a mile behind Merritt. The troops were making good progress by now, "passing at a rapid rate," noted Theodore Lyman, who watched them from the porch of Todd's Tavern. "In light order they were, many without knapsacks, or coats: most had thrown away all baggage but a blanket and haversack." Warren ordered its lead brigade forward. As it neared the field, the brigade ran into a mysterious officer imperiously barking orders. Asked to identify himself, the officer snapped, "Sheridan!" Sure enough, the commander of the cavalry corps was on the field, personally deploying the infantry regiments into line of battle, punctuating his instructions with an impatient "Quick! Quick!"[10]

By this time the sun had inched above the horizon, the day already ripening with heat. Robinson's men shoved back the Confederates' cavalry rapidly at first, for with infantry piling in, the rebels no longer made a determined stand. But the Federals were bone tired after the night march. Overcome with fatigue and heat exhaustion, many fell out of ranks. Presently Robinson's troops reached the edge of an open field. Their commander went forward and took a good hard look at the terrain ahead. About four hundred yards beyond he saw a grove of pine trees. The intervening ground rose slightly—not much, just enough to create a good field of fire and observation for the enemy. At the edge of the grove, Fitz Lee's cavalrymen had felled some of the pine trees to use as abatis, and, as Robinson watched, they furiously piled up fence rails to make a crude breastwork. Plainly the rebels had chosen the crest of the elevation (soon dubbed Laurel Hill) to make their main stand.

Warren and Robinson had a quick consultation. Warren wanted a prompt advance, before the enemy could complete his defenses or receive reinforcements. Robinson pointed out that only his first brigade was in position to attack at once. He preferred to wait for the rest of his division and have everyone go in at once. Warren reluctantly consented, then reversed himself. Delay would simply give the enemy time to deploy artillery; better to go ahead with the troops on hand. The brigade already in position belonged to Col. Peter Lyle. At Robinson's order, his men went forward. They got within sixty yards of the Confederate breastwork, received a staggering volley from its defenders, and took cover behind a shallow depression.[11]

Soon more brigades came on the field, including those from Charles Griffin's division. Each brigade went into action as soon as it arrived, in some cases so fast that the men did not know they were about to attack until they heard the actual command to advance. Warren tried to inspire them: "Never mind cannon! Never mind bullets! Press on and clear this road! It's the only way to get your rations!" A Union colonel who heard this exclamation thought it highly appropriate. Most of his men were ravenous; their haversacks contained not so much as a cracker.[12]

Robinson, on horseback, advanced with his troops, "knowing that my brave men would follow wherever I led the way." Instantly recognizable— a soldier who served under him thought him "the hairiest man in a much-bearded army"—the division commander was a reassuring sight; "Old Reliable," the men called him. He was trying to coordinate the units east of the Brock Road with those west of it, hoping to fashion a single hard blow out of the succession of brigade-strength attacks. But the task was hopeless. The rebels systematically let the Federals close to within sixty yards or so, then smashed each brigade with massed volleys. A minié ball struck Robinson in his left knee joint, breaking the leg. In great pain, he turned his horse to the rear as willing hands helped him from the saddle. Within a week the leg would have to be amputated, effectively ending his Civil War career.[13]

With Robinson down, the Union assault fell apart. The survivors retreated to their starting point. A colonel recalled that the withdrawal was nightmarish: "The sun was so hot, and the men so exhausted from the long run as well as from the five days and nights of fighting and marching, that this retreat, though disorderly, was exceedingly slow, and we lost heavily in consequence from the enemy's fire. My own experience was that, wishing very much to run, I could only limp along, using my sword as a cane."[14]

At some point during their assaults, the exhausted Federals realized that they were facing not merely cavalry, as their officers had assured them, but infantry as well. "Pretty dismounted cavalry—carrying knapsacks!" spat one man when he got a closer look at his assailants. The Confederates belonged to Anderson's First Corps, which had been on the march all night and now swung in from the Shady Grove Road west of Spotsylvania. The lead division belonged to Brig. Gen. Joseph B. Kershaw, who sent two of its four brigades hustling up to Laurel Hill, where they arrived just in time to help beat back Warren's initial charge. Jeb Stuart himself directed them into line. "Hold your fire until the Federals are well within range," he instructed, "and then give it to them and hold this position until the last man. Plenty of help is near at hand." Kershaw's other two brigades hastened on to Spotsylvania Court House to block an advancing Union cavalry division under James H. Wilson. (Wilson, in fact, briefly occupied the village before Sheridan ordered him to pull back, fearing that the position was too exposed.)[15]

With the repulse of his first attacks, Warren withdrew some three hundred yards to the tree line in front of Laurel Hill, brought up the rest of his corps, and began extending his line to the east. By this time he was certain that he had Confederate infantry in front of him. He informed Meade as much. Meade at first could not believe that the enemy's foot soldiers, with farther to march, reached Spotsylvania ahead of him, but Warren was adamant that it was so and that he needed reinforcements. Meade therefore ordered Sedgwick's VI Corps, which was approaching from Todd's Tavern, to deploy on Warren's left, after which both corps were to attack "with vigor and without delay."[16]

Meade, by this time, was a frustrated man. His orders in the recent Wilderness battles had been repeatedly questioned or ignored, the just-completed night march had been a botch, and now the presence of Confederate infantry at Laurel Hill announced that Sheridan's cavalry had not carried out his orders to seize the Po River bridges and block the enemy. He summoned Sheridan to his new headquarters at Piney Branch Church on the Catharpin Road and, when Sheridan appeared, read him the riot act. Not only had Sheridan failed to impede the Confederate infantry's advance to Spotsylvania, Meade charged, but he had also allowed Gregg's and Merritt's divisions to impede the advance of the Union infantry.

Sheridan, every bit as mad as Meade, pointed an accusing finger right back at the army commander. The rebel infantry had gotten by because Meade countermanded Sheridan's instructions to Gregg and Merritt, and thereby placed Wilson's division in an exposed position from which Sheridan barely extricated it in time. He could not, Sheridan continued, command the cavalry any longer if Meade was going to give orders to his subordinates. Further, he was sick of this business of screening the army, which as far as he could see resulted in "disjointed operations" that negated his cavalry's numerical edge over that of Jeb Stuart. If Meade would just leave him alone, he could draw his cavalry corps together and whip Stuart out of his boots.[17]

Sheridan's demeanor was not merely insubordinate but openly contemptuous, and the air was blue with obscenities as he harangued his superior officer. Meade went straight to Grant about the matter, undoubtedly hoping that Grant would agree to reprimand or relieve Sheridan—or perhaps even urge his arrest, as with Griffin on the first day in the Wilderness. Grant did none of these things. Instead he listened calmly as Meade relayed Sheridan's accusations, perking up only when Meade got to the part where Sheridan proclaimed he could whip Stuart if Meade would only let him. "Did Sheridan say that?" Grant asked. "Well, he generally knows what he is talking about. Let him start right out and do it."[18]

Although Meade could not have been happy at Grant's response, he dutifully composed an order for Sheridan to "proceed against the enemy's cavalry." It was probably no accident, however, that the order incorporated instructions that would carry Sheridan as far from the Army of the Potomac as possible. The cavalryman was directed to take his supply trains with him, and when those were exhausted to resupply himself at Haxall's Landing on the James River, more than sixty miles distant. Having disposed of the matter, however unhappily, Meade returned to the business of ejecting the Confederates from Laurel Hill.[19]

It took all afternoon for the Federals to prepare their next attack. Sedgwick's corps began arriving at midday, but slowly, and it required hours for him to deploy his troops to Warren's left and get them into proper position for an assault. Probably the delay could not be avoided. Thousands of men cannot be shuttled down crowded roads and wood lots in a twinkling, especially when they are as weary as the Federals were after their long night march. The obvious exhaustion of the troops appalled everyone who observed it. One of Grant's staff reported that the countryside was covered with stragglers. Warren noted that his troops dropped to sleep as soon as they stopped marching, that Robinson's men had fought "with great reluctance," and that his command had lost heavily from men who had simply hobbled into the surrounding woods, fatigued and wounded. He briefly feared a Confederate attack until it occurred to him that the rebels must be equally exhausted."[20]

The last of Sedgwick's divisions did not arrive until 5 P.M. An hour later, the corps was ready. As the sun slanted low in the western sky, the long deferred attack jumped off . . . just as Ewell's Confederate Second Corps began coming on the field.

The Union attack quickly degenerated into a cruel mockery of the concerted effort it was supposed to be. Despite the laborious preparations, only the troops east of the Brock Road, a single division from Warren's corps and a brigade from Sedgwick's corps, even advanced. West of the road, the Federals never received instructions to go forward. Some of the troops who did advance got lost. Others unexpectedly ran into one of Ewell's brigades. Undone by surprise, they broke for the rear. Another Confederate brigade actually counterattacked, driving forward six hundred yards before the Federals stopped it in a hail of gunfire. Although an expensive failure, the rebel counterattack nevertheless bled away what little remained of Union offensive spirit in Sedgwick's sector. Spotsylvania was now firmly in Confederate hands.

The engagement at Laurel Hill was emblematic of the two armies. For the Confederates, it was a great day that at once became part of the Army of Northern Virginia's epic. Veterans would thump their chests and tell of the cavalry's gallant delaying action against the encroaching Union army; of a courageous major who single-handedly snatched an artillery piece from capture "as if by a miracle"; of Anderson's dramatic arrival just in time to repel the first Federal infantry attack. The Army of the Potomac had no such memories. "The dim impression of that afternoon," recalled one soldier, "is of things going wrong and of . . . much bloodshed and futility." No one ever made a serious attempt to determine what exactly had gone awry. The failure at Laurel Hill was either ignored in most official reports or put down to the onset of night, the unfamiliarity of the ground, or the fatigue of the troops. Yet the Confederates, just as tired, fought with confidence, grit, and aggressiveness.[21]

That night and the next day the armies continued to gather, spreading out from Laurel Hill to the east and west. The position eventually occupied by Lee's army formed a semicircle around Spotsylvania Court House, with Anderson's corps on the left, Ewell's in the center, and A. P. Hill's on the right. The line began at the Po River about half a mile west of Brock Road. Just east of the road it curved north for nearly a mile before veering back south to guard the eastern approaches to Spotsylvania.

In the center of the line was an immense salient, dubbed the "Mule Shoe" from its outline on the map, that was the defining feature of the Confederate position. It owed its existence mainly to one of Ewell's division commanders, "Allegheny Ed" Johnson. Scouting out a position for his division on the night of May 8, Johnson had planned to continue the basically east-west orientation of the Laurel Hill line. But as he walked the ground he detected a low ridge that ran to the north. Like Laurel Hill, the elevation was barely perceptible by civilian standards, but as far as Johnson could tell it was high enough that if the Federals ever occupied it with artillery, the Confederate position would be compromised. He therefore thought the battle line should encompass it. Lee, when he learned of it, did not altogether like the Mule Shoe. It greatly lengthened his line and was vulnerable to attack on three sides. But it was hard to fault Johnson's reasoning. And anyway, Lee's engineers assured him the Mule Shoe could be held if packed with enough artillery.[22]

The Federals remained well north of Spotsylvania, with the V and VI Corps along the Brock Road, Hancock's II Corps on the western flank, and Burnside's IX Corps poised to the northeast. They had only a hazy notion of the exact Confederate position, which was well shielded by clouds of skirmishers and sharpshooters. One of these picked off John Sedgwick on the morning of May 9, as he inspected his advanced line near the Brock Road. Though far from a military genius, Sedgwick possessed an aura of avuncular masculinity that made him a natural leader. Just moments before his death, he bantered with an enlisted man who ducked every time a bullet snapped by. The rebels were too far away, he laughed. "They couldn't hit an elephant at that distance." The bullet that killed him plunged the entire army into mourning and dismayed even Grant, who opined that to lose Sedgwick was as bad as losing a whole division. It was known that Sedgwick wanted Maj. Gen. Horatio G. Wright to lead the VI Corps should anything happen to him, and out of deference to his wishes, Wright got the job. But no one believed Wright could fill Sedgwick's shoes.[23]

Lee, too, had to select a new corps commander—his second such decision in as many days. On May 8, as the Laurel Hill fight was heating up, A. P. Hill asked to be relieved from command of the Third Corps. He had been ill since the first day of the Wilderness fight, probably with chronic prostatitis. Lee replaced him with Jubal A. Early, one of Ewell's division commanders, a tough, accomplished leader though acerbic and often unpopular with troops, staff officers, fellow commanders, and pretty much anyone who had dealings with him. Lee called him "my bad old man." The one certainty was that Early had the instincts of a born fighter and knew how to drive men hard. A bit of Jubal Early on the Northern side would have served it well.[24]

Lee and Grant spent May 9 sizing up the new situation. Each believed he had the upper hand. "We have succeeded so far," Lee wrote President Davis, "in keeping on the front flank of [Grant's] army, and impeding its progress, without a general engagement, which I will not bring on unless a favorable opportunity offers, or as a last resort. Every attack upon us has been repelled and considerable damage done to the enemy." Grant had already written Halleck, "The result of the three days' fight at Old Wilderness was decidedly in our favor." And on the whole, affairs still seemed favorable. Although originally Grant had hoped to move the Army of the Potomac well beyond Spotsylvania, he was not greatly bothered that the Confederates beat him to the crossroads. After all, the main objective was Lee's army. Besides, the farther north he fought Lee, the farther Lee would be from refuge in the formidable Richmond entrenchments, and the more difficult it would be for him to send detachments against Butler's army, which had disembarked at Bermuda Hundred on May 5 and was presumably advancing toward Richmond from the south. "My efforts will be to form a junction with General Butler as early as possible," Grant concluded.[25]

As May 9 wore on, both armies rested, dug entrenchments, and prepared for the next big grapple. For the Federals, the first order of business was to locate the complete position of the Confederate army. Hancock's II Corps was ordered to search out the enemy's left flank while Burnside's IX Corps felt for his right. Nothing much occurred on Hancock's front—thinking that Confederate forces opposed him in strength, Hancock spent the morning at his Todd's Tavern position and did not carry out his assignment—but a division from Burnside's corps ran into Confederate forces northeast of Spotsylvania and got into a hot little skirmish. Coupled with other fragmentary reports, this suggested that Lee might be shifting his army to the east, possibly in hopes of interposing himself between Meade's army and its new base at Fredericksburg. Meade, alarmed, began casting about for ways to defend against such a thrust. Characteristically, Grant drew the opposite conclusion: If Lee were shifting eastward, this meant that he had weakened his left, or western flank. Hancock's corps received orders to find this vulnerable flank and strike it.

The main watercourse around Spotsylvania was the Po River, which flowed southeasterly to a point about two miles west-northwest of the village, then turned sharply south for two miles before resuming its southeasterly direction. On the map, the stream thus resembled a shallow Z. Just east of the point where the Po made the first of these turns was Laurel Hill, which the Confederate First Corps held in force. What lay west of the stream was anybody's guess. If Grant's hunch was correct, nobody was there at all.

No longer bewitched by the chimera of rebels hovering near Todd's Tavern, the lead elements of the Union II Corps moved out and reached the north bank of the Po (the upper bar of the Z) around 2 P.M. Grant, Meade, and Hancock observed its progress in person. Soon afterward a Confederate wagon train trundled into view along the Shady Grove Church Road about a half mile south of the stream. Succumbing to an urge to kibitz, one staff officer mused that Hancock's artillery ought to bombard the train while his infantry crossed to attack it. Meade was indignant—"And what good would you do? Scare a few niggers [*sic*] and old mules?"—but other voices endorsed the idea. Meade finally relented. Soon Union batteries were shelling the trains, creating a lively stampede among the flustered teamsters and mules. Several infantry regiments splashed across to screen construction of a pontoon bridge. That accomplished, Hancock's corps crossed the Po River in force.[26]

As Meade predicted, shelling the wagon train proved pointless: The Confederate brigade assigned to protect it made sure it got safely away. But at least the II Corps was now south of the Po and in position to do some mischief. By 6:30 P.M. Hancock's three divisions were headed east toward the Block House Bridge, which brought the Shady Grove Church Road to Spotsylvania and gave access to the Laurel Hill position. At daylight on May 10, the generals decided, Hancock would storm the bridge and strike Laurel Hill from the west. Once the II Corps was in action, Warren's V Corps would charge the hill from the north.[27]

It did not work out that way. Hancock's afternoon foray alerted the Confederates to his presence, and the rebel troops deployed at Laurel Hill took care to strengthen the Block House Bridge portion of their line. By morning, Hancock could make out the raw profile of fresh earthworks frowning at him from across the Po. He prudently decided not to throw his men into a river crossing under fire. Instead he would try to find a place farther downstream where they could reach the eastern bank unmolested.

Lee was well informed of Hancock's presence south of the Po River and, Union intelligence reports notwithstanding, he was not shifting his army to the northeast. On the contrary, he was hungry for the chance to attack from his current position, and Hancock's movement seemed to offer him the opportunity. The Confederate commander ordered the division nearest the Block House Bridge, that of Brig. Gen. William Mahone, to prepare for action, and sent a second division under Harry Heth circling around to confront Hancock from the south. If all went well, two powerful Confederate divisions would strike three small Union divisions while they were separated from the rest of Meade's army.[28]

This was vintage Lee aggressiveness and therefore the sort of thing that Hancock, like most Army of the Potomac leaders, kept constantly on guard against. Hence, it did not take him long to read the signs of the impending counterattack and pass his forebodings along to higher headquarters. Learning of Hancock's suspicions, Grant modified his plans. If the rebels were shifting troops to confront the II Corps, Lee must be weakening the Laurel Hill position to do it. New instructions went out for a general attack on the main Confederate line, scheduled for 5 P.M. Hancock received orders to recall two of his divisions to join the attack. His third division would stay in place so that Lee would not detect the new offensive.[29]

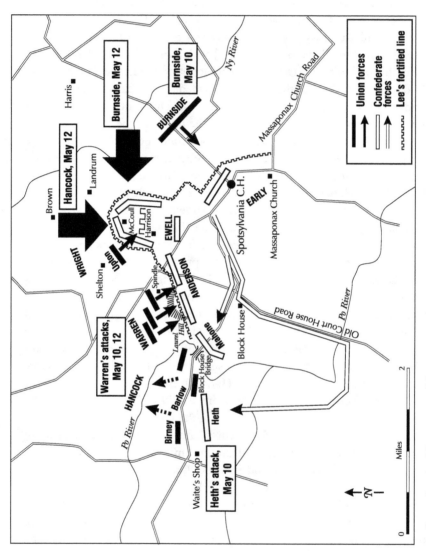

8. Spotsylvania, May 10–12, 1864.

Note: Mott's May 10 attack crossed the same ground as Hancock's May 12 attack.

That third division belonged to Brig. Gen. Francis C. Barlow, a thirty-year-old lawyer who had become one of the Army of the Potomac's finest combat leaders. He was probably the best man available for the assignment. He had his men dig in along the Shady Grove Church Road, facing south, with skirmishers deployed well forward to sound the alarm should the rebels attack. His troops did not have long to wait. Around 2:30 P.M., Heth's men came shouldering across the fields in massive lines of battle, while Confederate cannon posted near the Block House Bridge opened a strong supporting fire.[30]

Instantly fretful that Barlow's division might be gobbled up, Meade ordered Hancock to go back and supervise the situation personally. Hancock, who knew trouble when he saw it, told Barlow to fall back across the Po. Barlow complied but left some brigades to fight a rear guard action while the rest made it to safety. The men who stayed behind had a rough time of it. Heth's men stormed the Union fieldworks, "yelling," one Federal recalled, "as if they'd got a special license to thrash us." Hand-to-hand fighting broke out along some parts of the line, desperate enough in its own right, even more desperate for the Federals who knew that the rest of their division was pulling out and that if they remained too long they faced certain death or capture. Adding a final hellish touch, the woods behind them caught fire. Half-blind and choking from the heat and smoke, the survivors of Barlow's rear guard raced a thousand yards back to the Po River crossings.[31]

Afterward Hancock put the best face on this battle of the Po River, arguing stoutly that if Barlow's men had not gotten imperative orders to withdraw they would have thrown back Heth's division. But, in fact, the Federals did little more than avert disaster. They were no closer to beating Lee than they had been the day before. The Confederates, for their part, had once again demonstrated that man for man they outclassed the Army of the Potomac. They had not destroyed Barlow's division, but they certainly showed that they would seize the slightest opening to attack. Once again, Lee offered lethal proof that he was a very dangerous man.[32]

Perhaps none of this would have mattered much if the massive 5 P.M. assault had gone off as scheduled, but it did not. First, Gouverneur Warren, apparently anxious to neutralize criticism of his seeming lack of aggressiveness on May 8, insisted that the Laurel Hill position, which had previously seemed so strong, was now vulnerable. He must be allowed to strike immediately, not at 5 P.M. Meade gave him the go-ahead. But when Warren attacked, the position proved vulnerable not in the least. A hail of musketry and canister smashed the assault column within minutes. Aside from killing a good many men, the sole result of this early attack was to force the postponement of the general attack by an hour, so that Warren's troops could recover enough to participate.[33]

Next, in accordance with Murphy's Law, one division did not get the word and instead attacked according to the original schedule. This was Brig. Gen. Gershom Mott's division, which belonged to the II Corps but had remained at Todd's Tavern when Hancock's other division crossed the Po. Subsequently, it found itself temporarily attached to Wright's VI Corps. Ordered to connect the VI Corps, north of Spotsylvania, with Burnside's IX Corps east of the village, Mott's division had to spread itself very thinly in order to do so. It took nearly half its manpower just to maintain a tenuous skirmish line between the two corps, yet the division also received instructions to participate in the 5 P.M. general assault. Mott lodged a protest, telling Wright that it would take hours to retrieve the extended skirmish line into a compact attack formation. Wright told him to simply charge with the troops on hand, about 1,250 men—no more than an understrength brigade. Mott dutifully complied.[34]

The thin division moved forward down an open glade. Although Mott had only the vaguest idea of the Confederate position, the glade led straight for the tip of the Mule Shoe salient, packed with rebel cannon. Their gunners tracked Mott's infantrymen every step of the way. As the Federals crossed a country lane four hundred yards from the salient, the rebels opened fire with canister. Unsupported and exposed to shattering gusts of iron, Mott's men did what any troops in the world would have done. They ran, leaving their dead and wounded sprawled behind them.[35]

Warren had failed, Mott had failed—and the proposed general assault had yet to materialize. It did not appear at 6 P.M., either. Wright's VI Corps was ready, but the II and V Corps in front of Laurel Hill needed more time. After waiting thirty-five minutes for the laggards to deploy, Wright gave the order for his own attack to proceed alone. The striking column he had in mind was unusual, for Wright had eschewed the usual brigade and division organizations in favor of a task force created specifically for the occasion: twelve regiments, carefully picked from every division in his corps. The attack itself was also unusual, for unlike most Federal attacks since the campaign had begun, it was carefully planned and adroitly executed.

During the afternoon a strong Union skirmish line had cleared the rebel picket line from the VI Corps front. A corps of engineers lieutenant,

Ranald S. McKenzie, scouted forwarded and discovered a wooded area that offered a concealed approach to within two hundred yards of the Confederate trenchline. The division commander responsible for the VI Corps attack, Brig. Gen. David Russell, took a look for himself and agreed that it offered the best way to get at the rebel position. To lead the assault, Russell turned to his ablest brigade commander, Col. Emory Upton.[36]

Just twenty-four years old and three years out of West Point, Upton regarded the profession of arms as a Jesuit did the mission field. Utterly devoted to his vocation, he was impatient with the military ineptitude he observed all around him. In his stern estimation, most generals did not deserve to be corporals; he believed himself as qualified for high command as anyone in the army. On the latter score he was probably right. During the inconclusive sparring between Meade and Lee the previous autumn, the young colonel played a pivotal role in a deft attack on a fortified Confederate bridgehead over the Rappahannock River. Using tactics of his own creation, his brigade carried the enemy position at the first rush and bagged over a thousand prisoners. The victory was all the more impressive because the attacking force had been scarcely larger than that of the defenders.[37]

Collecting the colonels from all twelve regiments in the strike force, Upton led them to the edge of the wooded area that McKenzie had located. From where they stood, the ground sloped gently uphill to a salient in the Confederate trenches. The salient, Upton explained, was the objective point. The column would advance in four lines of three regiments each. Each line had a specific assignment. The first line would breach the rebel earthworks and continue onward, with the two flank regiments sweeping the trenches to the left and right while the third changed front to the left and opened an enfilading fire on the enemy in that direction. The second line would halt at the salient and open fire to the front if necessary. The third line would lie down behind the second and await orders. The fourth line would initially remain at the edge of the woods as a reserve. Upton would summon it when needed.

The most intriguing feature of Upton's scheme was its insistence on strict fire discipline during the advance. Until the enemy line was breached, no one was to use his musket. When the rebels opened fire, the attackers were simply to absorb the punishment and keep advancing. To respond would mean stopping to fire, and on previous occasions Upton observed that stopping drained too much momentum from the assault. To enforce the prohibition against firing, only the first line would advance with its muskets capped; that is to say, fitted with the mercury fulminate percussion caps that, when struck by the rifle hammer, ignited the powder. The other lines would move out with muskets loaded but uncapped, so that there would not be even the possibility of a man firing his weapon. As a final feature of the scheme, Upton ordered every officer in the assault column to continually repeat the command "Forward" until the works were carried.[38]

Upton would charge as part of the general assault, now slated for 6 P.M., and a few minutes before the hour he had his column formed in the woods and ready to go. Three artillery batteries opened fire on the Confederate line to prepare the way. But word came that the II and V Corps were not yet ready, so Upton waited. The minutes ticked by. Finally, Meade decided Upton's attack must proceed. The artillery bombardment had practically advertised that an assault was coming. The rebels must surely be getting suspicious.

At 6:35 P.M. the bombardment ceased. Upton rode to the front of his column and gave the order to attack. With a loud cheer, five thousand men rushed forward, worked their way through the abatis in front of the salient, and headed for the entrenchments. Two Confederate volleys ripped through their ranks while they crossed the open ground, but true to Upton's instructions, no one fired back. Instead with fixed bayonets the first line surmounted the breastworks and plunged onward, swamping the defenders and taking hundreds of prisoners. "Numbers prevailed," Upton wrote in his after action report, "and like a resistless wave, the column poured over the works, putting *hors de combat* those who resisted, and sending to the rear those who surrendered."[39]

It was a brilliant success, substantially aided by the fact that Confederate artillerists in the sector misinterpreted the hundreds of prisoners in Northern hands as a rebel counterattack and therefore ceased fire. By the time they learned the truth, they could not open up again for fear of hitting their comrades. But although in possession of the enemy fieldworks, Upton's men could not remain for long without supporting troops. Richard S. Ewell, the Confederate Second Corps commander, threw in reinforcements fast and hard, contained the breach, and began building strength to retake the salient. Help for Upton was supposed to come from Mott's division, but unknown to him, that division had already charged and been repulsed.

Even if they had come up as planned, the 1,250 men at Mott's disposal would have made scant difference. Any real assistance had to come from the VI Corps, and Wright was unsure what to do. He asked Grant, who barked unequivocally: "Pile in the men and hold it!" But once away from Grant, Wright's misgivings returned. It was getting dark, Upton's force was three-quarters of a mile in front of the rest of the corps, and Wright evidently doubted that reinforcements could arrive in time to retrieve the situation. Except for a single regiment, Wright committed no further troops.[40]

Isolated and increasingly beleaguered, Upton's men fell back to the salient's outer works, took cover on the exterior side, and fought off Ewell's counterattack. Upton went back to get his fourth line to bring it into action, but discovered that these troops had already entered the battle of their own accord. Finally he located Russell and asked for permission to withdraw. Russell granted it. When given the order, some of Upton's men refused to obey it—they had broken through, taken prisoners, won a great success! Only after repeated entreaties did they pull back. Overcome by their wasted sacrifice, many wept. Others cursed the fools in shoulder straps who nullified their victory.[41]

Upton's charge was the most successful Union strike of the day (at least for a time), but not the last. At 7 P.M., the II and V Corps finally launched their long-delayed attacks on Laurel Hill. It was not much of an assault. Having already failed on two occasions to breach the Confederate position, Warren was pessimistic about a third attempt. He made only a token effort to obey Meade's order. One of his divisions did not even advance; another went only a short distance before being told to return. "The charge will not be made this evening," a staff officer declared. "General Warren says the loss of life would be too great to risk it." Only the division where Warren was present in person made even the semblance of an attack, and this rapidly came apart, "a wild panic taking possession of the men." And although Warren rode among these troops to rally them, he made no apparent effort to renew the assault.[42]

Things were no better on Hancock's front. Having left Barlow's division and a brigade from Birney's division behind on the Po River, Hancock had only Gibbon's division and a brigade under J. Hobart Ward to make the assault. Gibbon's men took one look at the scowling Confederate works and flatly refused to attack. Ward's brigade did go forward and momentarily breached the rebel trenches before the inevitable counterattack hurled them back. With this repulse, the fighting on May 10 sputtered to a halt.[43]

In retrospect, it seems evident that the Federal high command erred by launching four separate attacks instead of one massive blow. Certainly this was not the initial plan. Yet only Mott's attack occurred by accident. The others were quite intentional. Meade approved Warren's request to strike ahead of schedule. He insisted that Upton go forward even though the II and V Corps were not yet ready. He had not suspended the Laurel Hill assault even though Upton's charge stalled. Why?

Since it was unlike Meade to launch such hasty attacks, a satisfactory explanation must look beyond him to the man who, continually peering over his shoulder, gave increasingly specific guidance about the handling of the Army of the Potomac: Ulysses S. Grant. Grant took a different approach to war than the cautious Meade. Like many commanders, Meade thought in terms of control. He preferred not to attack until he could be fairly sure of the outcome. Grant, on the other hand, thought mainly in terms of catching the enemy off-guard, forcing mistakes, and capitalizing on them when they occurred. He was certain that Lee's army was on the verge of collapse. In a dispatch to Halleck the next morning, he wrote optimistically, "I am satisfied the enemy are very shaky, and are only kept up to the mark by the greatest exertions on the part of their officers, and by keeping them entrenched in every position they take." True, his own losses were heavy—some twenty thousand men since the crossing of the Rapidan, he estimated—but Lee's losses must be even heavier, and on the whole, he considered the result of the battles to date "much in our favor." He urged Halleck to send reinforcements as soon as possible, for the sight of fresh troops would be very encouraging to the soldiers already engaged. Of his intentions, Grant wrote, "I . . . propose to fight it out on this line if it takes all summer." Although he gave little thought to the latter phrase, which was buried in the middle of his report, its note of pugnacity—artfully emphasized by Secretary of War Edwin Stanton when he saw the dispatch—electrified the North.[44]

Sizing up the events of May 10, Grant reached a number of conclusions, the most important of which was that Upton's charge, if properly supported, would have resulted in the decisive victory that had so far eluded him. Camp gossip blamed the failure, quite unfairly, on Mott's division. Grant accepted this assessment. Yet, in truth, the Army of the Potomac as a whole was behaving sluggishly, and this seemed particularly the case with the V Corps. The success of Upton's attack and the scapegoating of Mott's division diverted attention from Wright's indecision, while the fact that Ward's brigade had briefly cracked the rebel line obscured the failure of most of Hancock's troops to even attack. But Warren's tepid role in the evening attack was impossible to ignore. Assistant Secretary of War Charles A. Dana, who observed it, wrote Stanton that Warren's assault "was executed with the caution and absence of comprehensive *ensemble* which seem to characterize that officer," and he undoubtedly told Grant the same thing. Grant, who had earlier considered Warren an outstanding field officer, began to rethink his appraisal.[45]

Lee's assessment of the day's events was much different from Grant's. In a dispatch to the Richmond government composed that evening, he reported that although the enemy had made several infantry assaults against him during the day, these were "easily repulsed," except at Doles's salient—the point breached by Upton's force—but even then the line had been reestablished by dark. Moreover, General Early drove back an attempt to turn the army's left flank. In contrast to Grant's conviction that the Confederate army must be suffering heavy losses, Lee made a point of remarking, "Thanks to a merciful Providence our casualties have been small." All in all, his army was ably holding its own.[46]

Lee did have things to worry about, however, and they crystallized around three things. First was the ongoing threat to the Richmond-Petersburg sector from Butler's army, now firmly ashore at Bermuda Hundred and starting to probe toward one of the vital railroads linking the Confederate capital with the lower South. Even putting the best face on affairs, Butler's expedition was diverting badly needed reinforcements from Lee's army. And if the "Beast" advanced much farther, Lee might have to send some of his own troops to stop him. The bad news did not end there. Sheridan had left the Army of the Potomac and gone off on a major raid. Stuart was in pursuit with three brigades, but the Federals had already destroyed Lee's forward supply base at Beaver Dam Station on the Virginia Central Railroad. Over five hundred thousand rations of bread and nearly a million rations of meat went up in flames. True, Lee's army still had three days' supply of food on hand, and more supplies would soon be sent from Richmond, but the destruction of these rations was a serious inconvenience. Finally, and most important, Lee had so far been unable to wrest the initiative from Grant. If nothing else, this constant barrage of Union assaults, however easily repelled, was keeping him on the defensive. And without substantial reinforcements, that circumstance was unlikely to change.[47]

The next move was therefore up to Grant, and Lee had to prepare for it. He brought Heth's division back to Spotsylvania Court House, leaving only Mahone's division west of the Po River to guard against another attempt to turn his left flank. He was more concerned about the Mule Shoe salient, especially the sector that the Federals pierced so easily in their evening assault. Instructing Ewell to reestablish his entire line and be prepared for a renewal of the fighting at daylight, he even urged him to be on guard against a night attack, having heard erroneously that "it was a favorite amusement of [Grant's] at Vicksburg."[48]

Grant did not attempt a night attack, nor did he renew the battle next morning. But like Lee, he was impressed by Upton's success at the Mule Shoe. "A brigade today—we'll try a corps tomorrow," he reportedly said, and by noon of the eleventh he made up his mind that the best prospect was to attack over the same ground that Mott's division crossed in its ill-fated effort the day before. Further reconnaissance revealed for the first time the full outline of the Confederate position. The Union high command now had a fair idea of the shape and dimensions of the Mule Shoe salient, and realized that its apex must lie along Mott's axis of advance. A military truism held that the apex of a salient was difficult to defend, partly because creating the interlocking fields of fire characteristic of a good fortified position was impossible and also because the fire of its defenders tended to diverge, thus weakening its potency. A really strong assault stood a good chance of success, particularly if it employed the tactics that Upton displayed so effectively in his attack.[49]

By midafternoon, Grant committed the Army of the Potomac to this new course of action. He instructed Meade to move the II Corps behind the V and VI Corps under cover of night, so that it would be in position to join the IX Corps in a vigorous assault on the rebels at 4 A.M. Assuring Meade that he would make certain Burnside grasped the need to make a prompt, determined attack, he instructed him to order Warren and Wright to hold their corps as close to the Confederate line as possible, so as to seize any opportunity the main thrust might afford. He concluded pointedly, "There is but little doubt in my mind that the assault last evening would have proved entirely successful if it had commenced an hour earlier, and had been heartily entered into by Mott's division and the IX Corps."[50]

Hancock received his orders at 4 P.M. About two hours later he attended a briefing with Meade, Warren, and Wright. Warren, Meade instructed, would hold both his own line and that vacated by the II Corps. Wright's VI Corps would function as a general reserve. While Hancock made the main attack, supported by Burnside's IX Corps, Warren and Wright were to be prepared for anything, whether to attack on their fronts or move somewhere else and attack.[51]

The meeting adjourned. Hancock went back to his headquarters and had a second conference, this time with his own division commanders. The key man here was Barlow, whose division would spearhead the assault, reinforced by the divisions of Birney and Mott. (Gibbon would remain temporarily in place so as to deceive the enemy.) Barlow was nonplused about the assignment. He had heard nothing about the enemy's strength or position; nothing about the troops to be engaged in the movement, aside from his own division; nothing about the plan of attack—"or why any attack was to be made at that time or place." He had never seen the ground he was to attack, had never even visited the jump-off point, a farmhouse 1,400 yards north of the Mule Shoe apex. As if to further dampen his mood—literally—a heavy storm had just drenched the troops, the roads, the fields, everything.[52]

Barlow passed the word to move out. The same instructions went to the men of Birney's and Gibbon's divisions. "It did not take long to obey the order," one Federal recalled. "Each one had only to rise from the earth, shake himself in vain to get rid of the chills that were ever coursing up and down the spine on nights like this, wring the water out of his shoes, lift the cold, heavy musket from the stack, and all was ready." The division stopped first at corps headquarters to pick up two staff officers who supposedly knew the way. They seemed no happier about the operation than Barlow and scarcely more knowledgeable.[53]

A sort of gallows humor overtook the division commander. He began to find the whole operation hysterically funny. "I could hardly sit on my horse for laughter," Barlow recalled. "I remember that I finally said to Colonel Morgan [one of the staff officers], 'For Heaven's sake, at least, face us in the right direction, so that we shall not march away from the enemy, and have to go round the world and come up in their rear.'"[54]

Shortly after midnight Barlow's division reached the Brown house, which served as Mott's headquarters. The men were told to rest on their arms. Barlow, meanwhile, went to look for Mott, the one division commander with firsthand knowledge of the ground. If he found Mott—and in later years he could not recall that he did—he learned nothing of use. However, he did speak with Lt. Col. Waldo Merriam of the Sixteenth Maine. Merriam had participated in the May 10 attack and, Barlow wrote, had "advanced far enough to obtain some kind of impression as to the enemy's works and the intervening ground. He drew upon the wall a sketch of the position, and this was the sole basis on which the dispositions of my division were made. The intervening ground was open and comparatively free from trees and other obstructions, and from the information which he gave, we were able to form in such a position that a direct march forward brought us nearly upon the angle formed by the refusal of the enemy's line."[55]

Based on this information, Barlow made his dispositions, then lay down on the floor to grab a few hours' sleep before the attack was slated to begin. While he dozed, the other II Corps commanders arrived—by 2 A.M. Gibbon, Birney, and Hancock were all ensconced in the Brown house. Gibbon and Birney sat near the fire and, in low tones, shot the breeze. Hancock stretched out on a couch and asked to be awakened at 3:30 A.M. In the sodden fields around the snug farmhouse, only the most exhausted men were able to sleep. Pvt. John West Haley, who served in Birney's division, vividly remembered the fog and chill: "Our teeth chattered and our frames shook like leaves."[56]

Hancock arose at the appointed hour and went outside to observe the sky. Ordinarily at this season it would be light enough to conduct operations, but not this morning. The clouds were too heavy, and the fog was too thick. He delayed the attack by half an hour. The men stood in line of battle, cold, wet, miserable. When the order to advance came at 4:45 A.M., Private Haley recalled, it "wasn't half so disagreeable as one might think."[57]

Barlow's division spearheaded the advance in a formation similar to that of Upton's strike force two days previously. The divisions of Birney and Mott went in on Barlow's right, in conventional line of battle. Gibbon's division brought up the rear. All in all, about nineteen thousand men—fully a third more troops than had made Pickett's Charge at Gettysburg—began a swift but measured dash toward the Mule Shoe.[58]

Few of the senior officers believed the attack would succeed. The operation seemed too hastily planned, the instructions too vague, their previous experiences with Lee's veterans, entrenched or not, too forbidding. Such doubts surely transmitted themselves to the men in the ranks, but for the most part the troops were cold and drenched and glad to be moving again. The sheer weight of the attack must have provided some measure of visceral reassurance. Asked earlier why he had massed his column so heavily—would it not make a compact target for rebel artillery?—Barlow had snapped, "If I am to lead this assault, I propose to have men enough when I reach the objective point to charge through hell itself and capture all the artillery they can mass on my front."[59]

But, in fact, almost no artillery lay in Barlow's front. Misled by reports that the Federals were moving toward Fredericksburg, Lee ordered the guns at the salient withdrawn in anticipation of the need to make a sudden march to intercept Grant. During the night, pickets in front of the Mule Shoe discerned that the enemy was active on their front, and "Allegheny Ed" Johnson, whose division held the toe of the shoe, appealed to Ewell in person for the artillery's return. Ewell agreed, but not until 1 A.M., and his chief of artillery did not get the word until 3:30 A.M., just as Hancock was rising from his couch to prepare the attack. The cannoneers themselves were not notified until 3:45 A.M. or later. They were just beginning to reoccupy the Mule Shoe when the Union attack hit.[60]

Amazingly, the Confederate infantry did not seem prepared for an attack, either, though armies since time immemorial have stood to their weapons at dawn. Instead in some areas the rebel pickets were overrun without a shot fired—they must have been sleeping, one Federal guessed—while in others there was only the briefest spatter of musketry before the Union tide engulfed them. Just before the column reached the trench line, a shell arched overhead from one of the few cannon still in the salient. The Federals spontaneously broke into a dash. Within moments they were on the parapet.[61]

In some sectors a searing volley met the attackers full in the face. But in many areas they overpowered the defenders at once. The Union troops took many Confederate soldiers by surprise; too many Confederate weapons contained damp powder and failed to fire. Within minutes, the entire nose of the salient was overrun. Twenty rebel cannon fell into Union hands, most of them from the wayward artillery just returning to the salient. Hundreds of rebel soldiers raised their hands in surrender. Among the captives, it quickly developed, were two Southern generals: Ed Johnson and one of his brigade commanders, George H. "Maryland" Steuart.[62]

In fact, Johnson's division had virtually ceased to exist. As they saw the hundreds of prisoners, the dozens of captured guns, the sweep of empty trenches, the Federals realized that their apparently foredoomed attack had cracked Lee's defenses wide open. In the entire history of the Army of the Potomac, nothing like it had ever occurred. A courier spurred to Hancock with the news. He, in turn, breathlessly telegraphed Meade: "Our men have the works, with some hundred prisoners; impossible to say how many; whole line moving up. This part of the line was held by Ewell." The telegraph operator appended his own postscript: "General Hancock's troops are in second line works."[63]

These second line works were about a hundred yards behind the first, and beyond them lay a pine woodland, opaque in the morning mist. A few Federal units ventured into the treeline and blazed away at the Confederates who were fleeing to the rear. Most, however, were completely disordered by the attack. Clumps of men were everywhere, seizing prisoners, escorting them back to Union lines, rifling the Confederate bivouac areas for food and valuables. The dense column formation had dissolved into an unarticulated mass, packed with men twenty deep in some places. Further advance was impossible until this mob could be reorganized into the semblance of an army corps.[64]

A few hundred yards beyond the pines, word reached Confederate brigadier general John B. Gordon that something strange had happened at the front. It was hard to credit, because there had been no more firing than was usual when two armies were in contact. But from the dribs and drabs of information that excited men conveyed, it seemed evident that a sudden crisis had materialized, and after a few minutes came unequivocal news that Johnson's division had been overrun. As the commander of Ewell's reserve division, Gordon had standing orders to reinforce the front whenever help was needed. He now did what commanders in Lee's army seemed to do automatically. He counterattacked.

The first troops available were a thin brigade under Brig. Gen. Robert D. Johnston. Gordon extended them into a long, single-rank line and sent them forward to buy time. Then, as he began to organize a more orthodox strike with his remaining brigades, a familiar figure appeared on horseback: Robert E. Lee. Alerted to the disaster by clots of men running to the rear, Lee came up from the Harrison farmhouse several hundred yards away. Gordon spurred his own mount to join the army commander and asked, "What do you want me to do, General?"

Seeing that Gordon was already preparing a counterattack, Lee told him to continue. Then he rode to the center of the still-forming battle line, and Gordon suddenly grasped that Lee intended to lead the attack in person. Gordon would have none of that. Loudly enough so that the men could hear, the lanky Georgian informed Lee that this was no place for him. "Go back, General; we will drive them back. These men are Virginians and Georgians. They have never failed; they never will. Will you, boys?"

"No, no," the troops yelled back. Then, as at the Tapp farm six days previously, the chant of "Lee to the rear" went up. When Lee did not budge, Gordon and other officers interposed their mounts between him and the enemy. Finally a no-nonsense Virginia sergeant simply grabbed the reins of Lee's horse and swung him to the rear. Gordon ordered the charge. Three brigades went crashing forward in the gathering light.[65]

Although outnumbered, Gordon's troops had the advantage of being organized and purposeful in the face of an armed mob. After a short, fierce engagement they shoved Hancock's men back several hundred yards to the toe of the Mule Shoe. Two additional Confederate brigades also moved to the attack, and Lee sent for Mahone's Division west of the Po River. He pumped new units into the fight as fast as he could find them.

The Federals wavered between elation at their initial triumph and alarm that the Confederates were still hanging tough. At 5:55 A.M., Hancock fired off a second dispatch to headquarters, saying that all his troops were engaged. Wright's VI Corps must attack at once. Meade instantly complied. Within minutes, most of Wright's corps went forward, aiming generally at the same spot that Upton's men had hit on May 10. The Confederates in this sector, though hard-pressed, were able to hold, and shortly thereafter fresh troops came up to buttress the line. From this point on, although the fighting raged unabated, neither side made headway. The Federals could not regain the Mule Shoe; the Confederates could not force them to yield. Instead, separated by mere yards, the two armies stabbed and clubbed and shot each other.[66]

At their headquarters two miles from the fighting, Grant and Meade received a steady stream of reports. Hancock had clearly won an impressive initial victory—the taking of three thousand prisoners and twenty guns attested to that—but by 7:30 A.M. it was equally apparent that the situation in the Mule Shoe had reached a stalemate. Hancock was stymied, Wright seemed stalled at the outer works, and Burnside, who attacked at the same hour as Hancock, did not seem to be making much impression of any kind. That left Warren's V Corps as the sole force still uncommitted and able to influence the situation. Grant felt certain that if Lee was fending off three Union army corps at the Mule Shoe, he must surely be doing it by stripping troops from the rest of his line, and he began breathing down Meade's neck to send in the V Corps. Accordingly, Meade told Warren to prepare to attack to take the heat off the VI Corps. Thirty minutes later he instructed him to strike Laurel Hill at once.[67]

Warren balked. This would make the fourth sally against what by now seemed an impregnable sector. From what he could tell, Lee had not denuded this part of this line in the slightest, and in any case the enemy did not need many troops to hold the hill effectively. If Meade wanted him to attack, he should at least give him enough lead time to neutralize the most dangerous Confederate strongpoints first, and Warren said as much in writing. In the meantime, his only gesture toward an attack was to nudge his units tentatively in the direction of Laurel Hill.[68]

Little came of it. The men, wrote a staff officer, "had lost all spirit for that kind of work. Many of them positively refused to go forward." Those who did caught a savage blast from the entrenched Confederate artillery, especially the guns posted opposite Wright's front. One hapless regiment lost 103 out of the 190 men it carried into battle. Warren now lodged another objection with Meade: "My left cannot advance without a most destructive enfilade fire until the VI Corps has cleared its front." That brought an instantaneous response from Andrew Humphreys, Meade's chief of staff: "The order of the major-general commanding is peremptory that you attack at once at all hazards and with your own force, if necessary."[69]

Despite the sharp tone of his dispatch, Humphreys sympathized with Warren's objections, but he knew what Warren did not: Grant was fed up with Warren's temporizing and ready to remove him from command if he did not obey. Fifteen minutes later, hoping to spare an old comrade from this career-ending fate, Humphreys sent Warren a second note: "Don't hesitate to attack with the bayonet. Meade has assumed the responsibility and will take the consequences. Your friend, A. A. Humphreys." Warren at last bowed to the pressure. To his division commanders he sent terse, almost savage instructions, each of which concluded: "Do it."[70]

Warren's troops now attacked in earnest, some ninety minutes after Meade's original order to charge Laurel Hill. Moving out into the open, they at once came under a sustained and furious fire from the Confederate entrenchments. Where the ground provided some shelter, some units at least reached the screen of abatis in front of the rebel trenches. Where it did not, the fire simply swept them away like chaff. The dead and wounded men bleeding in the wet grass confirmed Warren's worst misgivings. Contrary to Grant's intuition, Lee had not taken any troops from this part of his line. He did not need to. A single Confederate division held Laurel Hill. Thoroughly entrenched in well-sited earthworks, with a beautiful field of fire in front of it and plenty of ammunition, that single Confederate division was enough to stop an entire Union corps.[71]

By noon practically the entire Army of the Potomac was in action. The II, VI, and IX Corps struggled for the Mule Shoe. The V Corps, repulsed at Laurel Hill, was being transferred piecemeal to the Mule Shoe sector, mostly to buttress Wright's advance. If sheer weight of numbers were the key, the Federals now ought to have crushed the salient for good. But numbers alone were not enough. In some sectors, Union commanders had trouble bringing their impressive weight to bear. In others, the objective had shifted in the minds of Union generals from the destruction of Lee's army to simply holding what had already been gained. Reinforced by the better part of two V Corps divisions, for example, General Wright used them not to revitalize his attack but to buttress his line against a potential Confederate counterstroke.[72]

Grant refused to abandon the offensive. He hoped that sustained pressure would crush the Confederate line. Lee, for his part, ordered the Mule Shoe held in order to buy time for the completion of a new system of earthworks at its base. The fighting raged all day and into the evening. Neither side gave an inch. Hour by hour the battle continued in the mud and the renewed rain. It was bad everywhere but worst, by common consent, at a salient on the western shoulder of the Mule Shoe known forever after as the Bloody Angle. Men on both sides recognized it as a critical position. "If Lee should recover the angle," explained one Federal, "he would be enabled to sweep back our lines right and left, and the fruits of the morning's victory would be lost."[73]

At the Bloody Angle the two armies stood yards apart, in some places divided only by a trench parapet. Wrote the commander of a VI Corps brigade that fought there: "Our men would reach over the logs and fire into the faces of the enemy, would stab over with their bayonets; many were shot and stabbed through crevices and holes between the logs; men mounted the works, and with muskets rapidly handed them kept up a continuous fire until they were shot down, while others would take their places and continue the deadly work." Pack mules brought up fresh ammunition from the rear. One soldier remembered firing four hundred rounds that day.[74]

These and similar accounts suggest a struggle of continuous ferocity, but human beings could never have sustained a battle at such a tempo except in a suicidal frenzy. In reality the fighting ebbed and flowed.

The same soldier who recalled firing four hundred times that day also remembered that "sometimes the enemy's fire would slacken, and the moments would become so monotonous that something would have to be done to stir them up." At times the combat subsided enough so that Confederate soldiers who wished to give up could have their surrenders accepted. A few men crawled away a few feet and fell fast asleep in the mud. One Confederate soldier actually changed clothes. A Vermont soldier testified that although each man in his regiment received about three hundred rounds that day, nowhere near that number were actually fired, for many of the paper cartridges were damp and useless. The casualty figures confirm the picture of sustained but modulated combat. The VI Corps lost about a thousand men in killed, wounded, and missing on May 12, out of a force of approximately sixteen thousand. Since it was engaged for about twenty hours in all, its loss rate averaged about fifty men per hour. By contrast, Pickett's assault column at Gettysburg sustained five thousand casualties in thirty minutes.[75]

None of which diminishes the misery and sacrifice of the men who struggled for the Mule Shoe. The emotional strain and physical exhaustion of the long contest were plainly immense, the overall casualties severe. By 3 A.M., when Lee's new line was finished and the last Confederate defenders abandoned the Mule Shoe, his army had sustained at least four thousand dead and wounded, with another four thousand taken prisoner by the Federals. The Union army lost over six thousand killed, wounded, and missing. The next morning revealed a grisly scene of dead men and horses half-trampled in the mud. The trenches were filled with corpses. Bodies that fell across the top of the earthworks had been pounded into unrecognizable pulp by dozens of musket balls and shell fragments. One officer could identify a fallen friend only by the color of the man's beard and a few scraps from a letter.[76]

Despite the losses, Grant interpreted the battle of May 12 as a success. That the enemy managed to repair the breach in his line struck the Union general in chief as less significant than the hundreds of captured rebel soldiers who were now en route, under guard, to Belle Plain. At 6:30 P.M., while fighting still sputtered at the Bloody Angle, he summarized the day in a dispatch to Halleck: "The eighth day of battle closes, leaving between 3,000 and 4,000 prisoners in our hands for the day's work, including 2 general officers and over 30 pieces of artillery [sic]. The enemy are obstinate and seem to have found the last ditch. We have lost no organization, not even a company, while we have destroyed and captured one division (Johnson's), one brigade (Doles'), and one regiment entire of the enemy."[77]

Some Confederates were defiant about the Mule Shoe debacle. Lee's adjutant, Lt. Col. Walter H. Taylor, conceded to his wife, "The 12th was an unfortunate day for us—we recovered most of the ground lost but c[oul]d not regain our *guns*. This hurts our pride—but we are determined to make our next success all the greater to make amends for this disaster. Our men are in good heart & condition—our confidence, certainly mine, unimpaired." He concluded stoutly: "Grant is beating his head against a wall. His own people confess a loss of 50,000 thus far."[78]

Lee was more subdued. Although he managed to construct a new defensive line across the base of the Mule Shoe, the losses of May 12 hurt. The following day he wrote President Davis requesting reinforcements. "We are outnumbered and constant labor is impairing the efficiency of the men."[79]

Fortunately for the Confederates, the Army of the Potomac was weary from its own ceaseless labors, and the rains continued to fall. The days that followed were frustrating ones for Grant. From the reports of Union skirmishers who gingerly probed Lee's new line, he concluded the enemy was now most vulnerable on his right flank, east of Spotsylvania Court House. On the evening of the thirteenth he put the V and VI Corps in motion, shifting them behind the II and IX Corps in hopes that they could attack Lee to advantage. Nothing come of it. Mud and rain badly slowed the troops who were to renew the offensive. Meade could not organize a massed attack before Lee saw the danger and blocked it. By the morning of the sixteenth, Grant conceded to Halleck that after five days of almost continuous rain, "All offensive operations necessarily cease until we can have twenty-four hours of dry weather." But, he added, "You can assure the President and Secretary of War that the elements alone have suspended hostilities and that it is in no manner due to weakness or exhaustion on our part."[80]

The sun returned the next day. True to his word, Grant sent the VI Corps on yet another trek, this time to the battlefield of May 12, where it supported the II Corps in a dawn assault on Lee's new line across the base of the Mule Shoe. In many respects the attack was a repetition of the charge made nearly a week before, but this time neither fog, damp powder, nor absent artillery hindered the Confederate defense. The result was simple slaughter.

Six divisions moved into Mule Shoe for a 4 A.M. assault, but spent so much time occupying and moving through the latticework of abandoned entrenchments—an area now dubbed "Hell's Half Acre"—that it was 8 A.M. before the attack was finally launched. The rebels knew full well the attack was coming. Lookouts in the court house belfry picked up the approach march on the previous day, and Ewell's pickets had deduced the exact objective. An artillery major "could not believe a serious attempt would be made to assail such a line as Ewell had, in open day, at such a distance." Still, "it was welcomed by the Confederates as a chance to repay old scores." Massed cannon hurled shell and canister at the Union infantry and smashed the attack almost unaided. Ewell's artillery chief was jubilant: "This attack fairly illustrates the immense power of artillery well handled." Meade was rueful: "We found the enemy so strongly intrenched that even Grant thought it useless to knock our heads against a brick wall, and directed a suspension."[81]

Perhaps a disgruntled Union infantryman put it best. The Wilderness, he wrote, was a soldier's battle. In those ravines and thickets, no one expected a lot of generalship. But Spotsylvania was different. "Here the Confederates are strongly entrenched, and it was the duty of our generals to know the strength of the works before they launched the army against them."[82]

Grant clung to his strategy of relentless assaults from the conviction that Lee must be in desperate straits: his capital was jeopardized by Butler's expedition, his supplies were interdicted by Sigel, Averell, Crook, and Sheridan, and all prospect of reinforcement was denied him by the relentless pressure of these five subsidiary offensives. But hard on the heels of the repulse of Hancock and Wright came word that the most important of these offensives had failed. Sigel was in retreat down the Shenandoah Valley, and Butler was in retreat to his defensive lines at Bermuda Hundred. This meant not only that two key threats to Lee had been eliminated but also that the Confederate commander could shortly expect to receive thousands of troops to replace his losses. "All this news was very discouraging," Grant conceded in his memoirs. It occurred to him that Lee must have known of these developments before he did. "In fact, the good news [for the enemy] must have been known to him at the moment I thought he was in despair, and his anguish must have been already relieved when we were enjoying his supposed discomfiture."[83]

His coordinated offensive suddenly in shambles, Grant realized that the Army of the Potomac could no longer remain at Spotsylvania. If the troops could not crack Lee's defenses while the Confederates were fighting unaided, what chance did they have once Lee began receiving the reinforcements that were surely on the way? Colonel Taylor was right—Grant really *was* beating his head against a wall. It was time to try something new, to slide past Lee's flank, to find some favorable battlefield. But even as he laid plans for new operations, Grant wondered: What had happened to wreck his grand design?

CHAPTER FOUR

The Collapse of Grant's Peripheral Strategy

In his final report, Grant claimed that early in the war he became convinced that there was only one way to break the Confederacy: first, by using "the greatest number of troops practicable against the armed force of the enemy," and then by hammering the rebel armies and resources "until by mere attrition, if in no other way, there should be nothing left to him" but submission. Although Grant made his report in the full glare of hindsight, there is no reason to suppose that this passage misstates his strategy for 1864. It certainly squares with the way he organized the Union effort in Virginia.[1]

By May 5, 1864, no fewer than 165,000 Federal soldiers menaced the Old Dominion. Grant and Meade had 122,000 men in the Wilderness. Benjamin F. Butler, with 27,000 more, steamed up the James River estuary toward Bermuda Hundred. Six thousand troops under Franz Sigel had begun a march up the Shenandoah Valley, while another 8,500 under Brig. Gens. George Crook and William W. Averell forged across the Allegheny Mountains toward targets on the Virginia and Tennessee River. To meet this threat, the Confederates could muster only about 90,000 troops of their own, and some of these would have to be transferred from the Carolinas. Given this preponderance of strength, Grant's coordinated offensives could scarcely fail to cripple the rebel war effort in Virginia. Yet in less than two weeks, the whole affair was a shambles. Every subsidiary offensive had been turned back or defeated. Reinforcements were speeding to Lee from tidewater and mountain country alike.[2]

How had such a thing come to pass? The answer, reduced to essentials, was simply this: With the exception of Grant and Sheridan, the Federal commanders feared the Confederates more than the Confederates feared the Federals. Time and again, Northern forces advanced with caution, took ominous rumors at face value, and failed to press home formidable numerical advantages. As a result, the Confederates in the eastern theater managed the one thing Grant explicitly sought to prevent: the exploitation "of their great advantage in interior lines of communication for transporting troops from east to west, re-enforcing the army most vigorously pressed," namely, Lee's.[3]

For nearly three weeks, however, it was not obvious that this was going to occur. The subsidiary offensives collapsed at different times, in different ways, for different reasons, and they were by no means totally bereft of success. The interdependent expeditions of Crook and Averell are a case in point.

Grant originally intended these expeditions to be a single massive raid led by Maj. Gen. Edward O. C. Ord, a trusted protégé who had been one of his corps commanders during the Vicksburg campaign. His instructions to Ord convey the sweep of his proposed campaign. Ord was to assemble about ten thousand men at Beverly, West Virginia, then strike southward and wreck the Virginia and Tennessee Railroad so thoroughly "that it can be of no further use to the enemy during the rebellion." He should also destroy whatever other Confederate war resources he could lay hands on. Then, once joined by a separate force under George Crook that would attack the Confederate salt works at Saltville, Ord would if practicable march northeast to Lynchburg, an important industrial center in central Virginia. If things went extremely well, he would go still further, marching through the piedmont, living off the land, and ultimately "establish[ing] a supply base on the James River"—which could only mean the James River estuary. All in all, Grant envisioned a raid from mountain highlands to tidewater flats.[4]

Nothing like this transpired, however, and for a simple reason: The commander of the Department of West Virginia, from which Ord's expedition would be launched, refused to cooperate. The commander's name was Maj. Gen. Franz Sigel, a thirty-nine-year-old German expatriate, failed revolutionary, and darling of the German American community. Slightly built, with a vague resemblance to Genghis Khan, Sigel cultivated a permanent sense of grievance against the Anglo-dominated army that had so often slighted him—for example, by once giving him command of the smallest corps in the Army of the Potomac. This, Sigel had complained in early 1863, was "exceedingly unpleasant," and he had asked to be relieved of duty. He got his wish with a vengeance. Not only was he removed from command but Halleck—who detested him—left him awaiting orders from March 1863 through the beginning of 1864.[5]

Sigel got out of the doghouse because of his impeccable political connections and his continued support of Lincoln, who doubtless appreciated Sigel's efforts to channel the German American vote away from one of his chief rivals for renomination, John C. Frémont. On February 29, 1864, Lincoln ordered Secretary of War Stanton to put Sigel in charge of the Department of West Virginia. David Hunter Strother, a staff officer stationed in the department, grasped the case exactly. "Halleck they say is indignant," he confided to his diary, "but the Dutch vote must be secured at all hazards for the Government and the sacrifice of West Virginia is a small matter."[6]

Grant had no intention of sacrificing West Virginia. Sigel could command the department, but the actual fighting would be left to competent professionals, Ord and Crook. Both men visited Grant's headquarters at the end of March, and Grant made clear to Sigel that he expected Sigel's full cooperation. Sigel, however, merely felt aggrieved, particularly with Ord. "All dispositions are made in such a manner as if I did not exist at all," complained the department commander, probably with great accuracy. He made life so hard for Ord that on April 19, Ord asked to be relieved of his assignment. Ord gave his reasons to Secretary of State William Seward, a political patron: "The force allowed me by General Sigel was about one-half what he was directed should be the least force of my column, and I now state that when I informed him that he was to come to a certain point with supplies that my men might not starve, he stated to me in so many words, 'I don't think I shall do it. I don't think I shall do it'; and I knew he would not." Ord got the impression that if the Beverly expedition were abandoned, the force slated for assembly there would go mainly to Crook, a good soldier. For that reason he chose to step aside.[7]

In the end, the great Beverly raid devolved into three smaller expeditions: the first, involving Crook and six thousand troops, to operate against the Virginia and Tennessee Railroad near Dublin Depot, Virginia; the second, two thousand cavalry under Averell, to strike the Confederate lead mines and salt works at Wytheville and Saltville; and, more or less at Sigel's own insistence, a third operation thrusting up the Shenandoah Valley, aimed vaguely at a link-up with Crook and Averell, and naturally under Sigel's personal command.

Crook departed first. With three brigades of infantry and two artillery batteries, he left Gauley Bridge, West Virginia, on May 2. A soldier of wide experience and good reputation, Crook was admired by his troops, who liked his unpretentious strength. One of his colonels, the future president Rutherford B. Hayes, declared flatly, "Crook is the best soldier we have ever served under." No better man could have led the expedition.[8]

Averell left three days later. A veteran of several campaigns with the Army of the Potomac, he was perhaps best known for his victory in a minor cavalry scrap at Kelly's Ford on the Rappahannock River in March 1863. Angered by taunting missives from Fitzhugh Lee, an old West Point classmate who led a brigade under Jeb Stuart, Averell blew up altogether when Lee baited him to cross the Rappahannock, pay a visit, and bring along some coffee. Union horsemen in those days had a reputation for being totally outclassed by their Confederate counterparts, but Averell won permission to make a foray against the rebel cavalry. He took a division across the river, got into a stiff little fight, killed Maj. John Pelham, Stuart's much beloved horse artillery commander, and left a note for his rival: "Dear Fitz, here's your coffee. Here's your visit. How do you like it?"[9]

The story had two divergent morals. On the one hand, the skirmish at Kelly's Ford was a symbolic turning point in the fortunes of the Union cavalry in the East and signaled that henceforth they could not be treated casually. On the other, the Confederate situation had been more tenuous than Averell supposed, and he had in fact traded a symbolic victory for a substantive one by getting skittish and beating a premature retreat.

Opposing Crook and Averell were perhaps 7,500 Confederates, scattered across 120 miles of rugged terrain. Leading them was Maj. Gen. John Cabell Breckinridge, a former U.S. vice president who had become an able soldier. Breckinridge had deployed his men so as to guard every avenue by which the Federals might advance, but he did not have enough troops at any one point to counter the enemy's punch. He could only hope to foresee the blow before it fell and concentrate all his forces to stop it. Success in such a strategy required two things. "We must trust to the earliest intelligence of enemy movements," he wrote, "and then to the promptest movements."[10]

In this spirit, the Confederates at the end of April watched the West Virginia mountains closely. They soon spotted Averell's cavalry but did not immediately locate Crook, the main threat. Indeed, on May 4, at Robert E. Lee's request, Breckinridge began shifting his three strongest brigades to the Shenandoah Valley to stop Sigel's advance, which Lee interpreted as a potential move to pitch into his rear as he moved to meet Grant. Breckinridge personally accompanied the three brigades and handed command of the remaining troops to Brig. Gen. Albert Jenkins. Jenkins, a native West Virginian, was a former U.S. congressman who had led a brigade in Jeb Stuart's cavalry during the Gettysburg campaign and been severely wounded. Barely thirty-three, he sported an enormous beard that made him seem much older. A talented man and a competent soldier, Jenkins could be relied upon to do his best in any situation.[11]

The situation quickly became grim. With barely enough troops to contain Averell, Jenkins suddenly confronted a new threat. On May 5, Confederate scouts spotted Crook's column as it approached Princeton, West Virginia. "Five regiments are now in view," the captain of the scouts reported via courier, "and more coming." Jenkins had barely a corporal's guard on hand to stop them. Although technically he commanded four thousand men, in reality most of them were still far distant, and in the fast-changing situation he was unsure even of their locations. Almost totally in the dark, Jenkins knew just two things. A strong enemy force was approaching, and he had just two hundred men available to oppose it.[12]

Jenkins's tiny band held a position at the New River Narrows, a few miles inside the Virginia border. Crook entered Princeton, less than a day's march away, on May 6. Jenkins fired off a taut message to Breckinridge, asking to retain one of the brigades earmarked to oppose Sigel. Breckinridge agreed.[13]

Next day, Crook's division crossed Wolf Creek Mountain at Rocky Gap, a shrewd move that placed him on Jenkins's flank. Jenkins fell back from the now-indefensible Narrows and headed for Dublin Depot on the railroad. It was the point on the railroad closest to Crook, and hence the logical place to make a stand. The brigade he had requested was already there, commanded by Col. John McCausland. McCausland and his men had been awaiting transportation to the Shenandoah Valley. When their appointed train arrived, its engineer was told to stand by.[14]

Evening of May 8 found Crook at Poplar Hill, just eight miles from Dublin. There he was joined by 400 cavalry under Col. John H. Oley, which raised his effective strength above 6,500. Jenkins, with about one-third that number, edged forward into the shadow of Cloyd's Mountain, a 2,600-foot ridge separating the two forces. He posted his troops on a high knoll facing the gap through which the Federals must advance. There he waited for morning and battle.

Crook's division broke camp at 5 A.M. on May 9 and began the long ascent up Cloyd's Mountain. Near the summit it ran into a handful of rebel skirmishers, chased them away, and continued to the top. Off to the east a tree-clad knoll offered better observation, so Crook, his staff, and Col. Carr B. White, the lead brigade commander, scrambled up its steep, rocky slope to see what they could see. The effort paid off. In the valley below they could view Jenkins's whole position, some two miles distant. Rebel infantry stood motionless behind rail fence breastworks. Nine artillery pieces gleamed in the morning sun. As the Federals watched, a new body of Confederates appeared and formed behind their comrades. Crook took in the scene through field glasses, then handed them to White and grunted, "The enemy is in force and in a strong position. They may whip [us], but I guess not."[15]

As Jenkins—now up to three thousand men, thanks to some last-minute reinforcements—made his final preparations, Crook deployed his three brigades for battle. Two of them came at the rebels head-on. The third, belonging to White, made a wide flanking movement around the Confederate right, crossing the mountain through dense woodlands and finally arriving on Shuffle Ridge, on whose western crest stood Jenkins's battle line. White formed his brigade, two regiments abreast, two deep, and advanced through a thick belt of trees toward the enemy. After a half mile or so his men came under heavy fire, but they far outnumbered the Confederates in the immediate area and soon had them under heavy pressure. Jenkins sent a small battalion to assist, but it was not enough. Finally he sent one of his largest regiments over from the left, and at that moment the rest of the Union division attacked.[16]

Crook led the attack himself, charging across a wide meadow against the Confederate front. Col. Horatio Sickel commanded the brigade on the right, Col. Rutherford B. Hayes the one on the left. Intense artillery and musket fire swept the meadow and ripped into dozens of men. Still, almost no one wavered. The Federals came forward smoothly, keeping good alignment. They were barely a hundred yards from the enemy when they ran smack into Back Creek.

No one had known the stream was there. It cut a ravine four feet deep and was wide enough to constitute a significant barrier. Crook's men tumbled down the banks, splashed into copper water, and lost all semblance of a line of battle. It took several minutes to reorganize them. Fortunately, the ravine was deep enough to give some protection against enemy fire. Otherwise, the Union attack might have fallen apart.

The Federals shook the water from their brogans and resumed the charge. The Confederates kept up a steady fire, but, as on the right, the Yankees proved unstoppable. Crook's men reached the rebel breastworks, fought the defenders hand-to-hand for a moment, and soon overwhelmed them through weight of numbers. Albert Jenkins struggled to rally his Confederates but was shot in the arm and captured. John McCausland then took command and fruitlessly tried to form a new defensive line. But Federal pressure proved too strong. The rebels began to retreat, first in an orderly fashion but then, thanks to the intervention of some four hundred cavalry in Crook's little army, with more and more haste until, by the time it reached Dublin Depot, McCausland's force had lost all cohesion. Only the timely arrival of a fresh regiment, the Fifth Kentucky, prevented a wholesale rout.

Led by Col. Howard Smith, the Kentuckians had boarded a train at Saltville the previous night. Originally some 750 strong, almost half the troops had to be left behind when their locomotive derailed. Scarcely four hundred were on hand to slow Crook's advance. Smith sized up the situation, formed his regiment, and marched through their retreating comrades. He soon found McCausland and reported to him for orders. Resist the further advance of the enemy, McCausland said. Cover the Confederate retreat. For more than an hour Smith did exactly that, fending off the Union horsemen and an assault by Hayes's brigade. He held on long enough for McCausland to make a clean escape, then followed with his own men. The Confederates crossed the New River and bivouacked for the night. Crook's men entered Dublin at dusk, bone-weary but jubilant.[17]

Victory had come at a cost. Over 100 Federals had perished in the brief charge, and 508 more had been wounded. An additional 72 were listed as captured or missing. The Confederates, for their part, reckoned their casualties at 72 killed, 262 wounded, and 200 captured or missing. That night ambulances roamed the battlefield, collecting the wounded.[18]

Next morning, Crook's men burned the Dublin telegraph office, the railroad station, and a large Confederate supply depot. Then they marched a few miles east to New River Bridge, a four-hundred-foot wooden railroad span. To protect it, McCausland had deployed sharpshooters and artillery on the opposite bank. Crook promptly brought up his own artillery, and a duel ensued. For two hours, Union and Confederate cannoneers traded salvoes, halting only when the rebels began to run low on ammunition. Finally, a company from Sickel's brigade went forward and successfully fired the bridge. Its destruction removed the

Confederates' sole reason for lingering. McCausland ordered a general retreat to Christiansburg, twelve miles to the east.[19]

The Federals made no attempt to pursue. In fact, they made no further offensive moves of any kind, but tamely headed back to West Virginia. Except for scattered enemy cavalry, easily shoved aside, Crook encountered no opposition on his homeward march except heavy rains that turned the mountain roads into gelatinous muck. On May 14 the division reached Union, a village just across the West Virginia border. The next day Averell's command rode into town, and Crook for the first time learned in detail how the cavalry had fared. The tale was not inspiring.

Averell had left Charleston late on May 2 and reached Logan Court House three days later. From that point his raid began in earnest, toiling across "pathless mountains and up tortuous streams" until he reached Jeffersonville on May 8. There he met the first enemy opposition and received reports of 4,500 Confederates at Saltville, whose extensive salt works formed his primary target. Averell took the reports at face value. Had he scouted more aggressively he might have discovered that only 1,300 rebels were in the town.[20]

Turning away from Saltville, Averell headed next for the lead mines of Wytheville, only to find them guarded by about 4,500 men under Brig. Gens. William E. "Grumble" Jones and John Hunt Morgan. A vigorous four-hour firefight ensued, during the course of which Averell was repeatedly forced back. "If we had 2 more hours of daylight we would have captured the whole force," Morgan wrote his wife. Averell's men had fought "elegantly," he allowed, but "our boys gave them no time to form"—just shoved them from position to position.[21]

Averell's column now turned eastward, following the Virginia and Tennessee Railroad, rode into Dublin Depot on May 11, found it smoldering from the efforts of Crook's men, and continued on its way. At Christiansburg Averell finally tore up a few miles of railroad track and some depots and shops, communicated with Crook—then just up the road at Blacksburg—and received orders to proceed along the railroad to Lynchburg, destroying the tracks as he went. Averell did nothing of the sort. Instead, he soon turned north to link up with Crook at Union. From that point the combined forces continued on to Meadow Bluff, where jaded troops had time to rest and draw supplies while Crook and Averell composed their after-action reports. What exactly had they accomplished?

Averell, of course, had achieved little, and so his report dwelled heavily on the courage and fortitude of his men, the physical obstacles overcome, and (reduced to essentials) the Confederates' failure to destroy his force. Crook had done more, though his modest account framed it less ably than did Rutherford B. Hayes in a letter to his uncle: "Our raid," Hayes enthused, "has been in all respects successful. We destroyed the famous Dublin bridge and eighteen miles of the Virginia and Tennessee Railroad and many depots and stores; captured ten pieces of artillery, three hundred prisoners, General Jenkins and other officers among them, and killed and wounded about five hundred, besides utterly routing Jenkins's army in the bloody battle of Cloyd's Mountain." If Crook refrained from criticizing his cavalry counterpart, Hayes was less charitable. "I see the papers call this 'Averell's raid,'" he wrote. "Very funny! The cavalry part of it was a total failure. General Averell only got to the railroads at points where we had first got in. He was driven back at Saltville and Wytheville."[22]

Hayes failed to recognize that, in a larger sense, *both* raids had failed. Grant had conceived them less to win battles and destroy Confederate war resources than to tie down the enemy and prevent the release of reinforcements from southwest Virginia to buttress Lee's army. Yet by May 11, one week after the Army of the Potomac crossed the Rapidan River, the threats posed by Crook and Averell had for all practical purposes evaporated. In Averell's case this was unimpressive but understandable. His modest force had encountered nothing but reversals from the time his raid began. But the withdrawal of Crook, an able general who had just won one of the most complete little victories of the war, is more puzzling. Why did he not keep up the pressure?

Crook's report addressed the question simply. At Dublin Depot, he wrote, "I saw dispatches from Richmond stating that General Grant had been repulsed and was retreating," which by implication meant that fresh Confederate troops might soon roll down the Virginia and Tennessee Railroad, turn the strategic tables, and leave him outnumbered in enemy country. It was a slender reed on which to base a decision as serious as the abandonment of his raid. The fact that Crook so readily accepted it is eloquent testimony to the faith of Federals everywhere in Robert E. Lee's ability to thrash all comers. Be that as it may, Crook's withdrawal, in combination with events unfolding in the Shenandoah Valley, would have significant impact on the campaign in eastern Virginia.[23]

While Crook and Averell raided against the Virginia and Tennessee Railroad, Franz Sigel marched up the macadamized Valley Turnpike with 8,940 troops, a force equivalent to the one that Grant had originally desired Ord to command. Sigel, in effect, had made this the main offensive of his military department, notwithstanding the fact that until recently Grant did not contemplate an advance up the Shenandoah Valley at all.

The Valley had seen much fighting since the beginning of war. Evidence of it lay all along the turnpike as Sigel's army made an approach march from Martinsburg, West Virginia, to its assembly point at Cedar Creek near Strasburg. "Graves and dead animals in all stages of decomposition marked the way," noted Col. David Hunter Strother, Sigel's aide de camp. Men and beasts had died for possession of the Valley's rich farmland, dubbed the "breadbasket of the Confederacy"; for its strategic geography, which offered the Confederates a sheltered avenue of invasion into the North (Lee had used it during the Gettysburg campaign); and for the foundries, storehouses, and railroad facilities at Staunton, where the harvest of the Valley was loaded aboard the trains of the Virginia Central Railroad and shipped east to feed Richmond and Lee's army. All this was at risk if Sigel's offensive succeeded, and for these reasons Breckinridge abandoned his headquarters at Dublin Depot and took his best troops north to confront the Federals in the Valley.[24]

Sigel left Cedar Creek on May 11. At Woodstock, the next village up the road, he learned from captured dispatches that Breckinridge, with between 4,000 and 4,500 troops, was on his way north to confront him. In the meantime, Sigel's army faced only 1,400 cavalry under Brig. Gen. John D. Imboden, who was desperate enough to call out the local reserve guard, composed of men ages forty-five and older. But Sigel, unsure of the enemy's dispositions, beset by guerrillas, and plagued by the same heavy rains that had stalled Grant's offensive at Spotsylvania, lingered at Woodstock until May 14. Even then he launched only a reconnaissance in force, which continued up the Valley Turnpike another twenty miles to New Market, a trim little village of seven hundred inhabitants.[25]

The reconnaissance was led by Col. August Moor, who had grave reservations about the assignment. For one thing, Sigel ordered him to take not the troops of his own brigade, with whom he was intimately familiar, but three infantry regiments, one thousand cavalry, and a battery of artillery whose abilities and weaknesses he did not know at all. For another, the entire force numbered 2,350 men, too much to withdraw easily if the Confederates materialized in strength, but not nearly enough to fight a pitched battle with any hope of success.

Moor lucked out. He encountered nothing but Imboden's cavalry, prodded it back during the course of the day, and by evening had reached New Market, where the strangers he commanded made bivouac in the

rain. At three o'clock next morning Moor ordered his troops to stand
to and sent patrols forward to see what had become of Imboden. They
reported that he had pulled out of the area around midnight, but at 7
A.M. a cavalry detachment returned with word that Imboden's cavalry
was about four miles south of New Market and that Breckinridge had
joined him. Soon he saw Confederate horsemen buzzing on the hills in
front of him, as if daring him to attack. Moor ignored the invitation.
Instead, he prepared for a defense against superior numbers.

Sigel, heartened by reports of Moor's advance the previous day, had
already ordered the rest of his army forward. It left Woodstock at 5 A.M. on
May 15, preceded by about a thousand cavalry under Brig. Gen. Julius H.
Stahel. As Moor's senior, Stahel assumed responsibility for the defense
of New Market. When a soft rain began to fall, he and the 3,350 men at
his disposal tried to stay dry, watched for the enemy, and waited for the
rest of their army to arrive.

Just south of the Federal line lay Shirley's Hill, a grassy eminence that
rose about 150 feet above the surrounding countryside. On its summit
stood Breckinridge and Imboden, and as the Federals kept their vigil
the two generals discussed the best course of action. Breckinridge had
reached the field around 3 A.M. In addition to the 735 cavalry under
Imboden, Breckinridge had two infantry brigades, under John Echols and
Gabriel C. Wharton, that had accompanied him from southwest Virginia.
These had a combined strength of a little over 3,000 men. The force
at his disposal also included 500 middle-aged men from the Augusta-
Rockingham Reserves, a tiny company of engineers, 332 independent
cavalry, eighteen fieldpieces, and 227 cadets from the Virginia Military
Institute, who had been offered for duty by the school superintendent
and reluctantly accepted by Breckinridge, who had no wish to put these
boys—most of them eighteen, the youngest just over fifteen—into harm's
way. All in all, the Confederate army had just 5,335 men with which to
stop Sigel's force of 8,940.[26]

At first Breckinridge expected to fight a defensive battle, but three
considerations led him to change his mind. First, the Federals failed to
attack. Second, a survey of the ground in front suggested the possibility
that, even with a smaller army, he could launch a successful attack: two
streams, the North Fork of the Shenandoah River and Smith's Creek,
would prevent his flanks from being turned by the enemy, and a series
of open hills would enable him to use his infantry and artillery in a
combined assault. Within five minutes, Imboden recalled, Breckinridge

had absorbed the topography and declared, "We can attack and whip them here, and I'll do it."[27]

Breckinridge reached his decision at around 10 A.M. An hour later he had his infantry maneuver on Shirley's Hill, "playing," explained an admiring subordinate, "the old strategic trick of countermarching his men with the view of multiplying their numbers in the eyes of the enemy." It worked. Reports flowed back to Sigel that the rebel army numbered ten, fifteen, twenty thousand strong. Though Sigel had sense enough to doubt the reports, they still conveyed an aura of danger and urgency.[28]

Confederate skirmishers, meanwhile, pressed aggressively against the Union line. Sigel ordered Stahel to fall back toward the main body, so that the rebels' efforts to eject them coincided with Sigel's positive order to retreat. The German American commander initially contemplated giving battle at Mount Jackson, a village about seven miles to the north, but soon reversed himself. "We may as well fight them today as any day," he concluded. "We will advance."[29]

Having mutually chosen to battle it out at New Market, Sigel and Breckinridge now assembled their full strength on the cultivated hills and valleys north of the town. Between the modest numbers at their command, the open terrain, and the streams on either flank, the brewing engagement was like a throwback to the eighteenth century, scarcely larger in scale than the 1781 contest between Cornwallis and Nathanael Greene at Guilford Court House. And the elegance with which Breckinridge conducted it would have done credit to the best ancien régime commander.

By 2 P.M. the situation had crystallized. Sigel had arrived and deployed on Bushong's Hill, about a mile north of New Market. Although his position was a strong one, he greatly diluted it by disposing his troops in two lines, one on the hill itself, the second about a thousand yards in front. Worse, he did not have his whole force present, for some units were still pursuing outmoded instructions to concentrate at Mount Jackson. In contrast to Sigel's wretched dispositions, Breckinridge placed his own infantry in a compact mass between the Shenandoah River and the Valley Turnpike, with most of his artillery astride the turnpike and Imboden's cavalry covering the ground between the turnpike and Smith's Creek.

Imboden soon discovered that the Federal cavalry was in his front, partially concealed by woodland. He got permission from Breckinridge to send a battery of guns east of Smith's Creek in order to take the Yankees under fire from their left flank. Meanwhile the former vice president

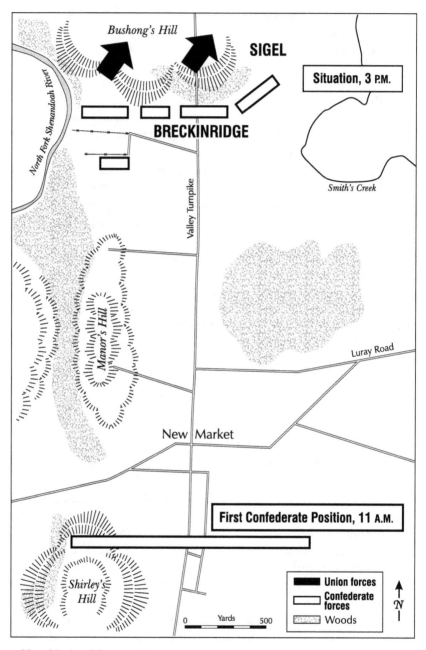

9. New Market, May 15, 1864

pressed ahead with Echols's and Wharton's brigade and personally supervised the handling of his artillery, cannily advancing the guns from one knoll to another and keeping the enemy under a steady barrage of shells. The Confederate infantry hit the Union first line, overlapped it on both sides, and soon sent its defenders hustling back toward Bushong's Hill. An Ohio soldier noted that his own regiment fired just one volley before it fell back. "It was Sigel's way of fighting," he sneered.[30]

The Union infantry and cavalry in the advanced line now joined with their comrades on Bushong's Hill. The Confederates pursued them closely. Breckinridge perceived that the strongest part of Sigel's position lay on the hill's summit, close to the Shenandoah River. He sent the bulk of his forces in that direction and led them personally. The rest of his troops kept up the pressure along the rest of Sigel's line—or tried to. The pace of the advance, the vagaries of terrain, and the smoke of battle now combined to create a gap in the Confederate line. Stahel's cavalry was in front of the gap, driven from its first position by Imboden's artillery but reestablished on good ground and laying down a hail of carbine fire. There was no doubt that the Federals could see the gap, and little doubt that they would exploit it as fast as they possibly could. What was shaping up into a Confederate triumph seemed about to fall apart.

Breckinridge reviewed his options. The obvious solution was to contract his lines so as to remove the gap, but his entire line was under heavy enemy fire; such a maneuver was out of the question. Then a staff officer spoke. "General, why don't you put the cadets in line? They will fight as well as our men."

"No, Charley," Breckinridge said, "this will not do, they are only children and I cannot expose them to such a fire as our center will receive."

"General," the officer insisted, "it is too late. The Federals are right on us. If our cadets are ordered up, we can close the gap in our center."

Breckinridge asked if the cadets could stand the hammering they would take. "Yes," he was assured, "they are the best Virginia blood, and they will."

Everyone close enough to hear the exchange turned to Breckinridge. His face was wet with tears. "Put the boys in," he said, "and may God forgive me for the order."[31]

The staff officer went to the cadets, who had been following behind the Confederate infantry, and led them toward the gap. They had been under fire briefly during the morning skirmishing and a handful had been wounded, but nothing could have prepared them for what happened when they marched up, resplendent in their tailored gray uniforms, and joined the main battle line. Shot and canister screamed into their ranks. Three cadets went down immediately, two of them ripped open and killed outright, the third writhing on the grass in agony until his heart stopped beating. Fifty yards further another cadet took a bullet full in the chest and collapsed. He had just enough time to tear open his clothing and see the wound before he died.

In the morning engagement the cadets' formation had been shaky when they first came under fire. Now it was not. They stayed in good order, stood the punishment, and closed up like veterans when their classmates fell dead or wounded. They reached a fence just beyond an orchard and, in doing so, sealed the gap in the Confederate line.

Men on both sides intuited that the battle hung in the balance. "The position was very critical," recalled one Confederate, "and for a time it seemed doubtful as to which [army] would be the first to give way." Sigel was already almost manic with excitement, wrote David Strother, "and rode here and there with Stahel and Moor, all jabbering in German. In his excitement he seemed to forget his English entirely, and the purely American portion of his staff were totally useless to him." Sigel now decided that dramatic action was needed to tilt the scales toward a Union victory. He therefore ordered a charge—with three regiments.[32]

The closest student of the battle, William C. Davis, estimates that these three regiments contained about 1,700 men, while the Confederates had between 2,600 and 2,800 troops immediately at hand to stop them. His assessment of Sigel is devastating but deserved: "Having begun his march with an army that outnumbered all of Breckinridge's forces almost two to one, he had now mismanaged and maneuvered himself into a position where he was ordering an attack that outnumbered *him* by more than three to two. The verdict is clear: Franz Sigel was not just an incompetent; he was a fool."[33]

Needless to say, the charge failed, and badly enough to disrupt the Union line, damage Union morale, and set the stage for the collapse of Sigel's army. The Confederates perceived the shift in momentum and took advantage of it. As Federal batteries began to pull out, the rebels pressed forward, intent on killing the artillery horses so as to render the guns immobile. The Corps of Cadets participated in the final Confederate attack, charged a Union battery, and captured one of its 12-pounder Napoleons. Other troops captured an additional four cannon, left on the soggy battlefield as Sigel ordered a general retreat.

The retreat, at least, went off without a hitch. Sullen Federal artillery kept Breckinridge at bay, while Imboden's cavalry utterly failed to seize and destroy the single bridge over which Sigel's army had to retreat across the rain-swollen Shenandoah. The Federals started crossing the river at 4:30 P.M., barely two and a half hours after the main phase of the battle had begun. They did not stop their retreat until they reached Strasburg, one day and thirty-two miles later. There Sigel received word that Averell and Crook had been successful in their raids against the Virginia and Tennessee Railroad. "We are doing a good business in this department," Strother wisecracked. "Averell is tearing up the Virginia and Tennessee Railroad while Sigel is tearing down the Valley turnpike." The remark was overheard and widely repeated, much to Sigel's indignation.[34]

The brief New Market campaign cost the Federals 96 killed, 520 wounded, and 225 missing or captured, for a total of 841 men—14 percent of the force engaged (nearly a third of Sigel's army did not even get into action, thanks largely to his mismanagement). Confederate returns are incomplete, but indicate losses of at least 43 killed, 474 wounded, and 3 missing, for a total of 531 or more. Among the dead were 10 VMI cadets. Another 45 cadets were hit during the action; thus about 25 percent of the tiny VMI contingent became casualties. For the rest of his life, it was said, Breckinridge could not think of them without weeping.

Of the battle itself, however, the Kentuckian took enormous satisfaction, and rightly so. If Sigel's handling of the battle was wretched, Breckinridge performed superbly. Many veteran officers would have endorsed one colonel's assessment that New Market was "the best planned and best managed fight in which I was engaged." As a combat commander, wrote General Echols, Breckinridge "had few if any superiors in either army." Certainly his adroit use of terrain, judicious deployment of a numerically smaller force, and imaginative handling of artillery made his the most brilliant piece of generalship of the spring campaign in Virginia, with the possible exception of Emory Upton's May 10 attack at Spotsylvania. If it took a Sigel to lose the campaign, it took a Breckinridge to gain so complete a triumph.[35]

Now came the ultimate penalty for the failure of Averell and Crook to continue their raids against the Virginia and Tennessee Railroad. The day before New Market, Lee had wired Breckinridge: "If you can drive back the different expeditions threatening the Valley it would be very desirable for you to join me with your whole force." On the morning of the battle, Breckinridge received word that both Averell and Crook were falling back into West Virginia. Relieved of the need to return to southwest Virginia to protect the railroad, Breckinridge was able to comply with Lee's request. At Staunton on May 19, he placed the brigades of Echols and Wharton on flatcars and headed down the Virginia Central Railroad, bearing 2,500 priceless infantrymen to reinforce Lee's beleaguered army.[36]

On the same day that battle was joined at New Market, John W. Joyce, a soldier in the Twenty-first North Carolina, wrote his wife: "[T]he yankes are poring in like flies. . . . [W]e past through Richmond Day before yesterday and they are [in] the greatist Exceitement in Richmond I ever sead in my life they are scared nearley to Death the Yankes are doing a heap of mischief where they go." Joyce scrawled the letter from Drewry's Bluff, Richmond's principal bastion on the James River below the city. The "Exceitement" he described stemmed from two sources: Butler's Army of the James, which had landed at Bermuda Hundred and was now maneuvering between Richmond and Petersburg; and a heavy cavalry raid by ten thousand troopers under Phil Sheridan, which had come within a few miles of the city, beaten the Southern cavalry in a pitched battle, and slain the legendary Jeb Stuart, one of the Confederacy's greatest heroes.[37]

The dual threat posed by Butler and Sheridan, coming at the capital from opposite directions, placed Richmond in its greatest jeopardy since June 1862, when George B. McClellan had brought the Army of the Potomac within five miles of the city. Butler showed up first, landing at Bermuda Hundred on May 5, but Sheridan moved faster, reached the city's outskirts sooner, and was the first of the two threats to culminate.

The raid, of course, had its genesis on May 8, when Meade and Sheridan raged at one another about the performance of the Union cavalry and Sheridan swore that he could whip Jeb Stuart out of his boots if Meade would only let him. Meade, prodded by Grant, issued the order that gave Sheridan his chance: "The major-general commanding directs you to immediately concentrate your available mounted force . . . proceed against the enemy's cavalry, and when your supplies are exhausted proceed . . . to Haxall's Landing, on the James River, there communicating with General Butler, procuring supplies, and return to this army." Sheridan at once assembled his division commanders, David McMurtrie Gregg, Wesley Merritt, and James Harrison Wilson. "We are going out to fight Stuart's cavalry in consequence of a suggestion from me," Sheridan announced. "In view of my recent representations to Meade"—which still warmed the air above army headquarters—"I shall expect nothing but success." Initially the three subordinates seemed startled. In the Army of the Potomac it was virtually unheard-of to launch a mounted raid for the express purpose of fighting the enemy's horsemen. But the trio quickly warmed to the idea, listened closely as Sheridan outlined his plans, and then went off to prepare their commands for the raid.[38]

The Cavalry Corps rode out at daybreak, May 9. It left behind the infantry battle still brewing around Spotsylvania and headed east toward the Telegraph Road, the main highway between Fredericksburg and Richmond. It moved at a walk, in one immense thirteen-mile column—seven brigades of horsemen, two of horse artillery, together with ambulances and wagon trains—in all, about twelve thousand men and thirty-two guns. It had one objective: to fight the enemy cavalry wherever it might be found.

Confederate scouts picked up the movement almost at once, for Sheridan made no attempt to conceal it. Given the strength of the Federal column, it would have made sense for Jeb Stuart to take every available horseman in pursuit. Instead, he left four of his seven brigades behind, possibly on his own initiative, possibly at the insistence of Robert E. Lee, who could not afford the absence of most of his cavalry at a time when Grant was likely to try and slip around his flank.

The two brigades of Fitzhugh Lee's division galloped after Sheridan around 1 P.M. A third brigade, under Brig. Gen. James B. Gordon, departed late in the afternoon. Stuart himself left the Army of Northern Virginia around 3 P.M. and, after a four-hour ride, caught up with Fitz Lee and his horsemen about twenty miles south of Spotsylvania, at the tiny hamlet of Mitchell's Shop. Gordon's brigade arrived shortly after nightfall.

During the day, Lee reported to Stuart, his troopers had tangled with Sheridan's rear guard on two occasions, the first at Jerrell's Mill, on the Ta River ten miles up the road, the second right at Mitchell's Shop. There had been no question of stopping the Union raiders or even slowing them down. Part of Sheridan's column was already at the North Anna River, nearly halfway to Richmond. Anxious to get ahead of Sheridan, Stuart ordered a night march. Fitz Lee would take one of his brigades, that of Brig. Gen. William C. Wickham, and continue straight after the Federals. Stuart would take Gordon and Lee's second brigade, under Brig. Gen. Lunsford L. Lomax, swing to the west, cross the North Anna River upstream, and try to hit Sheridan while his corps was astride the river and vulnerable to defeat in detail.

The gambit failed. Anticipating just such a move, Sheridan sent a detachment to guard against it and got his cavalry safely beyond the North

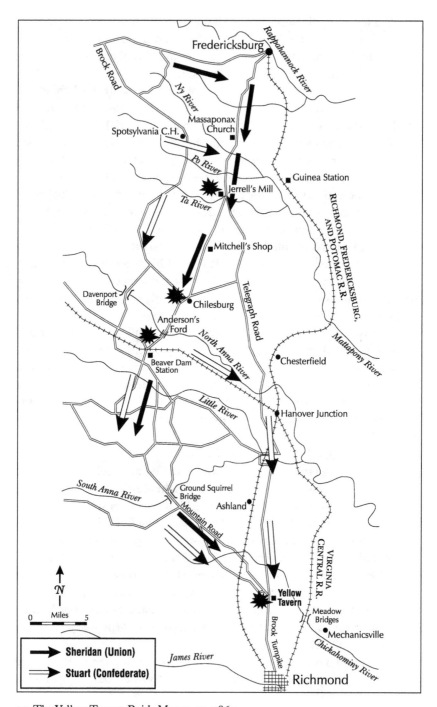

10. The Yellow Tavern Raid, May 9–11, 1864

Anna before Stuart could lay a glove on him. Instead, the Confederate cavalier encountered only the wreckage of the supply depot at Beaver Dam Station, on the Virginia Central Railroad just south of the North Anna River. Union troopers ravaged the depot overnight, burning a hundred railroad cars, two locomotives, a store of medical supplies, and 1.5 million badly needed rations of meat and bread. They also liberated between three hundred and four hundred prisoners of war, captured in the Wilderness and at Laurel Hill.

Stuart now issued new orders. The enemy had chopped down trees as they moved south, making direct pursuit too difficult. Therefore, Gordon would follow Sheridan's column, maintain contact, and ensure it did not double back to strike the Army of Northern Virginia from behind. Fitz Lee's division would head southeast, reach the Telegraph Road, and use its macadam surface to make better time in the effort to overtake Sheridan before he reached his probable objective, Richmond. Stuart fired off a stream of dispatches to the capital, warning of the enemy's approach and announcing, "Should he attack Richmond I will certainly move [in] his rear and do what I can; at the same time, I hope to be able to strike him if he endeavors to escape."[39]

The Confederate horsemen stayed in the saddle all day and well into the evening. Finally around 9 P.M. they halted at Taylorsville, just south of Hanover Junction. By then the men had been in the saddle for thirty-two hours and desperately needed rest. Stuart gave them six hours. At 3 A.M. they were under way again, and Stuart swore to overtake Sheridan if it cost every horse in his command.

Such desperate oaths were unnecessary. Sheridan had scant interest in reaching Richmond ahead of his adversary. Instead, the Union cavalry commander ordered his troopers into bivouac at 4:15 P.M. on the tenth, just across the Ground Squirrel Bridge on the South Anna River. Stuart imagined that Sheridan was maintaining a pace as killing as his own—he wrote Robert E. Lee hopefully that "the enemy's horses are broken down. They are shooting them in the road." But although this may have been the case for some of Sheridan's mounts, it was hardly true for most. And where Stuart fell asleep on the evening of May 10 in a state of stupefaction, his Yankee counterpart felt fresh enough to play with the children of the household where he made his headquarters for the night.[40]

May 11 dawned bright, mild, and lovely. At Ground Squirrel Bridge the bugles sounded "To Horse," and ten thousand Union troopers swung into the saddle and rode off toward Richmond, leaving a brigade of two thousand, under Brig. Gen. J. Irvin Gregg, to guard the rear. The men who stayed behind figured on an easy time. The bridge had been burned, the enemy would have difficulty reaching them. Instead, Gordon's brigade came barreling down upon them, having splashed across the South Anna River at an old ford whose fifteen-foot banks had seemed impassable. For the next several hours Gregg and Gordon carried on a running battle as Gregg attempted to shield the rest of Sheridan's command while Gordon attacked ferociously in an effort to get past. Though the Federals managed to hold on, the effort was costly, the fighting sometimes hand to hand. A second sharp encounter occurred near Ashland, when a second Union brigade under Brig. Gen. Henry Davies showed up to destroy the tracks of the Richmond, Fredericksburg, and Potomac Railroad. Fitz Lee's cavalry put a stop to that, but not before Davies's men had done significant damage.

Meanwhile, Sheridan's main column was advancing on the Mountain Road, the main highway from Richmond to Charlottesville. Stuart, riding with Fitz Lee's division, was coming down the Telegraph Road. The two roads intersected near an old hostel called the Yellow Tavern—yellow only by courtesy now, for it was abandoned, weather-beaten, and ravaged by soldiers of the Richmond garrison who periodically raided it for firewood. Here Stuart planned his decisive encounter with the enemy.

The brigade of Lunsford Lomax reached Yellow Tavern first, comfortably ahead of any Federals. It was 8 A.M. Lomax established a blocking position at the road junction. Wickham's brigade arrived a short time later, along with Fitz Lee and, soon after, Stuart himself. Stuart had three options available to him. He could withdraw into the Richmond defenses, as the outer ring of earthworks was barely two miles to the south; he could build on Lomax's position, directly across the Federals' path; or he could deploy his men so as to hit the Yankees in the flank as they rode by. For the present, he rejected the first option and combined the other two: Lomax assumed a position on the Telegraph Road just short of the intersection, with skirmishers thrown forward in the direction of the Mountain Road. Wickham's brigade deployed on a low ridge that overlooked a rivulet called Turner's Run. The position was about a half mile to the north of Lomax, and it faced due south, thus enabling Wickham's men to hit the Federal flank and rear if the Yankees tried to bull their way past.

With only three thousand troopers immediately on hand to stop Sheridan, Stuart reckoned the numerical odds at about three to one against him (they were actually even worse). Yet he hoped not only to defeat the

Federal column but to annihilate it. His own command was insufficient to do the job on its own, but if the substantial Richmond garrison emerged from its works, the rebel cavalry was well placed to cut off Sheridan's only line of retreat. The government was informed of Sheridan's approach and Stuart's own strength and situation. Surely it would send help. To make certain, he sent a staff officer, Maj. H. B. McClellan, to locate Gen. Braxton Bragg, the president's military adviser, and gain his assurance.

Long before McClellan could return, the first Union cavalry pounded up, a full division under Wesley Merritt. The Federals dismounted, formed line of battle, and crossed a field of new corn. Their seven-shot, breech-loading Spencer carbines barked relentlessly. They slammed into Lomax's line, captured two hundred prisoners, and sent the rest flying to the north to join Wickham's line on the ridge. Stuart nevertheless expressed satisfaction with the outcome. He had halted Sheridan's progress. He still held the ground that commanded Sheridan's line of retreat. And Sheridan was deep in hostile country, whereas Stuart's men stood not ten miles from the capital of the whole Confederacy.

The possibility of a foray by the city's garrison loomed as large in Sheridan's mind as it did in Stuart's, and as the initial battle subsided he sent two regiments and a section of artillery toward Richmond to see about it. They headed down the Brooke Turnpike, passed the unmanned outer fortifications, and got close enough to the city to hear the peal of bells, the whistle of locomotives, and other indications that "general alarm and bustling seemed to prevail in Richmond." But there was no sign of Confederate reinforcements. Hearing this welcome news, Sheridan waited for his remaining two divisions to reach the field. Then, as advertised, he would whip Stuart out of his boots.[41]

On the ridgeline to the north, Stuart entertained similar thoughts about Sheridan. A courier arrived with word that Gordon had driven the Union rear guard from Ground Squirrel Bridge. "Bully for Gordon!" he boomed jovially. At 2 P.M. McClellan returned from his interview with Braxton Bragg. The president's military adviser had assured him that the Richmond works were already held by four thousand "irregular" troops—meaning reservists and government clerks—and that three full brigades of veteran infantry were en route from Petersburg (where they had been gathering to fend off Butler's Army of the James). Stuart liked the sound of that. "He was pleased with the information I had brought from Richmond," McClellan recalled, "and expressed the intention of retaining his position on Sheridan's flank, and the hope that, aided by a strong attack by the infantry in Richmond, he might be able to inflict serious disaster on the enemy's cavalry." Stuart sent Bragg a note formally requesting that a Virginia brigade under Brig. Gen. Eppa Hunton should sortie against Sheridan's right flank. "If we make a combined attack on them," he wrote, "I cannot see how they can escape"—especially if Gordon's cavalry brigade also came up, as Stuart hoped and expected.[42]

Although the day had begun to darken with the clouds of an approaching thunderstorm, this bright vision of triumph still bathed Stuart's imagination when, at 4 P.M., Sheridan attacked. He had three massed divisions on hand. Neither Gordon nor Hunton nor anyone else had arrived to support the two slim Confederate brigades arrayed on the ridgeline just above Turner's Run. But Stuart, game as ever, opened fire with his artillery. At about the same time the skies opened, drenching the combatants. Lightning flashed and thunder rolled above the sound of the guns.

The two sides hacked and clawed at one another, most regiments dismounted, a few on horseback. It was over within thirty minutes. The Union charge was simply too strong. Sheridan did not even have his whole command engaged when the Confederate line cracked and the survivors withdrew to safety beyond the Chickahominy River some two miles to the east. The commander who led them away was Fitz Lee, not Stuart. While driving back a Federal thrust at the center of his line—exhorting his men, blazing away with his LeMat revolvers, defiantly on horseback—Stuart had been shot, almost casually, by a Michigan private named John Huff. The cavalier who had received scarcely a scratch in three years of war slumped in the saddle as blood poured from his abdomen and mingled with the spring rain. Fitz Lee had ridden up, his face taut with concern. "Go ahead, Fitz old fellow. I know you'll do what's right," Stuart had said. And to his cavalrymen, buckling under the weight of Sheridan's assault, he had commanded, "Go back, go back! I had rather die than be whipped."[43]

That night the Yankees triumphantly held the field of what Stuart had imagined would be the scene of his own triumph. The beaten Confederates made a cheerless bivouac in the rain, and an ambulance rattled along the muddy roads on a roundabout trek to Richmond. It finally halted in front of a handsome residence on Gracie Street, the home of Stuart's brother-in-law. Grief-stricken aides carried the general inside to his deathbed. He lingered another day, struggling to stay alive long enough for his wife and daughter to reach him. Gradually it became clear that this would never happen. Wavering between hope and resignation, he said, "I am resigned if it be God's will; but I would like to see my wife. But God's will be done." His next words were his last: "I am going fast now; I am resigned; God's will be done." And the eyes of Lee's army closed forever.[44]

While Stuart lay dying, Sheridan collected his wounded and continued his march, leaving Yellow Tavern around 11 P.M., skirting Richmond to the north and east and heading toward a junction with Butler's Army of the James. Confederates had sown the road with "land torpedoes" (land mines) and outraged Federals forced prisoners of war to find them and remove them. Infantry and artillery from the capital harassed the line of march, and by daylight Sheridan realized he could not squeeze between the city defenses and the rain-swollen Chickahominy River. He would have to cross the river and clear Richmond well to the east.

That meant getting control of the Meadow Bridges just northeast of the city, which in turn meant fighting off Fitzhugh Lee's cavalry, which sullenly held the opposite bank. The bridges were in a state of partial collapse and would have to be repaired. To do so required Sheridan's men to drive away the rebels by the only available avenue, the Virginia Central Railroad bridge that crossed the river a short distance east. Michigan troopers scrambled across the narrow span on hands and knees. If shot, they simply tumbled into the black water; there was nothing to hold on to. Meanwhile, Gordon's brigade pressed in from the west and Brig. Gen. Archibald Gracie's veteran infantry brigade advanced from Richmond. "It was the tightest place in which the [cavalry] corps ever found itself," wrote one officer.[45]

Sheridan seemed not to care. He soon had his troops in action in all directions—against Lee, against Gordon, against Gracie—and to a fretful artillerist he announced that there was nothing to worry about. "Why, what do you suppose we have in front of us?" he laughed. "A lot of department clerks from Richmond, who have been forced into the ranks." Far from being in a tight place, he could tear right into the capital if he wanted. "It isn't worth the men it would cost," he conceded, "but I'll stay here all day to show these fellows how much I care for them, and go when I get ready."[46]

Afterward, the cavalry leader claimed that while his men fought for control of the Meadow Bridges, scouting parties discovered a number of fording points across the Chickahominy. "This means of getting out of the circumscribed plateau I did not wish to use, however, unless there was no alternative, for I wished to demonstrate to the Cavalry Corps the impossibility of the enemy's destroying or capturing so large a body of mounted troops." And so the troopers remained, taking on all comers, knocking them back, and taking their sweet time in leaving. Finally around 4 P.M. the Meadow Bridges were clear of the enemy and repaired, the Federals crossed, and the Confederates had suffered a second defeat in as many days.[47]

Sheridan's cavalry then made its leisurely way to Haxall's Landing, far below Richmond on the James River estuary, where it encamped on May 14. Sheridan established contact with Union gunboats and sent a message to Grant detailing his success. "This has lasted six days," he wrote near the end. "If I could be permitted to cross the James River and go southward I could almost ruin the Confederacy."[48]

The raid had cost the Federals about six hundred casualties, the Confederates roughly the same, as well as the severe material losses inflicted at Beaver Dam Station (especially the priceless medical stores), and much temporary damage to the railroads. The hardest blow, of course, was the death of Stuart. Civilians greeted the news with shock, and Confederate horsemen still on duty at Spotsylvania "bowed their heads and wept like children." Robert E. Lee got word of Stuart's mortal wound on May 12, as he struggled to construct a new line across the base of the Mule Shoe. In shaken tones he told his staff what had happened, then added by way of tribute, "He never brought me a piece of false information."[49]

With the defeat at New Market and the end of Sheridan's Yellow Tavern raid, only one subordinate threat to Richmond yet remained: Benjamin F. Butler's Army of the James, firmly based at Bermuda Hundred and heading toward the southern defenses of the Confederate capital. But that threat lasted scarcely longer before it, too, was neutralized in one of the Civil War's most curious operations.

An air of unreality clings to the Bermuda Hundred campaign. It seems unlikely that the Confederate capital would be virtually undefended, yet such was very much the case. It seems equally strange that an army of thirty-six thousand could get within twenty miles of Richmond without a battle, yet Federal naval control of the James River estuary made it entirely practicable. Finally, it seems impossible that in the face of such an opportunity, the Union would entrust its exploitation to Ben Butler, a general devoid of combat experience. Yet it did. Taken together, these oddities comprised the campaign's basic truths.[50]

Each fact had a rational explanation. The slender garrison at Richmond reflected a deliberate choice on the part of the Confederate government. Unlike the Lincoln administration, which seldom garrisoned Washington with fewer than fifty thousand men, the Davis regime kept the fewest possible troops in the Richmond fortifications. Faced with limited military manpower and many hard choices, the Davis administration generally opted to maximize Confederate forces in the field. As of April 20, 1864, the Department of Richmond comprised only 7,133 troops. Should a crisis arise, the government counted on militia to help defend the city until reinforcements could arrive from elsewhere: coastal North Carolina, the Shenandoah Valley, or conceivably even the Army of Northern Virginia.[51]

The ease with which a Union army could ascend the James River estuary derived from the width of the river and the slender resources of the Confederate navy. Ever since the loss of Norfolk in May 1862, the rebels had conceded the estuary to Federal gunboats. They did not attempt to defend the James until it narrowed dramatically just north of Bermuda Hundred and twisted in a series of six hairpin bends or "curls" that greatly multiplied the beeline distance to Richmond. There the Confederates had sown electrically detonated mines, called "torpedoes" in nineteenth-century parlance. Beyond the last of these curls they had constructed Fort Darling, a massive earthen fort that commanded the river from the crest of ninety-foot Drewry's Bluff. Farther upstream lurked a squadron of Confederate rams and ironclads, able to block the narrow channel that led up to Richmond but not to challenge the Union navy in the broad tidal river. Thus, a Northern flotilla could easily land Butler's army at Bermuda Hundred, for it lay below the capital's river defenses. And with cooperation from the land forces, the navy might well be able to pick its way past the torpedoes, reduce Fort Darling, and support the army in its bid to seize Richmond itself.

As for Butler, the combat neophyte, while it was true that he lacked battle experience, it was equally true that Grant had supplied him with two corps commanders who possessed that experience abundantly. Maj. Gen. William F. Smith, who led the XVIII Corps, had fought in both the eastern and western theaters. Maj. Gen. Quincy A. Gillmore, chief of the X Corps, had waged a determined though unsuccessful campaign to batter through the defenses that guarded Charleston, South Carolina. Grant expected these two West Point officers, especially Smith, for whom he had great regard, to supply the military judgment that Butler lacked. He believed that they would be responsible enough to render it. He trusted that Butler would be sensible enough to accept it. As it turned out, Grant was wrong on both counts. But he could not have known that before the campaign took place.

The problem began with the fact that even a strategic situation as fraught with opportunity as Butler's was not devoid of complications. From the moment his army arrived at Bermuda Hundred, Butler had a knife at the vitals of the Confederacy. With Richmond fifteen miles to the north, the critical railroad city of Petersburg eight miles to the south, and the crucial Richmond and Petersburg Railroad rolling by just three miles beyond the waist of the Bermuda Hundred peninsula, Butler was poised to strike at three critical objectives. That was the opportunity. Yet the same proximity to these objectives which made his expedition attractive also made it dangerous, for the Confederates would react sharply to his presence. Indeed, the more he succeeded in his expedition, the more dangerous to the Confederates he would become. The more dangerous he became, the more strength they would assemble to oppose him— up to and including Lee's Army of Northern Virginia, for surely Lee would abandon his campaign against Grant before he would permit the Confederate capital to fall into enemy hands. Butler therefore believed he must conduct his own operations with prudence as well as flair.

He began, sensibly enough (and in accordance with Grant's explicit orders), by protecting his base of operations. At the waist of the Bermuda Hundred peninsula only about five miles separated the James and Appomattox Rivers. After landing on May 5, Butler spent the entirety of May 6 fortifying the narrow waist of the peninsula, , and he continued to improve the position for several days thereafter. In the meantime, he probed toward the Richmond and Petersburg Railroad. A brigade advanced on May 6; four brigades went forth the following day. Each foray resulted in a scrap with rebel forces. Each scrap underscored the danger inherent in threatening the Confederacy's lifeline so fundamentally. News of the battles along the Rapidan also reached Butler in garbled form. He had to consider what he would do in the event that Grant's offensive, like so many before it, crumbled beneath Lee's slashing counterattacks.

The military geography also gave him pause, especially when coupled with his rather vague written instructions from Grant. The primary order simply called for Butler to "seize upon City Point and act from there, looking upon Richmond as your objective point," and disavowed any intention of telling Butler how the operation was to be conducted. The one certainty was that he must "use every exertion to secure footing as far up the south side of the [James] river as you can, and as soon as possible."[52]

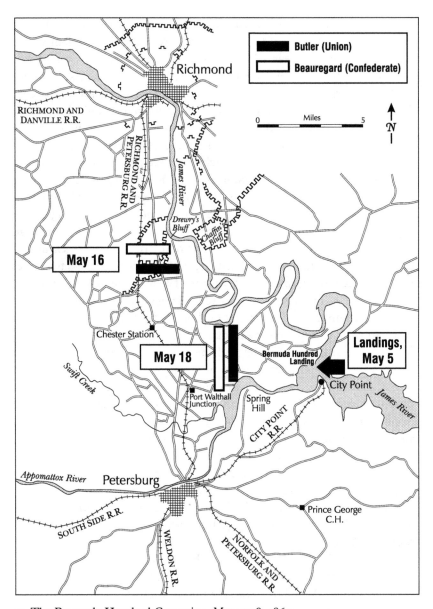

Butler (Union)

Beauregard (Confederate)

Richmond

RICHMOND AND
DANVILLE R.R.

0   Miles   5

N

RICHMOND AND PETERSBURG R.R.

James River

Drewry's
Bluff

Chaffin
Bluff

May 16

Chester Station

May 18

Bermuda Hundred
Landing

Landings,
May 5

City Point

James River

Swift Creek

Port Walthall
Junction

Spring
Hill

CITY POINT R.R.

Appomattox River   Petersburg

Prince George
C.H.

SOUTH SIDE R.R.

WELDON R.R.

NORFOLK AND
PETERSBURG R.R.

11. The Bermuda Hundred Campaign, May 5–18, 1864

Butler's orders thus required him to advance upon Richmond while hugging the right bank of the James River. Yet such a movement would leave his base and the rear of his army vulnerable to whatever Confederate reinforcements might come up from the Carolinas. That suggested the advisability of first capturing Petersburg or at least blocking the approaches from that direction. But a movement on Petersburg would have to be made in strength, and if Butler did so, he would, in effect, be marching directly away from the objective Grant had ordered him to attack.[53]

Butler solved the dilemma by concluding that it would be better to wait until Grant got closer before launching the Richmond offensive. In the meantime, he would make a subsidiary stab at Petersburg, aimed less at capturing the city outright than at destroying the railroad linking it with the capital. On May 9 he marched forth with nine brigades—more than in any previous foray, but still three short of the twelve brigades available to him. Around mid-afternoon his troops reached Swift Creek, two miles north of Petersburg, and found a force of Confederates posted on the opposite bank. The two sides sparred inconclusively, but the Federals made no attempt to advance any farther. Instead, Butler put wrecking crews to work tearing up the railroad.

Late that afternoon he met with his corps commanders, Smith and Gillmore, to discuss plans for the next day. With no news as yet from Grant, Butler thought it best to continue threatening Petersburg. He proposed to have the troops storm Swift Creek and advance as far as the Appomattox River just short of the city. The division at City Point would support the operation by launching a diversionary foray of its own. He asked Smith and Gillmore for suggestions. They had none, and so as far as Butler was concerned the matter was settled: His plan would be put into effect the following day.

However, neither corps commander liked the plan. It seemed unimaginative and likely to result in casualties out of proportion to its limited purpose. As soon as Butler departed, Gillmore turned to Smith and suggested an alternative. Why not withdraw to the Bermuda Hundred defenses, construct a pontoon bridge across the Appomattox River, and advance against Petersburg's rail communications with the south? Both men saw the advantages. Gillmore's proposal avoided a needless battle at Swift Creek. It got the Federals across the Appomattox River at a stroke, enabled the advance on Petersburg to be supported by the division at City Point, and offered the chance to destroy new railroads rather than simply add to the Richmond and Petersburg Railroad trackage already wrecked. At 7 P.M., Gillmore put the proposal in writing. He and Smith signed it and sent it to Butler.[54]

In theory, the two corps commanders were providing the inexperienced Butler with sound professional advice, just as Grant hoped they would. But they were going about it in a way far more likely to antagonize than edify. Butler fully recognized that, as a political general in command of a military department, he was in a tough situation. He knew that his superior, Grant, would have preferred for him merely to manage the administrative duties of the job and leave the actual field command to Smith. This, Butler had made clear, was unacceptable: He possessed and would exercise the right to command all troops in his department, and by taking such a stand he forced Grant to back down or take the politically expensive step of removing him. But he could anticipate that Smith and Gillmore, as professional soldiers and especially in light of Grant's preferences, would attempt to challenge his authority.[55]

Now the challenge had come, and in writing, which a seasoned lawyer like Butler easily read as an attempt by Smith and Gillmore to place their opposition to his plan officially on record. And as a seasoned politician he was shrewd enough to guess at the human truth behind the document he held in his hands. Smith and Gillmore had submitted this plan so promptly after his departure that clearly they must have doubted Butler's plan even as he had explained it to him and asked for their advice. Each man had simply been too gutless to disagree with Butler to his face, particularly without prior assurance that his opposite number shared the same misgivings.

Butler's response was immediate, decisive, and dripping with contempt. Settling his ponderous body at a writing table, he scribbled a blistering reply. "While I regret an infirmity of purpose which did not permit you to state to me, when I was personally present, the suggestion which you make in your written note, but left me to go to my headquarters under the impression that another and far different purpose was advised by you, I shall [not] yield to the written suggestions which imply a change of plan made within thirty minutes after I left you. Military affairs cannot be carried on, in my judgment, with this sort of vacillation."[56]

The whole point of this withering missive was to humiliate Smith and Gillmore and underscore his status as the man in charge, for by the time he wrote it Butler had decided to scrap his own plan: not just some of it but all of it. The evening had brought a dispatch from Stanton indicating that the Army of the Potomac had fought a pitched battle with Lee, that the Confederates were "in full retreat for Richmond," and that Grant was pursuing. (It even reported, erroneously, that a Union corps had already passed through Spotsylvania Court House.) A second dispatch indicated that Grant was "on the march with his whole army to form a junction with you."[57]

In Butler's mind, that news nullified the wisdom of any further diversions toward Petersburg. The Army of the James must turn to its main objective, Richmond, advancing as far as possible up the south bank of its namesake river and threatening the city at the earliest moment. The balance of Butler's biting letter informed Smith and Gillmore as much, and the next day the army withdrew to its Bermuda Hundred fortifications to prepare for the main offensive.

Butler began his advance on May 12, the same morning that Hancock stormed the Mule Shoe, though of course Butler had no inkling of the battles at Spotsylvania and serenely believed that Grant was pursuing Lee toward Richmond. Butler never intended to capture the Confederate capital (and his orders did not actually require him to try). He would simply demonstrate in front of it and divert Confederate attention until Grant could arrive with his main force. That was wise, because by May 12 the Davis government had amassed so many troops to hold the Richmond trenches that no attempt to storm them would have succeeded. What Butler did not know was that until a few days previously, the southern approaches to Richmond had been almost wide open.

When Butler's troops landed on May 5, the sole Confederate force available to block him was 750 troops under Maj. Gen. George E. Pickett, leader of the famous last charge at Gettysburg. Pickett was at Petersburg, wrapping up his final hours as commander of the First Military District of the Department of North Carolina and Southern Virginia. He had already received his orders to go by train to Hanover Junction, where he would rendezvous with the brigades of his division—currently scattered about on detached service—and join Lee's army along the Rapidan. The sighting of fifty-nine Union transports steaming up the James River plainly signaled that a major force was headed straight toward him. He promptly sent word both to his department commander, Gen. Pierre Gustave Toutant Beauregard, and to the authorities in Richmond. It took time for the Confederate high command to sort the matter out—Butler, it developed, had unintentionally landed at a point where Confederate military boundaries were overlapping and ill-defined—and Pickett endured a harrowing five-day ordeal in which he bore responsibility for opposing a Union army, yet with vastly inferior forces and limited authority to command even those. By May 10, he was so exhausted from nervous tension that he asked to be placed on a medical leave of absence.

By then, however, the high command had assembled additional troops in Butler's path: 1,350 by May 7; 2,668 by May 8; 7,500 by May 10. Coupled with a field force detached from the Richmond garrison—5,000 men under Maj. Gen. Robert Ransom—the total was more than sufficient to conduct a viable defense. In overall command of the defense was Beauregard, the fourth-ranking general in the Confederate army and widely regarded as one of the best.[58]

Beauregard arrived at Petersburg on the morning of May 10, the same day that Butler retired to his Bermuda Hundred lines in preparation for the Richmond offensive. Taking stock of the situation, he soon realized that an opportunity existed not merely to block the Union thrust but to launch a counterstroke that would send the Federals reeling if it did not destroy them entirely. True, the Northern army on his front might number as many as fifty thousand men (this was Pickett's anguished initial estimate), but by May 10 it was definitely known to be commanded not by Ambrose E. Burnside, as at first supposed, but by Benjamin F. Butler, the hated "Beast" Butler of New Orleans. The indecisive way in which Butler was handling his army—now forward, now back, probing gingerly with forces inadequate for the job—suggested that the Union force was in inexperienced hands. And the James River estuary, although a broad highway for a planned advance, would be a cul-de-sac should Butler's army have to retreat. All in all, it seemed advisable for the Confederates to take the offensive. The Richmond authorities—President Jefferson Davis, Secretary of War James A. Seddon, and the president's military adviser, Gen. Braxton Bragg—concurred, particularly because Butler's expedition was already a success in one respect: it was tying down thousands of troops badly needed by Lee.

Even so, it would take a few more days to ready the counterstroke, and in the meantime tensions in Richmond continued to build. The news from every side was bleak. Grant was on the attack at Spotsylvania. Averell and Crook had struck several targets in southwest Virginia. Sigel was advancing up the Shenandoah Valley. Butler was advancing up the James. Nor was this all. Acting in support of Butler's expedition, a force of three thousand cavalry under Brig. Gen. August V. Kautz had gone raiding into southside Virginia and burned two bridges on the Weldon and Petersburg Railroad, an important supply artery and the most direct route by which troops in the Carolinas could be redeployed to defend the capital. Until the damage could be repaired, Confederate reinforcements from the Carolinas would have to walk the ten-mile gap between the bridges, creating substantial delays.

Finally, Sheridan was at the northern fringe of Richmond. The Davis administration worried about the prospect of Sheridan's force piercing the thinly held entrenchments north of the city and urged Beauregard to gather all available troops at Richmond immediately. Beauregard demurred. He wanted to collect at Petersburg all troops coming up from the Carolinas before taking such a step, but Secretary of War James A. Seddon was adamant. "This city is in hot danger," he wired Beauregard, and ordered him to send the troops at once.[59]

Butler, in the meantime, had launched his demonstration toward Richmond. On May 13 he fought a preliminary engagement that won him control of the outer fortifications of the Confederate defensive complex at Drewry's Bluff. Still, he could go no further without a major battle and so he entrenched his army where it was and pondered his next move. Beauregard did the same. Having lingered at Petersburg until the last reinforcements arrived from the Carolinas, Beauregard finally reached Fort Darling around 3 A.M. on May 14. He promptly conferred with the engineer of the Richmond defenses, Col. W. H. Stevens. To assist in their discussion, Stevens produced a map detailing the strategic situation. Grant and Lee were at Spotsylvania; Sheridan was moving down the Virginia Peninsula toward the James River landings. The bulk of the Confederate force was at Drewry's Bluff, while a small detachment under Maj. Gen. W. H. C. Whiting covered Petersburg. Butler occupied a defensive position just south of Drewry's Bluff. Beauregard, who by now had some twenty thousand troops at his disposal, was certain he could take the offensive and force Butler to retreat, but at best such a victory would merely neutralize the Army of the James, not destroy it. To crush Butler would require at least fifteen thousand additional troops, and such a number could only come from Lee's army.

Getting those reinforcements was not out of the question, Beauregard thought, but it would require a daring expedient. Why not have Lee send the needed fifteen thousand at once, then fall back swiftly to the Richmond defenses where he could escape destruction from Grant's much larger army? As soon as the new troops arrived, Beauregard would attack, wreck Butler's army, then turn with his full command, join up with Lee, and deliver a crushing blow against Grant's army. Without pausing to commit the plan to paper, Beauregard sent Stevens galloping off to Richmond with instructions to lay it verbally before President Davis or his military adviser, Braxton Bragg.[60]

The sun was not yet up, Davis was ill, and his aides refused to disturb him at such an ungodly hour. But Stevens was able to meet with Bragg, who decided that he should discuss the matter with Beauregard in person. When the military adviser reached Fort Darling later that morning, Beauregard once again rehearsed the plan, ending with an exhortation: "Bragg, circumstances have thrown the fate of the Confederacy in your hands and mine. Let us play our parts boldly and fearlessly! Issue those orders and I'll carry them out to the best of my ability. I'll guarantee success!"[61]

Bragg rode back to Richmond to discuss the plan with Davis. From his demeanor, Beauregard evidently thought Bragg favored the idea, but in fact Bragg excoriated it, giving Davis seven objections, the most important of which were that Lee's army could not retreat such a distance (sixty miles) without grave danger and that the withdrawal was unnecessary: Beauregard's present force was ample to crush Butler "if promptly and vigorously used." Davis went in person to hear Beauregard's proposal, but purely as a courtesy, for he had already made up his mind to veto it. Beauregard, the president said, must attack with the troops on hand.[62]

It took another day for Beauregard to organize the attack, but Butler's army remained obligingly inert. The final plan called for the Confederate left wing, under Ransom, to make the main assault and cut Butler off from the James River, while the right wing, under Maj. Gen. Robert Hoke, would pin down the rest of Butler's army and lend support to Ransom's attack as needed. Meanwhile, the force under Whiting, which then was covering Petersburg, would advance northward and strike Butler's left rear.

The battle began before dawn on May 16. A dense fog shielded Ransom's approach but also threw his attack into disarray after it initially pierced Butler's lines. Although hundreds of prisoners fell into Confederate hands, along with a number of cannon, it proved impossible to press home the advantage and get around Butler's right flank. Hoke's supporting attack made some initial headway but ran into trouble. By midmorning it was apparent that Beauregard's attack had stalled. Whiting's small force, a mere footnote in the original plan, now became the Confederates' principal hope for restoring momentum to the offensive.

It never came. Whiting lost his powers of decision on May 16 and permitted a small blocking force of Federals to detain him all day. Some claimed that he was drunk. Whiting maintained that he was ill and suffering from exhaustion. But whatever the case, Whiting's troops played no role in the Battle of Drewry's Bluff, and the Confederate counterstroke failed to dislodge Butler's army. Nevertheless, the Federals retreated. The man who defeated Butler was not Beauregard but Butler himself.

Butler received word of the attack at dawn. Despite the fog, it soon became clear that the Confederates were striking most heavily on his right, the part of the line held by Smith's XVIII Corps. Butler assumed, calmly enough, that in order to concentrate against Smith, the Confederates must have reduced their strength opposite Gillmore's X Corps. He urged Gillmore to attack, but Gillmore never did. In the meantime, Smith, disconcerted by the fog and fearing the worst, instructed his units to fall back. Presently Gillmore did the same, and by early afternoon Butler's army had taken up a new position about a mile behind its original line.

The situation now was curious. The Confederates had not pursued; Butler could not know it, but Beauregard's army was worn and disorganized from the morning battle. Even so, Smith and Gillmore seemed to have no spirit for renewing the fight, and the commander of Butler's rear guard reported that a force of rebels—Whiting, of course—was advancing from Petersburg. All in all, it seemed pointless to linger in front of Drewry's Bluff any longer. Around 3 P.M., Butler gave the order for his troops to fall back to the Bermuda Hundred lines.

All told, the battle of Drewry's Bluff cost the Union about three thousand casualties, of whom nearly half had been captured. Confederate losses totaled about the same. In many respects, Butler had accomplished what Grant expected of him. He had landed at Bermuda Hundred, drawn reinforcements away from Lee, and made a strong demonstration toward Richmond. But his decision to retreat into Bermuda Hundred nullified everything. Beauregard promptly advanced to the waist of the peninsula, sealed it off with an entrenched line of his own, and restored the strategic equilibrium. True, he had not destroyed Butler's army, but he had neutralized it, and he was able to hold the Bermuda Hundred lines with a reduced force. Soon seven thousand troops were heading north by train to reinforce Lee's army, with a promise that more would follow.[63]

By May 18, all five of the subsidiary offensives set in motion by Grant had evaporated. Three—Averell, Sigel, Butler—had met outright defeat, while even the two success stories, Crook and Sheridan, were no longer in position to threaten Confederate targets or pin down Confederate troops.

The bad news came in rapid succession. That day, as Grant saw Hancock's troops recoil from their attack at "Hell's Half Acre," a dispatch arrived from Halleck, announcing the defeats at New Market and Drewry's Bluff in a few acid sentences. "[Sigel] is already in full retreat on Strasburg. If you expect anything from him you will be mistaken. He will do nothing but run. He never did anything else. . . . Butler has fallen back to-day. Do not rely on him."[64]

The import of the news was obvious. "Lee," Grant told his staff, "will undoubtedly reinforce his army largely by bringing Beauregard's troops from Richmond, now that Butler has been driven back, and will call in troops from the valley since Sigel's defeated forces have retreated." He met the new situation with the calm resolve for which he was famous. "The general," wrote Horace Porter, an officer on Grant's staff, "was not a man to waste any time over occurrences of the past; his first thoughts were always to redouble his efforts to take the initiative and overcome disaster by success." Grant's reaction to the news, Porter recalled, was to sit down at once and write out an order for the army to leave Spotsylvania. There was nothing further to be gained here if Lee was about to be reinforced. Instead, the Federals would swing a second time around Lee's right flank and seek battle on better ground. The movement, he stipulated, would begin the following day.[65]

CHAPTER FIVE

"Lee's Army Is Really Whipped"

Good commanders contemplate many possibilities at once. Grant had pondered the option of another slide around Lee's flank days before it became necessary to do it and could therefore respond to the defeat of Sigel and Butler immediately. Certain aspects of the prospective march were obvious. The lack of a viable supply line west of Spotsylvania, for example, required the Army of the Potomac to swing around to the southeast, so that it could continue to receive rations, ammunition, and reinforcements by water. Such a maneuver, however, would uncover the roads that led back to Belle Plain. Consequently, that base would no longer serve; a new one would have to be established farther south. Port Royal, a sleepy tobacco port on the lower Rappahannock River, answered the purpose, and Grant told Halleck he wanted future shipments of supplies and reinforcements sent there.[1]

But supply was not the main problem. Rather, it was how to destroy Lee's army or, as Grant preferred to think, complete its destruction. Confronted with a new turning movement, the Army of Northern Virginia could easily fall back a few miles to the North Anna River, an obvious defensive position. It could even retreat into the Richmond fortification belt. Either way, the Confederates would confront him behind entrenchments just as formidable as those at Spotsylvania. No, the rebels had to be caught in open country, where decisive victory was possible. But how to do it?

Since Grant could not force Lee to accept battle in the open, he would have to induce Lee to do so of his own accord. That meant, in turn, that he must offer Lee a reason to take the offensive, a prize worth the risk of fighting outside entrenchments. The prize was self-evident. If Grant wanted an opportunity to destroy Lee's army, he must first present Lee with a chance to destroy his own. Accordingly, the Union commander decided to make the turning movement using only the II Corps. The rest of the Army of the Potomac would remain at Spotsylvania. Lee would detect Hancock's corps and, if he were as aggressive as advertised, try to crush it. Then, once the rebel chieftain had committed himself to the attack, Grant would sweep down suddenly and destroy Lee's army before it could do serious harm to the exposed corps. The gambit was risky, but it offered the only chance to beat the Confederates in the open field. Indeed, Grant worried less about defeat than that Lee had lost his offensive spirit and would fail to take the bait.[2]

Grant received an encouraging sign on May 19, the day Hancock was slated to begin the movement around Lee's flank. Union troops spent the day shifting to new positions, abandoning their west-to-east orientation in favor of a line that ran past Spotsylvania Court House on a north-to-south axis, with the V, VI, and IX Corps holding the line while Hancock's II Corps assembled in the rear. Morning and noon passed without incident, but at 4:30 P.M. a large Confederate force suddenly appeared on the Federal right flank. The explosion of musketry from that direction served notice that Lee remained as bellicose as ever.

The flank was located near the Harris farm, not far from the main road leading down to Spotsylvania from Fredericksburg. If the rebels seized the road, they would jeopardize the Union army's most direct link with its Belle Plain base and probably gobble up dozens of valuable supply wagons. As always when Lee did something combative, Meade reacted defensively. "Move up a division in double-quick," he instructed Hancock. "The enemy have attacked us in force at the Harris house. The rest of your corps to follow." The order effectively nullified Hancock's turning movement, slated to begin that evening. It was more important to shore up the threatened flank.[3]

Col. Horace Porter of Grant's staff was napping at headquarters when the attack began. A black camp servant shook him awake; Porter later caricatured him as crying out, "Wake up, sah, fo' God's sake! De whole ob Lee's army am in our reah!" The colonel groggily peered outside his tent, saw Grant and his staff on horseback, and hastened to join them. Grant, animated but composed, told Porter, "The enemy is detaching a large force to turn our right. I wish you would ride to the point of attack, and keep me posted as to the movement, and urge upon the commanders of the troops in that vicinity not only to check the advance of the enemy, but to take the offensive and destroy them if possible. You can say that Warren's corps will be ordered to cooperate promptly."[4]

Porter galloped to the battlefield and within minutes located Brig. Gen. Robert O. Tyler, an old army friend who commanded a fresh division just arrived from Washington. It was the most unusual outfit in the army. Though temporarily styled a division, it had no brigade substructure and was not composed of infantry. Instead, it was made up of five regiments of heavy artillery, oversized units averaging 1,500 men each, created and trained to man the fortifications that ringed the Northern capital. Since no Confederates had ever attacked Washington, the artillerists had spent the war holding parades and polishing their big guns until Grant decreed that they should convert to infantry and join the Army of the Potomac. Steamers had brought them down to Belle Plain; they had marched the rest of the way. Though well disciplined—most of the troops had more than two years' service under their belts—this was their first battle.

The former heavy artillerists took a lot of heat from genuine infantrymen and even from their counterparts in the field artillery. A New York cannoneer explained, "There was a widespread belief among us that these men had enlisted in that arm because they expected to fight behind earthworks, or to safely garrison the forts which surrounded Washington." For that reason veterans catcalled, "How are you, heavies? Is this work heavy enough for you?" or "Why, dearest, why did you leave your earthworks?" Wounded men brandished their bloody limbs as the heavies moved up to the firing line. Some went so far as to expose a corpse in order to display its mangled face.[5]

The heavies blanched. But once in line of battle they stood the test of combat well, and when Porter arrived he could see them gamely delivering volleys in the grand old stand-up style of 1861. "Tyler, you are in luck today," he congratulated his old friend. "It isn't every one who has a chance to make such a début on joining the army. You are certain to knock a brevet out of this day's fight." Tyler nodded. "As you see, my men are raw hands at this sort of work, but they are behaving like veterans."[6]

The Confederates assailing the heavies belonged to Ewell's corps. Contrary to what Porter's camp servant (and many others) at first believed, they were not intent on crushing the Union right. They simply wanted to pinpoint its revised location. Lee's instructions had called for a reconnaissance, not a full-blown assault, but Ewell tapped his entire corps for the mission, apparently on the theory that only so large a force could

1. Lt. Gen. Ulysses S. Grant (National Archives).

2. Maj. Gen. George G. Meade (Library of Congress).

3. Gen. Robert E. Lee (Valentine Museum/Richmond History Center).

4. Maj. Gen. Benjamin F. Butler
(National Archives).

5. Gen. P. G. T. Beauregard (National
Archives).

6. Maj. Gen. Franz Sigel (Library of
Congress).

7. Maj. Gen. John C. Breckinridge (National Archives).

8. Maj. Gen. Philip H. Sheridan and subordinates. *Left to right*: Brig. Gen. Wesley Merritt, Brig. Gen. David McM. Gregg, Sheridan, Brig. Gen. Henry E. Davies, Brig. Gen. James H. Wilson, and Brig. Gen. A. T. A. Torbert (National Archives).

9. The Union VI Corps crosses Germanna Ford, May 4, 1864 (Library of Congress).

10. Ewell's breastworks at Saunders' Field: An early postwar photograph (MOLLUS, U. S. Army Military History Institute).

11. Wadsworth's Division in the Wilderness, May 6, 1864. A sketch by Alfred Waud (Library of Congress).

12. Union soldiers cheering Grant, May 7, 1864. A sketch by Edwin Forbes (Library of Congress).

13. "The Toughest Fight Yet": Alfred Waud's sketch of close quarters combat at the Mule Shoe, May 12, 1864 (Library of Congress).

Lieut. U.S. Grant &c. Wilderness May 7th 1864.

The roughest fight yet.   A R Waud

14. The charge of the VMI cadets at
New Market, May 15, 1864 (Virginia
Military Institute Museum).

15. Union council of war at
Massaponax Church, May 21, 1864.
Grant (*at left*) studies a map held by
Meade (partially obscured by Grant's
head and right shoulder) (National
Archives).

16. The Union base at Belle Plain on the Potomac River, ca. May 16, 1864. Federal sea power played an unheralded but crucial role in Grant's campaign against Lee (Library of Congress).

17. Dead Confederate after battle of Harris Farm, photographed on May 20, 1864 (Library of Congress).

18. Union troops in fieldworks, North Anna River, May 25, 1864. Though primitive, the living conditions shown were actually among the best of this arduous campaign (Library of Congress).

19. Destroyed railroad bridge over North Anna River, May 25, 1864. The disruption of Confederate transportation infrastructure played a significant role in Grant's strategy (Library of Congress).

20. Union burial detail at Fredricksburg, May 19 or 20, 1864 (National Archives).

21. Barlow's Division at Cold Harbor, June 3, 1864. This sketch by Alfred Waud depicts a brief moment of success, as Union troops gain a toehold in the Confederate trenches and take dozens of prisoners (Library of Congress).

hold its own should it encounter serious trouble. Even using everyone, he had barely six thousand infantry to do the job.[7]

The Confederates had left their entrenchments around 2:30 P.M. They detoured warily around the previously identified Union position, then struck out eastward toward the Fredericksburg road. Near the Harris farm they suddenly encountered Tyler's division and two additional heavy artillery regiments under Col. J. Howard Kitching, reinforced by a heavy artillery battalion. Believing erroneously that the Federals were about to charge, the commander of the lead Confederate brigade, Brig. Gen. Stephen D. Ramseur, launched a spoiler attack to throw them off balance. Soon most of Ewell's corps became engaged, and a three-hour fight ensued amid a drenching downpour. Some Confederates briefly broke through to a Federal wagon train but had time only to shoot a few horses and mules before being forced back. For the most part, they had their hands full just fending off Tyler's unexpectedly combative heavies. To be sure, the heavies showed inexperience. They "got a little mixed and didn't fight very tactically," a veteran officer conceded, "but they fought confounded plucky." In the end, Ewell's corps withdrew, having lost nine hundred casualties as the price for locating the Union right. The heavies tallied fifteen hundred killed and wounded of their own.[8]

Militarily pointless, the battle of Harris farm underscored the realities of 1864. A year previously, Ewell's corps would have contained twenty thousand men and would have mauled the heavies in short order. But the May 19 reconnaissance against the Union right flank had a shadow of that former strength. And significantly, the Federals whom the exhausted Confederates encountered were not weary veterans like themselves but fresh troops with full ranks. A Confederate corps of six thousand men had fought seven Union regiments totaling ten thousand. Ewell's expedition was a reconnaissance not of the Union right but of the Confederacy's future.[9]

The battle had two additional outcomes. First, the Army of the Potomac's veterans discarded their preconceptions of the heavies and accepted them as full-fledged comrades. Second, Grant gained new reason to believe that Hancock's impending turning movement might succeed. "My chief anxiety now is to draw Lee out of his works and fight him in the open field, instead of assaulting him behind his entrenchments," he told his staff next morning. "The movement of Early [Ewell] yesterday gives me some hope that Lee may at times take the offensive, and thus give our troops the desired opportunity."[10]

Hancock's II Corps finally began the movement after dark on May 20, marching eastward to Massaponax Church, where it picked up Brig. Gen. A. T. A. Torbert's cavalry brigade to act as escort. The combined force then continued to Guinea Station on the Richmond, Fredericksburg and Potomac Railroad. There the Union troopers drove away a small picket force of Confederate cavalry and turned south down the railroad tracks. The infantry followed by the same route. At 9 A.M. on May 21, Torbert's cavalry reached Milford Station, about seventeen airline miles southeast of Spotsylvania. Around noon, Hancock's lead division passed through nearby Bowling Green, crossed the Mattapony River, and halted. Hancock had now fulfilled his instructions. As Meade had directed, he had reached the right bank of the river, a position from which his corps could threaten Lee's line of communications.[11]

The threat, to be sure, was as yet more latent than real. Confederate communications were still intact, and Lee, if he chose, could easily withdraw to a new position behind the North Anna River. By continuing the march, however, Hancock's men would form a menace so serious and immediate that Lee would have no choice but to react at once. That was precisely what Grant desired, but only if it did not jeopardize the survival of the II Corps. Hancock briefly considered the option but rejected it. For one thing, he was already almost twenty miles away from the rest of Meade's army; it seemed imprudent to widen the gap even further. For another, Confederate prisoners captured in a sharp midmorning action at Milford Station proved to belong not to Lee's army at Spotsylvania but to several regiments of Pickett's division, which had previously been serving in the Bermuda Hundred sector. Their presence signaled the arrival of the first reinforcements to Lee's army, made possible by the collapse of Grant's peripheral strategy. That being the case, if Hancock continued to march, he might well run into more enemy troops than he could handle. He decided to fortify his present position and await developments.[12]

According to the logic of Grant's original plan, Lee would now evaluate Hancock's corps as a threat but also as isolated and vulnerable, which would entice him to leave his Spotsylvania entrenchments and attack. But Lee failed to take the bait. In fact, he failed even to recognize it as bait. Reading Hancock as neither an imminent threat nor an inviting target, he assumed that the II Corps advance to the Mattapony was merely the first stage of a general movement by the Army of the Potomac. And his scouts had spotted Hancock's night march so promptly (just three hours after it began) that it surprised Lee not in the least. He had been expecting that sooner or later Grant would try to get around his right flank. Now Grant was doing it. The Confederate commander ordered Ewell's corps to head for the North Anna River. Then, arranging for demonstrations against the Union forces at Spotsylvania to screen his withdrawal, Lee began a general retrograde movement.[13]

For the next thirty-six hours the two armies marched along roughly parallel routes. The Army of the Potomac followed the II Corps in a march that carried it generally southeast, from Spotsylvania to Guinea Station and thence to Milford Station and the neighboring village of Bowling Green. The Army of Northern Virginia headed directly for the North Anna River, equidistant between Spotsylvania and Richmond. Cavalry scouts kept a general eye on the rival forces, but otherwise the two armies were out of contact for the first time since May 5.

They had also left Spotsylvania County, the scene of four of the war's bloodiest battles: Fredericksburg and Chancellorsville as well as the recent struggles in the Wilderness and around Spotsylvania Court House itself. Now the armies were entering Caroline County, scarcely touched by war and one of the wealthiest counties in the region, rich in crops and livestock and with real estate valued at $4.8 million. According to the 1860 census, the county had a population of almost 19,000, including 11,500 slaves. The war, of course, had significantly reduced that figure. Many able-bodied white men had gone into the army. Other whites had fled to safer areas, in some instances taking along valuable property. As Charles A. Dana reported to Stanton, "The cattle of the plantations have all been driven from our line of march, and the negroes removed mostly to Danville."[14]

Even so, enough residents and slaves remained to keep the region under cultivation. Dana observed "fine, clear country." An artillerist termed it "the best agricultural region I had seen in Virginia." What happened next was predictable. Short on rations, famished after the Spotsylvania fighting, and eager for fresh victuals, some of Hancock's men left the ranks and plundered the county's sheep, chicken, cattle, and corn. The same occurred when the V, VI, and IX Corps passed through.[15]

By 1864 such unauthorized foraging—"marauding" was the term officially used—had become an old story, particularly in the western theater, where officers tended to see it as unfortunate but inevitable and (depending on whose goods were stolen) justified. Reaction among the Army of the Potomac's officer corps varied. Some were outraged. Capt. Oliver Wendell Holmes Jr. noted on May 23 that "straggling & marauding have become a great evil—Families are robbed and houses burned constantly by ruffians, chiefly, I suspect, noncombatants who move along the outskirts of the column." One of Meade's staff officers noted, "Some of the generals, particularly Birney and Barlow, have punished pillagers in a way they will not forget; and they will be shot if they do not stop outrages on the inhabitants."[16]

Other officers inclined to view such depredations as harmless fun. In the V Corps, Brig. Gen. Joseph J. Bartlett, coming upon a vast expanse of sheep carcasses and fleece, shrugged and remarked, "If sheep attack you, you are obliged to fight." And Provost Marshal Marsena Patrick believed that Grant's staff were "themselves, engaged in sheep stealing, fowl stealing, and the like. . . . I am *very* tired," Patrick confessed to his diary, "& feel very despondent about Grant's notions of discipline."[17]

In fact, Grant was anything but indifferent to this outbreak of marauding, less because of its effect on civilians—he explicitly approved of foraging if done by proper authority—than its impact on military efficiency. For that reason, orders went out for a full regiment to march at the rear of each corps with instructions to punish summarily anyone straggling from the ranks, "especially those who may be found going to farm-houses for the purpose of pillaging." (At least one division commander interpreted this as authorization to bayonet or shoot the offenders.) Grant was so concerned about the rash of thievery because he knew the hemorrhaging of troops from the ranks, if not curtailed, would interfere with his next bid to strike at Lee, who seemed to be taking up a new position behind the North Anna River along Caroline County's southern border.[18]

The North Anna River had its source in the foothills near Orange Court House and flowed through green, pleasant countryside, innocent of war aside from Sheridan's recent foray to the Richmond suburbs. Twenty-one miles north of the Confederate capital, it bisected the Telegraph Road, the main highway between Washington and Richmond, then turned sharply south and after four airline miles combined with the South Anna to form the Pamunkey River. Sandwiched between the North and South Anna lay Hanover Junction, a minor hamlet where the Virginia Central and Richmond, Fredericksburg and Potomac Railroads intersected. The latter was of little consequence to Lee, but the Virginia Central constituted his main link with the foodstuffs in the Shenandoah Valley. Because of that, he needed to hold Hanover Junction if at all possible. The North Anna provided a useful shield, since it was 150 feet across, steep-banked, and crossable only at a few points. But as a defensive line it had one glaring defect: its left (northern) bank was generally higher than its right (southern) bank, which meant that Union artillery would be able to command most of the crossing points. A close defense of the river line would therefore be difficult. Still, the stream would restrict Grant's options to a handful of bridges and fords, and it would require several hours to get an army corps from one side to the other. All in all, from Lee's perspective the North Anna was a good interim position.

He did not expect to fight there anyway—at least, not for several days. On May 22, as his three infantry corps converged on Hanover Junction, Lee penned a letter to President Davis explaining the situation. The enemy, he wrote, had left Spotsylvania and gone toward Bowling Green. "It appeared . . . that he was endeavoring to place the Mattapony river between him & our army, which secured his flank, & by rapid movements to join his cavalry under Sheridan to attack Richmond." To guard against this possibility, Lee had chosen to withdraw. "I should have preferred contesting the enemy's approach inch by inch; but my solicitude for Richmond caused me to abandon that plan." The Confederate chieftain assumed that Grant would do one of two things. He might continue his swing to the southeast and cross the Pamunkey River, which would enable him to approach Richmond from the east while using the Pamunkey or York River to keep his army stocked with food and ammunition. Alternatively, he might advance directly south toward Richmond, using the Richmond, Fredericksburg and Potomac Railroad as his supply line.[19]

If Grant did the latter, however, he would have to wait until the railroad was rebuilt, and Lee speculated that his opponent would welcome the delay. "During its reconstruction," he explained to Davis on May 23, "General Grant will have time to recruit and reorganize his army, which as far as I am able to judge, has been very much shaken." Lee's adjutant echoed those sentiments. Despite the withdrawal, wrote Lt. Col. Walter H. Taylor to his wife, "This does not look like a retreat. Our army is in excellent condition—as good as it was when we met Grant, two weeks since for the first time. . . . His losses have already been fearfully large. Our list of casualties is a sad one to contemplate, but does not compare with his terrible record of killed and wounded."[20]

Taylor did not expect a battle on the North Anna, either. "I think it probable he will make still another move to the right & land somewhere near West Point," on the York River at the confluence of the Pamunkey and Mattapony Rivers. West Point lay within a few miles of White House Landing, the place McClellan had chosen to supply his own Richmond offensive back in 1862. Grant appeared to have elected to follow the same course, though Taylor found his strategy puzzling. "Why Grant did not carry his new base without incurring the heavy losses he has sustained in battle, I can not say. If Fredericksburg was his destination [in the first days of the campaign] he c[oul]d have obtained possession of it without the loss of 100 men. The same can be said of West Point."[21]

Such thoughts were based on the assumption that Grant's objective was Richmond. Neither Lee, Taylor, nor any other Confederate appreciated that Grant's actual goal was the destruction of the Army of Northern Virginia, notwithstanding the fact that Lee's own goal was the destruction of the Potomac Army. In any event, contemplating the situation from Hanover Junction, Lee believed that goal was getting closer. Grant's army was much depleted by its horrific casualties in the Wilderness and at Spotsylvania, it was steadily losing thousands of veterans whose enlistments had expired, and its line of communications was becoming longer with every mile it advanced. The Army of Northern Virginia's situation was just the reverse. It had lost fewer men, its supply line to Richmond had grown shorter and less exposed, and as it reached Hanover Junction it had been reinforced by over ten thousand soldiers fresh from the victories at New Market and Bermuda Hundred. Even better, only forty miles now separated Lee's army from Beauregard's forces, and with two railroads linking Hanover Junction and Richmond, a concentration of all available Confederate troops in the region could quickly be made. "It seems to me our best policy [is] to unite upon [Grant's army] and endeavor to crush it," Lee wrote Davis on May 23. "I should be very glad to have the aid of General Beauregard in such a blow, and if it is possible to combine, I think it will succeed."[22]

Lee's assessment was optimistic but not unrealistic. The best present-day estimate of the strength of the two armies after Spotsylvania, including replacements and reinforcements, credits the Army of Northern Virginia with 51,000 to 53,000 men compared with just over 67,000 men in the Army of the Potomac. The Confederates' numerical disadvantage was as slight as it had ever been against their opponents. Moreover, a quarter of the Federal troops were new to active campaigning. Small wonder that Lee believed he had a real chance to destroy Grant's army. And small wonder he did not expect Grant to resume the offensive until he had rested and reinforced his battered force.[23]

Grant, of course, viewed the situation differently. Far from being afraid that Lee would take the offensive, he hoped that the Confederate commander would do so. Nevertheless, he knew from his intelligence service that Lee had received substantial reinforcements from the Shenandoah Valley and Bermuda Hundred. This last was especially galling. "The force under Butler is not detaining 10,000 men in Richmond, and is not even keeping the roads south of the city cut," Grant complained to Halleck on May 22. Under the circumstances, he thought it best to give up the Bermuda Hundred operation, retain a toehold at City Point, and bring the rest of the Army of the James north to link up with the Army of the Potomac. Let "Baldy" Smith take charge of the force; Grant would leave Butler to administer his now denuded Department of Virginia and North Carolina.[24]

Contrary to Lee's expectations, Grant had no intention of suspending offensive operations, but rather instructed Meade to march down to the North Anna crossings. The army got on the road early next morning, but Federal maps of the region proved woefully inadequate. As a result, the II and V Corps collided with one another while en route to destinations that turned out to be incorrectly described or nonexistent. It took several hours of delay and countermarching to sort things out. Still, by early afternoon the II Corps was approaching Chesterfield Bridge, which conveyed the main Richmond highway across the North Anna, while the V Corps had reached Jericho Mill, directly on the river about five miles upstream.[25]

At Jericho Mill the North Anna was waist-deep and about fifty yards across: an easy wade for infantry but nearly impassable for wagons or artillery because of steep banks on either side. Engineers went to work building a pontoon bridge. Meanwhile Warren threw a steady stream of regiments across via the ford. By midafternoon he had two full divisions on the south bank, and a third was preparing to cross. Rebel cavalry silently monitored the operation, and around 3 P.M. a lone South Carolina infantry regiment sparred briefly with Warren's picket line. A Southern prisoner, taken to Warren for questioning, assured him that an entire Confederate division—that of Cadmus Wilcox, from the Third Corps—lay in wait behind the Virginia Central Railroad, not two miles distant.[26]

The prisoner proved accurate enough about the presence of the division but wrong about its intentions. Around 5:45 P.M. it suddenly materialized and attacked, remorselessly, in full strength. The Union picket line caved in at once, followed by most of two infantry brigades (including the once distinguished Iron Brigade), which abandoned their positions and ran for the rear. For a half hour or so the Confederates held the upper hand, but gradually the Union line stiffened, buttressed by a dozen fieldpieces that dashed across the just-completed bridge. Their commander, Col. Charles S. Wainwright, ordered the cannoneers to hold on at all costs, and they did, forcing the rebels to take cover until Union infantry finally pried them loose. The fighting continued until dusk, after which Wilcox withdrew his force to nearby Noel's Station. The Confederates had lost 730 killed, wounded, and captured. Union casualties totaled 377.[27]

Soon after the battle of Jericho Mill commenced, a second engagement opened at Chesterfield Bridge. As his II Corps neared the crossing, Hancock discovered a redoubt manned by three Confederate regiments on the north bank, ordered up twenty cannon to bombard it, and deployed three brigades to capture it. The outcome was preordained. At 6 P.M. the Federals charged and overran the redoubt, forcing its defenders literally to swim for their lives. Although Hancock did not put his victorious troops across the river that evening, the northern bank overlooked the southern so handily that the rebels could never defend it. He knew that in the morning he could cross the river easily enough.[28]

As darkness fell on May 23, the Federals could feel well satisfied with their day's work. They had achieved one bridgehead across the North Anna River and would shortly secure another. If Lee remained in the area, he could now be attacked to advantage. If he withdrew—as there was every reason to suppose he would do, now that the North Anna line was compromised—the Federals might well be able to damage him as he fell back. Either way, things looked promising.

The Confederates, on the other hand, were rueful. The loss of Chesterfield Bridge was perhaps unavoidable, but the attack on Jericho Mill, though capably made, seemed an expensive mistake. Lee was furious that A. P. Hill, in authorizing the attack, had sent only one division. Confronting Hill the next morning, he demanded, "Why did you not do as Jackson would have done—thrown your whole force upon these people and driven them back?"[29]

Others regretted that the attack was made at all. Hill apparently based his decision on cavalry reports that only two Union brigades had crossed the river. Wilcox's division might well have clobbered such a force, but against an entire Union corps, victory was out of the question. A South Carolina officer gloomed, "The movement was a failure. . . . The truth is, General [W. H. F.] Lee's scouts had been miserably deceived. Instead of two brigades, resting and cooking, there were two corps of infantry [*sic*] between us and the river, perfectly prepared for us! It could hardly be expected that one small division, of four brigades, could rout all these!"[30]

That evening Lee summoned his chief engineer and several commanders to headquarters. Together they reviewed the situation. With Union troops across at Jericho Mill and practically so at Chesterfield Bridge, holding the river line was obviously impossible. The Army of Northern Virginia could retreat, of course, but that would mean abandoning Hanover Junction to the enemy, something Lee was loath to do. Gradually, after studying the map and discussing the local topography in detail, an ingenious solution emerged. When the meeting broke up, the engineers and commanders headed off to construct one of the most brilliant defensive positions of the entire war.[31]

Union orders for May 24 called for a general advance. The II Corps would consummate its crossing of the North Anna; the V Corps would move inland from its bridgehead, accompanied by the VI Corps, which had arrived at Jericho Mill overnight. Burnside's IX Corps, meanwhile, would cross the river at Ox Ford, about midway between the mill and Chesterfield Bridge. The early stages of the operation went off without a hitch. Aside from scattered small arms and artillery fire, the Confederates made no attempt at resistance. Two African American men from the neighborhood, who paddled across the river during the night, were taken to Meade for interrogation. "I have seen the negroes," he told Grant, "and think from what they say the enemy has fallen back beyond the South Anna."[32]

That tallied with other reports, and at 8 A.M. Grant wrote Halleck, "The enemy have fallen back from North Anna; we are in pursuit. Negroes who have come in state that Lee is falling back to Richmond." The new development altered plans for Smith's XVIII Corps. In the shifting circumstances it was no longer obvious where the corps could be used to best advantage. Smith should be placed in readiness to move, Grant told Halleck, but held until the situation developed further. "I will probably know to-day if the enemy intends standing behind South Anna."[33]

As the morning wore on, Warren and Wright overran the Virginia Central Railroad at Noel's Station. They encountered no one except two hundred Confederate soldiers inadvertently left asleep when Wilcox's division had withdrawn the previous night. These put up no resistance; most seemed glad to surrender. Hancock, meanwhile, got across Chesterfield Bridge and assembled his corps on the south bank. The only opposition he encountered was some desultory shell fire. It looked as if Lee had pulled out. The only corps commander who seemed stalled was Burnside. He had reached Ox Ford as ordered, only to discover that it was one of the few points on the river where the south bank overlooked the north. Furthermore, the far bank appeared to be held in force. "The prospects of success are not at all flattering," he wrote Grant, "but I think the attempt can be made without any very disastrous results, and we may possibly succeed."[34]

That sounded just like Burnside, and when noon came and went, with Burnside still on the north bank, Grant decided to prod him. "You will move your entire corps, with trains, to the south side of North Anna this afternoon," the dispatch began, and, after offering Burnside some suggestions about how to proceed, concluded, "You must get over and camp to-night on the south side." Burnside objected that he had been trying to do so all morning, but the enemy position was too daunting. However, he had discovered another crossing point, Quarles' Ford, a mile upstream, and had sent a division there. Once on the south bank, it would turn east and drive the rebels from Ox Ford.[35]

That was promising, at least, and the overall picture at headquarters was bright. Assistant Secretary of War Charles A. Dana captured the mood in two dispatches sent to Washington that day. The first, written during the early morning, declared, "The enemy have fallen back, whether to take up a position beyond the South Anna or to go to Richmond is uncertain. Reports brought by negroes favor the latter alternative. Warren, Burnside, and Hancock are pushing forward after the retreating army." A follow-up dispatch at 1 P.M. was even rosier: "Everything going on well. Warren has 500 prisoners, Hancock some 300, and Wright has picked up some. The whole number resulting from yesterday's operations will not fall short of 1,000. . . . The prisoners captured are in a great part North Carolinians. They are more discouraged than any considerable number of prisoners ever captured before. They say also that Lee has deceived them; that his army will not fight again except behind breast-works."[36]

In midafternoon, however, the picture changed abruptly. A V Corps division sent to help Burnside cleared Quarles' Ford but struck a line of Confederate entrenchments on its right front. Around 3 P.M., the II Corps encountered rebel skirmishers a half mile north of Hanover Junction. They seemed in no hurry to depart, so John Gibbon sent a regiment to dislodge them. When the regiment got nowhere, Gibbon reinforced it, gradually feeding in more troops until he had the bulk of his division in action. The Federals finally jarred the skirmishers loose and overran a line of entrenchments, only to discover a second, more formidable line farther on. Within minutes, a considerable force of Confederates poured forth from this second line, evidently intent on recovering the first. Gibbon fought them off, but not without difficulty, and from prisoners taken in this encounter Hancock got some sobering news: The enemy in his front belonged to Ewell's Second Corps, with at least one division from Anderson's First Corps nearby. Although the situation was unclear, plainly Lee's army had not withdrawn but was still somewhere around Hanover Junction.[37]

Burnside, meanwhile, remained on the north bank of the river, but Maj. Gen. John Crittenden's division had crossed the North Anna via Quarles' Ford and by 4 P.M. faced the west side of the bluff overlooking Ox Ford. Even so, a formidable line of earthworks, amply defended by infantry and artillery, stood atop the bluff, and the prospect of a successful attack looked as bleak from the south bank as it had from the north. It looked bleak, that is, to everyone except Brig. Gen. James H. Ledlie, who commanded Crittenden's lead brigade. Convinced that he faced only a rear guard, Ledlie unhesitatingly put his 1,500 men in line of battle and rolled forward, to the horror of Crittenden, who wondered if Ledlie knew that the rest of the division had not yet arrived. Brig. Gen. William Mahone's division held this sector, veteran troops under a solid commander, and from the protection of massive entrenchments the Confederates shattered Ledlie's brigade within minutes. At least a hundred Federals fell dead or wounded. Another hundred were taken prisoner. Afterward, observers claimed that Ledlie had been "thoroughly liquored up"—which he quite probably was. Incredibly, however, he escaped censure for the debacle at Ox Ford. Indeed, within weeks he replaced Crittenden in command of the division.[38]

By 6:45 P.M., as the last of Ledlie's brigade withdrew from the field, the situation facing the Army of the Potomac was becoming apparent. Lee's army was indeed still in the area, and it defended a new line that was, if anything, more formidable than holding the river crossings would have been. The position resembled an inverted V, with the vertex at Ox Ford and the shanks running southwest and southeast to cover Hanover Junction. The entire line was heavily entrenched—Lee's troops had thrown up earthworks all night and improved them during the day. The result, crowed Confederate Brig. Gen. Evander M. Law, was to place Grant "in what may be called a military dilemma. He had cut his army

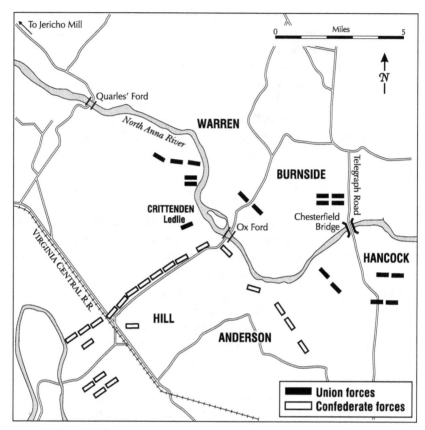

12. The North Anna, May 24, 1864

in two by running it upon the point of a wedge"—Ox Ford. "He could not break the point, which rested upon the river, and the attempt to force it out of place by striking on its sides must of necessity be made without much concert of action between the two wings of his army, neither of which could reinforce the other without crossing the river twice; while his opponent could readily transfer his troops, as needed, from one wing to the other, across the narrow space between them."[39]

By creating the inverted V position, Lee brilliantly retrieved a situation that had seemed badly compromised by the Federal lodgments at Jericho Mill and Chesterfield Bridge. But, one of his officers later maintained, he had larger aspirations than merely a successful defense. In 1873 his aide-de-camp, Lt. Col. Charles S. Venable, gave a speech in Richmond in which he declared that Lee had intended to exploit the Union army's divided condition by delivering the decisive counterstroke he had been aching to launch since the campaign's start: "He hoped much from an attack on Warren's corps, which, having crossed at Jericho ford, several miles higher up the North Anna, lay in a hazardous position, separated from the rest of the Federal army. General Hill, who was now sufficiently recovered to be in the saddle, at the head of his corps, was also sanguine of success in this attack; but the main plan miscarried through some mishap, though one or two minor successes on this our left flank—notably one by General Mahone's division—were effected." The main reason the Army of Northern Virginia failed to launch a full-scale attack, Venable continued, was the poor health of General Lee, who had come down with a debilitating gastrointestinal disorder. "As he lay prostrated by his sickness," Venable recalled, "he would often repeat: 'We must strike them a blow—we must never let them pass us again—we must strike them a blow.' But though he still had reports of the operations in the field constantly brought to him, and gave orders to his officers, Lee confined to his tent was not Lee on the battlefield."[40]

Did Lee intend to launch a major counterattack on May 24? Generations of Confederate military historians have maintained that he did. But aside from Venable's address, evidence that Lee planned to attack is scanty. Other officers in a position to know about the contemplated attack fail to mention it. No surviving contemporaneous correspondence alludes to such an operation, and the troop movements made on the night of May 23 and on May 24 were limited and defensive in nature. A. P. Hill did not make the slightest offensive foray on May 24, and his troops were arrayed in a single line of battle, with only two brigades in reserve. Anderson's First Corps remained on the defensive as well. And although Ewell's corps did launch a counterattack on the afternoon of May 24—against Gibbon's division—this attack was carefully limited in scope and obviously calculated to avoid a general engagement. Furthermore, although impressive defensively, the inverted V was not self-evidently a good position from which to launch an offensive. It lacked depth. In the event of a reversal it would have been difficult to sustain such a line and even harder to retreat from it, particularly with the Little and South Anna Rivers flowing immediately to the south.[41]

In any case, if Grant perceived himself in mortal peril from Lee's inverted V position, he failed to show it. The next day, May 25, Union scouts aggressively probed the Confederate line and by noon had an accurate grasp of its layout. "The enemy are evidently making a determined stand between the two Annas," Grant informed Halleck. Far from anticipating a counterattack, however, he assumed that Lee would remain on the defensive. "It will probably take us two days to get in position for a general attack or to turn their position, as may favor best."[42]

With the two armies firmly in contact once more, Grant was able to make major revisions to the entire campaign in Virginia. First, Butler's Bermuda Hundred operation was definitely on the scrap heap. Previously Grant had suspended Smith's movement because the situation was in flux. Now he ordered not only it but the bulk of Butler's army to land on the north bank of the Pamunkey River, opposite White House Landing, and march up to join the Army of the Potomac. Troops should be left to hold the James River as far as City Point, but just enough to do the job, and on the assumption that the enemy "will not undertake any offensive operations there, but will concentrate everything here."[43]

Grant also had plans for the Union forces in the Shenandoah Valley. Franz Sigel was gone, relieved on May 21 by Maj. Gen. David Hunter, a senior officer who had impressed Grant favorably when the two had met during the Chattanooga campaign. Hunter was already completing preparations for a renewed advance. Grant encouraged this, but thought in terms of a raid rather than the occupation of any fixed strategic point. He was more interested in the destruction of the infrastructure on which Lee's supplies depended. "If Hunter can possibly get to Charlottesville and Lynchburg, he should do so, living on the country," Grant wrote. "The railroads and canals should be destroyed beyond possibility of repair for weeks. Completing this he could find his way back to his original base, or from about Gordonsville join this army."[44]

As yet unclear to Grant was the next move against Lee. No one seriously suggested a direct attack on the scowling earthworks around Hanover Junction. The question was whether to turn the position by going west or east. An eastward turning movement would be simple, a mere repetition of the maneuver that had carried the army first to Spotsylvania and then to the North Anna. But for that very reason Lee would be expecting it, so the chance to capitalize on any mistakes Lee might make would be minimal. Moving to the west, around Lee's left flank, had the advantage of novelty. It also would place the Army of the Potomac squarely athwart the Virginia Central Railroad, thereby depriving Lee of his best communications line with the Shenandoah Valley. And it offered the chance for a direct attack on Richmond from the north, which would force Lee into a fight to the finish. Both options were debated at a council of war held on the evening of May 25, and Grant initially decided to head west, a move reportedly endorsed by Warren and artillery chief Henry J. Hunt.[45]

But the general in chief quickly reversed himself. Upon reflection, a movement west seemed too unworkable. It could not be supplied, at least not in a conventional sense, because communications with the new base at Port Royal would be compromised as soon as the Army of the Potomac got well under way. It was possible, of course, to live primarily off the land, as Grant had done during his Vicksburg campaign, but that expedient hinged on the ability of foraging parties to fan out across the countryside without serious molestation from the enemy, a condition that did not apply here. Successful foraging also depended on speed. With over sixty thousand human mouths to feed, and as many horses and mules, the Army of the Potomac would quickly exhaust any neighborhood from which it drew supplies. Unless it could move rapidly forward, it would soon begin to starve in the field. And a turning movement to the west could not be rapid, Grant realized, because the troops would have to cross three streams to get around Lee's army, pausing each time to lay pontoon bridges for the wagon trains and artillery. All in all, it was more prudent to shift toward the east.[46]

Grant therefore ordered Meade to prepare for a general movement in the direction of Hanovertown, a minor settlement on the Pamunkey River about fifteen airline miles east of Hanover Junction. His instructions to Meade were specific, stipulating not just where the army should go but exactly how it should proceed, right down to details about the order of march. Sheridan's cavalry had arrived the day before and was available to screen the movement. To deceive Lee about Federal intentions, James H. Wilson's division carried out an elaborate feint against the Confederate left on May 26, marching dismounted to look like infantry and getting into a noisy firefight using twelve cannon. The ruse worked: Lee briefly believed the Federals were going to move around his left flank.[47]

Before leaving the North Anna, Grant also saw to it that the local railroads were wrecked. Although it was still unusual for the Army of the Potomac to devote much effort to the destruction of Confederate economic resources, western armies had been doing it routinely for a full year. The work began on May 25 and continued the next day. Extensive details—often entire brigades and even divisions—were put to work on the job. Hundreds of men would line up on one side of the railroad, then, at a signal, would pick up the track, flip it over, and systematically dismantle it. Cross ties were piled up and set afire. Once a blaze got good and hot, soldiers placed the iron rails on the flaming coals until the metal sagged from the heat. Some parties even twisted the rails to make it that much harder for Confederate work crews to salvage them. At least eight miles of the Virginia Central Railroad received this treatment, as did the Richmond, Fredericksburg and Potomac Railroad as far north as Milford Station. It was hot work, but the destruction had a carnival aspect to it, and many men thoroughly enjoyed themselves.[48]

Although the destruction of the railroads was almost the sole achievement Grant could show for his three-day stint on the North Anna, his observations of the enemy buoyed his enthusiasm. "Lee's army is really whipped," he assured Halleck on May 26. He could read it in the faces and comments of the prisoners and above all in the Confederates' evident determination to fight only from the cover of earthworks. "A battle with them outside of intrenchments cannot be had. Our men feel that they have gained the *morale* over the enemy and attack with confidence. I may be mistaken," Grant concluded, "but I feel that our success over Lee's army is already assured."[49]

By the time he wrote, the preliminaries for the new turning movement had already begun. Artillerists and teamsters withdrew their limbers and wagon trains to the north bank of North Anna on the evening of May 25. The movement began in earnest the next day, spearheaded by two of Sheridan's cavalry divisions, under A. T. A. Torbert and David McM. Gregg, and a VI Corps division under David Russell. The cavalry marched until it neared the Pamunkey crossings around midnight. Next morning the lead brigade drove away a handful of Confederate cavalry and took control of Hanovertown. A battalion of the Fiftieth New York engineers constructed two pontoon bridges amid sporadic small arms fire. By 9 A.M. on May 27, Sheridan's cavalry was firmly on the south bank. Russell's division crossed two hours later.[50]

By then the rest of the Army of the Potomac was also well under way, having begun its movement soon after midnight on May 27. The V and VI Corps marched by one route while the II and IX Corps took a parallel route farther north. Despite inevitable delays as some units waited for others to clear the road, the army made good time. The II Corps marched until 11 P.M. and ended its march just three miles short of the Pamunkey crossings. The next day, May 28, the army completed its passage. Most of the infantry was across by noon. The last of them reached the south bank shortly after midnight on May 29.[51]

It was impossible to screen so large a maneuver for very long. By May 27 Lee knew that Grant had withdrawn from his immediate front and that a mixed force of infantry and cavalry had been spotted down by Hanovertown. These clues indicated that Grant was making another movement around his right flank. Accordingly, he gave orders for his army to fall back twelve miles to Atlee's Station, which left him barely nine miles from Richmond.

Both armies were now returning to the scene of their first encounters during the Peninsula campaign back in the spring and summer of 1862. Familiar landmarks put veterans of that campaign in a reminiscent mood, but aside from memories, the flat, featureless terrain had little to recommend it. Except for Richmond, at its far southwestern fringe, it had no settlements of consequence. Most of it was just worn-out farmland, sandy and bereft of nutrients from decades of relentless tobacco cultivation. Roads were frequent but sketchy, most of them little more than dirt tracks connecting the farms. Stands of pine and live oak trees grew in irregular patches, while here and there the soil was cut by black, evil-looking little creeks that fed into the region's principal streams, the Pamunkey River to the north and the Chickahominy River to the south. Both rivers and nearly all the creeks were as much swamp as water courses, which made them significant military obstacles.[52]

The largest creek was Totopotomoy Creek, which flowed sluggishly from its source just north of Richmond on an east-west line until it emptied into the Pamunkey River two miles below Hanovertown. The best place to stop Grant, Lee knew, was a low ridge that commanded the creek's southern bank. Trouble was, the Confederates had lost contact

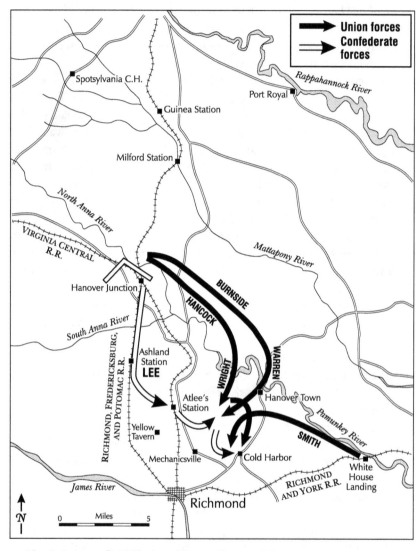

13. North Anna to Cold Harbor, May 27–June 1, 1864

with much of Grant's army, and until Lee had hard information that the Union army's main body had crossed the Pamunkey, he could not commit himself fully to the Totopotomoy line. There was always a chance that Grant might do something else—for instance, backtrack suddenly to Hanover Junction and come straight down the Telegraph Road. Until he knew for sure, Lee had to guard against several possibilities.

To get a solid fix on Grant's position, on the morning of May 28 Lee ordered Wade Hampton to make a reconnaissance in force toward the Hanovertown crossings, breach the enemy's cavalry screen, and find the Union infantry. Hampton departed at once with four cavalry brigades, a battery of horse artillery, and three regiments of mounted infantry, the latter just up from South Carolina and commanded by Brig. Gen. Matthew Butler (though led that day by Col. Benjamin H. Rutledge). Three-quarters of a mile short of Haw's Shop, the Confederates ran into a brigade of Union cavalry—the vanguard, as it happened, of a Federal reconnaissance in force designed to get a clear read on Lee's whereabouts. The battle that ensued was one of the largest, most severe cavalry fights of the entire war.

The Union brigade, belonging to the division of David McM. Gregg, was commanded by Henry E. Davies. It had no sooner reached the Haw's Shop intersection than Hampton's cavalry came barreling through, briefly driving in Davies's pickets before falling back a short distance to the west. Davies pursued, found that the Confederates had dismounted, taken a position astride the main road, and were scrambling to construct a barricade. A stream to the north and a mill pond to the south made the position impossible to turn. If the Federals were going to get past, they would have to go straight over the Confederates.

The rebels showed no inclination to let them. The fire that blazed forth from behind the barricade was so heavy and continuous that the Federals soon concluded the enemy force included infantry as well as cavalry. (They were fooled, in part, by the Enfield muskets carried by Butler's men.) Gregg brought up a second brigade but still lacked the muscle needed to dislodge the rebels. He called back to Sheridan for reinforcements. In the meantime, his troopers fired at the Confederates as fast as they could. Since the Federals had repeating carbines, the firepower thus created was tremendous. A Pennsylvania trooper estimated that the two hundred men in his unit fired eighteen thousand rounds. Their carbines got so hot that from time to time the troopers had to pause to let them cool.[53]

The battle continued like that, intense but inconclusive, for over five hours. Gregg impatiently told one of Sheridan's staff officers that with reinforcements he could "destroy the equilibrium and go forward." Unfortunately, the rest of the cavalry was mostly committed to screening the army. Plenty of infantry nearby and Sheridan asked Meade to give him two brigades, but Meade refused. Exasperated, Sheridan cast about for other troops, found Custer's brigade, which was resting nearby, and threw it into the fight. It entered the battle just as Hampton, having gotten the whereabouts of the V and VI Corps from prisoners, sent word for his brigades to disengage. They would have gotten away scot-free but for the inexperience of Butler's men, who mistook a Federal shift in position for a retreat and charged forward, only to be hammered by Custer's arriving brigade. At least eighty Confederates fell prisoner, and Custer's men went on to break the main Confederate line. The rebels eventually fought their way out to safety, but took significant losses in so doing.[54]

The battle of Haw's Shop cost Gregg's division 256 men dead, wounded, and captured. Another 41 were killed in Custer's brigade, including Pvt. John Huff, the Fifth Michigan trooper who had fatally shot Jeb Stuart just seventeen days earlier. Confederate losses, though never tabulated officially, were probably even worse. Union reports claimed that 187 rebel bodies were buried after the battle and 40–50 wounded men recovered from the field. But both sides had what they needed. From Union prisoners, Hampton discovered that the Union V and VI Corps were definitely on the right bank of the Pamunkey. From Confederate prisoners, Sheridan learned the positions of Anderson's and Ewell's corps.[55]

At 6 P.M. Lee brought Secretary of War James Seddon up to date on the situation. His army, he wrote, was in front of Atlee's Station on a line extending toward Totopotomoy Creek. He had heard nothing to suggest that the enemy had crossed the creek. Instead, he believed that Grant was assembling his army behind it. He passed along the report about the location of the V and VI Corps, adding cautiously, "I have not, however, received very definite information as yet either as regards their positions or numbers."[56]

Even so, the presence of two corps south of the Pamunkey strongly suggested that Grant was concentrating his entire army around Hanovertown, which meant that Lee could quit worrying about a Union thrust from the north. On the other hand, it did little to clarify Grant's next move. From Hanovertown he could march northwest, keeping the Totopotomoy between himself and Lee, then hit the Virginia Central Railroad near Ashland and so threaten Lee's left flank. Alternatively, he could advance to the southeast, cross the Totopotomoy lower down, pick up the Old Church Road, and threaten Lee's right. Or he could come straight at Lee to engage him in his current position. Whatever Grant did, Lee would have to react promptly to stop him. With only nine miles now separating the Army of Northern Virginia from Richmond, Lee was running out of maneuvering room. If Grant got around him, or pierced his line, the result would quite likely be complete defeat.

Meditating thus, Lee's thoughts turned, as they had repeatedly since the campaign commenced, to the prospect of reinforcements. True, his situation had improved since Spotsylvania. Breckinridge had come from the Valley and Pickett's division had finally arrived, as had one brigade from the division of Robert F. Hoke. But Grant still outnumbered him. Lee needed all the troops he could get. Only two reservoirs of manpower remained: the garrison at Richmond and Beauregard's force at Bermuda Hundred.

Beauregard was the key. In a real sense, the garrison and the Bermuda Hundred force were intertwined, for any reduction in the garrison would have to be offset by Beauregard. To be sure, the Creole had indicated a willingness to join forces with Lee, albeit on his own terms. A memorandum sent from Beauregard's headquarters to Braxton Bragg on May 18 had proposed, "If General Lee will fall back behind the Chickahominy, engaging the enemy so as to draw him on, General Beauregard can bring up fifteen thousand men to unite with Breckinridge and fall upon the enemy's flank with over twenty thousand effectives, thus rendering Grant's defeat certain and decisive." Then, having beaten Grant, the combined Confederate armies would turn on Butler's army and drive it away as well. President Davis had vetoed the proposal as too problematic, and ever since, Beauregard had been reluctant to part with any troops at all. Hoping, perhaps, to capitalize on Beauregard's desire to play the role of rescuer, Lee concluded a May 28 dispatch to Davis, "[Whatever Grant does] I shall endeavor to engage him as soon as possible, and will be near enough to Richmond for General Beauregard to unite with me if practicable. Should any field nearer to Richmond be more convenient to him, and he will designate it, I will endeavor to deliver battle there."[57]

Davis knew that Lee needed reinforcements badly and wanted to help him if at all possible. Unfortunately, the situation at Bermuda Hundred was also delicate. Yes, Butler had been thrown back, but his army was intact and safe behind entrenchments. It could emerge at any moment, and if it overwhelmed Beauregard's force, Richmond's rail communications with the rest of the Confederacy would soon be cut. And while Davis held Lee in far greater esteem than Beauregard, he understood that just as Beauregard bore responsibility for the defense of his sector, so too he must have authority over the troops under his command. Save for the most compelling of reasons, it would be wrong to peremptorily order him to send Lee reinforcements. Better to let him make the decision on his own.

Accordingly, Davis forwarded Lee's letter to Beauregard, sending it in the hands of a trusted aide who would not only deliver it but could give Beauregard detailed information concerning the state of affairs on Lee's front and in the capital. He also gave the aide a short letter of his own. A report was circulating in the capital that Butler was preparing to abandon Bermuda Hundred. "If it be true," Davis wrote, delicately but pointedly, "it will of course affect your own views in relation to the contents of the letter herewith transmitted."[58]

Davis next wrote Lee directly. "I have sent a copy of your letter to General Beauregard, and hope he may be able to reply satisfactorily to your inquiry in relation to his co-operation. He has been strengthening his defensive line, but reports his force but little more than half that of the enemy in his front. If he be holding nearly double his number inactive, and at the same time protecting our line of communication, along which we are bringing up supplies, it is doubtful whether he could be better employed at this time. I have sought to get reserve troops that might be placed with a part of Beauregard's, to relieve some to be sent away. The progress has been slower than our necessities demand. There are two reports in town, one that General Butler was withdrawing, and another, mentioned to me at this instant, that re-enforcements to the extent of 4,000 to 5,000 men had joined General Butler last night."[59]

Beauregard received both aide and letters and replied the next day: "The report you refer to of Butler breaking up his encampments in my front is only partially true, and indicates probably a change of position, not a withdrawal of part of his forces. . . . My force is so small at present that to divide it for the purpose of re-enforcing Lee would jeopardize the safety of the part left to guard my lines, and would greatly endanger Richmond itself." The next day, May 29, Davis and Beauregard visited Lee's headquarters—separately—and Lee did what he could to pull loose some troops from the Bermuda Hundred sector. Davis was loath to order it if Beauregard considered it militarily inadvisable and Beauregard told Lee no. At 9 P.M. Lee bowed, for the moment at least, to reality. "In conference with Genl Beauregard he states that he has only twelve thousand infantry and can spare none," Lee reported to Davis. "If Genl Grant advances tomorrow I will engage him with my present force."[60]

Ironically, at the same time that Beauregard was arguing to keep his present force, his opposite number, Butler, had just lost his battle to do the same thing. In the wake of his setback at Drewry's Bluff, two senior officers from the War Department, Brig. Gens. John Barnard and Montgomery C. Meigs, came down from Washington on a fact-finding mission made at Grant's behest. Their job was to check on the condition of Butler's army, decide if it could or should assume the offensive again, and, if not, determine how many troops would be needed to hold the position and how many could be sent to augment the Army of the Potomac. Barnard and Meigs were impressed by the strategic possibilities of the position Butler occupied and recommended that he resume the offensive. But Grant had already made up his mind to strip the army of as many troops as possible. The only relevant part of their report, therefore, was their estimate that City Point and the Bermuda Hundred line could be held with ten thousand troops. The other twenty thousand could go to reinforce the Army of the Potomac.[61]

Even before learning of the report, Grant had instructed Halleck to have Butler put the XVIII Corps on transports and send it around the Virginia peninsula to White House Landing on the Pamunkey River. The rapidly shifting situation on the North Anna led him to suspend the directive, but on May 26 he reinstated it. Butler of course had to comply. Still, he resisted the idea. Taking advantage of the fact that it would take time to assemble the needed transports, he used the interim to undertake an offensive against Petersburg, hoping to achieve enough results to convince Grant to suspend the transfer—or to commit Smith's troops so completely that they could not easily be withdrawn. His gamble failed, but only by a few hours. Late on the afternoon of May 28, just as he was about to launch the operation, word arrived that enough transportation had materialized. Reluctantly, he told Smith to put his command aboard the transports.[62]

On May 29 the Army of the Potomac sidled closer to its opponent, but gingerly: it lacked as yet a detailed grasp of Lee's position, although, as Theodore Lyman wrote his parents, Lee was plainly entrenched "in a sort of way that says 'I will fight you to my last gun and my last battalion!'" But so far only Hancock's II Corps and one division of the V Corps had neared Totopotomoy Creek. Wright's VI Corps was to the north, occupying a line between Hanover Court House and Crump's Creek. The bulk of the V Corps and all of the IX Corps were at Haw's Shop, with Sheridan's cavalry screening both flanks of the army.[63]

Lee, meanwhile, consolidated his line on Totopotomoy Creek. From west to east, it consisted of A. P. Hill's Third Corps, over by Shady Grove Church, followed by Breckinridge's slender division, then Anderson's First Corps, and, on the right flank, the Second Corps, now under a new commander, Maj. Gen. Jubal A. Early. Ewell had fallen ill with diarrhea. Much worse in Lee's eyes, he had proven unequal to the demands of his assignment. "Old Baldy" had disappointed Lee ever since Gettysburg. His conduct during the rest of 1863 had been lackluster, and his behavior during the current campaign was poor. True, Ewell had handled his corps effectively during the Wilderness fight. But that took place largely outside Lee's observation, whereas Lee had personally witnessed two serious enemy breakthroughs in Ewell's sector at Spotsylvania and had seen Ewell become unhinged during the Mule Shoe breakthrough on May 12, cursing his men hysterically until Lee ordered him to get control of himself. Further, Lee had been unimpressed by Ewell's needless and costly decision to give battle at Harris Farm on May 19. Ewell had to go. Thus, when Ewell fell ill on May 26 and temporarily relinquished command to Early, his senior division commander, Lee seized the opportunity to get rid of him. On May 29 he wrote an order giving "temporary" command of the Second Corps to Early and encouraged Ewell to leave the army to rest. In coming days Ewell would repeatedly insist that he was able to resume his post, but each time Lee tactfully but firmly rebuffed him. Ewell was out.[64]

And Early was in. Lee had long respected this rather cold, hard-bitten West Pointer, a lifelong bachelor who left the prewar army and became a district attorney in Virginia. Starting out as a colonel in the Confederate army, Early had risen steadily through the ranks, commanding a brigade after First Manassas and a division from Sharpsburg onward. Early exhibited a combination of aggressiveness and sound judgment that appealed to Lee, as well as an iron will. Early could make men follow him and didn't much care how he did it, a trait he shared with Stonewall Jackson, whose talents Lee sorely missed. Henceforth he would become Lee's most important subordinate.

"In many of the Federal accounts," wrote Confederate artillerist E.

Porter Alexander after the war, "it is assumed that Lee's attitude during [the Overland campaign] was strictly the defensive. Perhaps it should have been, but all who were near him recognized that never in the war was he so ready to attack upon the slightest opportunity." Alexander was correct. Lee had been actively looking for a chance to strike the enemy a hard offensive blow, and Early was to be his chosen instrument. An opportunity soon materialized. On May 30, cavalry scouts reported that the Union VI Corps was gone from in front of Hanover Court House. That ended any threat that the enemy might make for the Virginia Central Railroad. Lee intuited that, instead, Grant would fortify his current line, swing once again around the Confederate right, and make for the Chickahominy River. "This is just a repetition of their former movements," Lee explained to Richard H. Anderson. "It can only be arrested by striking at once at that part of their force which has crossed the Totopotomoy in General Early's front"—that is to say, Warren's V Corps. Accordingly, Early received discretionary orders to attack if he thought success was likely. Lee told Anderson to support Early. To Early he said, "We must destroy this army of Grant's before he gets to James River. If he gets there it will become a siege, and then it will be a mere question of time."[65]

Early got his troops on the move promptly, making use of two recently constructed military roads to shift his corps from Shady Grove Church Road to Old Church Road. Rodes's division was in the lead, followed by Ramseur, then Gordon. In the early afternoon Rodes's lead brigade (under Brig. Gen. George Doles) struck a Union skirmish line just west of Bethesda Church. Rodes put two brigades into line and shoved the Yankees eastward. Near Bethesda Church he encountered a full Union brigade but in short order sent it flying as well.

The Federals vanished northward along the Walnut Grove Church Road. Just beyond them were two additional brigades from Samuel Crawford's division. These took to their heels as well. The acerbic Charles Wainwright described the scene for his journal: "I waited to see how much of an attack it was, which I soon found out, for in five minutes Hardin's brigade were running, and the other two divisions, finding the enemy on their flank, were rather indiscriminately hurrying back to the Shady Grove road." He thought that if the Confederates had renewed attack at once, they would have won the battle, but instead a delay occurred during which Warren—calling on "Helen Damnation"—was able to restore the line.[66]

As at Jericho Mill a week previously, the V Corps artillery restored the equilibrium, greatly assisted by the fact that Early did not yet have enough troops on field to exploit the situation. Gordon was still on the road, Ramseur just arriving. Early wanted to continue the attack but also wanted Anderson to assist by advancing a division along the Old Church Road to take the enemy in the flank. The idea was to erect a strong line perpendicular to Warren and then smash the exposed flank. Unfortunately for the Confederates, communication between Early and Anderson was defective. Anderson failed to come up, and in the meantime Early waited. While he did, one of his division commanders, Maj. Gen. Stephen Dodson Ramseur, approached him, pugnaciously saying that he really wanted to hit a single enemy cannon that the enemy had posted well in front of the Union main line. Although Early advised against it, he did not forbid Ramseur to try.

As Ramseur deployed for action, Union artillery struck his division, and he sent a brigade under Brig. Gen. Edward Willis to clear out a battery that lay south of the Shady Grove Road. Willis did, only to find that this battery masked three more batteries farther north, as well as several regiments of Pennsylvanians. At two hundred yards the Federal cannon opened fire on the brigade with canister. Then, as Willis closed the range, Union infantry joined as well. The result, wrote one survivor, was the "heaviest and most murderous fire I had ever seen with grape, canister, and musketry." Their converging fire wrecked the brigade and mortally wounded Willis. Even so, the Confederates got within fifty yards of the Union line before stopping. The historian of the Thirteenth Pennsylvania wrote that "the slaughter was so sickening that Major Hartshone leaped to his feet and called upon his assailants to surrender. Some hundreds did so. Rebels or no rebels, their behavior and bearing during the charge had won the admiration of their captors, who did not hesitate to express it." Casualties in Willis's brigade approached 60 percent.[67]

While the attack was little short of a disaster, it nevertheless demonstrated that the Federal flank was held in strength. Without help from Anderson, Early could not turn the enemy position. At least, that is the way he chose to explain things to Lee: "If Anderson had moved down the road from Hundley's Corner, I think we could have struck the enemy a severe blow. As it is, all we have to regret is the loss of valuable officers and men in [Willis's] brigade, which is one I much deplore. The enemy was not discovered to be intrenched until the brigade was very close to his line, and the loss was sustained before re-enforcements could get up."[68]

Grant's headquarters that afternoon were near Haw's Shop. When Warren sent word he was being attacked, the general in chief ordered attacks along the Totopotomoy to relieve the pressure, especially by Hancock, who had the closest hug on the Confederate line. Hancock was reluctant to do it but complied nevertheless, and got all three of his divisions into action as darkness fell. The attack lasted but thirty minutes and achieved little but casualties. One heavy artillery regiment did manage to seize some enemy rifle pits, only to relinquish them when the order came to fall back.[69]

One other fight of note occurred on May 30. Considering the chain of events it set in motion, it was arguably the most important of all. During the afternoon, Matthew Butler's brigade of Confederate mounted infantry probed northeast from a dusty intersection known as Old Cold Harbor. By the banks of Matadequin Creek his troops got into a sharp skirmish with a brigade from Torbert's division of Union cavalry, which was posted in that area to screen the Union supply line to White House Landing. Butler made some progress early on, but the Federals could not permit the enemy to remain close to such a vital point, and Torbert soon threw in his entire division: three brigades against one. The Yankee troopers not only forced Butler's men away from Matadequin Creek, but pursued the Confederates nearly to Old Cold Harbor.[70]

That outcome meshed with Grant's thinking as it had developed after two full days along the Totopotomoy line. Plainly no opportunity existed to break Lee's defensive line. Just as plainly, however, Lee seemed inclined to maneuver outside the protection of earthworks—the abortive battle of Bethesda Church proved that. Grant therefore decided to move southward, beyond Lee's right flank, with Smith's XVIII Corps coming in from White House Landing to spearhead the shift. Lee, Grant felt sure, would catch wind of Smith's approach and try to put forces in his path, so at 6:40 P.M. he told Meade to order Sheridan, "with at least half a brigade, to swing down from the Union left and clear the way for Smith." According to Horace Porter, Grant hoped that Lee would send an entire corps against Smith. In that case, Grant intended to "move the whole army to the right, and throw it between Lee and Richmond."[71]

Smith's XVIII Corps—ten thousand men, with more coming—had already begun to disembark at White House Landing, having left Bermuda Hundred the previous day. It was a slow process, considering the limited wharf facilities, but Grant would shortly have a fifth infantry corps to pit against Lee's three. No one understood the implications of this more than Lee, who now breached protocol and wrote Beauregard directly for reinforcements. When the Creole responded that the War Department would have to determine which troops, if any, could be spared from the Bermuda Hundred front, Lee's patience gave way. At 7:30 P.M. he wired President Davis, "General Beauregard says the Department must determine what troops to send for him. He gives it all necessary information. The result of this delay will be disaster. Butler's troops (Smith's corps) will be with Grant to-morrow. Hoke's division, at least, should be with me by light to-morrow."[72]

Although as intent as any executive on getting what he needed, Lee seldom used words like "disaster" in official correspondence. It worked on Davis, who now flatly ordered Beauregard to help out. Beauregard, in point of fact, had actually thought better of his original response and ordered the transfer of Robert F. Hoke's division to Lee just minutes before the formal order from Richmond arrived. Events, men on both sides understood, were moving toward a climax. The decisive battle, sought now for so many days, was now almost certain to occur, somewhere between the Totopotomoy and the Chickahominy, and quite likely near the little crossroads called Cold Harbor.[73]

CHAPTER SIX

"The Hardest Campaign"

By the end of May, both armies had suffered the most severe and sustained casualties of their three-year existence. Neither side yet knew the full extent of those losses, although during the heavy rains that drowned operations to a halt at midmonth, Grant and Meade had gotten a shocking glimpse from the earliest official field returns. These tallied the army's remaining strength and its losses since the opening of the campaign. Leaving aside Sheridan's cavalry and the recent reinforcements from Washington, for which no returns were yet available, the Army of the Potomac and Burnside's IX Corps together numbered 56,124 men. Casualties for the month to date came to 3,841 killed, 22,298 wounded, and 10,733 missing, for a total of 36,872, or about 36 percent of the infantry and artillerists who crossed the Rapidan River twelve days before.[1]

The figure was staggering, higher by thirteen thousand than the casualties of Gettysburg. No one could absorb such a figure without reflection, and Grant voiced regret that so many men had been lost. Meade's response was laconic. "Well, general," he said, "we can't do these little tricks without losses." Meade sounded tough and professional, Grant uncharacteristically soft-hearted. But of the two, Grant's reaction more closely grasped the big picture.[2]

All campaigns involve casualties, and the Civil War had already spawned death and injury on a scale never seen in North America before or since. Few campaigns, however, are *defined* by their casualties. Antietam, notorious as the war's bloodiest single day, is equally recalled as paving the way for the Emancipation Proclamation. Gettysburg, the war's bloodiest engagement, has gone down in history as the South's high-water mark. But the Overland campaign, like Verdun, remains synonymous with sheer death and misery. "This is a hard campaign, putting in the shade all others," wrote Union general Robert McAllister. A South Carolinian agreed, calling it "the most severe and awful time we have ever experienced." From the opening battles in the Wilderness all the way to its conclusion at Cold Harbor, the campaign's preeminent feature was the scale of human suffering.[3]

That suffering could be seen most vividly on the roads that led away from the battlefields. These were filled with wagons, laden with bandaged, blood-stained men, slowly making their way to the rear. The burden of caring for the wounded was heavy on both armies, but of the two, the Confederates had the more manageable task. They suffered fewer casualties and in almost every instance—the Wilderness, Spotsylvania, New Market, and Drewry's Bluff—they held the battlefield after the fighting ended. The level of medical attention and supplies in the Army of Northern Virginia appears adequate, notwithstanding Sheridan's destruction of a large store of medical supplies during his Yellow Tavern raid.

Most important, the Confederate army enjoyed simple, secure, and reasonably short transportation links to the network of nearly fifty general hospitals established all over Virginia, including a vast eight thousand–bed medical complex on Chimborazo Hill outside Richmond. A wounded soldier could generally look forward to initial treatment at a field hospital, followed by a few hours' journey by ambulance to a rail station, then a quick train trip to his final destination. The sheer crush of wounded men was a problem—by May 24 the state's military hospitals contained over eighteen thousand patients—but by and large the medical evacuation system functioned smoothly.[4]

The situation was much worse on the Union side, which had to contend with the greater number of wounded and also had by far the more difficult challenge of getting them to the general hospitals that alone had the resources to provide consistent medical care. The medical director of the Army of the Potomac, Thomas McParlin, was an able administrator with sixty officers, 2,300 enlisted men, and nearly eight hundred ambulances at his disposal, to say nothing of the 699 regimental and brigade surgeons not under his direct command. They crossed the Rapidan River with supplies and equipment to handle twenty thousand casualties for eight days and to address the army's other medical needs for a full month. But the campaign was not a week old before McParlin had a serious crisis on his hands, and before things got better they got considerably worse.[5]

The structure in place for battlefield evacuation normally took a wounded man through three main stations: first, the field hospitals at regiment or sometimes brigade level, where he received initial care and was operated upon if necessary; then the division and corps hospitals, set up for more extended care; and finally the general hospitals with permanent care facilities. Washington had about sixteen such hospitals in 1864; nearby Alexandria had seven more. Ordinarily the wounded would have gone directly from field to general hospitals. But during the Overland campaign, evacuating them that quickly was impossible because such "normal" evacuation depended on the maintenance of a regular line of communications. The decision, at the end of the Wilderness fight, to transfer the Army of the Potomac's base to Belle Plain meant that the line stretching back to Culpeper could no longer be used. This denied wounded men a relatively short wagon trip over well-maintained roads and a speedy journey by train to Washington. Instead, they would have to go by way of Belle Plain with an initial stop at Fredericksburg on the Rappahannock River—about ten miles from the Wilderness and Spotsylvania battlefields and not quite as far again from Belle Plain.

Improvised on the spot, this conduit had four serious drawbacks. It was longer and far more cumbersome than the Culpeper route. It ran through territory recently held by the Confederates, only tenuously controlled by the Union, and full of rebel cavalry and guerrillas. And it required the creation of a fourth stage in the evacuation process—a so-called depot hospital system to provide intermediate medical care until transportation could be arranged to get the wounded to Belle Plain and aboard steamers for the trip up the Potomac River to Washington. Unfortunately, the depot hospital at first existed only in theory: No one was at Fredericksburg to set one up before the first wagonloads of wounded arrived. Making matters even worse, some wounded began the trek to Culpeper before the orders were revised, which gave them an extra twenty-four hours on the road.

A bleaker interim destination than Fredericksburg could scarcely have been found. Although the nearest town of any size, it had been shelled heavily during the battle there in December 1862, and many roofs still stood open to the heavy rains that poured down during the second week of May. It lay at the head of navigation of the Rappahannock, but the river was mined and the lower banks were said to be infested by guerrillas. The final stretch of the Richmond, Fredericksburg and Potomac Railroad ran northeast of the town to Aquia Creek, near the river that was its partial namesake. That railroad, however, had been wrecked after the Union army departed from the region in June 1863 and had not been rebuilt. A dirt road led from town directly to Belle Plain, but all bridges across the Rappahannock were down and anyway, the road was deeply rutted and the constant jostling of the wagons would have tortured the wounded and killed the more severely injured outright. Moreover, this road constituted the army's single avenue by which to receive supplies and reinforcements, which meant that wagons and ambulances bound for Belle Plain would compete head-on with wagons carrying desperately needed rations and ammunition coming the other way. And with a kind of negative perfection, Fredericksburg was filled from one end to the other with secessionists, dedicated to the Confederacy and coldly furious at the Yankees who had ruined their beautiful town. The city's mayor allegedly even turned over some of the first Union wounded to Confederate irregulars.[6]

For all these reasons, the wounded piled up at Fredericksburg—an estimated fourteen thousand arrived by May 12—and once there they experienced some of the most wretched conditions of the entire war. Most of the army's surgeons remained with the front line units, so trained medical professionals were in short supply. The enlisted attendants were for the most part men detailed for the job from their regiments and selected, often enough, in inverse proportion to the likelihood that they would perform as effective soldiers. Some behaved toward the wounded with compassion, but many exploited their helpless condition to rob them. Initially the wounded were not even placed in private homes. The officer in charge of keeping order apparently believed that only the few public buildings could be legitimately appropriated; civilian residences could be used only if their owners volunteered them. And of course, almost none of them did.

The Civil War occurred at a time in American history when public needs routinely outstripped government resources. To bridge the gap, concerned citizens often created voluntary associations. Hundreds existed by 1860, and the war spurred the creation of many more, including the United States Sanitary Commission, established in June 1861 to aid sick and wounded Union soldiers and, as events unfolded, to lobby the Medical Department to fashion a better standard of care. By 1864 the Sanitary Commission had five hundred agents and a network of lodges, convalescent camps, branch offices, and over seven thousand aid societies across the North and the occupied Confederacy. It financed its operations through donations and massive "Sanitary Fairs" that generated hundreds of thousands of dollars. (The New York Metropolitan Fair, held on the eve of the campaign, alone had brought in over a million dollars.) The

Commission was sufficiently well-heeled to staff and maintain five ambulances permanently with the Army of the Potomac; it also sent a number of physicians and nurses directly to Fredericksburg as soon as it learned that wounded men were there.[7]

The Commission workers, accompanied by members of a similar organization, the United States Christian Commission, began arriving in Fredericksburg around May 12. What they found was appalling. Nurse Cornelia Hancock, already a veteran of the field hospitals at Gettysburg, wrote her sister that "the scenes beggared all description." Two male physicians accompanied her. Eminent men in their professions, they had no previous military experience and were simply horrified. "Rain," Hancock continued, "had poured in through the bullet-riddled roofs of the churches until our wounded lay in pools of water made bloody by their seriously wounded condition." She quickly organized a detail to saw up the pews into improvised cots, so that the men could at least get out of the wet. To her mother she wrote, "I am the first and only Union woman in the city; the Secesh help none, so you may know there is suffering equal to any thing anyone ever saw, almost as bad as Gettysburg."[8]

Another woman who witnessed the scene at Fredericksburg was Clara Barton, a relief worker who operated on her own terms and had created her own struggling organization, one day to be called the American Red Cross. But on this occasion she signed on with the Massachusetts State Relief Agency, an association established specifically to help soldiers from the Bay State. En route from Belle Plain, Barton paused to assist the first wounded trickling down to the river landing, but once at Fredericksburg she absorbed the situation in one indignant glance and, as fast as she could, boarded a steamer back to the capital.

Once in Washington she accosted Massachusetts senator Henry Wilson. The situation, she stormed, was a scandal. Brave Union boys were dying in the rain, and a "dapper captain of 21" had informed her that "it was in fact a pretty hard thing for refined people like the citizens of Fredericksburg to be compelled to open their houses and admit these dirty, lousy, common soldiers, *and he was not going to compel it.*" Wilson's jaw clenched; he went straight to Secretary of War Stanton, telling him that if the War Department did not get an investigator on the scene at once, the Senate would. Stanton promptly dispatched Brig. Gen. Montgomery C. Meigs, the army's quartermaster general, with full authority to do anything—anything!—to fix the situation. Meigs arrived on the fifteenth. He promptly forced local residents to take in Union wounded, ordered construction of a second pontoon bridge to join one that had already been built, spurred efforts under way to rebuild the railroad to Aquia Creek, advised Washington of additional needed supplies, and suggested that the navy send a gunboat up the Rappahannock to clear the channel of mines. At Stanton's direct order he also launched a manhunt for Mayor Slaughter, whom Stanton wanted arrested and brought to Washington in irons.[9]

By May 23 a good line of evacuation had been established, and wounded men were streaming from Fredericksburg via wagon to Belle Plain, railroad to Aquia Creek, or river steamers down the now mine-free Rappahannock River. By then, however, the Army of the Potomac had left Spotsylvania, and new orders arrived to move the depot hospital to Port Royal, a village on the Rappahannock just seventeen airline miles southeast of Fredericksburg but far easier for the Union army to screen from its new position on the North Anna. Most medical workers went thither, but Port Royal was barely up and running before orders came to transfer everything yet again to White House Landing, which served as the army's base of operations once it crossed the Pamunkey.

The experience of a wounded man in this nomadic, makeshift system was necessarily pretty bad, but this was in keeping with the state of Civil War medicine more generally. This is not to say that surgeons of the 1860s were a pack of butchers. On the contrary, most of them were dedicated, professional, and familiar with the burgeoning knowledge about human physiology and pathology. Recent decades had witnessed the routine employment of safe anesthetics, such as ether and chloroform, which both reduced a patient's agony and made elaborate surgical operations possible for the first time. As a result, Civil War surgeons were capable of impressive feats, including some surprisingly intricate reconstructive surgery on faces mangled by flying projectiles. But medical science was still a few years short of the discovery that germs and bacteria were at the root of most disease and infections and that rigorous antiseptic hygiene could transform a patient's odds of survival. Up to four hundred thousand Union and Confederate soldiers paid for that missing information with their lives.

More culpably, wounded men often lost their lives because military commanders had yet to grasp the fact that prompt, aggressive medical intervention was what, in present-day parlance, would be called a "force multiplier." A quickly treated injured man is more likely to survive and re-turn to duty. Just as important, knowing that a combat injury need not be fatal improves his morale and helps him cope with the stress of battle. Of this realization even the best Civil War generals had scarcely a clue. Their attitude toward the wounded wandered between casual humanitarian concern and a "we-can't-do-these-little-tricks-without-losses" fatalism not far removed from indifference. As a result, commanders tried to keep a lid on the number of ambulances and medical wagons that accompanied the army, fearing their presence would prove an encumbrance, and—as Grant and Meade thrice demonstrated during the Overland campaign— they rarely factored medical evacuation into their operational plans. Mc-Parlin did not even get advance warning of an imminent change of base.

The failure of high-level authority to provide support for medical care at anywhere near the required level meant that the harried army surgeon at the other end of the medical hierarchy played an even more stone-hearted God than would otherwise have been the case, and wounded soldiers had to plead like souls before the seat of Judgment. Faced with an influx of wounded, the first job of a regimental surgeon was to sort these vessels of torn and broken humanity into men who were seriously stricken but likely to recover, those who were lightly wounded, and those who, in the surgeon's snap judgment, were beyond saving. The first group got priority, the second received treatment when time became available. Those identified as mortally wounded were made comfortable if possible but otherwise ignored.

A soldier earmarked for death need not necessarily be unconscious when the verdict was made. John C. Johnston, a Pennsylvanian in the VI Corps, was hit in the face by a shell fragment, left for dead, and about to be buried when his comrades noticed signs of life, revived him with water, and took him to the nearest field hospital. Although the surgeon refused to dress the wound, saying he would be dead in a few minutes, Johnston told him he was mistaken and convinced the doctor to treat him. Abram Buckles of the Iron Brigade had a similar experience. Hit in the chest in the Wilderness, he heard one surgeon tell another not to bother treating him: "No, that is a mortal wound, this boy must die and there is no use giving him further pain." When the field hospital shifted locations, he was left behind to die, but finally convinced a physician that if he could stumble to an ambulance under his own power, he would be evacuated. Incredibly, he did so, survived, and ultimately returned to his unit.[10]

Johnston and Buckles were the exceptions, however. For the most part, surgeons who pronounced a man mortally wounded knew their business all too well. They made such choices because it was a full-time job just to treat those who stood a good chance of living, and even then the task was overwhelming. "How heart rending to hear the groans & shrieks of dying men as we went over the battlefield that night with torches, hunting up the wounded," wrote a surgeon late in the campaign. "Rebs and Union lay side by side, praying loudly & fervently to God to have mercy on them, & when they saw a green sash on"—the emblem of an army physician—"scores of them would beg at the same time for him to help them, but the Surgeon cannot do very much on the field, except to administer a little cordial occasionally or ligate a bleeding artery & see that they are carefully handled by the stretcher bearers." At peak periods the doctors might work for days, almost without rest, and not infrequently under fire. One surgeon was dressing a soldier's wound when the man was hit a second time, fatally.[11]

Patching the wounded was the preeminent task at field hospitals—a visitor to one of them encountered a noise "which seemed to be one continuous sound: the tearing of linen for bandages." The second important task was surgery, often amputations. According to statistics compiled by the Union medical department, for example, during the battle of the Wilderness, Northern soldiers suffered 4,819 wounds in arms and legs, of which 560 (11.6 percent) required removal of the limb. More amputations undoubtedly occurred at depot and general hospitals. The same held true for the Confederates. A rebel artillerist who fell asleep near a field hospital awoke to find "a big pile of amputated arms, hands, legs and fingers within a foot or two of me. A horrid sight."[12]

During the campaign, Federal wounded were commonly left behind on the battlefield, where they fell into enemy hands. The hapless souls who met this fate often suffered from inadequate care. In part this was because the Confederates, understandably, gave priority to their own men. A Louisiana chaplain who visited some Union wounded on May 17 reported that "they were in a miserable condition. Many of them were several days without having their wounds dressed. I found many whose wounds were complete masses of maggots."[13]

The situation could be bad even when—as generally happened—Union surgeons stayed behind to look after them. By military custom these men were regarded as noncombatants and could perform their duties unhindered, but other complications arose. Dr. William Watson, who stayed behind in the Wilderness to care for 275 men, sent an urgent request through the lines for replenishment of his dwindling stock of food and medical supplies. He was told that nothing could be sent without Grant's permission, presumably because the rebels might use it. The Confederates, for their part, declined to provide anything, correctly pointing out that "nothing prevented us from recieving [*sic*] supplies from our own lines." In despair, Watson sent a second letter saying that many of the wounded had already died for lack of food, that he had issued his last cracker, and that "if relief is not afforded the men will die of sheer starvation." Whether anyone heeded the request is unknown.[14]

Watson spent three weeks in the Wilderness before returning to Union lines. The wounded in his care who survived, however, joined the more than nineteen thousand men on both sides who during the campaign became prisoners of war. In previous campaigns, many of these would have been paroled under an agreement between the Washington and Richmond governments reached in July 1862. The agreement provided for the prompt release of prisoners provided they refrained from performing military duties until exchanged for an enemy captive or captives according to an elaborate scale of equivalents (a lieutenant was worth four privates, a captain six, a colonel fifteen, and so on). Known as the Dix-Hill cartel after the Union and Confederate generals, respectively, who handled the negotiations, the system worked reasonably well until the Union army began to recruit African American soldiers in significant numbers, which the Confederates interpreted as nothing but an effort to incite servile insurrection. In December 1862 President Davis announced that when captured, black soldiers would be treated essentially as runaway slaves. When it became apparent that the Richmond government intended to make good on its threat, the Federals suspended the cartel in May 1863. It continued informally for several months—Grant paroled the Vicksburg garrison to save him the trouble of shipping thirty thousand captives to northern prison camps—then collapsed entirely when some of these Vicksburg parolees returned to duty without being properly exchanged.[15]

From that point onward, the prisoner of war camps began to fill while Union and Confederate officials wrangled over the Vicksburg parole irregularities and the treatment of African American captives. The two sides showed no signs of reaching agreement, particularly after the Federal government made Ben Butler—the "Beast" Butler of Southern infamy—its new prisoner exchange commissioner. In Confederate eyes the appointment seemed a calculated insult, all the more so because the same order concerning treatment of black prisoners had branded

Butler and his subordinate officers "robbers and criminals" who would be executed if caught.

As a result, soldiers on both sides embarked on the spring campaign of 1864 in the certainty that capture would mean many months of imprisonment. If anything, the knowledge made them more likely to avoid such a fate. The perils of capture were further underscored by reports of a recent massacre at Fort Pillow, Tennessee, where Confederate cavalry under Nathan Bedford Forrest shot down scores of African American and white Unionist troops after organized resistance ceased. Many had been killed while trying to surrender. The incident created a furor throughout the North and, because it took place just three weeks before the Army of the Potomac crossed the Rapidan, was much on the minds of its soldiers. Some thought it provoked in them a spirit of revenge. While on the North Anna, a Union officer wrote home that "our men are much opposed to taking prisoners since the Fort Pillow affair, and that has cost the Rebels many a life that would otherwise have been spared."[16]

As a rule, however, that was not the case; both sides took prisoners as readily as ever. Basic humanity and an incentive to encourage similar mercy from the enemy played a role, as did the weapons of the time. The semiautomatic rifles and machine guns of later wars fostered an ease of killing and a better-safe-than-sorry bias that did not yet exist. Muzzle-loading rifles, slow to reload and capable of hitting just one man at a time, made it advisable to take men—especially groups of men—alive whenever possible rather than risk a protracted and costly resistance by trying to shoot them. Similarly, the linear tactics of the day reduced confusion and made it easier to see when an enemy did and did not pose a mortal threat. Then too, prisoners of war have certain perennial uses, particularly as sources of information. Some men were captured specifically for that purpose.

Of the many engagements of the Virginia campaign, the Wilderness was the one in which by far the most men fell captive. It was a big battle anyway, and the tangled thickets made it common for individuals and sometimes whole units to be separated from friends. Once snared in a situation where capture seemed imminent, a man had just a second or two to consider the number of adversaries and the chances of successful escape. Union major Charles Mattocks described such a moment. Trying to supervise a detachment of sharpshooters in the dense woodlands, Mattocks lost his way and ran headlong into a Confederate regiment barely forty yards away. "Come in, come in," they chanted, coaxing him to surrender. Mattocks considered escape—he was on horseback—but figured "the thick bushes and the brook would impede my progress more than that of two or three hundred bullets. It was but a short moment, but I had time to weigh all the chances. It was simply death or capture, and I very ungallantly chose the latter. I raised my hat and started toward them."[17]

Others finding themselves in such a predicament elected to flee. A fortunate few even turned the tables. Seeing that he and seventeen of his men were about to be cut off during the fighting on May 5, for example, Maj. Holman S. Melcher of the Twentieth Maine gathered them in a huddle, explained the situation, and finished, "Now, my men, as for myself, I had rather die in the attempt to cut our way out, than be captured to rot in rebel prisons. Will you stand by me in this attempt?" They agreed, charged toward Union lines, and after a confused running battle not only reached safety but took thirty-two rebel captives. These had made their own split-second estimate, guessed wrong, and quickly regretted it. "When our prisoners discovered how few were their captors and how near their many friends," Melcher wrote, "they slackened their pace, refusing the orders to double-quick, and seemed inclined to turn on us." Melcher's drawn pistol served to dissuade them. That was not the only such incident. Down by the Orange Plank Road, the Seventh Pennsylvania Reserves charged the enemy so aggressively that it outran its neighboring regiments and became isolated. Called upon to surrender, the Seventh's colonel decided he had no alternative. He and 325 others lay down their arms—to discover that they had been captured by two understrength Georgia companies, perhaps fifty men in all.[18]

Away from the Wilderness, surrenders usually occurred in the context of an enemy breakthrough, the classic example being the sudden capture of three thousand men at the Mule Shoe. Such situations were far more delicate and dangerous, because soldiers passed almost instantaneously from furious resistance to hoped-for surrender. A single wrong move could make an attempted capitulation look like treachery. Swamped by the May 12 Union assault, Confederate captain McHenry Howard ordered his men to fire a volley, then abruptly regretted it as he realized the enemy's strength was overwhelming. Surrender seemed the only choice, but in that instant at least one of Howard's men obeyed his order. The smoke from the musket's discharge, Howard recalled, "seemed as if it would never dissipate." For a breathless second he thought the Federals would exact a penalty for "our firing when we were practically captured," especially when dozens of blue-clad soldiers surrounded Howard's trench and brought their bayonets down—but only, it turned out, "for the purpose of sweeping aside the bayonets of our men which were resting on the top, and we were ordered to scramble out."[19]

Once captured, prisoners went first to a holding area maintained by the provost guard, the nineteenth-century version of military police. When enough had assembled, they were marched away from the battlefield on foot. In the case of Confederates captured in the Wilderness and Spotsylvania, this meant a trip via Fredericksburg to Belle Plain, where they were temporarily held in a large circular valley known as "the Punch Bowl." There they were visited by the curious, including James Gardner, an employee of famed cameraman Mathew Brady, who photographed them for posterity, and Secretary of the Navy Gideon Welles, who showed up with a coterie of VIPs on May 15. Ever the Connecticut Yankee, Welles sized up the prisoners as "rough, sturdy-looking men, good and effective soldiers I should judge. Most of them were quiet and well-behaved, but some few of them were boisterous and inclined to be insolent." Welles more or less provoked the insolence by tactlessly inquiring "if they had not had enough of fighting, opposing the Union and lawful authority." A Tar Heel assured Welles that "Lee would be in Fredericksburg before the Union army could get to Richmond."[20]

The presence of roughly 7,500 Confederate POWs in Grant's logistical pipeline undoubtedly complicated the already daunting task of evacuating the wounded and supplying the army, but it could not be helped. Lee's provost guard, at least in the Wilderness, had a better solution. Instead of marching POWs south along their main supply line, they instead hiked them thirty miles west to Orange Court House, where they were placed on railway cars and dispatched to points south, mostly to a new POW camp of which few had yet heard: Camp Sumter, better known as Andersonville.

Andersonville had been in operation only a few months when the spring campaign began, but after that its population mushroomed. On April 1 the sixteen-and-a-half-acre log stockade harbored eight thousand Union captives. By May 8 that figure was up to 12,213, and on June 30, by which time the last prisoners taken during the Overland campaign arrived, the number topped twenty-six thousand. There were no barracks for the prisoners, who simply fashioned crude shelters from tent canvas and tree branches, and the main source of water was a stagnant creek that ran through the stockade. Rations were bad, sanitation worse, and disease rampant. A ten-acre extension opened in July failed to relieve the terrible overcrowding. Not all Union prisoners at Andersonville came from the Army of the Potomac, but most from that army who became prisoners wound up there. Once inside they stood about a one-in-three chance of dying: odds little different from their comrades still on the firing line.[21]

The equivalent of Andersonville, in terms of the most common destination for Confederate POWs taken in Virginia, was Point Lookout, Maryland, which experienced a similar population explosion: from 5,741 on April 30 to 14,489 two months later. The problem became so acute that in July the Federals put a new prison camp in operation at Elmira, New York. Converted from a disused recruitment and training facility, Elmira had regular barracks, but its record in other respects was scarcely better than Andersonville. The problem with such prisons was not intentional mistreatment but rather a callous clumsiness that killed men as surely as deliberate cruelty.[22]

Eventually the grim POW situation mingled with the attrition of the Overland campaign to produce a potent piece of Civil War mythology. Critics would claim that Grant intentionally fought a campaign of attrition in Virginia and that his failure to resurrect the exchange cartel was part of an overall design. They pointed especially to two comments Grant made in August 1864. In a letter to Ben Butler, he argued that while it might be hard on Federals held in Southern prisons not to exchange them, "it is humanity to those left in the ranks to fight our battles. Every man we hold, when released on parole or otherwise, becomes an active soldier against us at once either directly or indirectly." And in a letter to Secretary of State William H. Seward he insisted, "We have got to fight until the military power of the South is exhausted, and if we release or exchange prisoners captured it simply becomes a war of extermination." Yet Grant was not necessarily expressing an intentional policy rationale, but simply putting the best face on an existing situation. And the Confederate government did not unbend in its policy toward African American troops, either.[23]

Despite the policy, the Confederate government did in fact place some African Americans in POW camps. But a number of blacks captured during the Overland campaign faced consequences worse than imprisonment or the reenslavement that was officially prescribed. Confronted with the sight of Negroes uniformed in blue and carrying muskets, some Confederates gave vent to a cold, lethal rage. A small party of rebel cavalry, ranging in the wake of the departed Army of the Potomac, came upon an isolated detail of African American troops near Culpeper on May 8. "We captured three negro soldiers the first we had seen," one of the horsemen, Byrd C. Willis, noted tersely. "They were taken out on the road side and shot, & their bodies left there." Union prisoners at Orange Court House were roused one morning with the cry, "Hey thar you-uns, if yo want to see a nigger hang look 'round right smart." A New Jersey man peered out a window: "[S]ure enough they were just pulling up one of Burnside's black heroes in full uniform." Fitz Lee's cavalry reportedly executed two black soldiers captured at Fort Powhatan on the James River, and after Cold Harbor a black soldier captured on the picket line was taken into some nearby woods and shot.[24]

Confederate prisoners of war, seeing black troops for the first time, reacted with the same mixture of disgust and hatred made deeper, if anything, by their own humiliating status. Captured at the Mule Shoe, members of the Stonewall Brigade came upon a group of African American troops as they tramped toward Belle Plain. The blacks, wrote Confederate lieutenant J. L. Doyle, were "standing, grinning and jabbering" along the roadway and looking "revengefully at these ragged heroes of the Confederacy." According to Doyle, the onlookers shouted gleefully that it was lucky the prisoners were being guarded by whites, for if the U.S. Colored Troops had been their captors, they would not have lived to tell the tale. Another prisoner recalled hearing similar comments from a brigade of "impudent negroes," but took comfort in the knowledge that later, "those same negroes were shoved into the most dangerous places and the Rebels killed them by hundreds without mercy."[25]

Black soldiers were sometimes thought to be bent upon the same mayhem, especially in light of Fort Pillow. But during the Overland campaign they had few opportunities, and at least one Confederate prisoner found them rather benign. Marching to Fredericksburg he and his comrades encountered "the Negro troops of Burnside, who gazed upon us with as much curiosity as hatred as we filed through their midst." The guards earlier intimated that the blacks would massacre them, but "the Negroes offered us little, if any, more insult than their white companions had done before. For the most part we simply eyed each other with mutual curiosity and dislike."[26]

In addition to wounded men and prisoners, the campaign produced at least twelve thousand corpses. One might conclude, coldly, that the suffering of these men was over, but their deaths visited pain on countless families and friends. More prosaically, their rotting bodies often nauseated comrades yet living. Most soldiers who fought in the Overland campaign were veterans of previous battles. They had seen death before, and even the sight of headless or badly mangled corpses was not unusual. But because the fighting at Spotsylvania and later Cold Harbor kept them in the same trenches for days at a time, they found themselves eating, drinking, and sleeping in the immediate presence of hundreds of unburied bodies. This, for most of them, was something new.

The sheer number of bodies was shocking. "[M]en who have fought over many bloody fields in Va. say they never saw dead Yankees lie so thick on the ground as they do in front of the works where they charged," wrote one Confederate enlisted man from the Spotsylvania trenches. "The dead yankees are heaped up in piles half as high as a man, in front of our Breastworks," another agreed. Across no man's land a German soldier recorded in his diary: "Thousands of dead bodies are seen and the trenches are filled with them, 4 and 5 on top of each other." At Spotsylvania the condition of the corpses was often just as appalling, for many of the dead had fallen across the parapets of trenches and had been hit by hundreds of bullets. "Some lying between the lines are so completely riddled that it is impossible to raise them," wrote surgeon Daniel Holt. "A hole has to be dug side of them and they rolled into it for burial. They were a *complete jelly!*"[27]

The air hung heavy with the smell of death. After the Wilderness Northern troops were able to bury only those comrades who died within friendly lines, which meant that most of the Union dead remained in the thickets and fields. The atmosphere was filled "with the noisome odors that came up from the putrifying corpses," wrote a Confederate surgeon, and "perfectly pestilential from decaying bodies of men and horses," according to one of his Federal counterparts. "May God grant that I may never again experience such sensations or witness such scenes," vowed Chaplain James B. Sheeran of Louisiana. "The sights are shocking. The smell is still more offensive." Not all the unburied dead were even from the battles just fought. A Union battery in Burnside's corps spent the night of May 10 on the old Chancellorsville battlefield. "The ground . . . was littered with the accoutrements, arms and clothing of soldiers, and the bones and skulls of the dead," wrote an artillerist. "The stench arising from the mass of decayed human flesh and bone was sickening. The puddles of water made by the May showers were in some places covered with maggots."[28]

When the military situation permitted, soldiers from both sides went to retrieve their dead. Henry Keiser, Company G, Ninety-sixth Pennsylvania, described one such scene that took place on May 13, after the Mule Shoe's capture made it possible at last to bury the men who had perished in Upton's charge three days previously. By that time the bodies "were swollen and bloated so that they could scarcely be recognized." Nevertheless, Keiser and his comrades managed to locate the dead from their own company as well as one man from another company. They buried them all in a single trench with what slender dignity was possible in the mud-churned field: one blanket under the men and another on top, with boards from a cracker box to serve as headstones, each carefully inscribed with the name, company, and regiment of the man who lay beneath.

Getting a dead man's identity correct was a crucial but sometimes gruesome task. Keiser recalled that the regiment's colonel heatedly disagreed with the company lieutenant over the identity of one J. M. Ferree, "the Colonel contending that it was Ferree, while the Lieut. as strongly contending that it was not, saying that he had seen Ferree shot in the thigh and get behind a stump." This man was behind a stump, all right, but had been hit in a different part of the body. The colonel directed Keiser to reach into the dead man's pockets. In the right-hand pocket he found a broken pocketknife; in the left, Keiser put "the full length of my fingers into a pile of maggots, which had filled the pocket." The maggots helped confirm that it was in fact Ferree. The corpse had indeed been shot through the thigh, as the lieutenant recalled Ferree had been. The intervening rains had washed away the blood from the outside of the wound, but the maggots had gathered in the pocket where the blood remained. The misleading second wound, it was deduced, had been the coup de grace from a cross fire that killed Ferree as he sat behind the stump. Convinced, the lieutenant gave in.[29]

The unfortunate Private Ferree was nonetheless fortunate in three respects: He was buried with reasonable promptness, by comrades who knew him, and with a marker that made it likely his body could still be identified on the distant day when a burial party came to inter him permanently. That day most likely occurred sometime in June 1865, when a detail under Capt. J. M. Moore reached the Wilderness and Spotsylvania battlefields soon after the end of the war. By that time many more corpses had been temporarily interred, some by Union cavalry that passed through a month after the battle, others by local farmers who performed the burials through agreement with Federal authorities or simply to reduce the stench.

Captain Moore noted that at Spotsylvania most of the corpses had been buried by one Mr. Sanford, in compliance with an agreement made with Maj. Gen. William T. Sherman, who had passed through the area with his army after the final Confederate surrender. Over seven hundred tablets had been erected in memory of the deceased—presumably including Ferree—and although the warm weather and "unpleasant odor from decayed animal matter" made it impossible to remove the bodies at that season, they were at least re-covered with earth, especially those corpses imperfectly buried or partially exposed by erosion. The situation in the Wilderness was different. Here Moore and his men established two military cemeteries, one on the Orange Turnpike and the other on the Orange Plank Road, both where the fighting had apparently been fiercest. "It was no unusual occurrence to observe the bones of our men close to the abatis of the enemy," Moore reported, "and in one case several skeletons of our soldiers were found in their trenches. The bones of these men were gathered from the ground where they fell, having never been interred, and by exposure to the weather for more than a year all traces of their identity were entirely obliterated."

Moore impartially buried or reburied Union and Confederate dead alike, with name, rank, and regiment on their grave markers if available; if not, then with the standard inscription, "Unknown U.S. soldiers, killed May 10, 1864," in the case of Federals who could not be identified. This, too, proved a temporary arrangement. In a few years the Union dead were removed to a permanent military cemetery established at Fredericksburg, which became the final resting place for 15,273 Union soldiers killed in the four major battles—Fredericksburg, Chancellorsville, the Wilderness, and Spotsylvania—that took place in the region. More than 83 percent of the dead are listed as unknown. Some of those killed later in the campaign wound up at Cold Harbor National Cemetery. No Confederate dead were permitted in these cemeteries. After the war, local women formed associations to create special resting places for them: 600 in a little cemetery just northeast of Spotsylvania Court House; 3,300 more (including 2,184 unknown) in the Confederate Cemetery in Fredericksburg. Still others joined the 30,000 Confederates buried in Oakwood and Hollywood Cemeteries, Richmond.[30]

While most who perished on the battlefield had to wait years before finding a permanent grave, those who died of their wounds in Washington quickly gained a final resting place. In a few cases, relatives arrived to bring the body home for burial. In others, shipment arrangements were made by "military agents": civilian businessmen who for a fee would attend to such things and, in addition, could track down "any facts about any living or deceased friend or relative, or their affairs, or about Pensions, Bounty, Pay, Patents, Contracts, or any other matter whatever," so that grieving heirs could get whatever was coming to them. But most of those who died from wounds in the Overland campaign were interred in a brand-new burial ground on a verdant hill just across the Potomac River, recently created by the Federal government on land confiscated from the family of rebel general Robert E. Lee. The first soldier to be interred was Pvt. William Christman, buried on May 13. Named for the Greek Revival mansion that surmounted the hill, it was designated Arlington National Cemetery.[31]

For the soldiers who remained with the armies as May wore on, what increasingly dominated the psychic landscape of the soldiers was fatigue, stress, and animal misery. Every campaign brought hardship, but the relentlessness of the Overland campaign stunned everyone. "The world has never seen so bloody or so protracted a battle as the one being fought and I hope never will again," Grant wrote his wife, Julia. His correspondence during this period often opened with a reference to its duration. "We have now ended the sixth day of very heavy fighting," Grant prefaced one dispatch to Washington. "The eighth day of battle closes," another began, and in a letter to his wife, "The ninth day of battle is just closing." Other men kept count as well. "We have been fighting continuously for six days"; "the battle . . . has been raging here for twelve days with more or less ferocity"; "the fifteenth [day] in which our men have been in line of battle." On May 17, welcoming the rains that forced a suspension in Grant's campaign, a soldier explained to his girl back home: "We need the rest as we have worked day and night sence we started. In all other fights it has not lasted but two or three days but we have been in [this one] about two weeks."[32]

It is impossible to overestimate the impact of this grinding tempo on the soldiers forced to endure it. Set aside the crack of gunfire, the screech of shells, the ceaseless fear of wounds and death. Sheer existence was an ordeal. Modern armies possess immense logistical support systems to sustain the fighting soldier—not just field kitchens and hospitals but field showers, laundry services, and detachments whose sole function is to locate, purify, and transport fresh water. With the exception of rudimentary field hospitals, Civil War armies had none of these things. The individual soldier not only had to march, fight, dig entrenchments, and perform picket duty. He also had to feed himself, find his own water, clean his own clothes, and bury his own dead. Unsurprisingly, he could not do it all. In the Wilderness, for example, exhausted men fell asleep as soon as possible after the first day's battle. When the combat recommenced next morning, most had no time for breakfast. They fought with coffee in their bellies or nothing at all.

Even when the men had time to prepare meals, the raw material was uninspiring and, for the Confederates, unplentiful. Confederate sergeant John Worsham recalled that at this stage of the war he and his comrades received a half pound of bacon or beef each day, supplemented by a pound and a half of flour or corn meal, or a pound of corn bread or hard bread: just about half the officially prescribed ration. Coffee, for its part, was so scarce that it was issued literally "given us in the grain and in quantity so small that the grains were counted out to each man." In the Army of Northern Virginia everyone, from private to field officer, fared much the same. While at Spotsylvania, General Jubal Early visited Robert E. Lee's headquarters and received an invitation to stay for supper. The meal, he recalled, consisted of "a scanty supply of hard crackers, fried fat bacon, and a beverage made as a substitute for coffee out of parched wheat, without sugar." It was routine for Confederate troops to rifle the haversacks of dead Federals for food. One Virginian was so hungry that when he found blood on a piece of hardtack, he simply cut off that part and ate the rest.[33]

Federals got more than their Southern counterparts, but it amounted to an almost steady diet of salt pork and hardtack, the latter being a thick cracker about four inches square and about as chewy as a stone. Men would nibble it if need be, but whenever possible preferred to soak it in water until soft, then create "a sort of mush . . . wh[ich] they call 'Son of a b——h.'" Rations sometimes gave out entirely for a day or two when soldiers on the march outstripped supply wagons or the mud made it impossible to get supplies up to the front. "I know a man who gave $9 for 9 hard pieces of bread, our crackers," wrote a man in the VI Corps. "A person at home can't hardly imagine or believe how a soldier has to suffer in all kinds of hardships."[34]

On the positive side, Union soldiers occasionally got the boon of fresh beef, for the Army of the Potomac brought with it over a thousand head of cattle, to be killed and issued to the troops as necessary. As with so many other things, the care and ultimate slaughter of the cattle became an additional duty for the common soldier, for the commissary would issue the cattle, in all their mooing, cud-chewing glory, directly to corps, divisions, brigades, and ultimately individual units. One artillery battery received a steer that they failed to kill immediately. Instead, they held on to the animal against the day when their regular rations might fail, and over the course of a week or so the beast became a sort of pet. Finally an order came down that the army was about to move and all remaining steers were to be slaughtered. When an army butcher showed up to perform the chore, the artillerists pleaded for the creature's life. The butcher would have none of it. "Gettin' tender-hearted!" he spat. "I shouldn't wonder if you men would be a-killin' men before night."[35]

Until they left Spotsylvania, the infantrymen were stuck with whatever their commissaries gave them, but cavalry had the luxury of being able to forage. "We got great loads of smoked pork—Meal, some Flour—& Butter etc.," wrote one of Sheridan's troopers the day after reaching Haxall's Landing, soon converting the confiscated goods into "Fried Pork—SlapJacks—Corn pone—Hoe Cake—Bread and gravy—a little butter—and a little molasses, with coffee plenty, etc., etc." If the trooper's palate found such unaccustomed grub sumptuous, his stomach had a different reaction. His next diary entry reports: "about sick—vomiting and purging—Ate too freely, and too rich, after so long a time of almost utter fasting."[36]

During the campaign, water was often in short supply. Men had nothing to wash away the cotton in their mouths, the dust, the acrid taste of black powder. "No water could be found as no springs or running brooks were in the Wilderness," recalled Col. Wesley Brainerd. "Men died from thirst, many from excitement and sun-stroke." He amended his statement to say that there was indeed "one little stream, almost dry, called Piney Branch Creek," but it was available only to the troops who happened to be fighting near it, "though muddy water was carried from it to considerable distances."[37]

Men endured what they had to in order to live, but at times it hardly seemed worth the trouble. Late in the campaign a Union surgeon growled, "I am tired to death lying here drinking Chickahominy swamp water in which a thousand dead horses are macerating." His life, he continued, had settled into a hellish routine: "It is drink this water, eat half cooked fresh beef before it is half dead, run to sink [i.e., the latrine] every fifteen minutes, and sleep with stenches under your nose sufficient to cause a turkey buzzard or carrion crow to contract typhoid fever, then up and fight three or four hours and *keep doing it until you get used to it.*"[38]

Nature itself conspired against the soldiers. A Massachusetts man ran into a patch of poison ivy. "I do not feel very well today," he wrote his wife. "[M]y eyes are almost shut up and they [his messmates] are all laughing at me." The woods were infested with ticks. Father William Corbin, a chaplain in the Irish Brigade, awoke one morning to find himself and another priest "literally covered" with them. In his memoirs he devoted a long paragraph to this episode. To remove the ticks, he informed his readers, "you must break the body and leave the head embedded in your flesh. Father Ouellet and I had to go through this morning exercise by way of making our toilet. During the day we suffered terribly. The heads of those pests were still in deep and caused a burning sensation that was anything but comfortable." Later they washed their skin with salt water, which helped a bit, but day after day their body sweat aggravated the raw wounds "so as to throw us in a fever, and we passed whole nights in sleepless agony." Writing in 1894, Father Corbin realized his staid Victorian readers might find it odd that he should dwell so heavily on such a thing. That, he said, was precisely the reason: "Hundreds, thousands, I may say, have written up those conflicts and painted them in the bloodiest colors. Whereas few, if any, have entered at length into the details of other trials and sufferings incurred by the poor soldier while serving his country."[39]

Wood ticks were not the only torment. Mosquitoes and gnats lavished attention on one and all, while cavalrymen endured a hazard unique to their branch: the horse fly. "Their bites or stings, and the after touches, seem to create misery in the marrow of one's bones," attested a Pennsylvania trooper.[40]

Probably the worst plague was lice. Col. Rufus Dawes of the Sixth Wisconsin ordered his men one day to construct breastworks and later rode over to see how they were progressing. Far from wielding spades or axes, the soldiers were stripped to the waist and utterly absorbed in the business of killing "gray backs." Quite unabashed, the men explained that having located the first shade from the Virginia sun in weeks, they must improve the opportunity. Often the only effective solution was to boil the afflicted clothing. This sometimes had unintended side effects— the clothing shrank. "Once a man brought to me one of his shrunk up shirts in a package, to be franked by mail," Dawes recalled. "He said he thought it would about fit the baby."[41]

Usually the men had no time to kill lice or even change their uniforms, and given the mud and dirt it seemed pointless even to try. "I have not changed my clothes since May third," Dawes wrote his wife on May

25. When soldiers finally did don fresh clothing, the act was frequently important enough to merit mention in one's pocket diary or a letter to the folks back home. The getting of shelter was another newsworthy event. The First New Jersey Cavalry slept under canvas for the first time on May 25, more than three weeks after leaving their winter encampment.[42]

For the most part, the men slept on the ground, often in their trenches, shielded only by a gum blanket. Under idyllic conditions—a bed of hay or straw underneath, a canopy of stars overheard, a pleasant night breeze—this had qualities to recommend it. But conditions were usually anything but idyllic. Drenching rain and seas of mud made sleep sometimes as miserable as staying awake, and even dry ground had disadvantages. "I shall always believe," wrote Pvt. Theodore Gerrish, "that the soil of Virginia is at least several degrees harder than any other State in the Union." But whatever the discomforts that attended it, most men lusted for sleep. A Union general estimated that the army was getting by on but "two to four hours per day. It is the hardest campaigning I have ever seen. Before it commenced, I would not have believed that I could have gone through it." A Pennsylvania soldier wrote that in twenty-five days he got one night's sleep, "and this was the average for the whole army."[43]

Poor or inadequate food, bad water, pests, and fatigue steadily ground both armies down, sapping the troops of strength and wrecking their health. Almost everyone suffered from diarrhea, fever, or some other malady. A substantial percentage became sufficiently ill to require evacuation. Statistics for the Army of the Potomac and IX Corps, for example, list the number of sick transported from Fredericksburg to Washington at 4,225: more than 16 percent of total evacuations. Confederate losses due to illness, like virtually every other statistic for this period, are unknown but probably similar in proportion to overall strength. At times it seemed as if neither side could endure the strain. Confederate general Bryan Grimes echoed the opinion of blue and gray officers when he informed his wife on May 19: "This is the fifteenth day since we have met them [the enemy]. Have been fighting more or less every day. If they would retire beyond the river and give us a breathing spell, it would be decidedly advantageous. Nearly all are fagged out and need rest."[44]

The toll on soldiers was not only physical but psychological as well, for the Overland campaign kept soldiers in almost perpetual tension and danger. During the nineteenth century such a state was still fairly rare. Except in sieges, when troops might be under continual threat of bombardment (though relatively safe, as a rule, in deep trenches or bombproofs), combat was a matter of a few hours or even minutes. Soldiers would enter the fighting from a state of almost complete security. They might suffer horrendous losses during that brief interlude of battle—casualties of 40, 50, even 60 percent were not uncommon—but afterward they returned to a state of security once again, for days, weeks, even months. This had critical implications for their ability to withstand the ordeal of war. "Courage," argues Lord Moran in his classic study, *The Anatomy of Courage,* "is a moral quality. It is . . . the fixed resolve not to quit; an act of renunciation which must be made not once but many times by the power of the will. Courage is will power." Most men had it, but virtually any man could lose it. "In the trenches"—Lord Moran was a veteran of the Western Front in 1914–18—"a man's will power was his capital and he was always spending." When his capital ran out, "he was finished."[45]

Lord Moran wrote in 1945, when physiologists and psychologists had as yet a comparatively sketchy grasp of what happens to human beings under stress. Although quite right about "courage," if defined as the ability to function effectively in the face of danger, he was—as he implicitly conceded elsewhere in his book—wrong about its being purely a moral quality. Certainly it requires an effort of will for a person consciously aware of danger to choose to remain in its presence. But this effort of will gets a strong assist from the body's ability to adapt to stress: to maintain, in ways that are half-conscious, half-visceral, what military psychiatrist Jon Shaw has termed "an illusion of personal safety"—the irrational confidence that whatever happens to those around him, the subject himself is likely to survive.[46]

A soldier thus had two lines of psychological defense: a conviction, consciously cultivated and maintained, that facing danger was a moral imperative; and an illusion of personal safety whereby he and his biochemistry conspired to believe that despite the danger he would continue to exist. By 1864 most veterans found the illusion of personal safety impossible to maintain in any conscious way, so they sought it indirectly. Many took refuge in Christianity and its promise of eternal life. Revivals swept both armies during the winter of 1864, especially in the Army of Northern Virginia, which witnessed an estimated seven thousand conversion experiences in the months before the campaign. A Mississippi private may well have honestly recalled that the night before the battle of the Wilderness, "I slept a solid dreamless sleep as peaceful as a child. Mentally I had already given up my life to the keeping of our Lord, and said in my soul, 'Not my will, but Thine be done.'" "Death must come sometime," a devout New Yorker reminded his family, "and it makes but little difference where a man dies if he has the right feeling. . . . [R]emember me at the throne of Grace and I will you."[47]

Others took their fatalism straight. From Spotsylvania, Major Dawes soberly warned his wife that "the probabilities of coming out safe are strongly against me," adding, with a grandeur of perspective she probably failed to appreciate: "If we may only finish this horrible business here, our lives are of poor moment in comparison." Late in the campaign a soldier in the Second Michigan described the ferocity of the fighting and asked his readers to "imagine yourself as target for a thousand shots a minute and then think what a slim chance a soldier has to come out of this all safe." Such sentiments reduced stress biochemically as well as transcendentally. Experiments in behavioral psychology have demonstrated that subjects who possess no ability to control a painful stimulus experience less stress than those who do. Curbing the belief that one's battlefield choices could affect one's survival was thus a powerful adaptive technique.[48]

Even so, it was rare for soldiers to face the full logic of their fatalism. Soldiers who resigned themselves to the will of God routinely thanked Him for sparing their lives and espoused, tacitly or overtly, a theory of divine protection. Or they simply contradicted themselves: Two sentences after asking his family to imagine facing a thousand shots a minute, the same Michigan soldier reassured them, "You must not worry too much about me for I have been in danger for most of two years and been in some of the hardest fighting of the war and have not been hurt yet."[49]

The illusion of personal safety, for its part, did not obviate the shortness of breath, pounding heart, and urge to flee that characterizes the somatic response to danger; it simply made these sensations manageable. Some had a more difficult time than others. A Union doctor described a young soldier in the Wilderness "going to what may have been his death, with pallid face and trembling lips, yet with his head erect and eyes to the front." It was, he thought, a "wonderful example of mind over matter." In the same battle, Col. Wesley Brainerd recounted seeing something he had heard about but never previously observed. Veterans whom he knew to be brave men "dropped out of the ranks by twos, and threes, by the score, and stepped to the rear to attend to the demands of nature. No one laughed, no one blamed them, for all felt that peculiar feeling experienced only in the presence of *death.*"[50]

Brainerd went on to say that he considered the incident "a striking illustration" of the fact that a soldier often feels greater fear before an action than during it: "The actual reality, met face to face, serves only to stimulate and embolden him." He was describing the effect of adrenaline, which tends initially to provoke flight but, if one remains in a dangerous situation, just as effectively unleashes ferocious activity. Yet the body's supply of adrenaline is not inexhaustible. Constant exposure to danger outstrips the body's ability to synthesize new supplies. Stress becomes much harder to manage. A Union officer testified after ten days of combat, "It is dreadful to be kept in a constant state of excitement like this."[51]

The illusion of safety, by definition irrational, paradoxically requires a certain amount of genuine safety to sustain. Soldiers placed in harm's way for too long a period, Lord Moran and others have observed, decrease in effectiveness until they become almost useless. In contemporary terms, they have succumbed to combat stress reaction, sometimes called post-traumatic stress disorder. Just how debilitating this disorder may be is somewhat controversial. According to one theory, its effects are deep, long-lasting, and persistent. But according to another—the so-called stress evaporation hypothesis—it is superficial, nonpersistent, and rarely dysfunctional.

During the Second World War, for example, one American physician concluded that lack of sleep, induced by intense anxiety, was the most critical factor in "combat fatigue" (as it was then diagnosed). He treated patients with massive sedation that guaranteed a solid period of rest. Thirty percent of his patients returned to combat duty within a day; over 70 percent after forty-eight hours. In this respect the armies' interlude at the North Anna River undoubtedly played an important role in preserving the troops' effectiveness. For two days the armies broke contact, re-creating a sense of relative safety, and although many units were in combat at one time or another during the next week, the fighting was intermittent, not continual. One gets a sense, from the first-person narratives of this period, that the men found new energy and spirit—to use Lord Moran's metaphor, they were able to replenish some of their capital—like the Tar Heel who informed his wife on May 26: "I have slept undisturbed for two nights, and also slept a good portion of the day time and feel considerably revived."[52]

Yet it is still difficult to avoid the conclusion that the campaign gradually eroded the troops' military effectiveness. Observers saw it in their increasing reluctance to assault positions vigorously and in the brittleness of even crack units like the Iron Brigade, which in two years had compiled a reputation as the Army of the Potomac's toughest outfit, only to run like sheep at Jericho Mill. This outcome was, in a sense, overdetermined. Not only did casualties and fatigue grind down the armies. By the nature of combat, the losses fell heaviest on the bravest, most dutiful soldiers, who in life had emboldened others with their example. The problem was particularly acute in Union army, which had two additional sources of strain: lack of confidence in the new recruits, bounty jumpers, and Heavy Artillery regiments that made up its replacements, and veteran regiments whose enlistments were about to expire. "Our time is reduced to 19 days but from present appearance they will be terrible days," commented a Union officer late in the campaign. "The 2nd RI has got but 4 days more and if they get into a fight I don't think they will stand a minute. it makes all the difference in the world with mens courage. they do dread awfully to get hit just as thier time is out." Such was the common impression of "short timers." In reality, most of these units ably acquitted themselves to the very end. But the perception that they were unreliable was at least as important as the reality.[53]

What was being purchased by all this death, injury, and suffering? As the month wore on, soldiers and civilians alike grappled with the question. Their opinions mattered because they had direct implications for morale and motivation. Soldiers who think they are winning generally fight better than those who think they are losing. Perception has a way of becoming reality. And in a people's war, civilian opinion matters just as much. It factored into the willingness to sacrifice for the cause and, especially in the North, into the willingness to support leaders who wished to continue the war. And although armies were fighting all across the South in the spring of 1864—most notably in Georgia, where Sherman and Johnston were locked in a struggle for Atlanta—public opinion was disproportionately focused on the conflict in Virginia. Seen as a duel between Grant and Lee, with the Bermuda Hundred expedition and Union raids all part of Grant's master plan to subdue Lee and seize Richmond, the Virginia campaign was considered the war's decisive theater.

The dominant opinion among Federal soldiers during the first two weeks of May was that the campaign was going well. They thought— quite mistakenly—that they had hurt Lee worse in the Wilderness than he hurt them. It impressed them even more that after the first round they were still on their feet, something that had rarely occurred when the Army of the Potomac tangled with Lee. As one soldier put it, "We attacked Lee and were not repulsed, which is saying a good deal." An even more important factor in making the Wilderness seem like a victory was Grant's decision to continue south afterward.[54]

But the strongest evidence of all was the victory at the Mule Shoe, which was far and away the greatest victory the Army of the Potomac had yet achieved over its adversary. Hitherto it had either failed to break the Confederate lines at all or else sustained devastating counterattacks that nullified any gains. At the Mule Shoe, however, the Federals had not merely broken Lee's line. They had captured over three thousand prisoners and twenty fieldpieces, and had fended off everything Lee could throw at them, finally forcing Lee to construct a new trenchline a mile to the rear.

To most bluecoats that looked much like triumph. "We have had the best of the fighting so far and its my opinion that Genl Grant has got Lee in a pretty tight spot," declared one Yank on May 16. Wrote another: "We have been fighting for 10 day's now & I think on the whole the Rebs have got rather the worst of it. . . . On the whole I think Grant has outgeneralled Lee."[55]

The Lincoln administration was also pleased. Upon receiving the first reports of the Wilderness battle, John Hay, Lincoln's personal secretary, confided in his diary, "The President thinks very highly of what Grant has done. He was talking about it today with me and said 'How near we have been to this thing before and failed. I believe if any other General had been at the Head of that army it would now have been on this side of the Rapidan. It is the dogged pertinacity of Grant that wins.'" Wrote Secretary of the Navy Gideon Welles after the Mule Shoe, "[E]verything looks auspicious for the republic."[56]

If the soldiers and administration were upbeat, the Republican newspapers were positively ecstatic. On May 9, the *New York Times* trumpeted, GLORIOUS NEWS---DEFEAT AND RETREAT OF LEE'S ARMY . . . IMMENSE REBEL LOSSES," and the *New York Herald* announced, "VICTORY!—Splendid Success of General Grant." On May 10 the *New York Tribune* editorialized, "There is no longer any doubt. Gen. Grant has won a great victory." It went on to say (erroneously) that Lee was in retreat toward Richmond, that Hancock had driven through Spotsylvania, and that the II Corps headquarters were fully twenty miles south of the Wilderness battlefield. "The military power of the Rebellion," concluded the *Tribune*, "has received a fatal blow."

The Democratic press was more subdued. In an election year it could not afford to admit that the Lincoln administration was winning the war, yet it could not sound defeatist, either. It therefore had to walk a line between supine cheerleading and callow pessimism. Thus, on May 6, the *New York World* soberly warned readers to "fortify their minds against discouragement" in the event of Union reversals. It joined in the general exuberance after the Wilderness—"VICTORY CERTAIN . . . A RACE FOR RICHMOND" read its May 10 headline, but just a day later it opined that public feeling remained divided between "hope and solicitude," with hope leading by just a little.

Both Republican and Democratic papers got their news from a mixture of correspondents' reports and official dispatches, which they interpreted as best suited to their preferred editorial slants. Every New York paper (except perhaps the *World*) had at least six correspondents with the Army of the Potomac. And although news reporters with the army managed to get dispatches to their home newspapers—it was a young reporter, Henry Wing, who actually got the very first report, official or otherwise, out of the Wilderness fight—the papers still relied on periodic communiqués from Secretary of War Edwin M. Stanton (who relied in turn on dispatches from Grant and Assistant Secretary of War Dana).[57]

Ostensibly composed as official dispatches to Maj. Gen. John A. Dix, commander of the Department of the East, with headquarters in New York City, these communiqués were in fact fed directly to the Associated Press. Stalwart in tone and accurate in detail, they nevertheless contained restrained but shrewd editorializing. For example, one communiqué noted that a quartermaster's request for more supplies mentioned that the enemy were retiring, on the strength of which Stanton argued that "the enemy's strength has always been most felt in his first blows, and these having failed and our forces not only maintained their ground but preparing to advance, lead to the hope of full and complete success."[58]

But the most famous communiqué went forth to Dix late on May 11: "Dispatches from General Grant, dated at 8 o'clock this morning, have just reached this Department. He says: 'We have now ended the sixth day of very heavy fighting. The result to this time is much in our favor. Our losses have been heavy as well as those of the enemy. I think the loss of the enemy must be greater. We have taken over 5,000 prisoners in battle, whilst he has taken from us but few, except stragglers. I propose to fight it out on this line if it takes all summer.' The Government is sparing no pains to support him." Copies of the communiqué went directly to every pro-administration governor in the North.[59]

The Republican press loved that one and made the final sentence of Grant's dispatch a battle cry. The Democratic *World* interpreted it differently on May 13. "We must frankly state our impression that the military aspect is not very hopeful," and put its own downbeat spin on Grant's famous phrase. "Even Grant is profoundly impressed with a sense of the herculean magnitude of his task: '*I propose to fight it out on this line if it takes all summer.*' Heroic and resolute words, assuredly; but still the words of a man before whom difficulties are looming in portentous proportions."

But that was before the Mule Shoe. In its entire career, the Army of the Potomac had never done anything like it: pierced Lee's main line, captured one of his divisions, taken twenty of his guns. The North went wild. Even the *New York World* exulted on May 14: "All doubt is at an end. After a series of desperate battles, contested on both sides with matchless valor, skill, and obstinacy, the Army of the Potomac has won a decided, if not a decisive victory." While it could be doubted that the first week of the campaign was "adverse to our arms," the *World* maintained, the battle on May 12 "is a great step toward the final possession of Richmond."

The Republican press was even less restrained. "TRIUMPHANT NEWS!!! THE REBEL ARMY ROUTED! crowed the *Ohio State Journal* for May 16, 1864: RICHMOND TO BE ABANDONED! HOW ARE YOU, JEFF DAVIS?" The May 14 *New York Times* editorialized, "The veteran army of Robert E. Lee is breaking up. Or rather, it is being defeated, demolished, crushed and annihilated by the courage of our soldiers and the masterly generalship of their Commander." This, it insisted, was "not fancy, but joyous fact—grim, solemn, terrible, sanguinary fact."

And expensive fact: The Northern press was in no doubt that the loss of human life in Virginia was high. On May 12—even before it got word of the fight at the Mule Shoe—the *New York Tribune* overestimated Union losses at forty thousand. The *New York Times* on May 15 put total casualties at twenty thousand. On May 18 the *New York Herald* estimated the Army of the Potomac's loss—excluding Sheridan's cavalry—with fair accuracy at thirty-five thousand. Yet none of this seemed disheartening. On the contrary, taken in context it seemed to reinforce the opinion that the Waterloo of the Civil War was at last at hand, with Grant playing the role of Wellington.

That perception quickly diminished. It soon became obvious that Lee was not crushed but had simply withdrawn to a new line. The opposition Democrats were quick to point this out. "It is now definitely settled that so far no victory has been won," opined the *World* on May 17. True,

Hancock had stormed the rebel works, captured prisoners, and at one point controlled thirty rebel cannon. "But the rebels . . . contested the field vigorously for the rest of the day, recovered some of their lost guns, repulsed all the attacks made upon them, and the battle at the close was, as all previous ones have been, indecisive."

Republican papers had to acknowledge the same thing, especially after word of Sigel's defeat at New Market and Butler's reverse at Drewry's Bluff. But unlike the Democrats, they subjected these events to considerable spin control. Sigel, said the *New York Times*, prudently withdrew in the face of superior numbers, while both the *Times* and *Tribune* pointed to the "signal advantages" gained by Butler's foray toward Richmond and the concomitant cavalry raid by August Kautz. Regarding the main offensive itself, the *Times* continued its optimistic tone but with a newly defensive tinge. On May 19 it opined: "We know the great losses his [Grant's] army has already suffered; we hear privately and otherwise of the fearful mud of Virginia; we learn that the soldiers are greatly exhausted with their recent fighting and marching. But we have seen also, under Grant's management in the West and in the East, what can be accomplished by able generalship."

This, as May wore on, became increasingly a minority opinion. The *Times* would later complain of a public backlash after May 12, as euphoria gave way to despondency. Even those inclined to put the best face on things began to discuss the state of events more guardedly. One soldier who wrote his mother on May 17 contrasted encouraging reports from other points with "our somewhat negative success here." Remarked one Union surgeon, "It is true that we have driven the enemy at every point; still to all appearance their lines are as complete and strong as ever." Secretary of the Navy Welles recorded in his diary for May 17 that there was "a painful suspense in military operations. It is a necessary suspense, but the intense anxiety is oppressive, and almost unfits the mind for mental activity." The suspense was so bad because Welles anticipated that shortly "one or more bloody battles will take place in which not only many dear friends will be slaughtered but probably the Civil War will be decided as to its continuance, or termination."[60]

At least one of Welles's colleagues was not optimistic even to that degree. On May 23 Secretary of the Treasury Salmon P. Chase wrote a friend, "The people are crazy or I am. I don't *see* the recent military successes. Most earnestly do I pray that we may see them hereafter. All under God depends on Grant. So far he has achieved very little and that little beyond computation."[61]

The New York worthy George Templeton Strong noted the bad feeling in his own circles. The sentiment downtown, he wrote on May 17, was despondent, despite the lack of news from the front to justify it. "People have taken up with an exaggerated view of Grant's hard-won success in opening the campaign, and now, finding that the 'backbone of the Rebellion' is not 'broken at last' into a handful of incoherent vertebrae, and that Lee still shews fight, 'on the Po' or elsewhere, they are disappointed, disgusted, and ready to believe any rumor of disaster and mischief that the wicked ingenuity of speculators can devise and inculcate."[62]

Strong referred more than anything else to the New York gold market, where gold and greenbacks were traded at rates of exchange tied heavily to perceptions of Union military success or failure. The worse the Union appeared to fare, the higher gold went. At the moment, according to market commentary, those perceptions were linked almost exclusively to Grant's campaign in Virginia. On May 4, the day the Army of the Potomac crossed the Rapidan, gold stood at 179½; that is, it took $179.50 in greenbacks to buy a hundred dollars in gold. Grant's reported success in the Wilderness brought down the price to 168 on May 10; after that it spiked a bit, then slid to 170 upon confirmation of the Mule Shoe victory. After that it started to climb: 173½ when the market closed on Monday, May 16; 177¼ the next day, and 184 on Wednesday, May 18.[63]

The Wednesday spike was due to an out-and-out attempt to capitalize on the death and suffering of the campaign. On May 18 the New York *Journal of Commerce* and *New York World* published a proclamation from President Abraham Lincoln that threw the market into a frenzy. After regretting that the Almighty had seen fit to make the United States "the monumental sufferer of the nineteenth century," the proclamation ran, the president got down to business: "It is not necessary that I should tell you that the first Virginia campaign under Lieutenant-General Grant, in whom I have every confidence, and whose courage and fidelity the people do well to honor, is virtually closed." True, Lincoln continued, Grant had shown "discreet ability" and "inflicted great loss upon the enemy." But in view of the stalemate in Virginia and reversals elsewhere, he, Abraham Lincoln, was proclaiming a day of fasting, humiliation, and prayer, calling for four hundred thousand new recruits to replace the hundred thousand three-year veterans about to depart, and threatening an "immediate and peremptory draft" on any Northern state that failed to meet its quota.[64]

The proclamation was bogus, planted by one Joseph Howard Jr., who was apparently in cahoots with a nest of Wall Street speculators hoping to take advantage of the turmoil that was bound to grip the market when the proclamation came out. Every New York paper got a copy, but only the two major Democratic papers were unlucky enough to publish it. Stanton, misinterpreting their misfortune as intentional sabotage, had their publishers arrested, despite the fact that the publishers had recognized their mistake, printed a retraction, and—in the case of the *New York World*—raced to retrieve bundles of their newspaper from the packet steamer *Scotia,* bound for London. (The proclamation would have savaged American diplomatic and financial interests overseas had it reached Europe; the War Department sent a fast dispatch vessel to overtake the *Scotia* before it cleared the Narrows.)

Stanton, most agreed, overreacted, and in so doing he added meat to Democratic charges that the Lincoln administration lacked respect for civil liberties. Even the city's Republican newspaper publishers petitioned for the release of their Democratic colleagues, who were set free on May 23. (Joseph Howard got off after just three months' confinement in New York harbor's Fort Lafayette; Henry Ward Beecher, an influential abolitionist and clergyman, persuaded the administration to let him go.) Underscoring the futility of Stanton's gesture, within a week gold had risen above 184—and it continued rising for the rest of the Overland campaign. Initially jubilant, the Northern public had been disappointed, and it was becoming less and less sanguine about the prospect of a great victory.[65]

Southern opinion, by contrast, remained upbeat throughout the campaign. True, there were a few guarded voices, but these were impressed far more by Union raids against Virginia's transportation network than by the fortunes of Lee's army. In Richmond, Confederate war clerk John B. Jones noted in his diary for May 13 that Union cavalry under August V. Kautz, having cut the Weldon Railroad, had now cut the Danville Railroad as well: "All communication with the country from which provisions are derived is now completely at an end! And if supplies are withheld that long, this community, as well as the army, must be without food in ten days!" Even the victory at Drewry's Bluff did not improve his spirits: "The battle yesterday decided nothing, that I am aware of. . . . If Butler remains near Richmond and Petersburg, and is reinforced, and Grant is strong enough (two to Lee's one) to push toward Richmond, our perils and trials will be greater than ever."[66]

But most Confederates were confident—and unimpressed by Grant's continuation of his offensive. Grant, wrote one of Lee's soldiers to his wife, "is twice as badly whiped now as was Burnside or Hooker." True, so far he was rather pigheadedly refusing to acknowledge it, "but I think before he gets through with Lee he will have to own up." Another man wrote home that the bluecoats were refusing any longer to charge the Confederate works, adding, "Thus far Grant has shown no remarkable generalship— only a bulldog tenacity and determination in a fight, regardless of the consequences or the loss." A third Southerner estimated the Union loss at "50 to 60,000 all told—They still move against us, but feebly." Even Grant's advance to the North Anna did not alter Confederate opinion. "I cannot but think that Lee is as well prepared to fight now as he ever will be," noted Confederate ordnance chief Josiah Gorgas on May 25. Lee's army had been reinforced, and the two opposing forces must now be near parity. That gave the actual advantage to the Confederates. "We can still fall back upon our entrenchments, but Grant is irretrievably ruined if defeated. He has never before ventured so far from his gunboats."[67]

Southern reporting of the Virginia campaign was typically a mirror image of press coverage in the North. On May 9, the same day that New York papers were heralding a Union victory in the Wilderness, the *Richmond Examiner* was reporting "THE GREAT BATTLE ON THE RAPID ANN— THE ENEMY REPULSED AT ALL POINTS AND IN RETREAT ON FREDERICKSBURG." It assured its readers, "If we win this round, the game is our own. Nothing can prevent the collapse of the war party in the United States and the collapse of its financial system."

Other papers picked up the theme of a decisive battle in progress. "GREAT NEWS FROM VIRGINIA!" boomed the *Charleston Mercury* on May 18. "Northern Admissions of the Defeat of Grant . . . Beauregard's Victory over Butler." The enemy, it exulted, "has failed disastrously in this last and desperate attempt." After Spotsylvania, the *Raleigh Daily Confederate* opined that "the repulses of the foe have been attended, to him [the enemy], with a slaughter wholly disproportionate to ours, and such a loss as his army cannot be able to afford." One more victory, declared the *Southern Literary Messenger,* and the "disheartened and disappointed North will be made to see the necessity of peace."[68]

Yet Grant continued to advance, thereby creating a phenomenon that required explanation. An interpretation soon arose to account for the discrepancy: Grant was beaten, but he either did not know it or could not afford to admit it. The May 10 *Richmond Examiner* observed that although

Lee had "whipped Grant" in the Wilderness, Grant's movement toward Spotsylvania indicated that Grant did not believe himself whipped. Yet the battle of Laurel Hill demonstrated that, however Grant may have felt, his men were demoralized, "and that they now feel, when opposed to our men, that they are in the presence of their masters." Grant might yet get closer to Richmond, but he now commanded "the ruins of an army." Similarly, the *North Carolina Semi-Weekly Standard* argued that Lee was beating Grant so badly that under ordinary circumstances the Yankee would have abandoned his offensive. He continued to attack out of sheer desperation: "Grant is in that condition when his final withdrawal is to him and his country the loss of all."[69]

The image of Grant driving forward a decimated, demoralized army became a prominent theme of Confederate editorials as the campaign unfolded. It showed not the determination of Grant and the Lincoln administration but rather their callous inhumanity. The image was especially pronounced in the May 16 *Richmond Examiner,* which announced, "There are butchers of humanity to whom the sight of the fellow creature's blood affords an intoxicating pleasure; they are indifferent to whose blood it is. . . . His government and his brother Generals will not baulk him in the present instance. A large part of the army now in his hands is composed of the regiments enlisted for three years, and their term expires in this coming summer. They have resisted every inducement to re-enlist. . . . The Government is entirely willing that Grant should save it the trouble and mortification of giving the discharge to these veterans."

Nevertheless, warned a May 20 editorial, "Grant . . . is no contemptible antagonist. We may believe him doomed; still he is dangerous. . . . He has deliberately counted on 'depletion,' and a fearful depletion too— fearful to any man of less obstinacy and less selfishness. If he can effect, with every assault on our lines, not an equal, but a proportionate depletion of our ranks, then the satisfactory solution to the problem is, from his point of view, a mere question of arithmetic, a mere question of time. He would coolly throw away a hundred thousand of his men if, by that means, he could put fifty thousand of ours *hors de combat.*" A subsequent editorial likened Grant to a gambler fanatically committed to a flawed gambling system: "He shall stake pile after pile until his last man is gone."[70]

The piles of chips in question were, of course, the lives of the men under Grant's command. Lee had his own chips—not as many, and not dwindling quite as fast, but in rough proportion to Grant's losses. And every one of these losses translated, not just into a figure on a muster roll but also a missing comrade and a family member dead, wounded, captured, or missing. Sometimes it seemed as if nothing could justify so much misery and grief. After the battle of the Wilderness, a Massachusetts senator, reading the first vivid news accounts of the fighting, exclaimed, "If that scene could have been presented to me before the war, anxious as I was for the preservation of the Union, I should have said: 'The cost is too great; erring sisters, depart in peace.'"[71]

The Wilderness, Laurel Hill, Cloyd's Mountain, the Mule Shoe at Spotsylvania, New Market, Drewry's Bluff, the engagements along the North Anna. So many battles, so many dead, and still, as May gave way to June, no one yet knew the outcome of the campaign.

CHAPTER SEVEN

"It Seemed Like Murder"

Cold Harbor—technically "Old" Cold Harbor, to distinguish it from equally unremarkable "New" Cold Harbor a mile west—was nothing but a weathered tavern where five roads met. But the roads were of critical importance, for they connected with the region's major highways, especially the ones leading down to the Chickahominy River crossings. The Army of the Potomac's direct route to the James River led through those crossings and, consequently, through Cold Harbor. Both Grant and Lee understood this fact perfectly. The key to the campaign now seemed to rest at the heart of this obscure, star-shaped intersection.

The hamlet's population could normally be counted on one hand, but on May 31 it numbered several thousand: Butler's brigade of mounted infantry, which had been shoved away from Matadequin Creek the previous day, and Fitzhugh Lee's two-brigade division of cavalry, just arrived after a long hard ride from the Confederate army's opposite flank. Fitz Lee commanded the combined force and had spread it in an arc to cover Cold Harbor's eastern approaches. He deployed pickets well forward to provide early warning of a Union attack and put most of the troopers to work throwing up fence rails, logs, and earth into hasty breastworks.[1]

Pickets, scout reports, and common sense told Lee that Sheridan's cavalry was out beyond his line and probably had him outnumbered. He keenly needed reinforcements. Periodically he sent a staff officer down the road to his rear to see if Robert F. Hoke's infantry division was anywhere in sight. Lee had been told of its rail transfer from Bermuda Hundred and that it had orders to march to Cold Harbor from Mechanicsville. Around 3:30 P.M. Hoke's lead brigade came into view: four North Carolina regiments under Brig. Gen. Thomas L. Clingman. Lee sent them over to extend the left (northern) end of his line. A half hour later, the Federals attacked.[2]

They came from the northwest, two brigades under Wesley Merritt and George Custer, advancing astride the road that led to Matadequin Creek and the Old Church Hotel. They came dismounted, their Sharps and Spencer carbines sputtering. Lee's troopers and Clingman's infantry unceremoniously repelled them. Thwarted in their first attempt to gain the intersection, the Union commanders nevertheless got two benefits from the attack: They now had a better sense of the Confederate position, and understood that they faced a combined force of infantry and cavalry. Their division commander, A. T. A. Torbert, conferred quickly with Merritt, who commanded the brigade closest to the rebel flank. They decided that Merritt would use part of his force to pin the enemy in front; the rest would work around to his flank and rear.[3]

The plan worked admirably, in part because it was adroitly executed, but also because Clingman's brigade was inexperienced, understrength, and badly posted. It had spent most of the war in North Carolina, where it had seldom fought a regular engagement, and had left one of its regiments at Bermuda Hundred to screen its section of the trenches. Moreover, at Hoke's direction, Clingman had placed one of his remaining regiments, the Fifty-first North Carolina, 500 yards in advance of the brigade. Presumably intended to provide warning of an enemy thrust, the Fifty-first simply found itself outflanked and isolated by Merritt's second attack. Still worse, Clingman had stationed himself with this regiment, so that for several crucial minutes he too was isolated and unable to supervise the rest of his brigade. Eventually he cut his way back to them, but not in time to organize a revised defensive line. Instead, the brigade collapsed to the rear, thereby uncovering the flank of Lee's division.[4]

With their position compromised, Lee ordered his troopers to withdraw. Seeing the Confederates about to pull out, Custer ordered one of his battalions to charge, mounted, with drawn sabers. The charge, wrote Custer in his report, "produced the desired effect. The enemy, without waiting to receive it, threw down their arms and fled, leaving their dead and wounded on the field." The critical Cold Harbor intersection was now in Union hands.[5]

For Torbert's cavalry it had been a glittering moment, marred only by the fact that the division's third brigade, under Thomas C. Devin, had somehow failed to join the attack. But this mistake only underscored the achievement of Merritt and Custer, for with two slender brigades

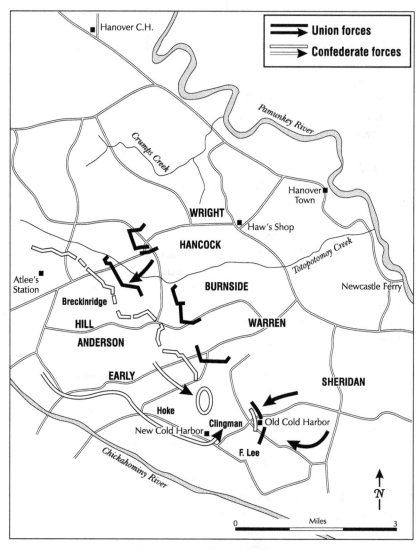

14. Situation, May 31, 1864

they had put to flight four Confederate brigades. Sheridan, who arrived after the fight had ended, warmly praised the troops in his report: "The fight on the part of our officers and men was very gallant; they were now beginning to accept nothing less than victory." But a few hours' reflection sobered him a bit. From scouts and prisoners he learned that another of Hoke's brigades had come up, the Confederate cavalry was still dangerous, and a second infantry division might be moving up as well. Torbert mustered only three brigades—three thousand troopers against several times as many as rebels—and the nearest infantry support was miles away. Late that evening Sheridan ordered Torbert to fall back and reported his decision to Meade. "Lee's line of battle is in front of Mechanicsville, and, with the heavy odds against me here, I do not think it prudent to hold on."[6] Torbert's men withdrew quietly—so quietly, in fact, that the Confederates never realized they had left.

Miles to the north, the Army of the Potomac spent the day feeling Lee's defenses along the Totopotomoy, looking for an opening. By evening it was clear that there was no opportunity in front, but there were indications that Lee was shifting his army to the right, possibly to dart around the Army of the Potomac and strike Smith's XVIII Corps. Nothing would please Grant more: For weeks he had craved a chance to fight Lee in the open. But whether Lee intended to take the offensive or simply to block Grant's shortest route to the James River, he would have to go to Cold Harbor. Sheridan was already there; the XVIII Corps was en route. At 9:45 P.M. orders went forth to Wright's VI Corps to pull out of line and march to Cold Harbor as well.[7]

Ironically, that was just what Lee wanted. Although he did not yet know, as the Federals supposed he did, that Smith had reached White House Landing, he strongly believed that Grant was making another turning movement. Any such movement would go through Cold Harbor; the Union cavalry's seizure of the crossroads only confirmed the enemy's intentions. Accordingly, Lee planned an ambush. That afternoon, even before Torbert's attack, he issued orders for Richard Anderson's corps to pull out of line and march to Cold Harbor. Anderson would unite with Hoke and drive off Sheridan's cavalry. The two forces would then be poised to strike the head of the Union column while it was strung out on the road. Lee hoped to hit the enemy hard, forcing him to suspend his flank movement and contract his line. The attack might even create favorable conditions for a general engagement. But at a minimum, Lee wanted to stop reacting to what the enemy did. He wanted to force the enemy to react to him.[8]

Unlike Grant, Lee selected for this movement not the corps at the far end of his line, as was the Federal practice, but the corps in the center, and he counted upon Early and A. P. Hill to fill in the gap made when Anderson departed. This move was riskier, but it reflected Lee's confidence in his subordinates and, just as important, his confidence that the enemy would not detect and capitalize on the maneuver. As a result, not only did Anderson get an earlier start than Wright but his corps also had fewer miles to march.

Thus the night of May 31 found two rival army corps moving by parallel routes to Cold Harbor, each expecting to launch an attack. Preceding them was Sheridan's cavalry, for upon getting Sheridan's report that he had relinquished Cold Harbor, Grant instructed Meade to send him back there, post haste, to hold the intersection "at all hazards." Sheridan got the word around 1 A.M.; two hours later his weary troopers began to reoccupy the crossroads—which, fortunately for Sheridan, the enemy never realized he had abandoned. Sheridan's horsemen sneaked back into Old Cold Harbor before dawn. Weary as they were, they fully expected to be hit hard at daylight, and used the remaining hours of darkness to improve their position. Along some parts of the line, breastworks had to be built from scratch. At others the troopers discovered they could reverse the recently vacated Confederate works. Either way, they worked until they had good protection. Then at least some of them lay down to sleep, their carbines close beside them.[9]

A mile to the northwest, Anderson's corps began arriving after midnight. Only the division of Maj. Gen. Joseph B. Kershaw, over by Beulah Church, was in position to attack; the other two divisions were farther to the rear in support. Kershaw would strike Cold Harbor in the morning. Hoke had orders to cooperate and, upon hearing the battle open on Kershaw's front, would advance to his aid. Between them, Kershaw and Hoke commanded about ten thousand men. Sheridan had no more than five thousand with which to stop them.[10]

Confederates attacked soon after daybreak: first a protracted mutter of skirmishing, then, at 8 A.M., a charge by a regular battle line. Merritt's brigade, entrenched in the woods northwest of Cold Harbor, could not see the rebels but could hear the shouted orders of their officers as they advanced. When at last the Confederates came into view, the troopers held their fire, letting the enemy close the range. Some of them, perhaps, noticed that the enemy was advancing without skirmishers. And undoubtedly a number of men noticed a gray-clad officer, resplendent on horseback and evidently leading the attack, because when at last they opened fire, this officer went down in the first volley. The troopers worked their Spencer repeater carbines feverishly, with terrible effect, smashing the attack within minutes. A second enemy thrust met the same fate. And that was all. After that, the front was quiet, and Sheridan, who had expected to make a last-ditch stand, found that he could breathe easier. "I have been very apprehensive," he confessed in a report to Meade's chief of staff at 9 A.M., "but General Wright is now coming up." With the arrival of the VI Corps infantry, the cavalry's troubles were over.[11]

Plainly, Lee's counterstroke had fizzled. How did such a vital operation misfire so abjectly? Fingers started pointing almost at once. Anderson, it transpired, had decided to precede the attack with a reconnaissance in force. Joseph B. Kershaw, who led the division spearheading the attack, gave the mission to his old brigade, which on June 1 was under the command of Col. Lawrence Massillon Keitt, who had joined the brigade just two days previously, at the head of his regiment, the Twentieth South Carolina Infantry. With 1,100 men on its roster, the outfit easily doubled the brigade's strength—wags dubbed it "the 20th Army Corps"—but it brought complications. Having spent most of its service on garrison duty, few of its men had combat experience. Nor did Colonel Keitt. What he did have, to the misfortune of the brigade and to his personal extinction, was a commission that antedated by four months that of the brigade's senior colonel, John S. Henagan. As a result, Keitt replaced Henagan as brigade commander.[12]

It was Keitt, therefore, who received the order to make the reconnaissance; Keitt who tapped his own Twentieth South Carolina to lead the brigade; Keitt who failed to deploy skirmishers, as an experienced officer would have done; and Keitt who rode into battle on the magnificent horse so conspicuous to the Michigan troopers who killed him. The gallant but unseasoned officer was mortally wounded before he could experience a moment of regret. Dozens of his men met the same fate, and those who survived the massive short-range first volley from Sheridan's guns were completely undone by their sudden total immersion in combat. "They actually groveled upon the ground and attempted to burrow under each other in holes and depressions," wrote Robert Stiles. He and another officer rode in and tried to rally them. "It was to no avail. We actually spurred our horses upon them, and seemed to hear their very bones crack, but it did no good; if compelled to wriggle out of one hole they wriggled into another."[13]

By itself, the debacle of Keitt's brigade need not have derailed Anderson's attack. But it did create confusion, and it also revealed the inadequacy of the coordination arrangements with Hoke's division, which should have launched its own attack when Keitt went in but instead apparently did not realize an attack had even been made. In any event, a kind of paralysis set in. Hoke continued to wait; Kershaw did not renew the assault; and before long the other two divisions spontaneously began to entrench where they stood. Corps commanders exist precisely to wield a strong hand in such situations, but Anderson either did not act or acted ineffectually. Whatever the explanation, Lee's counteroffensive had come to nothing.[14]

Fortunately for the Confederates, the Federals were having troubles of their own. Wright's VI Corps reached the field at midmorning. By 1 P.M. it had taken the place of Sheridan's cavalry in the hasty breastworks north and west of Old Cold Harbor. But Smith's XVIII Corps was still toiling toward the battlefield under the blistering tidewater sun, delayed, incredibly, by orders that had misdirected it not once but twice.[15]

Disembarking at White House Landing, Smith found instructions to take his command to New Castle, up the Pamunkey in the vicinity of Hanovertown. Smith got his men most of the way to that objective, encamped for the night, and next morning received renewed instructions to go to "New Castle Ferry" and take position between the V and VI Corps. The order seemed urgent, so Smith put his troops on the road without breakfast. Arriving at the ferry, however, he discovered nothing but the river and a flat featureless plain surrounded by hills. Of the thousands of troops constituting the V and VI Corps, there was not a trace.

Neither the location nor its emptiness made sense, so Smith sent a captain to find Grant, tell him that he was certain there had been a mistake in his order, and ask that it be rectified. In the meantime, he occupied the hills in case the enemy should somehow materialize and put artillery on them. Then, on the off-chance that Grant might need him on the north side of the river—and probably to obscure the snafu from his troops— Smith put his engineers to work constructing a bridge across the river, quite as if everything was as it should be. Presently up came Colonel Babcock of Grant's staff. Yes, there had been a mistake. The destination named in his order should not have been New Castle Ferry but Cold Harbor.[16]

Smith suspended work on the bridge, recalled his corps from the hills, and put them on the road again, first back the way they had come, then eventually south on the road to Cold Harbor. "The day was intensely hot, the dust stifling, and the progress slow," Smith recalled, particularly after his infantry caught up to the slow-moving supply wagons that trailed the VI Corps. Overheated and worn out, soldiers began to fall by the wayside. Grant had placed Smith under Meade's operational command, and in the early afternoon Smith received the first instructions from his new commander. In one respect, the order was an improvement over its predecessors, in that it accurately described his destination. But in another it was even more frustrating, because it ordered Smith to "hold the road from Cold Harbor to Bethesda Church"—a distance of three miles—and also to cooperate with Wright in a general attack. Smith calculated that he had about ten thousand men on hand, nowhere near enough to carry out both parts of the order. He therefore decided to execute the second part. He would join the attack.[17]

Smith reached Cold Harbor in midafternoon. He found Wright, who had orders from Meade to attack at once, but had instead decided, sensibly, to await the arrival of the XVIII Corps and, in the meantime, to interpret "attack" to mean simply sending out a strong line of skirmishers. Exactly *why* Meade wanted an attack was not expressed in the orders, but Wright could probably infer, if he did not know for a fact, that the aim of headquarters was to wreck Lee's army, and it could be more easily done before the Confederates had fully entrenched. Presumably Hoke's and Anderson's men were still digging in; presumably a good, strong, prompt attack would hurt them badly.

Wright had three divisions—under Thomas H. Neill, David Russell, and James Ricketts—deployed in an arc that ran from the road south of the tavern to Mechanicsville Road. When Smith reached the field, he used his three XVIII Corps divisions, led by Charles Devens, William T. H. Brooks, and John H. Martindale, to extend the line farther north, bending it back so that the final Union position resembled an archer's bow. It was an awkward deployment, from Smith's perspective, because Martindale's entire division was needed to shield his exposed right flank from attack, leaving just two divisions to assault the Confederates in front. Wright's corps was in a similar fix, with Neill's division facing southward to guard against any threat that might materialize from the Chickahominy river bottoms.[18]

Even the four divisions that would make the attack needed time to get into position, reconnoiter the Confederate lines through field glasses, and coordinate arrangements with neighboring outfits. These tasks rapidly burned up what daylight was left, and at 6 P.M., with the sun sinking fast, Wright suggested to Smith that it was now or never. Smith agreed. The long Union battle line rolled forward.[19]

At most points, about 1,200 yards separated the Union jumping-off point from the Confederate lines, and contrary to what headquarters might suppose, the rebels were dug in—not completely, perhaps, but well enough. Artillery opened on the Union brigades almost immediately. As the Yankees closed the range, they began taking small arms fire, too. "The whole line thundered with the incessant volleys of musketry," recalled a VI Corps surgeon, George Stevens, "and the shot and shell of the artillery shrieked and howled like spirits of evil." In most sectors the heavy Confederate fire stopped the attack dead in its tracks, but at one point, close to where the VI and XVIII Corps came together, troops from both outfits discovered a ravine that offered a covered approach most of the way to the rebel line. Exploiting the ravine, they worked up close and for a few minutes gave the enemy a very hard time of it.[20]

The Southerners in this sector belonged to Clingman's brigade, which was experiencing its second debacle in as many days. Clingman had spotted the ravine and, by his account, was about to extend his line to cover it when he was informed that Johnson Hagood's neighboring brigade would take care of it. Not only did Hagood not take care of it; unbeknownst to Clingman, he took his brigade to another part of the line, so that when the Federals struck there was no one covering the ravine at all.[21]

The first Federals up the ravine belonged to Emory Upton's brigade, spearheaded by the recently arrived Second Connecticut Heavy Artillery, which with fifteen hundred men outnumbered the brigade's other regiments combined. Upton got his men within seventy yards of Clingman's line and traded volleys, followed closely by a second brigade under William S. Truex that used the covering fire from Upton to gain the Confederate flank and rear. Within minutes Truex had seized several hundred prisoners and seemed on the verge of breaking the rebel line beyond possibility of repair. But no fresh Union brigades were available to exploit the breach, while on the Confederate side Kershaw took personal

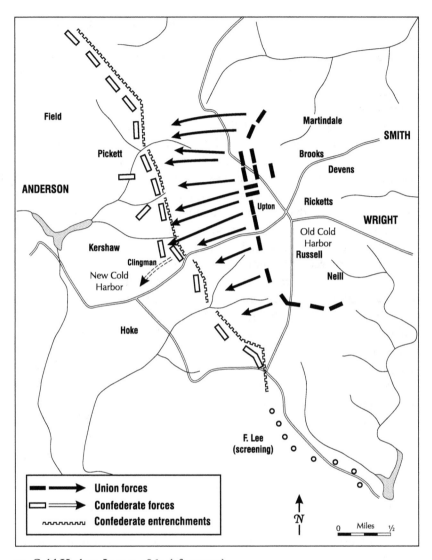

Field

Martindale

SMITH

Pickett

Brooks

Devens

ANDERSON

Upton

Ricketts

WRIGHT

Kershaw

Old Cold
Harbor
Russell

Clingman

New Cold
Harbor

Neill

Hoke

F. Lee
(screening)

Union forces

Confederate forces

Confederate entrenchments

N

0   Miles   ½

15. Cold Harbor, June 1, 1864 (afternoon)

charge of the defense and threw in portions of at least four Southern brigades to retrieve the situation. Truex went down, wounded. Upton stubbornly clung to the foothold his men had gained until he saw that it was hopeless. By then darkness had fallen over the battlefield, and he led his survivors to safety, angry and bitter that the gallantry of his men had gone for nothing.[22]

Several thousand Federals fell killed or wounded in this attack, compared with probably six hundred Confederates. Nothing had been achieved commensurate with the cost. Though portions of the XVIII Corps did capture an advanced line of Confederate rifle pits, the main line remained as strong and intact as ever. Still, partial successes here and there offered hope that a second, more powerful assault in the morning would break the enemy line for good. Accordingly, Grant gave orders for Hancock's II Corps to march down to Cold Harbor, link up with Wright and Smith, and renew the offensive at dawn.[23]

It had been a frustrating day at headquarters. Bad enough was the colossal staff blunder that sent the XVIII Corps on a wild goose chase up to New Castle Ferry, but it also appeared that Warren had completely failed to attack a Confederate column that had marched, in plain view, across his front toward Cold Harbor. Wright, for his part, was late in attacking, and then did so only after being reinforced by Smith's wayward corps. Assistant Secretary of War Charles Dana captured the mood in a 5 P.M. dispatch to Washington. Grant and Meade, he wrote, "are intensely disgusted with these failures of Wright and Warren. . . . Meade says a radical change must be made, no matter how unpleasant it may be to make it; but I doubt whether he will really attempt to apply so extreme a remedy."[24]

Word of the late afternoon attack improved the atmosphere, but not much. Although Wright optimistically reported that everything was going well and that his troops had taken many prisoners, he added that "a large [force] of the rebel army is in our front, and I think that you should send me re-enforcements to-night, if possible." Grant got wind of some of the particulars of the battle and concluded that "the attacks were . . . not followed up as they should have been." And Meade was just beside himself. Theodore Lyman heard him splutter about Warren and Wright, then unload upon Lt. Francis Farquhar, a staff officer who materialized from Smith's corps headquarters. Farquhar reported that General Smith had arrived and attacked as ordered, but had on hand little ammunition, no transportation, and considered his position precarious. "Then, why in Hell did he come at all for?" roared the exasperated army commander.[25]

Farquhar relayed Meade's outburst, verbatim, to Smith, which did nothing to calm Smith when late that night he received orders to renew the attack next morning, vigorously and with his entire force. "Your order for an attack in the morning is received," Smith crisply replied. "I have endeavored to represent to you my condition. In the present condition of my line an attack by me would be simply preposterous." He went on to explain that he lacked ammunition, that his line was too much extended, and that, if attacked, he would have a tough time simply holding his own. Smith's assessment had merit, particularly with regard to his critical ammunition shortage, but it is never a good idea to characterize the directives of one's superior as "preposterous." Smith's military career went into eclipse from that moment on.[26]

Meanwhile, Hancock's II Corps was making a forced night march, guided by a topographical engineer from Meade's headquarters, Capt. William A. Paine, whose original assignment had been to lead the corps to the Via House, near Bethesda Church. When Hancock received new orders, making Cold Harbor his destination, they included a revised route of march which, Paine believed, was needlessly long. He offered Hancock that brief, fatal phrase: I know a shortcut. Hancock, anxious to make all possible speed and having every reason to trust the judgment of a topographical engineer, told him to go ahead.

Paine took the lead division—infantry, artillery, and trains—down a country lane that, sure enough, would have shaved a couple of miles from the trip save for one thing: After a while it grew too narrow for the artillery teams and their caissons. Officers and cannoneers sweated and strained in the darkness, trying to find some way to use the lane, but it was impossible, and Hancock finally gave orders for the division to countermarch to the main road and use the route laid out by headquarters.[27]

Between the mistake and the confusion that attended its rectification, the II Corps lost hours in its march to reach Cold Harbor. The lead division arrived around 6:30 A.M., but its men were exhausted from their all-night trek, the rest of the corps was strewn out for miles behind it, and all in all it was obvious that for several hours Hancock's men would be in no condition to attack. Furthermore, Smith's corps was just beginning to receive its resupply of ammunition. Meade delayed the attack and at 1:30 P.M. issued a directive that it should take place at 5 P.M. A half hour later

Grant overruled him: "In view of the want of preparation for an attack this evening," he wrote, "and the heat and want of energy among the men from moving during the night last night, I think it advisable to postpone assault until early to-morrow morning. All changes of position already ordered should be completed to-day and a good night's rest given the men preparatory to an assault at, say, 4.30 in the morning." A circular went out, informing the corps commanders of the new schedule, and enjoining them to "employ the interim in making examination of the ground in their fronts, and perfecting their arrangements for the assault."[28]

In after years men would claim that a great opportunity was lost on June 2. But if so, it would be a mistake to pin the blame on hapless Captain Paine. Even if Hancock had clung to the route assigned him, it is unlikely that he could have reached Cold Harbor with his troops well closed and in shape to make the attack at daylight. And in any case, the XVIII Corps would still have been short on ammunition—a foreseeable consequence of its rapid transfer from Bermuda Hundred. The improvised, opportunistic nature of Grant's campaign was outrunning the ability of his army, or any army, to keep up.

A more realistic opportunity on June 2 existed on the opposite end of the line and for the Confederates. The Federals had shifted so much of their strength toward Cold Harbor that Lee reasoned they must have weakened their right in order to do so. Accordingly, he gave Jubal Early, who held the Confederate left, orders to "get upon the enemy's right flank and drive down in front of our line." That afternoon Early glimpsed his chance. Burnside's IX Corps, opposite his sector, was in the process of revising its line in order to cover the army's flank more effectively, while maintaining a solid connection with Warren's V Corps farther south. By that hour, most of A. P. Hill's Corps had departed to join the force at Cold Harbor, but Henry Heth's division remained, comprising the far left flank of the Army of Northern Virginia. Early went to Heth in person, telling him, as Heth recalled it, "that the enemy were retiring from our front, and that he proposed to attack, and asked me for a brigade to assist him." Heth staunchly replied that he would assist the attack not with a brigade but with his entire division. So it was agreed. Early went back to his corps and gave the order to advance.[29]

The battleground was familiar. Early's men were marching toward Bethesda Church, just as they had done two days previously, only this time the Federals were posted around the church rather than north of it and—more important—Early was rolling forward with four divisions. The attack took Burnside by surprise. The Confederates snapped up the better part of a 600-man picket detachment in the first moments of the attack, and in short order Early's corps had flanked two IX Corps brigades and bruised a V Corps division that Warren sent over to help. "It was a quick bold move," wrote E. Porter Alexander, "&, had there been more troops to give it force, it might have produced important results." Unfortunately for Early, he lacked numbers. The Union flank bent but did not break, and enough Northern artillery and infantry presently deployed to halt his drive for good.[30]

With the close of this second battle of Bethesda Church, Lee had lost his third bid in four days to wrest the initiative from Grant. True, Early had several hundred prisoners to show for his attack, but he had not achieved Lee's goal: a counterattack fierce and successful enough to get Grant's attention and make him react to Lee. That meant that Grant would continue to pursue his own program, which practically everyone on both sides could guess meant a renewed attack at Cold Harbor the next morning.

Lee made the Cold Harbor sector as strong as he could. Two of A. P. Hill's divisions went thither, as did Breckinridge's slim division down from the Shenandoah Valley. During the afternoon the enemy made a half-hearted stab to capture Turkey Hill, which rose up from the Chickahominy River bottoms and commanded the right flank of the Confederate line. Confederate troops were already supposed to occupy the hill but through an oversight had not. Lee sent two divisions under Breckinridge and Cadmus Wilcox to clear out the Federals from Hancock's corps who were working their way up the eastern slope. Around 6 P.M. they did so, in a brief, furious fire fight that cost both sides several hundred casualties. But with Turkey Hill in his possession, Lee knew he had a good, solid defensive line with which to face the coming assault.[31]

That is, he had a good general line. On some parts of the front—perhaps many—the exact line was not established until after dark, when troops could work in relative safety under cover of night. During the day Confederate commanders and engineers carefully surveyed the terrain immediately in front of their current positions, looking for ground with the best possible fields of fire. At nightfall they appeared in the existing trenches to organize the new lines. In one sector the process worked thusly: Engineers set a cord in the trenches, marked at intervals with white cloth. Picked men held the cord, and every hundred feet or so stood an engineer officer. A new line had previously been selected by estimation or triangulation, and at a signal the officers advanced a precise number of paces until the cord demarcated the revised position. Once on the new ground they made final adjustments, then working parties came up with picks and shovels and began to dig.[32]

The ravine that had given Clingman such trouble the previous day was now held by the brigade of Evander M. Law, one of the First Corps' most experienced officers. He took one look at the line he had inherited—bent back sharply at almost a right angle, in open ground and "ill-adapted to resist an attack"—and concluded that if the enemy attacked this point he would break through. Accordingly, Law decided the best solution was to construct a new line across the base of the angle, sacrificing a few yards to the enemy in exchange for a shorter line and a better field of fire. At nightfall he set forth with an armload of stakes and, assisted by staff officers, personally laid out the revised position.[33]

Scenes like that were repeated all along the Confederate line, as infantrymen and artillerists labored to create the deadliest killing fields they could devise. Six hundred to a thousand yards away, their Union counterparts knew intuitively what the rebels were doing and grasped all too clearly what was likely going to happen in the morning. Horace Porter of Grant's staff recalled a scene that was poignant or chilling, depending on one's point of view: "As I came near one of the regiments which was making preparations for the next morning's assault, I noticed that many of the soldiers had taken off their coats, and seemed to be engaged in sewing up rents in them. This exhibition of tailoring seemed rather peculiar at such a moment, but upon closer examination it was found that the men were calmly writing their names and home addresses on slips of paper, and pinning them on the backs of their coats, so that their dead bodies might be recognized upon the field, and their fate made known to their families at home."[34]

Most Federals shared the same fatalism. At Meade's headquarters, Theodore Lyman heard no great hopes for a successful assault: The enemy had enjoyed thirty-six full hours in which to perfect his defenses. "The whole army," recalled artillerist Frank Wilkeson, "seemed to be greatly depressed the night before the battle of Cold Harbor."[35]

Early that evening a steady rain began to fall. It continued most of the night, turning the ground to slop and exacerbating the misery of the soldiers. Toward morning it petered out, leaving behind a gray patchy fog that clung to low spots in the ground. Union infantry stood to in their sodden rifle pits while artillerists manned their guns. Orderlies took the horses of colonels and generals and led them to the rear: To be mounted on this or any other battlefield was suicidal, so the officers would go forward on foot. Punctually at 4:30 A.M. a courier rode up to the Tenth Massachusetts Battery on Hancock's front. Its right-hand gun fired a single round as a signal, and the attack was on.[36]

For ten minutes or so, the Union artillery hurled shot and shell at the Confederates, hidden among the raw earthworks in front. Then word came that the infantry was going forward, and the fire ceased so that the batteries would not hurt friendly troops. Smoke from the guns drifted off the field. The troops sprang up from the rifle pits and charged ahead. Instantly the slouch hats of rebel soldiers appeared on the works and the enemy line "glowed brightly with musketry" while canister from rebel cannon tore the Union ranks.[37]

What followed was the worst half hour the Army of the Potomac experienced in its four-year existence. Not only had the Confederates been given a day and a half to improve their positions, but the Union line bulged slightly outward, in the direction of the enemy trenchline, so that the II, VI, and XVIII Corps actually diverged as they advanced and were, therefore, exposed to cross fires from the concave rebel lines. Even worse, the high command made no effort to coordinate the attack. Meade simply established a common time when everyone was to go forward. Such a plan, fumed Baldy Smith, "is denounced by the standard writers on the art of war, and belongs to the first period in history after man had ceased to fight in unorganized masses. Giving up the few advantages belonging to the assailants, it increases largely the chances of successful defense, and would never be adopted by a trained general." Nor did the corps commanders do much better. Hancock apparently did not coordinate his attack with Wright, while Wright, approached by Smith concerning his own plan, responded simply that he would "pitch in" to the Confederates at the appointed hour. Unable to interest Wright in a coordinated assault, Smith accepted the reality that he must simply attack directly ahead.[38]

Hancock went forward at 4:40 A.M. He had two divisions in the assault: Francis Barlow on the left, John Gibbon on the right, each attacking on a two-brigade front with two brigades following in immediate support. Hancock's third division, under David Birney, stayed back in reserve. Barlow struck the slim Confederate division of John C. Breckinridge south of the Gaines's Mill Road, whose entrenchments were near the crest of an extensive ridge. By sheer happenstance his two lead brigades— Nelson Miles and John C. Brooke—hit a portion of the line not manned in strength. The overnight rain had turned the trenches in this sector into rivers of mud, causing George M. Edgar, colonel of the Twenty-sixth Virginia Battalion, to take misplaced pity on his men and permit everyone except a strong picket line to leave the trenches and sleep uphill, where the drainage was better. Miles and Brooke's brigades found this hole and, in a brief, savage clash with clubbed muskets and bayonets, overwhelmed its few defenders. Moments later they plunged onward and opened fire on the massed Confederates they found around them, most of them just emerging from bedrolls. Some were shot while still beneath blankets. Colonel Edgar, rushing his troops back toward their trenches in an attempt to retrieve the disaster, was soon shot dead. Miles's troops seized 125 prisoners, many from Edgar's battalion—who at least had a few hours' sleep to sustain them when they were marched off into captivity. Brooke's brigade took 300 more. The Federals also captured eight artillery pieces, which they spun around toward the Confederates and attempted to reload.[39]

Like the charge at the Mule Shoe three weeks previously, Barlow had achieved a stunning initial success, and was just as unable to capitalize upon it. Gibbon's division did not come up on his right. Delayed by a brigade commander who, incredibly, failed even to awaken his men, much less deploy them, Gibbon was a full fifteen minutes behind Barlow in reaching the Confederate works. Barlow had two brigades coming up in direct support, but the enemy, fully aroused by now, was pouring rifle and artillery fire into them more furiously, said one veteran, than he had ever witnessed before. "It had the fury of the Wilderness musketry and with the thunders of the Gettysburg artillery super-added," he wrote. "It was simply terrific."[40]

The Confederates now did as they nearly always did in such situations: They counterattacked without regard for the enemy's strength or their own. The sight of a gray battle line pounding up froze the Northerners in their tracks. The fear was particularly acute among Brooke's leftmost regiment, the sizable but inexperienced Seventh New York Heavy Artillery. "What was to be done?" asked one of its members. "We had lost all semblance of organization—a veritable mob with no means to turn the captured guns upon the enemy. In this dilemma, each man decided that question for himself. Green soldiers though we were, our short experience had taught us to know just when to run, and run we did, I assure you." First to fall upon Barlow's men was the Second Maryland, which recovered the guns and shoved the Yankees back down the slope.

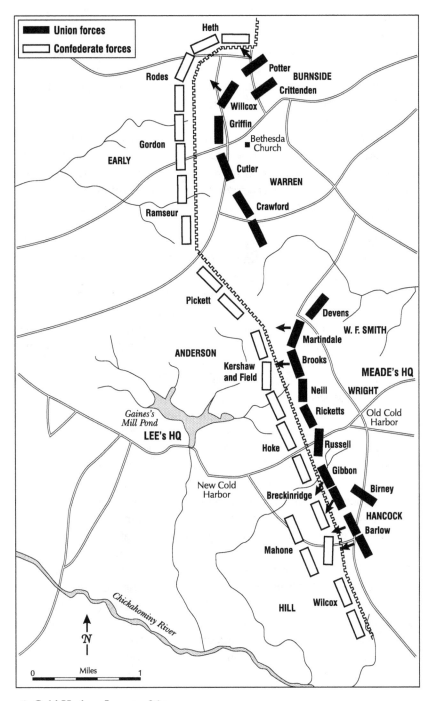

Legend:
- ■ Union forces
- □ Confederate forces

Heth

Rodes

Potter

BURNSIDE

Crittenden

Willcox

Griffin

Bethesda Church

Gordon

EARLY

Cutler

WARREN

Crawford

Ramseur

Pickett

Devens

W. F. SMITH

Martindale

ANDERSON

Brooks

MEADE's HQ

Kershaw and Field

Neill

WRIGHT

Gaines's Mill Pond

Ricketts

Old Cold Harbor

LEE's HQ

Hoke

Russell

New Cold Harbor

Gibbon

Birney

Breckinridge

HANCOCK

Barlow

Mahone

Chickahominy River

HILL

Wilcox

N

0   Miles   1

16. Cold Harbor, June 3, 1864

Moments later, a small Florida brigade came up and sealed the breach permanently.[41]

Fifty yards below the rebel entrenchments, Barlow's men found a patch of dead ground that gave them some cover from enemy fire. Unable to move up, unwilling to retreat, they just hung on, gouging the dirt with tin cups, bayonets, anything, to carve out shallow rifle pits. Their organization, already thrown into disarray by the swift advance, breach of the enemy line, and repulse, was further frayed when one of the brigade commanders, Brooke, was badly wounded by canister and the officer who replaced him was killed almost immediately. Worse, only one of Barlow's two follow-up brigades ever arrived in support. Through some mix-up, the other remained immobile. The reserve division, Birney, did not come up, either.[42]

Gibbon's men did come up, but never made it to the rebel earthworks. Instead, the lead brigades found their line of advance barred by a swamp whose existence no one had known. One brigade skirted it to the right, the other to the left, and they charged onward, taking heavy losses, especially among officers, as they scrambled up the ridge. Most of the troops never got within fifty to a hundred yards of the ridge. One colonel was spotted briefly on the parapet of the Confederate works, but fell almost instantly. (So many bullets riddled his corpse that when his brother came to retrieve the body, three days hence, he was identifiable only by the distinctive buttons on his sleeve.) All in all, Hancock's corps suffered nearly three thousand casualties in less than an hour. A rueful private in Gibbon's division summed things up: "We felt it was murder, not war."[43]

Wright's VI Corps, immediately to the north of Hancock, never got seriously under way. It, too, had two divisions in the lead attack, under David Russell and James Ricketts, but Wright was highly conscious that his outfit occupied the center of the convex Union line and was thus most exposed to Confederate cross fires. An advance immediately at 4:30 A.M. would have exposed the flanks of his forces in the attack; consequently, Russell, on the left, decided to stand fast until Gibbon's division arrived on line with his own and could afford some protection from enfilading fire. The sight of Gibbon's men being cut to ribbons, however, led him quickly to suspend his attack, and at least one of Russell's brigades, that of Emory Upton, never entered the fight at all. On the right, Ricketts did advance but got nowhere. "We never even reached the enemy's works. We advanced under a murderous fire in our front from the enemy's artillery, sharpshooters[,] and when in range of its main line of battle . . .

were simply slaughtered." Paradoxically, the heavy enemy fire may have actually saved the VI Corps from severe losses, by quickly convincing its leadership to suspend the assault.[44]

North of the Gaines's Mill Road, the XVIII Corps jumped off promptly at 4:30 A.M. Like its sister corps, it also had two divisions—under Martindale and Brooks—in the lead assault, but unlike them it had no reserve to exploit success: The third division, Devens's, was strung out trying to hold the corps' extended front. Even then, fully two miles separated the XVIII Corps from Warren's V Corps, its neighbor on the right.

The dearth of a reserve proved academic, however, since the corps achieved no success, though not for lack of trying. Smith had identified two ravines on his front that offered at least partial protection from enemy fire, and he tried to funnel his troops in their direction. Martindale's division, on the right, went in first. Like Upton in his charge on May 10, the troops advanced with fixed bayonets and uncapped muskets to discourage impromptu firing before they reached the enemy works. But despite these tactics and the effort to use terrain to advantage, nothing whatever could prevent them from taking a frightful pounding at the hands of the defenders. Brooks's division, on the left, was so badly exposed to enfilading fire that Smith ordered him to suspend his attack pending assistance from the VI Corps. The carnage in Martindale's division, which continued its assault, was horrifying. A captain in the Twelfth New Hampshire wrote: "To give a description of this terrible charge is simply impossible, and few who were in the ranks of the 12th will ever feel like attempting it. To those exposed to the full force and fury of that dreadful storm of lead and iron that met the charging column, it seemed more like a volcanic eruption than a battle, and was just about as destructive. . . . The men went down in rows, just as they had marched in the ranks, and so many at a time that many in the rear thought they were lying down." To a Massachusetts man in reserve, the division in front of him "seemed to melt away like snow falling on moist ground."[45]

Like Hancock's men, Smith's did not retreat to their starting point when the charge failed, but rather halted where they could find cover and began to dig in. A staff officer regarded this as evidence of the troops' "staunchness." Just as likely, it reflected their realization that the path to the rear was just as drenched in fire and just as deadly as the way forward.[46]

Farther to the right, Warren and Burnside kicked off their own attack around 6 A.M., ninety minutes after Meade's stipulated time, though it made no difference: No Confederate forces redeployed during the interim, or needed to. Burnside, on the army's extreme right, made the principal assault, supported by two brigades from Warren's corps—Warren felt his line too attenuated to attack with more. Burnside succeeded in driving in the pickets on Lee's left flank, but concluded he could not assail the main line without bringing up artillery, and suspended the assault until that could be done.[47]

Meade spent the early hours of the attack at Wright's headquarters in a farmhouse northeast of Old Cold Harbor. The first word he got of the assault came from Hancock and announced Barlow's breaching of the rebel line. Though within minutes this was followed by news that Barlow had been forced to fall back, that initial report gave Meade a picture of the battle that dominated his thinking for several hours. Barlow's success, while temporary, demonstrated the basic soundness of the concept behind the attack. The Confederate line *was* stretched, it did have weak points, and a determined general assault would surely find them. Consequently, when Hancock at 6 A.M. reported the stalled condition of his corps and opined guardedly "that if the first dash in an assault fails, other attempts are not apt to succeed better," Meade responded that he was to continue the attack and support it well, so that any advantage gained could be held. A Captain Cadwallader from Wright's staff indicated "some progress," and though at first Meade heard nothing directly from Smith, he too seemed to be advancing. At 7 A.M. Meade relayed the situation to Grant, concluding his dispatch with a question: If these attacks do not at first succeed, should they be continued? Grant replied with advice that, in effect, left the issue in Meade's hands: "The moment it becomes certain that an assault cannot succeed, suspend the offensive," wrote the general in chief, "but when one does succeed push it vigorously, and if necessary pile in troops at the successful point from wherever they can be taken."[48]

Meade decided to keep pressing the attack. To a message from Hancock that implied the II Corps commander thought otherwise, he replied, "No orders have been sent you suspending or rescinding the original order to attack. . . . I desire every effort be made to carry the enemy's works. Of course if this is deemed impracticable, after trial, the attack should be suspended, but the responsibility for this must be on your judgment. I cannot give more decided orders. Report promptly."[49]

That dispatch was date-stamped 7:40 A.M. Within the hour Meade's chief of staff, Andrew Humphreys, got a telegram from Wright complaining that "the major-general commanding has entirely misapprehended my message by Captain Cadwallader." The VI Corps, he explained, was ahead of its neighbors on either side. He thought he could carry the enemy's main line opposite his center, but he could not properly support the assault without help on his flanks, particularly from the XVIII Corps. Seizing upon Wright's belief that he could carry the rebel position, Meade and his staff urged all three corps commanders to renew their attacks. At 8 A.M. Humphreys wrote Smith: "General Wright has been ordered to assault at once and to continue his attack without reference to your advance, and the commanding general directs that your assault be continued without reference to General Wright's: General Wright had but a very short time before the receipt of your communication, through Major West, reported that he was waiting for your advance to enable him to assault." Perhaps thirty minutes later Meade received word from Hancock that he considered the assault failed "long since," but indicated a willingness to attack again if other corps on the right gained any success. Meade shot back that Wright "thinks he can carry the enemy's main line if he is relieved by attacks of the Second and Eighteenth Corps. . . . It is of the greatest importance no effort should be spared to succeed. Wright and Smith are both going to try again, and unless you consider it hopeless I would like you to do the same."[50]

Hancock replied, more or less, that he did consider it hopeless. "An assault can be promptly repeated if desired," he wrote, "but division commanders do not speak encouragingly of the prospect of success since the original attacks failed. Unless success has been gained in other points, I do not advise persistence here." In short, if Meade ordered him to attack, he would do so. Otherwise, he would use the discretion Meade had given him and decline.[51]

The orders that Wright and Smith received bestowed no such discretion. The situation was just as bleak on their fronts as Hancock's, but unlike Hancock they would have to renew the attack. Smith flatly refused. Wright evidently conveyed the order to his divisions, but allowed them to "attack" merely by stepping up the fire from their current positions. No one went forward.[52]

After the battle, a story spread that the Army of the Potomac refused direct orders to assault the Confederate works. "To move that army farther, except by regular approaches, was a simple and absolute impossibility, known to be such by every officer and man of the three corps engaged," reported Wright's chief of staff. An officer in the XVIII Corps declared that he would not lead another attack if Jesus Christ himself should order it. And William Swinton, a war correspondent who accompanied the army, wrote in 1866, "Some hours after the failure of the first assault, General Meade sent instructions to each corps commander to renew the attack without reference to the troops on his right or left. The order was issued through these officers to their subordinate commanders, and from them descended through the wonted channels; but no man stirred; and the immobile lines pronounced a verdict, silent, yet emphatic, against further slaughter."[53]

Some troops undoubtedly believed they *were* disobeying an order to attack. But if the episode was a mutiny, as some have suggested, then it was a mutiny in which practically everyone participated save Meade. Even Grant seemed to grasp the situation. A bit later in the morning one of his staff officers, Colonel Comstock, came snooping around on Smith's front. He went down the line, observing the troops and the enemy's position, then pronounced himself satisfied and went away. At 11 A.M. Grant mounted his horse and, if Horace Porter can be believed, during the next ninety minutes collected the views, directly or through his staff, of every corps commander from Hancock on the left to Burnside on the right. "Hancock now reported that the position in his front could not be taken," Porter recalled. "Wright said that a lodgment might be made in his front, but that nothing would be gained by it unless Hancock and Smith were to advance at the same time. Smith thought that he might be able to carry the works before him, but was not sanguine. Burnside believed that he could break the enemy's line in his front, but Warren on his left did not agree in this opinion." Convinced that further attacks would be futile, at 12:30 P.M. Grant wrote Meade: "The opinion of corps commanders not being sanguine of success in case an assault is ordered, you may direct a suspension of farther advance for the present."[54]

For all practical purposes, that ended the third and final battle of Cold Harbor. An hour later a circular went out from Meade's headquarters, announcing the suspension of all further offensive operations, telling the corps commanders to entrench the positions they currently held, and asking them to investigate the prospects for breaching the enemy line "by regular approaches"—that is, by siege. At 2 P.M. Grant summed things up in his daily communiqué to Halleck: "We assaulted at 4.30 o'clock this morning, driving the enemy within his intrenchments at all points, but without gaining any decisive advantage. Our troops now occupy a position close to the enemy, some places within 50 yards, and are intrenching. Our loss was not severe, nor do I suppose the enemy to have lost heavily. We captured over 300 prisoners, mostly from Breckinridge's command."[55]

The Union loss was indeed severe, as Grant would soon discover and perhaps already knew. In later years a myth would circulate that the Army of the Potomac "lost ten thousand [killed, wounded, and missing] in twenty minutes"—a factoid sometimes modified to seven thousand men in half an hour. The figures are wrong, though not by much. An exact number cannot be determined because the Army of the Potomac only recorded casualties for the entire period it spent at Cold Harbor—June 1 through 15. Most estimates agree that the army lost seven thousand men on June 3, the majority of these in the first hour of the attack.[56]

The Army of Northern Virginia, by contrast, suffered fewer than fifteen hundred casualties in all, and of these, up to two-thirds occurred on the Confederate left, opposite Burnside. Scarcely five hundred men were killed or wounded in the sectors where the main Federal assault occurred. Indeed, Southern memories of the battle are of a contest almost grotesquely lopsided. A man in the Fourth Alabama recalled: "Our artillery . . . was cutting wide swaths through their lines. . . . Heads, arms, legs, and muskets were seen flying through the air at every discharge." Blazing away at Martindale's division, the men in Law's brigade were "in fine spirits, laughing and talking as they fired." Elsewhere some troops loaded muskets for others to keep up the fastest, most lethal fire. "I could see the dust fog out of a man's clothing in two or three places at once where as many balls would strike him at the same moment," said a Confederate officer. "In two minutes not a man of them was standing." Another wrote that the enemy dead lay heaped "like hogs in a pen."[57]

At his headquarters near Gaines's Mill, Lee got the first news of the battle about ninety minutes after it began. A. P. Hill simply showed a courier the blue-coated bodies lying atop one another and said, "Tell General Lee it is the same all along my front." Robert Hoke sent word that the dead and wounded literally covered the ground and he had not yet lost a man killed.[58]

Around 11 A.M. a delegation from Richmond showed up, headed by John H. Reagan, the Confederacy's postmaster general. The battle was still in progress to the east. Trying to sound knowing, Reagan remarked that the artillery fire seemed heavier than usual. True enough, Lee replied, but it didn't matter much. He waved his hand to indicate the ceaseless musketry that sounded to Reagan like the tearing of some gigantic sheet. "It is that," Lee explained, "that kills men."

"General," Reagan inquired, "if the enemy breaks your line, what reserve have you?" This was a sore subject with the commander, and he became animated. "Not a regiment," he responded, exaggerating only slightly, "and that has been my condition ever since the fighting commenced on the Rappahannock. If I shorten my lines to provide a reserve, he will turn me; if I weaken my lines to provide a reserve, he will break them."[59]

By the same logic, having just won what would prove his last great victory in the field, Lee had no ability to launch a counterstroke, though Meade warned his corps commanders to prepare for such a contingency. The extended front, slim Confederate numbers, and the enemy's own formidable defensive powers prevented it, although Union reports assert that during the afternoon and evening, Confederate forces launched local attacks, vainly trying to dislodge the Yankees from their advanced positions.[60]

So the two armies settled down, improved their earthworks, and let evening come. The Union wounded lay between the lines in agony. When possible their comrades would try to recover them. In other instances they crawled to the rebel lines, gave themselves up as prisoners, and in exchange got medical attention. And by some outraged reports the rebels picked off anyone who moved.[61]

For three days the wounded lay between the lines. Neither side asked for a truce until June 5, when Grant suggested in a letter to Lee that "when no battle is raging either party be authorized to send to any point between the pickets or skirmish lines, unarmed men bearing litters to pick up their dead or wounded without being fired upon by the other party." Lee objected. Such an arrangement, he observed, would lead to confusion. Better to handle matters through a regular flag of truce. Next day Grant responded by saying that he would order unarmed men bearing litters to go between the lines carrying white flags. Lee objected that such an arrangement was not the same as a regular flag of truce. Meanwhile, the lives of the wounded ebbed away, and the stench of the dead grew suffocating. Things went back and forth in this way until the evening of June 7, when the two commanders finally reached agreement. It was a sorry episode in both men's careers.[62]

By June 7—more than four days after the last major Union attack— nearly all the wounded had been smuggled to safety by comrades or, more usually, had perished. "Every corpse I saw was as black as coal," wrote one Federal. "It was not possible to remove them. They were buried where they fell. . . . I saw no live man lying on this ground. The wounded must have suffered horribly before death relieved them, lying there exposed to the blazing southern sun o' days, and being eaten alive by beetles o' nights."[63]

CHAPTER EIGHT

The Campaign's Significance

With the truce, the Overland campaign came to a close. The debacle at Cold Harbor ended Grant's last opportunity to defeat Lee in the field, his avowed objective from the time the Potomac Army crossed the Rapidan. The Army of the Potomac had run out of room in which to maneuver. Its offensive, begun a month previously, now reached uneasy equilibrium in the sandy trenches and rifle pits between Totopotomoy Creek and the Chickahominy River. Grant therefore made plans to abandon the overland route in favor of a shift south of the James River against the railroads connecting Richmond with the Deep South. It was a different concept than the one underlying the campaign just ended. The Overland campaign had been intended to destroy Lee's army in the open field. The new offensive, presently dubbed the Petersburg campaign, would do so by choking off the lifeblood of supplies on which the Army of Northern Virginia depended.

Such an operation had been in the back of Grant's mind since before the campaign began, but mainly as a fallback option in the event he was unable to defeat Lee north of Richmond. That scenario had now become reality. The rebels were fighting on the defensive so persistently that a battle in the open was impossible, and, as he confessed to Halleck on June 5, it would require "a greater sacrifice of human life than I am willing to make" to persist in trying to break up Lee's army through direct assault (assuming it could be done at all).

Since the new campaign would require time to organize, Grant would hold the Army of the Potomac in its cheerless Cold Harbor entrenchments long enough to pin Lee while other expeditions began the isolation of his army by destroying Richmond's supply lines north and west of the city.

Sheridan's cavalry would dismantle the Virginia Central Railroad, then link up at Charlottesville with a column under Maj. Gen. David Hunter, who had relieved the luckless Sigel and was now marching southward up the Shenandoah Valley. After these operations were completed, he informed Halleck, "I will move the army to the south side of James River. . . . Once [there] I can cut off all sources of supply to the enemy, except what is furnished by the [James River] canal." The canal passed through Lynchburg, an important railroad and logistics center 150 miles west of Richmond. The city was Hunter's ultimate objective. If he reached it, the canal would be cut as well.[1]

But to Grant's chagrin, neither Hunter's nor Sheridan's expeditions came to much. Lee's cavalry under Wade Hampton stopped Sheridan at Trevilian's Station, a few miles short of Charlottesville. Hunter got nowhere near that town, but instead continued his march west of the Blue Ridge Mountains instead of turning east as Grant expected. As a result, although Hunter defeated a scratch Confederate force at Piedmont on June 6 and soon inflicted severe damage on the Virginia Military Institute at Lexington, he forfeited his chance to wreck the Orange and Alexandria Railroad between Charlottesville and Lynchburg. Nor did he capture Lynchburg. Instead, on the evening of June 10, Lee detached the Second Corps under Jubal Early and transferred it to that town by rail. A week later it skirmished with Hunter and drove him into West Virginia, thereby opening a path for an exciting raid down the Shenandoah Valley into Maryland. The foray mortified the Lincoln administration, briefly threatened Washington, and forced the recall of the entire Union VI Corps.[2]

By that time, Grant had the Army of the Potomac across the James River by way of the longest pontoon bridge in American military history. In so doing he stole a march on Lee but proved unable to capture Petersburg before Lee's army arrived in force to defend it. As a result, a new belt of earthworks went up, dwarfing anything the Overland campaign had seen, and both armies settled in for what would become a ten-month siege. For most of that period, Lee's army stubbornly kept open at least one of the railroads linking Petersburg with the Deep South. Only on April 2, 1865, a bare week before Appomattox, would the siege finally end.[3]

Inevitably, the lengthy deadlock at Petersburg colored perceptions of the Overland campaign. Had Grant's crossing of the James resulted in the town's seizure (as might well have occurred), the Overland campaign would appear the tenacious prelude to a brilliant final act. But the Petersburg stalemate made the campaign seem a failure. Even so, Northern disappointment might have been mild but for the campaign's horrendous casualties. From May 4 through June 12, the day Grant crossed the James River, the Army of the Potomac (and IX Corps) lost about fifty-five thousand men killed, wounded, or captured—to say nothing of the subsidiary offensives, which probably lengthened the casualty list by ten thousand. So much broken humanity—and for what? Morale plummeted on the Northern home front. Grant, many snarled, was nothing but a butcher. The price of gold nearly doubled, and by late August Lincoln was thinking seriously about what he would do if he lost the November election.[4]

Fortunately for Lincoln's administration and Grant's place in history, by the end of summer Northern hopes revived. A naval victory at Mobile Bay on August 5, and especially Sherman's capture of Atlanta on September 2, served notice that the Union would eventually prevail. Additional victories followed, ensuring Lincoln's reelection and extinguishing the South's bid for independence. In the afterglow of final Union triumph, it became possible to see the Virginia campaign of 1864 in a more favorable light. What seemed like a defeat—or at best a standoff—could now be read as a bold step on the road to victory. Yet no firm consensus on the campaign emerged. Then and now, it remains controversial.

Those who have defended Grant's generalship based their case on four arguments. First, they have maintained, he was the first Union commander to deprive Lee of the initiative: As soon as Grant took the field, Lee danced to Grant's tune, not the reverse. Second, Grant's relentless pressure put a breaking strain on Lee's army and laid the groundwork for its ultimate surrender. Third, while Grant lost fifty-five thousand men in a one-month campaign, that was no more than Lee lost in proportion to the size of his army—and Lee could not make good his losses. More imaginative defenders have argued that Grant lost far fewer men to gain a winning position than previous commanders in the East—McClellan, Burnside, Hooker, and Meade—squandered in a fruitless succession of campaigns.[5]

Finally, the defenders asserted, Grant's strategy must be seen in its widest context. He had to pin his Confederate adversary to prevent Lee from sending reinforcements to aid Joe Johnston against Sherman. He also had to shield Washington, which ruled out an immediate seaborne movement to the south side of the James River. And he had to maintain a pressure on Lee persistent enough that it would not adversely affect Lincoln's chance for reelection. Grant accomplished all these goals, thereby helping to ensure that Sherman took Atlanta and that Lincoln got a second term. Furthermore, he had planned all along for the possibility that he might have to defeat Lee through a siegelike attritional struggle. That, maintained his proponents, showed uncommon foresight.

Grant's detractors conceded some of these points. Yes, he deprived Lee of the initiative, placed a breaking strain on Lee's army, and ultimately pinned Lee to the Richmond-Petersburg trenches. But to them Grant's strategy has seemed, at best, unimaginative and, at worst, a waste of Northern flesh and bone. Writing in 1884, John C. Ropes, a gifted amateur historian of the conflict, caustically pronounced the Overland campaign a failure: "With any resources less than those of the United States, the campaign, as Grant conducted it, must have come to a dead halt." He continued bitterly: "It was so wasteful, so thoughtless of men's lives, that it required large reinforcements, an adversary numerically much weaker, and very patient and much-enduring soldiers."[6]

Southerners agreed. In the words of artillerist E. Porter Alexander, Grant "was no intellectual genius, but he understood arithmetic. . . . [He] knew that if one hundred thousand men couldn't [defeat Lee] two hundred thousand might, & that three hundred thousand would make quite sure to do it. That was the game which he deliberately set out to play." Or as Jefferson Davis tartly put it in his memoirs, Grant could afford a policy of attrition—he could replace his losses while the Confederacy could not. However: "To those who can approve the policy of attrition without reference to the number of lives it might cost, this may seem justifiable, but it can hardly be regarded as generalship."[7]

This interpretation continues to have adherents. Clifford Dowdey, writing in 1960 on Grant's situation after reaching Petersburg, commented icily: "Grant's total losses exceeded the number of men . . . with which Lee began the campaign. . . . Grant had eviscerated the army he inherited. The flower of the Army of the Potomac was gone." Military historian Bevin Alexander went so far as to claim that Grant's tactics in the Overland campaign "came close to losing the war."[8]

By contrast, most scholars have concurred that Lee's handling of the Overland campaign was a defensive masterpiece. Some have held it up as an example of the course Lee should have followed all along: a life-husbanding strategy of fighting behind fieldworks and making limited counterattacks, in contradistinction to the go-for-broke ripostes of Chancellorsville or the full-scale offensives of the Maryland and Gettysburg campaigns. But if so, it was a defensive masterpiece by default, for during the Overland campaign Lee constantly itched for a chance to unleash on Grant the same trademark counterattack he had administered to McClellan, Pope, and Hooker. He came close to his goal on May 6, when Longstreet arrived on the Orange Plank Road and rolled up Hancock's line "like a wet blanket." But critics have noted that because of a faulty precampaign deployment, Longstreet's two divisions nearly reached the field too late. Had their arrival been delayed by an hour, or had Burnside come up in support of Hancock as planned, Lee probably would have met with a clear defeat in the Wilderness.

As it was, the Wilderness ended in tactical stalemate with Grant still in possession of the initiative, something none of Lee's previous adversaries retained after the first major clash of arms. Lee spent the rest of the campaign furiously trying to wrest it away from Grant. His efforts, though unsuccessful, were costly. A recent reappraisal of his losses during the campaign suggests that the Army of Northern Virginia lost 11,125 casualties in the Wilderness, 12,451 at Spotsylvania, and 1,550 along the North Anna River. As a result, by the time significant openings for a counterthrust presented themselves, particularly at Bethesda Church on May 30 and June 2, the army lacked sufficient strength to capitalize upon them. All in all, the Army of Northern Virginia lost almost thirty-three thousand killed, wounded, and missing during the Overland campaign, a ratio of loss to original strength as severe as that in the Army of the Potomac. The best that can be said of Lee's performance in the Overland campaign is that he evaded Grant's attempt to destroy him between the Rapidan and the James. In all other respects he fell short of both his own expectations and the objective requirements for success.[9]

However one assesses their performance, the success or failure of the Virginia campaign did not rest on the shoulders of Grant and Lee alone. Their chief subordinates also played a vital role, and in this respect Grant was often poorly served. The subsidiary offensives in western Virginia, for example, came to little. William W. Averell retreated without inflicting significant damage on the Confederate salt and lead mines in southwestern Virginia. George Crook destroyed Dublin Depot and the Virginia and Tennessee railroad bridge across the New River, then tamely withdrew, thereby easing pressure on the Confederates in that region. Franz Sigel, for his part, was completely out of his depth. No reason save sheer incompetence can account for his defeat at New Market. David

Hunter's subsequent advance showed the ease with which Confederate opposition in the Valley could be swept aside (though Hunter presently committed some foolish blunders of his own).

Ben Butler's failed Bermuda Hundred campaign is often placed in the same category with Sigel's New Market debacle, though with less justice. The fact is, Butler had a more difficult assignment than Sigel and performed it better than is usually conceded. Grant's written instructions called for Butler to seize City Point, then advance toward Richmond, "holding close to the south bank of the James River as you advance." Executing these orders required Butler to place his army squarely between the Richmond garrison and the substantial Confederate forces arriving from the Carolinas, giving him two threats to worry about, from opposite directions. The arrangement would have been awkward for even a seasoned combat general. In retrospect, an advance by way of the north bank of the James would have been more prudent, but Grant's directive ruled this out.[10]

Nevertheless, until mid-May Butler pinned down practically all the reinforcements earmarked for the Army of Northern Virginia, by which time Grant, according to his original timetable, was supposed to have beaten Lee or shoved him into the Richmond entrenchments. Even after the Drewry's Bluff defeat, the Army of the James distracted thousands of enemy troops. More important, he complicated the Confederate military problem by maintaining a standing threat against the Richmond-Petersburg chokepoint.[11]

A second criticism leveled at the Bermuda Hundred operation was the awkward command arrangement whereby professionals like Maj. Gens. W. F. Smith and Quincy Gillmore were to supply Butler with sound tactical advice to offset his inexperience. A better alternative (as Barnard and Meigs recommended after their inspection tour on May 23–24) would have been to retain Butler in administrative charge of the Department of Virginia and North Carolina while placing Smith in command of its field forces. But this commonsense solution overlooked two points: Butler specifically wanted to handle troops in combat, an ambition the Lincoln administration could not afford to thwart; and Smith was temperamentally unsuited to play second fiddle to anyone, particularly an amateur general like Butler. Grant would ultimately solve the problem by stripping Smith's XVIII Corps away from Butler and sending it off to operate with the Army of the Potomac. Unfortunately, this was done so hastily that, as we have seen, the corps was in effect mislaid by Grant's staff and arrived at Cold Harbor exhausted and short on ammunition. As a result, the corps played an indecisive role at Cold Harbor while the remaining troops at Bermuda Hundred were placed firmly on the defensive, so that they no longer posed a threat to the Richmond-Petersburg sector.[12]

Perhaps even more awkward than the command arrangement between Butler, Smith, and Gillmore was the one between Grant and Meade. After the war, division commander John Gibbon argued that with the best will in the world, Grant's over-the-shoulder observation of Meade left him "shackled and sensible of the fact that he [was] deprived of that independence and untrammeled authority so necessary to every army commander." Better a single poor commander, Gibbon continued, than two good ones. A recent student of the Cold Harbor campaign endorsed this view, asserting that Grant lacked sufficient knowledge of the Potomac Army to give it specific orders, while "Meade did not feel deep personal responsibility for managing operations that Grant had broadly planned."[13]

Hardly. It is true that some of Meade's letters home to his wife betray understandable irritation at the way in which Grant's presence with the army overshadowed him. But it goes too far to judge a man by what he writes to loved ones in unguarded moments. Better to look at what Grant thought of Meade's performance. Seen in this light, Meade comes off rather well. On May 13 Grant recommended him (together with Sherman) for promotion to major general in the regular army. "General Meade," he wrote, "has more than met my most sanguine expectations. He and Sherman are the fittest officers for large commands I have come in contact with." When some of his staff suggested that Meade occupied an "anomalous position" and that it wasted time to issue orders through him instead of directly to corps commanders, Grant neatly deflected their arguments. As commander of all the Union armies, he could not afford to get drawn into the day-to-day direction of a single field command. Nor could he afford lightly to dismiss a general who had served a long time with the Army of the Potomac, knew its subordinate officers thoroughly, and at Gettysburg had won the army's only victory over Lee. Besides, "General Meade and I are in close contact on the field [indeed, they usually made their headquarters next to each other]; he is capable and perfectly subordinate, and by attending to details he relieves me of much unnecessary work, and gives me more time to think and mature my general plans. I will always see that he gets full credit for what he does."[14]

Whether Grant actually saw to it that Meade got full credit for his efforts is debatable (Meade was not even present at the Appomattox surrender negotiations), but the two commanders worked smoothly together. Late in May the captain in charge of Meade's cavalry escort wrote that Grant "has made no parade of his authority, he has given no orders except through Meade, and Meade he treats with utmost confidence and deference. The result is that even from the most jealously disposed and most indiscreet of Meade's staff, not a word is heard against Grant." Meade himself testified in a letter to his wife concerning a visit from two U.S. senators on May 18: "Both were very complimentary, and wished me to know in Washington that it was well understood that these were my battles. I told him that such was not the case; that at first I had maneuvered the army, but that gradually, and from the nature of things, Grant had taken the control; and that it would be injurious for the army to have two heads." Amusement rather than rancor infused Meade's next comment: "I see one of the newspaper men is puzzled to know what share we each have in the work, and settles it by saying Grant does the grand strategy, and I the grand tactics. Coppée in his *Army Magazine* says, 'the Army of the Potomac, directed by Grant, commanded by Meade, and led by Hancock, Sedgwick and Warren,' which is a quite good distinction, and about hits the nail on the head."[15]

The real problem in the Potomac Army's command structure lay not in the personal relationship between Grant and Meade but in their contrasting command styles. By temperament and experience, Grant possessed a *coping* style of generalship, that is, a style aimed at shaping any outcome toward a desired objective. The classic example of this was the turn south after the Wilderness, a battle which, as historians have rightly pointed out, was as bad a setback for Union arms as the battle of Chancellorsville. Generally speaking, a coping style is the best form of generalship: It displays less fear of improvisation, encourages a faster reaction time, and displays a keener sense of the nonlinear nature of war, whereby small events can produce large results, in much the way that a small dusting of snow can trigger an avalanche.[16]

Meade's essential command philosophy was based on the assumption that good generalship consists in *control*—to use resources and to manipulate variables so as to guarantee success. Since in war that is impossible, almost by definition—the enemy will systematically seek to undermine one's effort at achieving control—the next best thing is to avoid losing. This mentality was squarely in the McClellan tradition that shaped not only Meade but, with the exception of Horatio Wright, each of his infantry corps commanders. Grant perceived the grip of this tradition on the army but underestimated its strength. He thought that, simply by guiding Meade, he could force the army to adapt to his style. It is often said that Grant de facto commanded the Army of the Potomac. But it was Meade, not Grant, who remained the principal influence on the army's organizational culture. And Meade perpetuated the emphasis on control. He never caught Grant's vision. Though he obeyed Grant's orders like a good soldier, he was never a true partner in the way that Sherman had been in the West or that Sheridan would increasingly become in the East.

Meade's instincts were reflected in his infantry corps commanders, whose principal hallmark was a cautious, half-defensive mind-set that harmonized poorly with the demands of a campaign aimed at the destruction of Lee's army. In most cases this was accompanied by sheer mediocrity. Burnside is the preeminent example, but even "Uncle John" Sedgwick, though beloved by the troops and respected by his fellow officers, turned in a weak performance in the Wilderness and at Laurel Hill. His successor, Horatio G. Wright, spent most of the campaign simply learning to handle his expanded responsibilities. He was also unfortunate enough to receive his severest tests during the Mule Shoe attacks of May 10 and 12, when he had just assumed command of the VI Corps. Winfield Scott Hancock, for his part, was reliable enough that Meade and Grant usually put his II Corps at the forefront of any major operation. But on several occasions he fumbled, most notably at the Mule Shoe on May 12. There he could well have wrecked Lee's army had he kept his nineteen thousand troops under control rather than letting them dissipate into a disorganized mob.

Perhaps the most intriguing Federal corps commander was Gouverneur Warren. He was neither casual in the performance of his duty, as Sedgwick seemed to be, nor inept, like Burnside, nor did he get disoriented by reversals in the way that Wright occasionally did. But he was notoriously less dependable than Hancock, often because his professionalism rebelled at the things he was called upon to do. Warren had an irritating way of doing the wrong thing for the right reasons. On May 6, for example, his V Corps failed to renew its attack on the Orange Turnpike because Warren understood the strong Confederate fieldworks in front of him made success impossible. Two days later, instructed by Meade to "cooperate" with Sedgwick in attacking Laurel Hill, Warren pronounced his own emphatic verdict on the business of having two generals presiding over a battle. "General Meade," he clipped, "I'll be

God d——d if I'll cooperate with Sedgwick or anybody else. You are the commander of this army and can give your orders and I will obey them; or you can put Sedgwick in command and he can give the orders and I will obey them; or you can put me in command and I will give the orders and Sedgwick will obey them; but I'll be God d——d if I'll *cooperate* with General Sedgwick or anybody else." Maj. Gen. James H. Wilson, to whom Warren later told the story, replied that if Warren had used such language to him, Wilson would have placed him under arrest. But he understood Warren's point: "He doubtless meant to rebuke Meade, who had apparently directed cooperation without carefully considering that it was a formless and almost meaningless use of words where positive orders would have been far more creditable to himself as well as more certain to secure the best efforts of the general to whom they were directed."[17]

It is difficult not to admire Warren's moral courage. Yet he employed it more often to second-guess his superiors than to pitch aggressively into the enemy. The worst example of this behavior occurred on June 1, when Warren failed to attack Confederates marching across the front of his V Corps or counterattack Early's Second Corps after the second fight at Bethesda Church. Such failures infuriated Grant. After all, the whole point of the campaign was to get the Confederates to fight in the open, and he expected senior subordinates to seize every opportunity when they did.[18]

Of all the Union corps commanders, only Sheridan did notably well during the Overland campaign, and then only on his own terms following a debut in the Wilderness that was at best insubordinate and at worst culpably negligent. Fortunately for him—and, ultimately, the Union cause—Grant was an indulgent patron, for Meade would have removed him from command after Sheridan's blowup on May 8 (and quite possibly court-martialed him as well). Sheridan had scant interest in screening and reconnaissance, the usual roles for Civil War cavalry. He preferred raiding, but even more than that, straight-up combat against all comers, infantry and horsemen alike. Under fiery "Little Phil" the Union cavalry began a swift transformation from auxiliary arm to one of the principal factors in the North's ultimate victory. Capitalizing on both the size of the Potomac Army's mounted force and the firepower generated by its repeating carbines, Sheridan made the cavalry something it had never been during the Civil War: an arm of battlefield decision. The seizure and defense of Old Cold Harbor on May 31 and June 1 against infantry opposition were the first milestones on a road leading to the destruction of a Confederate corps at Cedar Creek in October 1864 and the cornering of Lee's army in April 1865.

Senior leadership on the Confederate side was generally better than for the Federals, particularly in the subsidiary theaters. Breckinridge and Beauregard clearly outclassed Sigel and Butler. The former's performance at New Market was a small masterpiece. Beauregard, despite his vainglory, performed a vital service in defeating Butler, and it is not at all clear that another commander—George Pickett or Robert Ransom, for example—could have done it. Lee was fortunate to have had the assistance of such officers. They eviscerated Grant's peripheral strategy and ensured that by late May Lee received a major infusion of reinforcements just when he most urgently needed it. Beauregard cannot even be seriously faulted for holding on to Hoke's division until May 31. He was correct in his estimate of the Federals facing him at Bermuda Hundred and mindful of the acute danger that would face the Confederates in Virginia should Butler break out of Bermuda Hundred.

Regrettably for Lee, his good fortune in having Breckinridge and Beauregard to assist him was largely offset by the indifferent performance of three corps commanders. As on so many battlefields, A. P. Hill exercised a curiously weak grip on his divisions. Ewell served effectively in the Wilderness but lost Lee's confidence thereafter, particularly when on May 12 he let the shocking loss of Johnson's division overthrow his equilibrium. After an impressive debut at Laurel Hill, Richard H. Anderson was lackluster as commander of the First Corps, and the fizzled June 1 attack at Old Cold Harbor robbed Lee of an offensive opportunity he had coveted since the campaign's start. Jeb Stuart's adroit screening of Lee's army turned to tragedy when he elected to fight Sheridan on singularly unfavorable terms at Yellow Tavern. Only two of Lee's corps commanders did well in the Overland campaign, and for different reasons they had little opportunity to shine. A near-fatal throat wound knocked Longstreet out of action just three days into the campaign. And by the time Jubal Early got command of the Second Corps, it had been so badly bled by hard fighting that his aggressive, well-conceived thrusts near Bethesda Church generated little but casualties.

Even so, the Army of Northern Virginia handily outperformed the Army of the Potomac, exhibiting superior leadership at the division, brigade, and regimental levels. Its troops showed more aggressiveness on the attack, tenacity on the defense, and greater esprit in general. In all likelihood it would have contained its adversary between Spotsylvania and the North Anna but for Union sea power, which was in many respects the Confederates' most dangerous nemesis. The Bermuda Hundred campaign would obviously have been impossible without it, but the Overland campaign was just as dependent on bases at Belle Plain, Port Royal, and White House Landing. Without the North's wealth of steamers, barges, and gunboats, Grant would have had a far more difficult time in turning Lee out of his formidable defensive positions.

The scale of this enterprise was immense. Exact figures are unavailable, but some idea can be had from the amount of shipping required to sustain Grant's operations in the Richmond-Petersburg sector in March 1865. According to War Department figures, it came to 190 steamers, 60 steam tugs, 40 sail vessels, and 100 barges—a total of 390 vessels at a cost to the government of $48,000 per day (to say nothing of the supplies this flotilla actually transported). In May 1864 the Army of the Potomac required logistical support on a similar scale. Indeed, at one point during the Overland campaign, Halleck warned Grant that he was using up nearly all the available shipping on the Atlantic coast.[19]

Yet overall, this represented a fine exploitation of superior Northern resources. A resource that was signally underutilized during the campaign, however, was one that marched with the Army of the Potomac everywhere it went: a IX Corps division under Brig. Gen. Edward Ferrero, two-thirds of which was composed of African American troops. At a time when Halleck was sending forward every available replacement to fill the ranks of the Army of the Potomac—some forty-eight thousand went forward during the course of the campaign—Ferrero's division stayed in the rear to guard the supply trains. Apart from a few brushes with Confederate cavalry and guerrillas, it remained as aloof from the fighting as if it had been in Vermont.

The reason for this, of course, had everything to do with white assumptions about blacks. Even Grant, who in the West found that black troops performed capably in battle, still had reservations about them, and the officers in the Army of the Potomac had even more. One man explained to his brother that the black troops "do not amount to any certain sum in a fight," and it was better to use troops on which one could depend. Then too, the rebels might kill them if captured. But the definitive judgment was pronounced by one of Meade's staff officers, who observed the division after the Wilderness fight. "As I looked at them, my heart was troubled and I would gladly have seen them sent back to Washington. Ah, can we not fight our own battles without these humble hewers of wood and drawers of water, to be bayoneted by the unsparing Southerners? We do not dare trust them in the line of battle. Ah, you may make speeches at home, but here, where it is life or death, we dare not risk it. They have been put to guard the trains and have repulsed one or two little cavalry attacks in a creditable manner; but God help them if the gray-backed infantry attack them!" It was a mistaken judgment. The "humble hewers of wood" would eventually be thrown into action at Petersburg, where they would fight at least as well as their white counterparts.[20]

In the end, few would remember the failure to use Ferrero's troops, nor would many consider the massive exploitation of Federal sea power, or the vital contribution, for good or ill, of the key Union and Confederate subordinates. Instead, the spring 1864 Virginia campaign would be recalled primarily as a great duel between Grant and Lee. And the duel motif, more than anything else, created the popular image of Grant the hammerer or, less charitably, Grant the butcher.

This image is unfair: Grant's Vicksburg campaign and his pursuit of Lee from Petersburg to Appomattox are two classic examples of bold, deft, mobile warfare. And even during the Overland campaign it was no part of Grant's program to win by attrition. He honestly believed that Lee was on the ropes and that a few good, hard blows would destroy his army. Yet the image has stuck, in no small measure because so many have found reasons to cherish the image of Grant the remorseless, head-down fighter.

To begin with, Grant partisans, confronted with the campaign as it actually panned out, put the best face on it that they could. Also, twentieth-century military commentators saw Grant's attrition strategy as tough-minded and modern. But perhaps the most enduring wellspring of the image has come from Southerners—not merely to disparage Grant but to create and sustain the myth of the Lost Cause.

The Civil War is rife with myths, but the Lost Cause is by far the most potent of these. It has many components—that the antebellum South was an idyllic age out of Sir Walter Scott, that the slaves were docile and content, that the war was contrived by an overweening, tyrannical North—but militarily its central element is the conviction that the South did not lose because of inadequate generalship or internal stresses. Rather, it failed because the stronger battalions beat it to death. Nowhere could this truth be better displayed than in the contest between Lee, the greatest of the Confederate generals, and Grant, the Northern commander who bested him.

It should be obvious, then, that the collisions between Grant and Lee would be fertile ground for mythology, and none greater than the Overland campaign. After all, at the beginning of the campaign, Lee occupied the same line from which he had previously repelled John Pope, Ambrose Burnside, Joseph Hooker, and George G. Meade. But once the campaign began, Lee's army never saw the Rapidan again. Thus, at first glance it certainly looks as if the defeat of Lee began during this campaign. The task of the mythmakers was to demonstrate how Lee nevertheless outgeneraled Grant at every turn.

The structure of their mythic reading of the campaign is simple: Lee shrewdly traps Grant in Wilderness, where Union advantage in numbers and artillery will count for less. Grant suffers the equivalent of a Chancellorsville defeat, but doggedly refuses to retreat and instead tries to slip around Lee's flank. Lee anticipates the move and blocks Grant at Spotsylvania. Grant again loses heavily, draws off, and shifts another time around Lee's flank. Lee once more anticipates and parries so adroitly that Grant has no choice but to shift a third time.

This third shift culminates in Cold Harbor, a shatteringly one-sided Confederate victory. But Grant simply slips once again around Lee's flank, crosses the James River, and attacks Petersburg. Although Lee defeats this effort, he is now effectively pinned to the defense of Richmond-Petersburg, where with dwindling men and resources he staves off defeat for another ten months.

The emphasis in this résumé is on Lee's superior generalship and Grant's superior numbers, which enable Grant to absorb successive losses and still press south. The outcome is inevitable and classically summed up by Col. E. P. Alexander, the famous artillerist of the Army of Northern Virginia: "However bold we might be, however desperately we might fight, we were sure in the end to be worn out. It was only a question of a few months, more or less."[21]

How to explain an outcome in which Lee fought an adroit campaign yet still found himself shackled, like Prometheus, to the cities of Richmond and Petersburg? Alexander at least was willing to give Grant credit for a well-conducted campaign. Most Southerners were not so generous. Typical were the words of Edward Pollard, editor of the *Richmond Examiner* and author of one of the earliest Southern histories of the war, *The Lost Cause* (1866):

No one will deny this man [Grant] credit for many good qualities of the heart and great propriety of behaviour. He had that coarse, heavy obstinacy, which is as often observed in the Western backwoodsman as in a higher range of character. But he contained no spark of military genius; his idea of war was to the last degree rude—no strategy, the mere application of the *vis inertiae;* he had none of that quick perception on the field of action which decides it by sudden strokes; he had no conception of battle beyond the momentum of numbers. Such was the man who marshalled all the material resources of the North to conquer the little army and overcome the consummate skill of Gen. Lee. He, who was declared the military genius of the North, had so little idea of the contest, such little appreciation of the higher aims and intellectual exercises of war that he proposed to decide it by a mere competition in the sacrifice of human life.

In modified form, this mythical interpretation insinuated itself into most analyses of the campaign. Thus, although Grant ultimately prevailed, he did so through sheer weight of numbers. Lee outgeneraled him at every step.[22]

Why this insistence on Lee's having outgeneraled Grant? For white Southerners, Lee was the embodiment of the Confederate Cause. His fate reflected on the fate of the Confederacy. As Frederick Porcher, a proslavery secessionist, put it in 1861: "It may be that slavery is doomed. Be it so. . . . All that we ask is that it may perish manfully." If Lee, the South's paladin, met defeat only because of the weight of overwhelming numbers, then surely he—and the Confederacy—had perished manfully. To allow that Grant was a superior general in his own right, and that Grant's generalship as well as his superior numbers explained Lee's defeat, would have obscured the mythical impact of a just, righteous Confederacy unflinchingly meeting its fate.[23]

This interpretation emerged even as the campaign was under way. It is curious how in May 1864, most Southerners viewed Lee's fifty-mile retreat from the Rapidan to the gates of Richmond with relative calm. They did it by insisting, in effect, that Grant was beaten but too stupid to know it. That sentiment was redolent in a May 10 *Richmond Examiner* editorial which asserted that while Grant did not see himself as being whipped after the Wilderness fight, his men did. It concluded that although Grant might still get closer to Richmond, he commanded "the ruins of an army." The same view was present in the comment of Lee's adjutant on May 15—"Grant is beating his head against a wall"—as well as a *Charleston Mercury* editorial on June 10: "[Grant] lacks strategy, he lacks caution, he lacks versatility, and he lacks the common instinct of humanity that teaches a care for life. . . . Grant's army, fully double Lee's in the beginning, has now been depleted down to an equality with, if not inferiority to, the Confederate army. Altogether Richmond was never safer, nor the Confederate cause on higher or firmer ground."[24]

Obviously, this argument had a certain truth. Grant's offensive did reach stalemate by the end of June, and as this recognition set in, the North became discouraged enough that in August Lincoln predicted his own defeat in the fall 1864 elections. But the victories at Mobile Bay, Atlanta, and in the Shenandoah Valley dispelled the gloominess and showed convincingly that the North was winning the war. Hood's disastrous defeat in front of Nashville in December 1864 wrecked the Army of Tennessee and made it almost impossible to stop Sherman in his northward march to join Grant via the Carolinas in early 1865. However, none of these Northern victories or Southern failures are part of the Lost Cause explanation for Confederate defeat. The mythical focus has remained firmly on Lee and his duel with Grant, a duel in which he outfought the Yankee chieftain but went down under overwhelming numbers. That defeat came as a result of neither Northern prowess nor Southern military mistakes. And as regarded Grant, it required only a slight shift from the wartime emphasis on Grant the unsuccessful butcher to the postwar portrayal of Grant the successful (but still unworthy) butcher.

Paradoxically, despite this dominant interpretation, few Confederates could reconcile themselves to the idea that defeat had really been inevitable. Thus much of the Southern literature on the Civil War searches for potential turning points—lost opportunities—most of which focus on the theater in which Lee operated. The assumption runs that Lee could have won if subordinates (or fate) had gotten out of his way. Some of the most powerful lost turning points precede 1864: if Stonewall Jackson had not been killed, for example, or if Longstreet, or Ewell, or Stuart had not failed Lee at Gettysburg. But the Overland campaign also had its powerful "might have beens."

In the Wilderness: What if Longstreet had been prepositioned to reach the battlefield on May 5, not the following morning? Or what if Longstreet had not been wounded in the flank attack on May 6? A local success might have translated into the rolling up of Grant's whole army. By the same token, John B. Gordon insisted—and many have believed—that his evening flank attack against the Union right might have succeeded in rolling up Grant's whole army if executed earlier in the day. (To add more resonance to this possibility, Gordon, never a stickler for veracity, made up an account of Lee personally approving the attack after Ewell and Early had vetoed it.)[25]

At Spotsylvania: What if those artillery pieces had not been withdrawn from the Mule Shoe salient? What if they had not been so slow to return? At the North Anna: What if Lee had been able to capitalize on his ingenious trapping of Grant's army with the inverted V defense. What if, at the decisive moment, he had not been incapacitated by illness? A King Lear quality resonates in the words that are quoted of him as he lay raging in his sick bed: "We must strike them a blow!"[26]

With the exception of Gordon's flank attack, the other "might have beens" were foiled by adverse fate: Longstreet's accidental wounding by his own men, a prudent but mistaken decision to withdraw the artillery, Lee's illness brought on by stress and exhaustion. Each of these explanations buttressed an Army of Northern Virginia—and by extension a Confederate South—defeated by fate and overwhelming numbers, not by its own military mistakes or lack of will. The Overland campaign thus became the *locus classicus* for the Lost Cause myth.

Those shrouds of myth are seductive. Historians of the campaign have tended either to succumb to them and craft a narrative that substantially follows the mythic emphasis—a story line that plays up, for example, Lee's valor, foresight, and crafty generalship as opposed to Grant's clumsiness, doggedness, and superior numbers—or, more rarely, to challenge the myth directly, point by point. But either way, historians can be trapped in the agenda of the myth and fail to look beyond it. The most obvious example is the "duel" motif itself. Many accounts barely notice that the Virginia campaign of spring 1864 involved not one Union offensive (Grant versus Lee) but four: Grant along the Rapidan, Butler at Bermuda Hundred, Sigel in the Valley, Crook/Averell in southwest Virginia—to say nothing of subsequent cavalry raids by Phil Sheridan and August V. Kautz. Indeed, from a Southern perspective, the campaign's most striking feature was the sheer number of Union offensives, which worried the Confederate high command and strained its resources more than Grant's offensive against Lee. Yet most accounts continue to emphasize the duel between

Grant and Lee, relegating other offensives to sideshows, with little attempt to analyze operations as Grant and Lee did, as an integrated whole.

Will we ever shake the grip of this myth? One doubts it. We need it too much. Though perhaps no longer necessary as an explanation of Confederate defeat, it has a more universal resonance. Sooner or later, everyone loses. The dreams of youth are left behind, the promising career falters, the fatal diagnosis is pronounced. The idea of facing inevitable defeat with courage, dignity, and humanity—as Lee is rightly said to have done—therefore has powerful attraction.

But if we need the myth of Lee, so too perhaps we need the countermyth of Grant. The world is as full of obstacles as it is of losses, and to get anywhere in life one must possess grit, drive, determination, persistence. And so we also need the image of Grant: Grant the implacable, Grant the hammerer, Grant the man who, despite everything, keeps moving on.

Notes

PREFACE

1. Qtd. in J. F. C. Fuller, *Grant and Lee: A Study in Personality and Generalship* (Bloomington: Indiana University Press, 1957), 78.

2. Leo Tolstoy, *War and Peace* (New York: New American Library, 1968), pt. 3, ch. 1, p. 988; pt. 2, ch. 28, p. 944.

3. Edward Porter Alexander, *Military Memoirs of a Confederate: A Critical Narrative* (1905; rpt., New York: Da Capo, 1993), 557–58.

I. CAMPAIGN PLANS AND POLITICS

1. Daniel E. Sutherland, *Seasons of War: The Ordeal of a Confederate Community, 1861–1865* (New York: Free Press, 1995), 342–43.

2. Theodore Lyman to his family, April 12, 1864, in *Meade's Headquarters, 1863–1865*, ed. George R. Agassiz (Boston: Atlantic Monthly Press, 1922), 81.

3. Qtd. in Bruce Catton, *Grant Takes Command* (Boston: Little, Brown, 1968), 56.

4. This sentence needs two minor qualifications. First, one other man, Winfield Scott, had held the rank of lieutenant general, but only honorifically. Second, Grant's predecessor, Halleck, actually requested that Grant replace him once Grant became a lieutenant general.

5. David Donald, *Lincoln* (New York: Simon and Schuster, 1995), 410. The jibe about Halleck's being a "first-rate clerk" is quoted in Stephen E. Ambrose, *Halleck: Lincoln's Chief of Staff* (Baton Rouge: Louisiana State University, 1962), 162.

6. Qtd. in Ambrose, *Halleck*, 163.

7. U.S. War Department, *War of the Rebellion: A Compilation of the Official Records of the Union and Confederate Armies*, 128 vols. and index (Washington: GPO, 1880–1901), series 1, vol. 36, pt. 1, 12 (cited hereafter as *OR*, followed by the volume

number, part number, and page number; all references are to series 1 unless otherwise indicated).

8. U. S. Grant, *Personal Memoirs*, 2 vols. (New York: Charles L. Webster, 1885), 2:143; entry for April 30, 1864, in *Lincoln and the Civil War in the Diary and Letters of John Hay*, ed. Tyler Dennett (1939; rpt., New York: Da Capo, 1988), 178–79.

9. Albert Castel, *Decision in the West: The Atlanta Campaign of 1864* (Lawrence: University Press of Kansas, 1992), 90, 106; *OR* 32, pt. 3, 246.

10. *OR* 33, 394.

11. *OR* 32, pt. 2, 412, 413.

12. See *OR* 33, 1144, 1185, 1283–84. This interpretation of Halleck's response to Grant follows Brooks D. Simpson, *Let Us Have Peace: Ulysses S. Grant and the Politics of War and Reconstruction, 1861–1868* (Chapel Hill: University of North Carolina Press, 1991), 54–55. For a more critical assessment, see Herman Hattaway and Archer Jones, *How the North Won: A Military History of the Civil War* (Urbana: University of Illinois Press, 1983), 513–15.

13. *OR* 33, 482, 804. The figure excludes nine thousand troops belonging to the District of North Carolina.

14. For Butler's pre-1864 career, see Hans L. Trefousse, *Ben Butler: The South Called Him BEAST!* (New York: Twayne, 1957).

15. For a detailed discussion of the Bermuda Hundred plan, see William Glenn Robertson, *Back Door to Richmond: The Bermuda Hundred Campaign, April–June 1864* (Baton Rouge: Louisiana State University Press, 1987), 14–24.

16. *OR* 33, 794–95, 885–86, 904–5.

17. The sniping at Meade is detailed in Bruce Tap, *Over Lincoln's Shoulder: The Committee on the Conduct of the War* (Lawrence: University Press of Kansas, 1998), 178–87.

18. For Meade's substantive contribution to the victory at Gettysburg, see Edwin B. Coddington, *The Gettysburg Campaign: A Study in Command* (New York: Scribner, 1968); for the period afterward, see Andrew A. Humphreys, *Gettysburg to the Rapidan: The Army of the Potomac, July, 1863 to April, 1864* (New York: Scribner, 1883). Grant's assessment is in his *Memoirs*, 2:117.

19. Jay Luvaas, "The Campaign that History Forgot," *Civil War Times Illustrated* 8, no. 7 (August 1969): 11–42; Humphreys, *Gettysburg to the Rapidan*, 49–70.

20. Andrew A. Humphreys, *The Virginia Campaign of 1864 and 1865* (1883; rpt., New York: Da Capo, 1995), 10–11.

21. The Federal plan is discussed in Gordon C. Rhea, *The Battle of the Wilderness, May 5–6, 1864* (Baton Rouge: Louisiana State University Press, 1994), 49–58.

22. *OR* 32, pt. 3, 246. Union plans for Sigel's department are discussed in William C. Davis, *The Battle of New Market* (Garden City NY: Doubleday, 1975), 20–23.

23. *OR* 34, pt. 3, 333. In a confidential letter to Grant, Halleck opined that in the case of Banks, whose Red River campaign ended in debacle, Lincoln

would probably consent to his removal from command. "[B]ut he will do so very reluctantly, as it would give offense to many of his friends, and would probably be opposed by a portion of his Cabinet. Moreover, what could be done with Banks? He has many political friends who would probably demand for him a command equal to the one he now has." Halleck added that the same would be true in the cases of Butler, Sigel, and others. *OR* 34, pt. 3, 332.

24. Lyman to his family, July 20, 1864, *Meade's Headquarters*, 192; Simpson, *Let Us Have Peace*, 57.

25. *Augusta (Georgia) Constitutionalist*, January 22, 1864, qtd. in Larry E. Nelson, *Bullets, Ballots, and Rhetoric: Confederate Policy for the United States Presidential Contest of 1864* (University: University of Alabama Press, 1981), 11; *OR* 32, pt. 3, 679–80. For accounts of Longstreet's proposal, see Douglas Southall Freeman, *R. E. Lee: A Biography*, 4 vols. (New York: Scribner, 1934–35), 3:259–61; Jeffry D. Wert, *General James Longstreet: The Confederacy's Most Controversial Soldier* (New York: Simon and Schuster, 1993), 369–72.

26. Lee to Davis, March 25, 1864, *Lee's Dispatches*, ed. Douglas Southall Freeman (1915; rpt., Baton Rouge: Louisiana State University Press, 1994), 144; *OR* 33, 1144, 1185, 1283–84.

27. *OR* 33, 1085–86, 1087, 1097–98, 1120–21, 1124.

28. Undated letter ca. January 1864, in "With the First New York Dragoons: From the Letters of Jared L. Ainsworth," ed. Richard J. Del Vecchio, unpublished manuscript, Harrisburg Civil War Round Table Collection, U.S. Army Military History Institute, Carlisle Barracks PA (Cited hereafter as HCWRTC, USAMHI.)

29. *OR* 33, 1063.

30. Lee to Davis, April 13, 1864, *Lee's Dispatches*, 156–57.

31. *OR* 33, 1128. Lee's supply difficulties are summarized in Steven E. Woodworth, *Davis and Lee at War* (Lawrence: University Press of Kansas, 1995), 260–61.

32. *OR* 33, 1247–50; John G. Barrett, *The Civil War in North Carolina* (Chapel Hill: University of North Carolina Press, 1963), 202, 213–20.

33. This overview follows William A. Tidwell, with James O. Hall and David Winfred Gaddy, *Come Retribution: The Confederate Secret Service and the Assassination of Lincoln* (Jackson: University Press of Mississippi, 1988), 105–14. Despite the title, the book contains much about Confederate intelligence activities in general, particularly in the eastern theater.

34. *OR* 33, 1268. Another scout reported that the clothing of these troops was "too new and overcoats of too deep a blue for old troops," which suggested that their numbers must include many recent recruits. *OR* 33, 1265.

35. *OR* 33, 1332.

36. *OR* 33, 1290. The Army of the Potomac's strength as of April 30, 1864, is given in *OR* 33, 1036. Lee estimated the IX Corps at "23,000 men, 7,000 of which are negroes." *OR* 33, 1326. At the end of April he placed the corps "on the Orange & Alexandria Railroad between Fairfax Court House and Alexandria."

Lee to G. W. C. Lee, April 30, 1864, *The Wartime Papers of R. E. Lee*, ed. Clifford Dowdey and Louis H. Manarin (New York: Bramhall House, 1961), 707. Thus, his estimate of the entire Union force arrayed against him was 98,000. The Army of Northern Virginia's strength on April 20, 1864, is given in *OR* 33, 1297. A recent study, based on samplings from compiled service records, estimates that on May 5, 1864, Lee's army contained 65,995 men divided as follows: First Corps, 11,200; Second Corps, 17,620; Third Corps, 22,650; field artillery, 5,205; Cavalry Corps, 9,320. See Alfred C. Young III, "Numbers and Losses in the Army of Northern Virginia," *North and South* 3, no. 3 (March 2000): 14–29. These estimates are helpful, although they should be used with caution pending the opportunity for a detailed examination of Young's data and methodology.

37. Qtd. in Stephen W. Sears, *To the Gates of Richmond: The Peninsula Campaign* (New York: Ticknor and Fields, 1992), 151.

38. Entry for February 19, 1870, William Allan, "Memorandum of Conversations with General Robert E. Lee," in *Lee the Soldier*, ed. Gary W. Gallagher (Lincoln: University of Nebraska Press, 1996), 17.

39. Most European armies held a similar view in the decades before the First World War, although they were influenced far more by the Austrian-Prussian War of 1866 and the Franco-Prussian War of 1870–71 than by the American Civil War. Military thinkers respected the firepower that could be generated by emerging, technologically advanced artillery, machine guns, and small arms, but believed that a strong spirit of the offensive could overcome it. On this point, see Michael Howard, "Men against Fire: The Doctrine of the Offensive in 1914," in *Makers of Modern Strategy: From Machiavelli to the Nuclear Age*, ed. Peter Paret (Princeton NJ: Princeton University Press, 1986), 510–26.

40. There are no official returns for the First Corps on the eve of the Wilderness campaign. This estimate is Longstreet's own. See Longstreet, *From Manassas to Appomattox* (1896; rpt., Secaucus NJ: Blue and Gray Press, 1985), 553–54; *OR* 33, 1297–98. The figures for the remaining corps represent combat officers and men "present for duty." (See also note 36, above.) The "aggregate present" numbers, which include teamsters and other noncombatant personnel, are 20,710 for the Second Corps, 25,391 for the Third Corps. The hypothesis regarding Hill's prostatitis is outlined in James I. Robertson Jr., *General A. P. Hill: The Story of a Confederate Warrior* (New York: Random House, 1987), 11–12. For Lee's misgivings about Ewell, see entry for March 8, 1868, William Allan, "Memorandum," in *Lee the Soldier*, 11.

41. *OR* 33, 1298. The aggregate present figure for Stuart's cavalry was 9,700. In addition, the army's artillerists numbered 4,854 present for duty, 5,547 aggregate present. The April returns show the total number for the army as a whole, including the provost guard, battalion scouts, and other unattached commands (but excluding Longstreet) as 54,344 present for duty, 62,913. Most authorities believe the army's actual strength when the campaign began was about 64,000–65,000.

See, e.g., Rhea, *Wilderness*, 21; Douglas Southall Freeman, *Lee's Lieutenants*, 3 vols. (New York: Charles Scribner's Sons, 1942–44), 3:345. But see also Alfred C. Young's estimate in note 36, above. The best biography of Stuart is Emory M. Thomas, *Bold Dragoon: The Life of J. E. B. Stuart* (New York: Random House, 1986).

42. The Union strength figures are from *OR* 33, 1036. The numbers given in the text represent combat officers and men "present for duty"; for the army as a whole this figure was 102,869. The "aggregate present" figure for the army was considerably higher—127,471—while the more exacting "present for duty, equipped" figure was only 97,273. Grant's observation about Warren is in his *Memoirs*, 2:214–15.

43. For the IX Corps in April 1864, the "aggregate present" figure was 21,357. *OR* 33, 1045.

44. This information is compiled from biographical data in Ezra J. Warner, *Generals in Blue: Lives of the Union Commanders* (Baton Rouge: Louisiana State University Press, 1964).

45. This information is compiled from biographical data in Ezra J. Warner, *Generals in Gray: Lives of the Confederate Commanders* (Baton Rouge: Louisiana State University Press, 1959).

46. Qtd. in G. F. R. Henderson, *Stonewall Jackson and the American Civil War*, 2 vols. in 1 (1898; London: Longmans, Green, 1949), 1:19.

47. Col. William H. Palmer to Douglas Southall Freeman, June 25, 1920, qtd. in Freeman, *Lee*, 3:331. It should be noted that although, in its essentials, this exchange between Hill and Lee did occur, close examination of the evidence suggests that Palmer misidentified the target of Hill's criticism.

48. My estimate of the number of Confederate conscripts received is an educated guess based on the troop returns of the Army of Northern Virginia for January–April 1864, as well as the report of the Bureau of Conscription, April 30, 1864. The latter indicates that from December 1863 through March 1864 some 4,588 conscripts (and 1,355 volunteers) were assigned to the Confederate army from Virginia, North Carolina, and South Carolina. I have assumed that most of these went to Lee's army. The conscription bureau report is in *OR*, series 4, vol. 3, 354–64. It was Col. Charles S. Wainwright who estimated that a third of the Potomac Army was green. Entry for May 1, 1864, *A Diary of Battle: The Personal Journals of Colonel Charles S. Wainwright, 1861–1865*, ed. Allan Nevins (1962; rpt., Gettysburg PA: Stan Clark Military Books, n.d.), 345.

49. Charles E. Davis Jr., *Three Years in the Army: The Story of the Thirteenth Massachusetts Volunteers* (Boston, 1893), 270. See also Martin T. McMahon, "From Gettysburg to the Coming of Grant," in *Battles and Leaders of the Civil War*, 4 vols., ed. Clarence C. Buel and Robert U. Johnson (New York: Century, 1887), 4:91–93.

50. As of March 28 the number of veterans who had reenlisted was 26,767 (*OR* 33, 776). Since veterans were required to make their decision several months

before their terms of service ended, that figure is reasonably close to the final total. Most soldiers counted their terms of service from the time of their original enlistment, but War Department regulations stipulated that they must be calculated from the date of muster into federal service. The two dates were often four to eight weeks apart. It made for hard feelings on the part of some veterans, particularly in the Pennsylvania Reserve regiments, where a few soldiers refused to do duty. See *OR* 33, 924. See also Benjamin F. Ashenfelter to his father, April 23, 1864, Benjamin F. Ashenfelter Letters, HCWRTC, USAMHI.

51. Frank Wilkeson, *Turned Inside Out: Recollections of a Private Soldier in the Army of the Potomac* (1887; rpt., Lincoln NE: Bison Books, 1997), 30–32.

52. J. F. J. Caldwell, *The History of a Brigade of South Carolinians, Known First as "Gregg's" and Subsequently as "McGowan's" Brigade* (Philadelphia: King and Baird, 1866), 124.

53. Samuel D. Buck, *With the Old Confeds: Actual Experiences of a Captain in the Line* (1925; rpt., Gaithersburg MD: Butternut Press, 1983), 102.

54. *OR* 36, pt. 1, 277.

55. Benjamin F. Ashenfelter to his father (with addendum for his mother), April 23, 1864, HCWRTC, USAMHI. For expressions of confidence in the army's leadership, see, e.g., William H. Martin to his wife, April 6, 1864, William H. Martin Letters, HCWRTC, USAMHI.

2. THE WILDERNESS

1. *OR* 33, 1321.

2. *OR* 33, 1266.

3. *OR* 36, pt. 1, 277, 894.

4. B. L. Wynn, "Lee Watched Grant at Locust Grove," *Confederate Veteran* 21 (1913): 68; *OR* 51, pt. 2, 888.

5. Wynn, "Lee Watched Grant," 68; Robertson, *A. P. Hill,* 231–32; Jedediah Hotchkiss, *Virginia,* vol. 3 of *Confederate Military History,* 12 vols., ed. Clement A. Evans (1899; rpt., Secaucus NJ: Blue and Gray Press, n.d.), 434.

6. The two principal roads Longstreet expected to use were the Pamunkey and Catharpin Roads.

7. His initial orders to Ewell were to seek battle, but he soon revised them.

8. Wilkeson, *Turned Inside Out,* 49.

9. Rhea, *Wilderness,* 85–86.

10. *OR* 36, pt. 2, 948.

11. *OR* 29, pt. 2, 819.

12. Lee to Davis, May 4, 1864, *Lee's Dispatches,* 169–74. Davis's letter to Lee, dated May 2, has not been found, but its contents may be inferred from Lee's response. Gordon C. Rhea, in his admirable *Battle of the Wilderness,* 87–89, has Lee responding to several dispatches from Davis misdated May 4 but more probably

written on May 5. The most telling indication of the misdating is Davis's report of many Union transports at Bermuda Hundred and City Point. No transports appeared at those places until the following day.

13. *Supplement to the Official Records of the Union and Confederate Armies* (Wilmington NC: Broadfoot, 1996), pt. 1, vol. 6, 787 [Cited hereafter as *OR Supplement*]; *OR* 51, pt. 2, 888.

14. Armistead L. Long, *Memoirs of Robert E. Lee* (1886; rpt., Secaucus NJ: Blue and Gray Press, 1983), 326–27; Charles S. Venable, "General Lee in the Wilderness Campaign," in *Battles and Leaders*, 4:241.

15. Robert Stiles, *Four Years under Marse Robert* (1903; rpt., Marietta GA: R. Bemis, 1995), 244–45. Stiles mistakenly wrote "plank road" instead of "turnpike."

16. Qtd. in Rhea, *Wilderness*, 124.

17. Rhea, *Wilderness*, 124–26.

18. Edward Hagerman, *The American Civil War and the Origins of Modern Warfare: Ideas, Organization, and Field Command* (Indianapolis: University of Indianapolis Press, 1988), 12–13, 123–25, 139–41. See also Paddy Griffith, *Battle Tactics of the Civil War* (New Haven CT: Yale University Press, 1987), 123–35.

19. Lyman to his parents, May 18, 1864, *Meade's Headquarters*, 99–100.

20. *OR* 36, pt. 2, 404, 403. For more critical assessments of Meade's reasoning, see Edward Steere, *The Wilderness Campaign* (Harrisburg PA: Stackpole, 1960), 99–104; Rhea, *Wilderness*, 103.

21. *OR* 36, pt. 2, 332; James Harrison Wilson, *Under the Old Flag: Recollections of Military Operations in the War for the Union, the Spanish War, the Boxer Rebellion, Etc.*, 2 vols. (New York: D. Appleton, 1912), 1:379.

22. An acid but merited assessment of the Union cavalry's performance in the Wilderness campaign may be found in Gordon C. Rhea, "Union Cavalry in the Wilderness: The Education of Philip H. Sheridan and James H. Wilson," in *The Wilderness Campaign*, ed. Gary W. Gallagher (Chapel Hill: University of North Carolina Press, 1997), 106–35. The subtitle is misleading since, as Rhea makes clear, neither Sheridan nor Wilson learned anything from their experience in the Wilderness.

23. First quote: Thomas Francis Galwey, *The Valiant Hours: Narrative of "Captain Brevet," an Irish-American in the Army of the Potomac* (Harrisburg PA: Stackpole, 1961), 195. Second quote: Timothy J. Reese, *Sykes' Regular Division, 1861–1864: A History of Regular United States Infantry Operations in the Civil War's Eastern Theater* (Jefferson NC: McFarland, 1990), 300.

24. Entry for May 5, 1864, *A Surgeon's Civil War: The Letters and Diary of Daniel M. Holt, M.D.*, ed. James M. Greiner, Janet L. Coryell, and James R. Smither (Kent OH: Kent State University Press, 1994), 182–83.

25. *OR* 36, pt. 2, 676.

26. *OR* 36, pt. 2, 418, 419, 420, 404.

27. William W. Swan, "The Battle of the Wilderness," *Papers of the Military*

Historical Society of Massachusetts, 14 vols. (1881–1918; rpt., Wilmington NC: Broadfoot, 1989), 4:150. Cited hereafter as *PMHSM.*

28. William H. Powell, *The Fifth Army Corps* (London: G. P. Putnam's Sons, 1896), 608.

29. Qtd. in Rhea, *Wilderness,* 163.

30. A detailed account of Warren's attack is in Rhea, *Wilderness,* 145–74.

31. Wilkeson, *Turned Inside Out,* 50.

32. Mary Genevie Green Brainard, *Campaigns of the 146th Regiment, New York State Volunteers* (New York: G. P. Putnam's Sons, 1915), 195; Wilkeson, *Turned Inside Out,* 66–67.

33. Lyman to his family, May 15, 1864, *Meade's Headquarters,* 90–91 (and note); Theodore Lyman, "Addenda to the Paper by Brevet Lieutenant-Colonel W. W. Swan, U.S.A., on the Battle of the Wilderness," *PMHSM,* 4:167–68.

34. Hazard Stevens, "The Sixth Corps in the Wilderness," *PMHSM,* 4:189–90.

35. Stevens, "The Sixth Corps in the Wilderness," 190.

36. Charles S. Venable, "General Lee in the Wilderness Campaign," in *Battles and Leaders,* 4:241.

37. Henry Heth, *Memoirs,* ed. James L. Morrison (Westport CT: Greenwood Press, 1974), 182–83.

38. Lyman to his parents, May 15, 1864, *Meade's Headquarters,* 91; Stevens, "The Sixth Corps in the Wilderness," 192.

39. Stevens, "The Sixth Corps in the Wilderness," 180.

40. Wilbur Fisk to Montpelier (Vermont) *Green Mountain Freeman,* May 9, 1864, in *Hard Marching Every Day: The Civil War Letters of Private Wilbur Fisk, 1861–1865,* ed. Emil and Ruth Rosenblatt (Lawrence: University Press of Kansas, 1992), 215.

41. Gen. L. A. Grant, "In the Wilderness," *National Tribune* (Washington DC), January 28, 1897, qtd. in Carol Reardon, "The Other Grant: Lewis A. Grant and the Vermont Brigade in the Battle of the Wilderness," in *The Wilderness Campaign,* ed. Gary W. Gallagher (Chapel Hill: University of North Carolina Press, 1997), 210.

42. Robert McAllister to his family, May 6, 1864, in *The Civil War Letters of General Robert McAllister,* ed. James I. Robertson (1965; rpt., Baton Rouge: Louisiana State University Press, 1998), 416.

43. Stevens, "The Sixth Corps in the Wilderness," 192.

44. *OR Supplement,* pt. 1, vol. 6, 704.

45. *OR Supplement,* pt. 1, vol. 6, 715, 704.

46. *OR Supplement,* pt. 1, vol. 6, 715; Caldwell, *History of a Brigade of South Carolinians,* 128.

47. Heth, *Memoirs,* 183.

48. *OR* 36, pt. 2, 411.

49. Rhea, *Wilderness,* 230–31.

50. William Royall, *Some Reminiscences* (New York: Neale, 1909), 30.

51. In his memoirs, Harry Heth asserted that Hill, not Lee, was responsible for the failure to reorganize the line. He claimed to have remonstrated with Hill to do so, that Hill had flatly refused, and that Heth had then unsuccessfully tried to locate Lee. But other sources clearly indicate that Lee made the decision. For a discussion of this point, see Robertson, *A. P. Hill,* 241–42.

52. Horace Porter, *Campaigning with Grant* (1897; rpt., Bloomington: Indiana University Press, 1961), 53–54.

53. Porter, *Campaigning with Grant,* 54; *OR* 36, pt. 2, 412, 415.

54. *OR* 36, pt. 2, 405.

55. Charles A. Page, *Letters of a War Correspondent* (Boston: L. C. Page, 1899), 52; Rhea, *Wilderness,* 320–24.

56. William Henry Locke, *The Story of the [11th Pennsylvania] Regiment* (Philadelphia: J. B. Lippincott, 1868), 325–26; Galwey, *The Valiant Hours,* 197–98.

57. William L. Royall, *Some Reminiscences* (New York: Neale, 1909), 30; *OR Supplement,* pt. 1, vol. 6, 777–78; Caldwell, *History of a Brigade of South Carolinians,* 133.

58. Edward Porter Alexander, *Fighting for the Confederacy,* ed. Gary A. Gallagher (Chapel Hill: University of North Carolina Press, 1989), 357.

59. Lyman to his family, May 16, 1864, *Meade's Headquarters,* 93–94.

60. William Marvel, *Burnside* (Chapel Hill: University of North Carolina Press, 1991), 351.

61. G. Moxley Sorrel, *Recollections of a Confederate Staff Officer* (1905; rpt., New York: Bantam, 1992), 201.

62. R.C., "Texans Always Move Them," *The Land We Love,* vol. 5, 481–82. A good account of this episode is in Rhea, *Wilderness,* 299–301. See also Freeman, *Lee,* 3:288.

63. *OR* 36, pt. 2, 440.

64. *OR* 36, pt. 2, 441; Rhea, *Wilderness,* 329.

65. Sorrel, *Recollections,* 202.

66. Fisk to *Green Mountain Freeman,* May 9, 1864, in *Hard Marching Every Day,* 217.

67. Longstreet, *From Manassas to Appomattox,* 568; Lyman to his family, May 16, 1864, *Meade's Headquarters,* 95–96.

68. Qtd. in Gregory A. Mertz, "No Turning Back: The Battle of the Wilderness, Part II—The Fighting on May 6, 1864," *Blue and Gray Magazine* 12, no. 5 (June 1995): 19.

69. *OR* 51, pt. 2, 893.

70. E. P. Alexander, *Fighting for the Confederacy,* 363.

71. *OR* 36, pt. 2, 952.

72. John B. Gordon, *Reminiscences of the Civil War* (New York: Scribner, 1903), 244.

73. Gordon, *Reminiscences*, 246–47.

74. Rhea, *Wilderness*, 407–8.

75. Hyland C. Kirk, *Heavy Guns and Light: A History of the Fourth New York Heavy Artillery* (New York: C. T. Dillingham, 1890), 159–60.

76. Kirk, *Heavy Guns and Light*, 162–64; qtd. in Rhea, *Wilderness*, 419.

77. Gordon, *Reminiscences*, 248.

78. Porter, *Campaigning with Grant*, 69–70.

79. Catton, *Grant Takes Command*, 204; Lyman to his family, May 18, 1864, *Meade's Headquarters*, 102n.; *OR* 36, pt. 2, 481.

80. Lyman to his family, May 18, 1864, *Meade's Headquarters*, 102.

81. Porter, *Campaigning with Grant*, 79. See also Catton, *A Stillness at Appomattox*, 91–92.

3. "GRANT IS BEATING HIS HEAD AGAINST A WALL"

1. Francis Cordrey, "The Wilderness: What a Private Saw and Felt in That Horrible Place," *National Tribune*, June 21, 1894; William D. Matter, *If It Takes All Summer: The Battle of Spotsylvania* (Chapel Hill: University of North Carolina Press, 1988), 15.

2. *OR* 36, pt. 2, 970.

3. *OR Supplement*, pt. 1, vol. 6, 656. In his report to Longstreet, Anderson says Lee used the term "Longstreet's Corps," not "your corps," but Anderson probably did so out of consideration for Longstreet's feelings. Lee habitually used the term "Anderson's Corps" for as long as Anderson remained in command.

4. It is sometimes asserted that Anderson intended to reach Spotsylvania as fast as possible and would have kept going, forest fire or no forest fire. Joseph Cantey Elliott says as much in his *Lee's Noble Soldier: Lieutenant General Richard Heron Anderson* (Dayton OH: Morningside House, 1985), 86. But Anderson's report to Longstreet, cited above, states that he would have bivouacked the men, as Lee explicitly directed, had it not been for the fire.

5. Col. Charles S. Wainwright, entry for May 8, 1864, *A Diary of Battle*, 355–56; Marsena Patrick, entry for May 7, 1864, *Inside Lincoln's Army: The Diary of Marsena Rudolph Patrick, Provost Marshal General, Army of the Potomac*, ed. David S. Sparks (New York: Thomas Yoseloff, 1964), 370.

6. For Sheridan's early encounter with Meade, see Philip H. Sheridan, *Personal Memoirs*, 2 vols. in 1 (1888; rpt., New York: Da Capo, 1992), 1:193–94. Sheridan's characterizations of the fighting around Todd's Tavern are in *OR* 36, pt. 2, 515. The assessment of Sheridan's performance in the Wilderness summarizes the argument of Gordon C. Rhea, "Union Cavalry in the Wilderness: The Education of Philip H. Sheridan and James H. Wilson," in *The Wilderness Campaign*, 106–35.

7. *OR* 36, pt. 2, 552.

8. *OR* 36, pt. 2, 551.

9. *OR* 36, pt. 2, 551, 539.

10. Lyman to his parents, May 18, 1864, *With Grant and Meade*, 103–4; qtd. in Matter, *If It Takes All Summer*, 55.

11. Charles Lawrence Peirson, "The Operations of the Army of the Potomac, May 7–11, 1864," PMHSM, 4:214–15.

12. Gordon C. Rhea, *The Battles for Spotsylvania Court House and the Road to Yellow Tavern, May 7–12, 1864* (Chapel Hill: University of North Carolina Press, 1997) [cited hereafter as Rhea, *Spotsylvania*], 53.

13. *OR* 36, pt. 1, 594; Harold Adams Small, ed., *The Road to Richmond: The Civil War Memoirs of Major Abner R. Small, of the Sixteenth Maine Volunteers* (Berkeley: University of California Press, 1939), 80; Jack D. Welsh, *Medical Histories of Union Generals* (Kent OH: Kent State University Press, 1996), 282.

14. Peirson, "The Operations of the Army of the Potomac," 216.

15. *OR* 36, pt. 1, 597; John Coxe, "Last Struggles and Successes of Lee," *Confederate Veteran* 22 (1914): 357; Rhea, *Spotsylvania*, 65–66. Anderson subsequently sent three more brigades from Field's Division to Spotsylvania. Matter, *If It Takes All Summer*, 69.

16. *OR* 36, pt. 2, 540–41, 545.

17. For accounts of the Meade-Sheridan exchange, see Porter, *Campaigning with Grant*, 83–84; and Sheridan, *Memoirs*, 1:199–200.

18. Porter, *Campaigning with Grant*, 84.

19. *OR* 36, pt. 2, 552. Meade's criticism of Sheridan receives endorsement in Rhea, "Union Cavalry in the Wilderness: The Education of Philip H. Sheridan and James H. Wilson," in *Wilderness Campaign*, 106–35.

20. *OR* 36, pt. 2, 527, 540, 541.

21. H. B. McClellan, *The Life and Campaigns of Major-General J. E. B. Stuart* (Boston and New York, 1885), 408; Thomas W. Hyde, *Following the Greek Cross; or, Memories of the Sixth Army Corps* (Boston: Houghton Mifflin, 1894), 191.

22. W. W. Olds, "Trees Whittled Down at Horseshoe," SHSP 33 (1905): 20–22.

23. Martin T. Martin, "The Death of General John Sedgwick," in *Battles and Leaders*, 4:175; Porter, *Campaigning with Grant*, 90.

24. Robertson, *A. P. Hill*, 240, 247; qtd. in Charles C. Osborne, *Jubal: The Life and Times of General Jubal A. Early*, CSA (Baton Rouge: Louisiana State University Press, 1992), 228.

25. Lee to Davis, May 9, 1864, *Lee's Dispatches*, 176; *OR* 36, pt. 1, 3. Grant's only word from Butler to date was a telegram received on May 6, reporting successful landings at Bermuda Hundred and City Point and the apparent achievement of surprise (*OR* 36, pt. 2, 430).

26. Qtd. in Rhea, *Spotsylvania*, 110.

27. Rhea, *Spotsylvania*, 111–12; Matter, *If It Takes All Summer*, 125–26.

28. Rhea, *Spotsylvania*, 113–14; Matter, *If It Takes All Summer*, 129–30.

29. *OR* 36, pt. 2, 599–600.

30. Rhea, *Spotsylvania*, 136–37.

31. Rhea, *Spotsylvania*, 137–40; Matter, *If It Takes All Summer*, 145–48.

32. For the battle of the Po River, see Rhea, *Spotsylvania*, 135–41; Matter, *If It Takes All Summer*, 141–48.

33. For Warren's May 10 attack, see Rhea, *Spotsylvania*, 143–49; Matter, *If It Takes All Summer*, 148–54.

34. *OR* 36, pt. 2, 603.

35. For Mott's May 10 attack, see Rhea, *Spotsylvania*, 165–68; Matter, *If It Takes All Summer*, 160–61.

36. *OR* 36, pt. 1, 667–68.

37. Humphreys, *Gettysburg to the Rapidan*, 43–46.

38. *OR* 36, pt. 1, 667. For an illuminating discussion of why so many Civil War infantry charges failed, see Paddy Griffith, *Battle Tactics of the Civil War* (New Haven CT: Yale University Press, 1987), 137–64.

39. I have followed the timing in Rhea, *Spotsylvania*, 169. Upton states that the artillery preparatory fire stopped at 6 P.M. and that he charged twenty minutes later. *OR* 36, pt. 1, 668.

40. Qtd. in Rhea, *Spotsylvania*, 174.

41. Rhea, *Spotsylvania*, 174. For accounts of Upton's charge, see Rhea, 168–77; Matter, *If It Takes All Summer*, 161–67; and Catton, *A Stillness at Appomattox*, 113–16.

42. Qtd. in Rhea, *Spotsylvania*, 178.

43. Rhea, *Spotsylvania*, 177–81; Matter, *If It Takes All Summer*, 150–54.

44. *OR* 36, pt. 1, 4.

45. *OR* 36, pt. 1, 66–67. Of the II Corps attack, Dana wrote simply, "The rebel lines were gained, but not held."

46. *OR* 36, pt. 2, 982. The identical dispatch went to Jefferson Davis and the president's military adviser, Braxton Bragg.

47. Rhea, *Spotsylvania*, 187–88.

48. *OR* 36, pt. 2, 983.

49. Qtd. in Catton, *A Stillness at Appomattox*, 116.

50. *OR* 36, pt. 2, 629.

51. Humphreys, *Virginia Campaign*, 89–91.

52. Francis C. Barlow, "The Capture of the Mule Shoe," PMHSM, 4:246.

53. Qtd. in Rhea, *Spotsylvania*, 222.

54. Barlow, "The Capture of the Mule Shoe," 247.

55. Barlow, "The Capture of the Mule Shoe," 249.

56. John West Haley, entry for May 12, 1864, *The Rebel Yell and the Yankee Hurrah*, ed. Ruth L. Silliker (Camden ME: Down East Books, 1985), 155.

57. Haley, entry for May 12, 1864, *Rebel Yell*, 155.

58. The estimate of II Corps strength in the May 12 attack is drawn from Matter, *If It Takes All Summer,* 189.

59. John D. Black, "Reminiscences of the Bloody Angle," in *Glimpses of the Nation's Struggle: Papers Read before the Commandery of the State of Minnesota, Military Order of the Loyal Legion of the United States* (St. Paul MN: H. L. Collins, 1898), 4.

60. Matter, *If It Takes All Summer,* 174–79, 189–91; Rhea, *Spotsylvania,* 225–28.

61. *OR* 36, pt. 1, 335–36; Rhea, *Spotsylvania,* 230, 232–34; Matter, *If It Takes All Summer,* 191–96.

62. Rhea, *Spotsylvania,* 232–44; Matter, *If It Takes All Summer,* 194–99.

63. *OR* 36, pt. 2, 656.

64. Rhea, *Spotsylvania,* 244.

65. Freeman, *R. E. Lee,* 3:317–19.

66. *OR* 36, pt. 2, 656–57; Rhea, *Spotsylvania,* 255–82. The Confederate side of the Mule Shoe fight is ably re-created by Robert K. Krick in "An Insurmountable Barrier between the Army and Ruin: The Confederate Experience at Spotsylvania's Bloody Angle," in *The Spotsylvania Campaign,* ed. Gary W. Gallagher (Chapel Hill: University of North Carolina Press, 1998), 80–126.

67. *OR* 36, pt. 2, 662.

68. *OR* 36, pt. 2, 662.

69. *OR* 36, pt. 2, 663.

70. *OR* 36, pt. 2, 663, 668, 669, 671. Grant in fact gave Meade a written order to relieve Warren if Warren did not attack. See *OR* 36, pt. 2, 654.

71. The May 12 Laurel Hill attack is described in Rhea, *Spotsylvania,* 285–88.

72. *OR* 36, pt. 2, 675.

73. G. Norton Galloway, "Hand-to-Hand Fighting at Spotsylvania," in *Battles and Leaders,* 4:171.

74. Lewis A. Grant, "Review of Major-General Barlow's Paper on the Capture of the Salient at Spotsylvania, May 12, 1864," *PMHSM,* 4:269; Galloway, "Hand-to-Hand Fighting at Spotsylvania," 4:173.

75. Galloway, "Hand-to-Hand Fighting at Spotsylvania," 4:173; Elisha Hunt Rhodes, entry for May 13, 1864, *All for the Union: The Civil War Diary and Letters of Elisha Hunt Rhodes,* ed. Robert Hunt Rhodes (New York: Vintage, 1992), 144. Humphreys, *Virginia Campaign,* 104, estimates the VI Corps loss at 840. Rhea, *Spotsylvania,* 311, believes the actual loss must have exceeded 1,000. George R. Stewart, *Pickett's Charge: A Microhistory of the Final Attack at Gettysburg, July 3, 1863* (New York: Houghton Mifflin, 1959), 263, places the Confederate loss in that action at 6,467 out of 10,500 engaged.

76. Rhea, *Spotsylvania,* 311–12. Matter, *If It Takes All Summer,* 266–67, estimates the Union loss on May 12 at 7,000–8,000 and Confederate casualties at 5,000–6,000, including the 3,000 captured from Johnson's division.

77. *OR* 36, pt. 1, 4.

78. Taylor to his wife, May 15, 1864, *Lee's Adjutant: The Wartime Letters of Colonel Walter Herron Taylor, 1862–1865*, ed. R. Lockwood Tower (Columbia: University of South Carolina Press, 1995), 160.

79. Lee to Davis, May 13, 1864, *Wartime Papers of R. E. Lee*, 729.

80. *OR* 36, pt. 2, 810.

81. Meade to his wife, May 19, 1864, in *The Life and Letters of George Gordon Meade*, 2 vols. (New York: Scribner, 1913), 2:197.

82. Wilkeson, *Turned Upside Down*, 88–89.

83. Grant, *Memoirs*, 2:238.

4. THE COLLAPSE OF GRANT'S PERIPHERAL STRATEGY

1. *OR* 36, pt. 1, 12.

2. *OR* 33, 762, 1036, 1045, 1053, 1201, 1298, 1299, 1334.

3. *OR* 36, pt. 1, 12.

4. *OR* 33, 758. The strength figure is taken from Grant to Sigel, March 29, 1864, *OR* 33, 765, specifying that the Beverly expedition should include "not less than 8,000 infantry, three batteries of artillery, and 1,500 picked cavalry." In dispatches to Sherman and Meade, Grant estimated Ord's force at between 10,000 and 12,000. See *OR* 32, pt. 3, 246; and *OR* 33, 828.

5. Stephen D. Engle, *Yankee Dutchman: The Life of Franz Sigel* (Fayetteville: University of Arkansas Press, 1993), 158.

6. Entry for February 28, 1864, *A Virginia Yankee in the Civil War: The Diaries of David Hunter Strother*, ed. Cecil D. Eby (Chapel Hill: University of North Carolina Press, 1961), 213.

7. *OR* 37, pt. 1, 526. Sigel, for his part, insisted that an expedition from Beverly was unpromising, owing to the poor condition of the roads, and that the complement of 10,000 men required by Grant could not be assembled without compromising the crucial Baltimore and Ohio Railroad. According to Sigel, Ord became so "diffident" with regard to these obstacles that he asked to be relieved. See Franz Sigel, "Sigel in the Shenandoah Valley in 1864," in *Battles and Leaders*, 4:487. Sigel presented his objections to Grant, who found them unimpressive. See *OR* 33, 844–45.

8. Rutherford B. Hayes to his uncle, May 19, 1864, *Diary and Letters of Rutherford Birchard Hayes*, 5 vols., ed. Charles Richard Williams (Columbus: Ohio State Archaeological Society, 1922), 2:464.

9. Bruce Catton, *Glory Road* (Garden City NY: Doubleday, 1952), 154–55; Stephen W. Sears, *Chancellorsville* (Boston: Houghton Mifflin, 1996), 83–91.

10. *OR* 33, 1325. For details of Breckinridge's career, see the able biography by William C. Davis, *Breckinridge: Statesman, Soldier, Symbol* (Baton Rouge: Louisiana State University Press, 1974).

11. *OR* 37, pt. 1, 719; Warner, *Generals in Gray*, 154–55.

12. *OR* 37, pt. 1, 720.

13. *OR* 37, pt. 1, 721.

14. *OR* 37, pt. 1, 44–45.

15. Frank Moore, ed., *Rebellion Record: A Diary of American Events*, 12 vols. (1861–68; rpt., New York: Arno Press, 1977), 11:14–15.

16. *OR* 37, pt. 1, 46.

17. For details of the battle of Cloyd's Mountain, see Howard R. McManus, "Cloyd's Mountain," *Civil War Times Illustrated* 18 (1980), and idem., *The Battle of Cloyd's Mountain: The Virginia and Tennessee Railroad Raid, April 29–May 19, 1864* (Lynchburg VA: H. E. Howard, 1989). A good, brief treatment of the battle is in Richard R. Duncan, *Lee's Endangered Left: The Civil War in Western Virginia, Spring of 1864* (Baton Rouge: Louisiana State University Press, 1998), 56–63.

18. McManus, *Battle of Cloyd's Mountain*, 41.

19. *OR* 37, pt. 1, 45.

20. *OR* 37, pt. 1, 41; Duncan, *Lee's Endangered Left*, 75–77.

21. Qtd. in James A. Ramage, *Rebel Raider: The Life of General John Hunt Morgan* (Lexington: University Press of Kentucky, 1986), 212.

22. Hayes to his uncle, May 19, 1864, *Diary and Letters of Rutherford Birchard Hayes*, 2:463; Hayes to his wife, May 25, 1864, 2:465–66.

23. *OR* 37, pt. 1, 12.

24. Entry for May [10], 1864, *A Virginia Yankee*, 223.

25. William C. Davis, *Battle of New Market* (Garden City NY: Doubleday, 1975), 62.

26. Davis, *Battle of New Market*, appendix A, "Strength of Commands in the New Market Campaign," 193–97.

27. John D. Imboden, "The Battle of New Market," in *Battles and Leaders*, 4:483.

28. Davis, *Battle of New Market*, 89.

29. Qtd. in Davis, *Battle of New Market*, 98.

30. Qtd. in Davis, *Battle of New Market*, 108.

31. Qtd. in Davis, *Battle of New Market*, 122.

32. Entry for May 15, 1864, *A Virginia Yankee*, 226.

33. Davis, *Battle of New Market*, 131.

34. Entries for May 16 and 21, 1864, *A Virginia Yankee in the Civil War*, 229–30.

35. Davis, *Battle of New Market*, 183.

36. *OR* 37, pt. 1, 735.

37. John W. Joyce to his wife, May 15, 1864, HCWRTC, USAMHI.

38. *OR* 36, pt. 2, 552; Sheridan, *Memoirs*, 1:200–201.

39. *OR* 51, pt. 2, 912.

40. *OR* 51, pt. 2, 913.

41. *OR* 36, pt. 1, 834–35.

42. H. B. McClellan, *The Campaigns of Stuart's Cavalry* (1885; rpt., Secaucus

NJ: Blue and Gray Press, 1993), 412; Stuart to Bragg, May 11, 1864, "Stuart's Last Despatch," *SHSP* 9 (1881): 138.

43. McClellan, *Stuart's Cavalry*, 415.

44. McClellan, *Stuart's Cavalry*, 417.

45. Theodore F. Rodenbrough, "Sheridan's Richmond Raid," in *Battles and Leaders*, 4:191.

46. Rodenbrough, "Sheridan's Richmond Raid," 4:191.

47. Sheridan, *Memoirs*, 1:209.

48. *OR* 36, pt. 2, 778.

49. Entry for May 13, 1864, Alexander R. Boteler diary, William E. Perkins Library, Duke University, Durham NC; Robert E. Lee Jr., *Recollections and Letters of Robert E. Lee* (New York: Doubleday, Page, 1904), 124–25.

50. The estimate is of Butler's field force at Bermuda Hundred and City Point: 17,990 infantrymen and artillerists in Smith's XVIII Corps; 17,926 in Gillmore's X Corps, for a total of 35,916. Robertson, *Back Door to Richmond*, 59. It does not include 4,701 cavalry on detached duty. Robertson, 63n. 29.

51. *OR* 33, 1299.

52. *OR* 33, 885, 794–95.

53. Butler might have avoided this difficulty by landing his main force at City Point, as Grant's order perhaps implied he should do, and marching on Richmond via Petersburg. But Butler reasoned that to operate from City Point would add at least fifteen miles to the distance separating him from Richmond, his main objective. He therefore simply occupied City Point with one division and put the rest of his troops ashore across the river at Bermuda Hundred. (Grant, for his part, understood well ahead of time that Butler intended to do this and made no objection.)

54. Robertson, *Back Door to Richmond*, 119. See also *OR* 36, pt. 2, 35.

55. On Grant's preferences and Butler's response, see Adam Badeau, *Military History of General U. S. Grant*, 3 vols. (New York: D. Appleton, 1885), 2:246–47.

56. *OR* 36, pt. 2, 35.

57. *OR* 36, pt. 2, 587.

58. The troop estimates are from Freeman, *Lee's Lieutenants*, 3:459, 462, 471.

59. *OR* 36, pt. 2, 986.

60. Beauregard later did put the plan on paper. *OR* 36, pt. 2, 1024.

61. P. G. T. Beauregard to Henry Wise, October 3, 1873, "A Letter from General Beauregard to General Wise Regarding the Battle [of Drewry's Bluff]," *SHSP* 25 (1897): 207.

62. *OR* 36, pt. 2, 1024–25. For Beauregard's belief that Bragg favored the plan, see G. T. Beauregard, "The Defense of Drewry's Bluff," in *Battles and Leaders*, 4:199; Alfred T. Roman, *The Military Operations of General Beauregard*, 2 vols. (1884; rpt., New York: Da Capo, 1994), 2:201. For secondary accounts of the discussions surrounding Beauregard's proposal, see Robertson, *Back Door to*

Richmond, 149–53; T. Harry Williams, *P. G. T. Beauregard: Napoleon in Gray* (Baton Rouge: Louisiana State University, 1955), 214–17.

63. These figures are based on estimates in Robertson, *Back Door to Richmond*, 217.

64. *OR* 36, pt. 2, 840–41.

65. Porter, *Campaigning with Grant*, 125.

5. "LEE'S ARMY IS REALLY WHIPPED"

1. *OR* 36, pt. 2, 906.

2. Porter, *Campaigning with Grant*, 131.

3. *OR* 36, pt. 2, 911.

4. Porter, *Campaigning with Grant*, 126–27.

5. Porter, *Campaigning with Grant*, 128; Wilkeson, *Turned Inside Out*, 84–85.

6. Porter, *Campaigning with Grant*, 127.

7. Matter, *If It Takes All Summer*, 317.

8. Quoted in Bruce Catton, *A Stillness at Appomattox*, 129. Matter, *If It Takes All Summer*, 328–29.

9. For accounts of Harris Farm, see Matter, *If It Takes All Summer*, 317–29; Gordon C. Rhea, *To the North Anna River: Grant and Lee, May 13–25, 1864* (Baton Rouge: Louisiana State University Press, 2000), 170–88; Gary W. Gallagher, *Stephen Dodson Ramseur: Lee's Gallant General* (Chapel Hill: University of North Carolina Press, 1985), 113–14; Pfanz, *Ewell*, 392–93.

10. Porter, *Campaigning with Grant*, 131.

11. J. Michael Miller, *"Even to Hell Itself": The North Anna Campaign, May 21–26, 1864*, 2d ed. (Lynchburg VA: H. E. Howard, 1989), 12–21; Rhea, *North Anna*, 212–54.

12. *OR* 36, pt. 2, 49; *OR* 36, pt. 1, 341; *OR* 36, pt. 3, 47.

13. *OR* 36, pt. 3, 801, 812.

14. *OR* 36, pt. 1, 76.

15. *OR* 36, pt. 1, 75; Wilkeson, *Turned Inside Out*, 103.

16. Entry for May 23, 1864, *Touched with Fire: Civil War Letters and Diary of Oliver Wendell Holmes Jr.*, ed. Mark De Wolfe Howe (New York: Da Capo, 1969), 130; Lyman to his parents, May 23, 1864, *Meade's Headquarters*, 117.

17. Eugene A. Nash, *History of the Forty-fourth Regiment New York Volunteer Infantry in the Civil War, 1861–1865* (Chicago: R. R. Donnelly, 1911), 193; Marsena Patrick, entry for May 22, 1864, *Inside Lincoln's Army*, 375–76.

18. *OR* 36, pt. 3, 96, 135.

19. Lee to Davis, May 22, 1864, *Lee's Dispatches*, 192.

20. Lee to Davis, May 23, 1864, *Lee's Dispatches*, 195; Taylor to his wife, May 23, 1864, *Lee's Adjutant*, 162.

21. Taylor to his wife, May 23, 1864, *Lee's Adjutant*, 162.

22. This estimate is drawn from a recent study by Alfred C. Young III, "Numbers and Losses in the Army of Northern Virginia," *North and South* 3, no. 3 (March 2000): 19. Freeman, *R. E. Lee*, 3:356, estimates that somewhat fewer reinforcements—8,500—joined the Army of Northern Virginia when it reached Hanover Junction. Miller, *North Anna*, 7, believes the total was considerably higher, on the order of 12,700 men. Lee to Davis, May 23, 1864, *Lee's Dispatches*, 195.

23. Miller, *North Anna*, 7–9.

24. *OR* 36, pt. 1, 7.

25. *OR* 36, pt. 3, 82.

26. *OR* 36, pt. 3, 126.

27. Miller, *North Anna*, 61–87; Rhea, *North Anna*, 292–94, 303–18.

28. Miller, *North Anna*, 56–60; Rhea, *North Anna*, 294–303.

29. Clement A. Evans, ed., *Confederate Military History*, 3:460. The author of this volume, Maj. Jedediah Hotchkiss, quite likely witnessed or heard about this incident soon after it occurred.

30. Caldwell, *History of a Brigade of South Carolinians*, 155.

31. Miller, *North Anna*, 88–89; Rhea, *North Anna*, 320–23; Freeman, *R. E. Lee*, 3:355–56; E. P. Alexander, *Fighting for the Confederacy*, 389–90; Maj. Jedediah Hotchkiss, entry for May 23, 1864, *Make Me a Map of the Valley: The Civil War Journal of Stonewall Jackson's Topographer*, ed. Archie P. McDonald (Dallas: Southern Methodist University Press, 1973), 207.

32. *OR* 36, pt. 3, 148.

33. *OR* 36, pt. 3, 145.

34. *OR* 36, pt. 3, 166.

35. *OR* 36, pt. 3, 167.

36. *OR* 36, pt. 1, 77–78.

37. *OR* 36, pt. 3, 159; Miller, *North Anna*, 108–18; Rhea, *North Anna*, 325–35, 342–44, 346–50.

38. Miller, *North Anna*, 100–107; Rhea, *North Anna*, 335–42; John Anderson, *The Fifty-seventh Massachusetts Volunteers in the War of the Rebellion* (Boston: E. B. Stillings, 1896), 99.

39. E. M. Law, "From the Wilderness to Cold Harbor," in *Battles and Leaders*, 4:136.

40. C. S. Venable, "The Campaign from the Wilderness to Petersburg," SHSP 14 (1886): 534.

41. Venable also remembered at least one critical detail incorrectly. According to him, Lee was "confined to his tent" on May 24, but other eyewitnesses recalled him as being on the front, observing the enemy advance through binoculars, during the early afternoon. (See Miller, *North Anna*, 108.) Still, there is no reason to question Venable's sincerity, and the overall portrait he paints is accurate. Lee certainly did covet the chance to wreck Grant's army, and Venable himself

stated that the North Anna was not the only place where Lee believed he had the opportunity. "He hoped to strike the blow at the North Anna, *or between the Annas and the Chickahominy*" (emphasis added). Venable, "Campaign," 534.

42. *OR* 36, pt. 3, 183.

43. *OR* 36, pt. 3, 183.

44. *OR* 36, pt. 3, 183.

45. Wainwright, entry for May 26, 1864, *A Diary of Battle*, 388.

46. For an excellent picture of the extent of the supply requirements of the Army of the Potomac during the Overland campaign, see [Thomas Wilson], "Feeding a Great Army," *Civil War Times Illustrated* 4, no. 10 (1966): 28–35. Indirect but useful light on the subject is shed by John G. Moore, "Mobility and Strategy in the Civil War," *Military Affairs* 24 (1960): 68–77.

47. *OR* 36, pt. 3, 183; *OR* 36, pt. 1, 880; Wilson, *Under the Old Flag*, 1:421–22; *OR* 36, pt. 3, 834.

48. Miller, *North Anna*, 123–24. The destruction is briefly but vividly described in St. Clair A. Mulholland, *The Story of the 116th Regiment, Pennsylvania Volunteers in the War of the Rebellion*, ed. by Lawrence Frederick Kohl (New York: Fordham University Press, 1996), 230.

49. *OR* 36. pt. 3, 206.

50. *OR* 36, pt. 1, 782.

51. Louis J. Baltz III, *The Battle of Cold Harbor, May 27–June 13, 1864*, 2d ed. (Lynchburg VA: H. E. Howard, 1994), 13–14, 22–23.

52. Lyman to his mother, May 28, 1864, *Meade's Headquarters*, 130.

53. William P. Lloyd, *History of the First Regiment Pennsylvania Reserve Cavalry* (Philadelphia: King and Baird, 1864), 95.

54. J. H. Kidd, *Personal Recollections of a Cavalryman* (Ionia MI: Sentinel Printing Co., 1908), 324; Sheridan, *Memoirs*, 1:218; *OR* 36, pt. 1, 821–22; Baltz, *Cold Harbor*, 15–22.

55. Baltz, *Cold Harbor*, 22. See also Gordon C. Rhea, "'The Hottest Place I Was Ever In': The Battle of Haw's Shop, May 28, 1864," *North and South* 4, no. 3 (April 2001): 42–57.

56. *OR* 36, pt. 3, 843.

57. *OR* 36, pt. 2, 1021–22, 1024; *OR* 51, pt. 2, 945, 947, 948. For a discussion of Beauregard's reluctance to assist Lee save on his own terms, see Williams, *Beauregard*, 222–25. Lee to Davis, May 28, 1864, *Wartime Papers of R. E. Lee*, 753–54.

58. *OR* 51, pt. 2, 966.

59. *OR* 51, pt. 2, 965–66.

60. *OR* 36, pt. 3, 849; Lee to Davis, May 29, 1864, *Wartime Papers*, 756.

61. *OR* 36, pt. 3, 68–69, 140–41, 178.

62. Robertson, *Back Door to Richmond*, 235.

63. Lyman to his parents, May 30, 1864, *Meade's Headquarters*, 133–34.

64. Pfanz, *Ewell,* 388–89, 396–403.

65. E. P. Alexander, *Military Memoirs of a Confederate,* 534; *OR* 36, pt. 3, 851; J. William Jones, *Personal Reminiscences of General Robert E. Lee* (1874; rpt., Richmond VA: U.S. Historical Society Press, 1989), 40.

66. Wainwright, entry for May 30, 1864, *A Diary of Battle,* 393.

67. Charles B. Christian, "The Battle at Bethesda Church," *SHSP* 37 (1909): 238; O. R. Thomson and William H. Rauch, *History of the Bucktails* (Philadelphia: Electric Printing Co., 1868), 320.

68. *OR* 51, pt. 2, 975.

69. Baltz, *Cold Harbor,* 52–53.

70. Baltz, *Cold Harbor,* 54–55; Ernest B. Furgurson, *Not War but Murder: Cold Harbor, 1864* (New York: Knopf, 2000), 64–67.

71. *OR* 36, pt. 3, 323; Porter, *Campaigning with Grant,* 161.

72. *OR* 36, pt. 3, 850.

73. *OR* 36, pt. 3, 856.

6. "THE HARDEST CAMPAIGN"

1. *OR* 36, pt. 1, 71.

2. Charles A. Dana, *Recollections of the Civil War* (1898; rpt., Lincoln: University of Nebraska Press, 1996), 199.

3. McAllister to his family, May 20, 1864, *Civil War Letters,* 424; Edward E. Sill to [unnamed], May 16, 1864, Duke University Library, qtd. in Mac Wyckoff, *A History of the Third South Carolina Infantry, 1861–1865* (Fredericksburg VA: Sgt. Kirkland's, 1995), 186.

4. H. H. Cunningham, *Doctors in Gray: The Confederate Medical Corps,* 2d ed. (Baton Rouge: Louisiana State University Press, 1960), 51–53, 65, 118–19, 125.

5. *OR* 36, pt. 1, 211, 216.

6. *OR* 36, pt. 2, 829.

7. William Quentin Maxwell, *Lincoln's Fifth Wheel: The Political History of the U.S. Sanitary Commission* (New York: Longmans, 1956); *OR* 36, pt. 1, 216.

8. Cornelia Hancock to her sister, n.d., *South after Gettysburg: Letters, 1863–1868,* ed. Henrietta Stratton Jaquette (New York: T. Y. Crowell, 1956), 92.

9. Stephen B. Oates, *A Woman of Valor: Clara Barton and the Civil War* (New York: Free Press, 1994), 229–34; *OR* 36, pt. 2, 829, 852, 854–55.

10. Undated newspaper clipping re John C. Johnston, ca. 1947, in Fair Family Papers, HCWRTC, USAMHI; Craig L. Dunn, *Iron Men, Iron Will: The Nineteenth Indiana Regiment of the Iron Brigade* (Indianapolis: Guild Press of Indiana, 1995), 246–47.

11. Alexander Neil to friends, June 8, 1864, *Alexander Neil and the Last Shenandoah Valley Campaign* (Shippensburg PA: White Mane, 1996), 34–35.

12. Galwey, *TheValiant Hours,* 213–14; *OR* 36, pt. 1, 225; entry for May 5, 1864, *FourYears in the Confederate Artillery:The Diary of Private Henry Robinson Berkeley,* ed. William H. Runge (Chapel Hill: University of North Carolina Press, 1961), 73.

13. James B. Sheeran, entry for May 17, 1864, *Confederate Chaplain, a War Journal,* ed. JosephT. Durkin (Milwaukee: Bruce, 1960), 88.

14. William Watson, *Letters of a Civil War Surgeon,* ed. by Paul Fatout (1961; rpt.West Lafayette IN: Purdue University Press, 1996), 81–82.

15. The Union provost marshal reported the capture of 13,584 POWs between May 1 and July 31. (7,078 between May 1 and 12 alone). Probably the lion's share, say 12,000 in all, were from the Overland campaign (*OR* 36, pt. 1, 280). Official Army of the Potomac returns show 8,342 captured or missing during campaign (*OR* 36, pt. 1, 188). Deducting 10 percent for dead or deserters leaves 7,608 POWs. Thus about 19,600 men fell captive during the Overland campaign alone.The text of the Dix-Hill agreement in *OR,* series 2, vol. 4, 266–68. Davis's proclamation regarding African American POWs is in *OR,* series 2, vol. 5, 797.

16. Holt to his wife, April 20, 1864, *A Surgeon's CivilWar,* 179; Brewster to his mother, May 24, 1864, *When This CruelWar Is Over:The CivilWar Letters of Charles Harvey Brewster,* ed. DavidW. Blight (Amherst: University of Massachusetts Press, 1992), 304.

17. Entry for May 10, 1864, *"Unspoiled Heart":The Journal of Charles Mattocks of the Seventeenth Maine,* ed. Philip N. Racine (Knoxville: University ofTennessee Press, 1994), 134, 136.

18. William B. Styple, ed., *With a Flash of His Sword: The Writings of Major Holman S. Melcher, Twentieth Maine Infantry* (Kearny NJ: Belle Grove, 1994), 174–76; Rhea, *Battle of the Wilderness,* 166–67. According to John I. Faller of the Seventh Pennsylvania Reserves, Colonel Bolinger of the Seventh could not see the rest of his brigade and pushed too far forward, "driving everything before him until suddenly the enemy closed in on our rear and cut off our retreat." A desperate attempt made to get out in another direction failed. "[F]inding we were completely surrounded the Colonel was compelled to surrender, to save his regiment from being cut to pieces. . . .We surrendered to MajorVan Valkenburg commanding the Sixty-first Georgias [*sic*].The Colonel and 325 officers and men were made prisoners." Milton E. Flower, ed., *Dear Folks at Home: The CivilWar Letters of Leo W. and John I. Faller, with an Account of Andersonville* (Carlisle PA: Cumberland County Historical Society, 1963), 116.

19. McHenry Howard, *Recollections of a Maryland Confederate Soldier and Staff Officer under Johnston, Jackson, and Lee* (Baltimore: Williams and Wilkins, 1914), 297.

20.The Brady photographs are reproduced inWilliam A. Frassanito, *Grant and Lee:TheVirginia Campaigns, 1864–1865* (NewYork: Scribner, 1983), 54–60; entry for May 16, 1864, in *Diary of Gideon Welles,* 3 vols., ed. Howard K. Beale (New York: Norton, 1960), 2:32.

21. The most thorough study of Andersonville is William Marvel, *Andersonville: The Last Depot* (Chapel Hill: University of North Carolina Press, 1994).

22. *OR,* series 2, vol. 8, 996–97; Lonnie R. Speer, *Portals to Hell: Military Prisons of the Civil War* (Harrisburg PA: Stackpole, 1997), 241–48.

23. *OR,* series 2, vol. 7, 607, 615.

24. Entry for May 8, 1864, Byrd C. Willis, "Reminiscences," qtd. in Sutherland, *Seasons of War,* 360; William B. Styple and John J. Fitzpatrick, eds., *The Andersonville Diary and Memoirs of Charles Hopkins* (Kearny NJ: Belle Grove, 1988), 59; Edward G. Longacre, *Army of Amateurs: General Benjamin F. Butler and the Army of the James, 1861–1865* (Harrisburg PA: Stackpole, 1997), 110; Noah Andre Trudeau, *Like Men of War: Black Troops in the Civil War, 1862–1865* (Boston: Little, Brown, 1998), 214.

25. W. G. Bean, *The Liberty Hall Volunteers: Stonewall's College Boys* (Charlottesville: University Press of Virginia, 1964), 192; "My Experience in the Confederate Army and in Northern Prisons," *http://www.innova.net/~vsix/elmiradoc18.htm* [visited December 5, 1998]

26. Raymond J. Herek, *These Men Have Seen Hard Service: The First Michigan Sharpshooters in the Civil War* (Detroit: Wayne State University Press, 1998), 107; Henry E. Handerson, *Yankee in Gray: The Civil War Memoirs of Henry E. Handerson* (Cleveland: Press of Western Reserve University, 1962), 73.

27. Lewis Warlick to his wife, May 19, 1864, McGimsey Papers, SHC, UNC–Chapel Hill; Michael F. Rinker to his parents, May 17, 1864, Michael F. Rinker, VMI Archives, Lexington VA; undated entry ca. May 15, 1864, Maurus Oestreich diary, HCWRTC, USAMHI; Holt to his wife, May 16, 1864, *A Surgeon's Civil War,* 190.

28. Terry L. Jones, ed., *The Civil War Memoirs of Captain William J. Seymour: Reminiscences of a Louisiana Tiger* (Baton Rouge: Louisiana State University Press, 1991), 118; Sheeran, entry ca. May 13, 1864, *Confederate Chaplain,* 88–89; Charles A. Cuffel, *History of Durell's Battery in the Civil War* (Philadelphia: Craig, Finley, 1903), 182.

29. Henry Keiser, diary entry for May 13, 1864, HCWRTC, USAMHI.

30. *OR,* series 3, vol. 5, 317–19; Frederick H. Dyer, *A Compendium of the War of the Rebellion,* 3 vols. (Des Moines IA: Dyer, 1908), 1:19; Furgurson, *Not War but Murder,* 258–59; "Fredericksburg National Cemetery" *http://www.nps.gov/frsp/natcem.htm* [visited August 12, 2000]; "Confederate Cemeteries," *http://www.nps.gov/frsp/rebcem.htm* [visited August 12, 2000].

31. Item in the Peter Ostre Letters, Gregory A. Coco Collection, HCWRTC, USAMHI; "Arlington National Cemetery," in John Cannan, *The Spotsylvania Campaign, May 7–21, 1864* (Conshohocken PA: Combined Books, 1997), 200–201.

32. Grant to his wife, May 13, 1864, *The Papers of Ulysses S. Grant,* ed. John Y. Simon, 18 vols. (Carbondale: Southern Illinois University Press, 1967–), 10:443;

OR 36, pt. 1, 4; Meade to his wife, May 11, 1864, *Life and Letters*, 2:194; Marion Hill Fitzpatrick to his wife, May 15, 1864, *Red Dirt and Isinglass: A Wartime Biography of a Confederate Soldier*, ed. Henry Vaughan McCrea (n.p: H. V. McCrea, 1992), 485; Charles Minor Blackford to his wife, May 19, 1864, *Letters from Lee's Army; or, Memoirs of Life in and out of the Army in Virginia during the War between the States*, ed. Susan Leigh Blackford (New York: Scribner, 1947), 245; Margery Greenleaf, ed., *Letters to Eliza from a Union Soldier, 1862–1865* (Chicago: Follett, 1970), 90.

33. John H. Worsham, *One of Jackson's Foot Cavalry* (New York: Neale, 1912), 195. See also J. Tracy Power, *Lee's Miserables: Life in the Army of Northern Virginia from the Wilderness to Appomattox* (Chapel Hill: University of North Carolina Press, 1998), 72–73; Jubal A. Early, *Autobiographical Sketch and Narrative of the War between the States* (1912; rpt., Wilmington NC: Broadfoot, 1989), 295. An inveterate Yankee hater, Early mentioned the meal specifically to refute Northern allegations that Confederate prisoner of war camps deliberately mistreated their captives. "This was what the foremost commander of the age was reduced to in the then critical condition of his health," he wrote. "Such fare, if furnished to a sick or wounded Federal soldier, would have been regarded as evidence of a barbarous purpose to cause his death" (295–96). John O. Casler, *Four Years in the Stonewall Brigade* (1893; rpt., Dayton OH: Morningside House, 1971), 208.

34. Entry for June 3, 1864, *Touched with Fire*, 139; entry ca. May 22, 1864, Maurus Oestreich diary, HCWRTC, USAMHI.

35. Hyland C. Kirk, *Heavy Guns and Light*, 218; qtd. in Catton, *Grant Takes Command*, 243.

36. Samuel Cormany, diary entries for May 15, 16, 1864, *The Cormany Diaries: A Northern Family in the Civil War*, ed. James C. Mohr (Pittsburgh: University of Pittsburgh Press, 1982), 426.

37. Wesley Brainerd, *Bridge-Building in Wartime: Colonel Wesley Brainerd's Memoir of the Fiftieth New York Volunteer Engineers*, ed. Ed Malles (Knoxville: University of Tennessee Press, 1997), 209.

38. Daniel M. Holt to his wife, June 8, 1864, *A Surgeon's Civil War*, 198.

39. Charles Harvey Brewster to his wife, May 24, 1864, *When This Cruel War Is Over*, 304; William Corby, *Memoirs of Chaplain Life* (Notre Dame IN: Scholastic Press, 1894), 235–36.

40. Samuel Cormany, diary entry for May 22, 1864, *The Cormany Diaries*, 428. Cormany for some reason called the creatures "gnats," but his description of their bites leaves little doubt of their identity.

41. Rufus Dawes to his wife, May 31, 1864, Rufus Dawes, *Service with the Sixth Wisconsin Volunteers* (Madison: State Historical Society of Wisconsin, 1962), 280.

42. Dawes to his wife, May 25, 1864, Dawes, *Service with the Sixth Wisconsin Volunteers*, 277; Henry R. Pyne, *Ride to War: The History of the First New Jersey Cavalry* (New Brunswick NJ: Rutgers University Press, 1961), 206.

43. Theodore Gerrish, *Army Life: A Private's Reminiscences of the Civil War* (1882;

rpt., Gettysburg PA: Stan Clark Military Books, 1995), 189; McAllister to his family, May 25, 1864, *Civil War Letters*, 426.

44. *OR* 36, pt. 1, 236; Pulaski Cowper, comp., *Extracts of Letters of Major-General Bryan Grimes, to His Wife: Written While in Active Service in the Army of Northern Virginia* (Wilmington NC: Broadfoot, 1986), 53.

45. Lord Moran, *The Anatomy of Courage* (1945; rpt., Garden City Park NY: Avery, 1987), 61, 63–64.

46. Qtd. in Zahava Solomon, *Combat Stress Reaction: The Enduring Toll of War* (New York: Plenum Press, 1993), 40–41.

47. Gardner H. Shattuck Jr., *A Shield and a Hiding Place: The Religious Life of the Civil War Armies* (Macon GA: Mercer University Press, 1987), 99; Thomas D. Cockrell and Michael B. Ballard, eds., *A Mississippi Rebel in the Army of Northern Virginia: The Civil War Memoirs of Private David Holt* (Baton Rouge: Louisiana State University Press, 1995), 238; Simon B. Cummins [151st New York] to his parents, May 11, 1864, "Diary of the Battle of the Wilderness" *http://www.pasty.com/book/diary.html* [visited June 14, 1999].

48. Rufus Dawes to his wife, May 14, 1864, *Service with the Sixth Wisconsin*, 255; Edgar Clark to his wife, June 12, 1864, "Edgar Clark Letters," *http://www.izzy.net/~jclark/edgar/ejmain.htm*.

49. Edgar Clark to his wife, June 12, 1864.

50. Gaff, *On Many a Bloody Field*, 342; Brainerd, *Bridge-Building in Wartime*, 207.

51. Brainerd, *Bridge-Building in Wartime*, 207; Brewster to his mother, May 15, 1864, *When This Cruel War Is Over*, 297. For a good discussion of adrenaline and its relationship to Civil War combat, see James M. McPherson, *For Cause and Comrades: Why Men Fought in the Civil War* (New York: Oxford University Press, 1997), 39–42.

52. Albert E. Cowdrey, *Fighting for Life: American Military Medicine in World War II* (New York: Free Press, 1994), 140; Fitzpatrick to Amanda, May 26, 1864, *Red Dirt and Isinglass*, 491.

53. Brewster to his mother, June 2, 1864, *When This Cruel War Is Over*, 313.

54. Charles J. Mills to his mother, May 10, 1864 (addendum dated May 11), Charles J. Mills Letters, Gregory Coco Collection, HCWRTC, USAMHI.

55. George W. Whitman to Mother, May 16, 1864, *Civil War Letters of George Washington Whitman*, ed. Jerome M. Loving (Durham NC: Duke University Press, 1975), 118; Henry Matrau to his mother, May 15, 1864, and Matrau to Cousin Rusha, misdated May 30; probably May 13, *Letters Home: Henry Matrau of the Iron Brigade*, ed. Marcia Reid-Green (Lincoln: University of Nebraska Press, 1993), 76, 78.

56. John Hay, entry for May 9, 1864, *Inside Lincoln's White House: The Complete Civil War Diary of John Hay*, ed. Michael Burlingame and John R. Turner Ettlinger

(Carbondale: Southern Illinois University Press, 1997), 195; entry for May 13, 1864, *Diary of Gideon Welles*, 2:30.

57. J. Cutler Andrews, *The North Reports the Civil War* (Pittsburgh: University of Pittsburgh Press, 1955), 526.

58. *OR*, series 3, vol. 4, 278.

59. *OR* 37, pt. 1, 427.

60. Charles J. Martin to his mother, May 17, 1864, Charles J. Martin Letters, Gregory Coco Collection, HCWRTC, USAMHI; Holt to his wife, May 17, 1864, *Letters of Civil War Surgeon*, 190; entry for May 17, 1864, *Diary of Gideon Welles*, 2:33.

61. Chase to Alfred P. Stone, May 23, 1864, *The Salmon P. Chase Papers*, 5 vols., ed. John Niven (Kent OH: Kent State University Press, 1993), 4:386.

62. Entry for May 17, 1864, *The Diary of George Templeton Strong*, 4 vols., ed. Allan Nevins and Milton Halsey Thomas (New York: Macmillan, 1952), 3:447.

63. Gold prices are taken from closing figures reported in the *New York Times*.

64. *OR*, series 3, vol. 4, 386–87.

65. Allan Nevins, *War for the Union*, 4 vols. (New York: Scribner, 1959–71), 4:68–69.

66. John B. Jones, entries for May 13, 17, 1864, *A Rebel War Clerk's Diary*, 2:208, 213.

67. Lewis Warlick to his wife, May 19, 1864, McGimsey Papers, SHC-UNC–Chapel Hill; Charles M. Blackford to his wife, May 19, 1864, *Letters from Lee's Army*, 246; John Hampden Chamberlayne to Martha Burwill Chamberlayne, May 15, 1864, *Ham Chamberlayne, Virginian: Letters and Papers of an Artillery Officer in the War for Southern Independence, 1861–1865*, ed. C. G. Chamberlayne (Richmond VA: Press of the Dietz Printing Co., 1932), 220; entry for May 25, 1864, *The Journals of Josiah Gorgas, 1857–1878*, ed. Sarah Woolfolk Wiggins (Tuscaloosa: University of Alabama Press, 1995), 111.

68. *Charleston Mercury*, May 18, 1864; *Raleigh* (NC) *Daily Confederate*, May 25, 1864; *Southern Literary Messenger* 38, no. 6 (June 1864): 378.

69. *Richmond Examiner*, May 10, 1864; *North Carolina Semi-Weekly Standard*, May 17, 1864.

70. *Richmond Examiner* editorials, May 20, 25, 1864, *Soldier and Scholar: Basil Lanneau Gildersleeve and the Civil War*, ed. Ward W. Briggs Jr. (Charlottesville: University Press of Virginia, 1998), 314–15, 321.

71. Nevins, *War for the Union*, 4:23.

7. "IT SEEMED LIKE MURDER"

1. *OR* 36, pt. 3, 858.

2. *OR* 36, pt. 3, 858.

3. *OR* 36, pt. 1, 805.

4. Baltz, *Cold Harbor,* 67–69.

5. Baltz, *Cold Harbor,* 65–69; *OR* 36, pt. 3, 822.

6. *OR* 36, pt. 1, 794; *OR* 36, pt. 3, 411.

7. *OR* 36, pt. 3, 405.

8. Freeman, *R. E. Lee,* 3:375; Clifford Dowdey, *Lee's Last Campaign: The Story of Lee and His Men against Grant, 1864* (Boston: Little, Brown, 1960), 284–86; *OR* 36, pt. 1, 1058–59; *OR* 51, pt. 2, 974.

9. Sheridan, *Memoirs,* 1:221; *OR* 36, pt. 3, 469.

10. Confederate strength is drawn from estimates, prepared by Alfred C. Young III, which credit Hoke's division with 6,850 effectives at the end of May. Kershaw's division had 5,180 effectives on May 5. Deducting its losses in the battles from May 5 through May 31 leaves 3,421 effectives available on June 1. Young, "Numbers and Losses," *North and South* 3, no. 3 (March 2000): 17, 19, 26–27. Union strength is estimated from the returns for Sheridan's Cavalry Corps on May 31. See *OR* 36, pt. 3, 426. Noah Andre Trudeau, *Bloody Roads South: The Wilderness to Cold Harbor, May–June 1864* (Boston: Little Brown, 1989), 265, places the Confederate and Union strength slightly higher, at 12,000 and 6,500, respectively. Roy Morris Jr., *Sheridan: The Life and Wars of General Phil Sheridan* (New York: Crown, 1992), 174, estimates that only 3,000 Union cavalry defended Cold Harbor, but this figure seems low.

11. *OR* 36, pt. 3, 469–70.

12. Baltz, *Cold Harbor,* 75.

13. Stiles, *Four Years under Marse Robert,* 274.

14. Baltz, *Cold Harbor,* 71–79.

15. Wright's last division reached the field at 2:10 P.M. *OR* 36, pt. 3, 455.

16. Baltz, *Cold Harbor,* 81–82; William F. Smith, "The Eighteenth Corps at Cold Harbor," in *Battles and Leaders,* 4:222–23.

17. Smith, "The Eighteenth Corps at Cold Harbor," 223.

18. Baltz, *Cold Harbor,* 85–86.

19. *OR* 36, pt. 1, 1000.

20. George T. Stevens, *Three Years in the Sixth Corps* (Albany NY: S. R. Gray, 1866), 349.

21. Baltz, *Cold Harbor,* 85.

22. Baltz, *Cold Harbor,* 89–91; *OR* 36, pt. 1, 671.

23. *OR* 36, pt. 3, 440.

24. *OR* 36, pt. 1, 85.

25. *OR* 36, pt. 3, 455; Grant, *Memoirs,* 2:268; Lyman to his parents, June 1, 1864, *Meade's Headquarters,* 138.

26. *OR* 36, pt. 1, 1001; *OR* 36, pt. 3, 505.

27. Baltz, *Cold Harbor,* 118; *OR* 36, pt. 1, 344.

28. *OR* 36, pt. 3, 482, 478, 479.

29. Taylor, *General Lee*, 247; Early, *Memoirs*, 363; Lee to Seddon, June 2, 1864, *Wartime Papers*, 762; Heth, *Memoirs*, 188–89.

30. Baltz, *Cold Harbor*, 124–29; E. P. Alexander, *Fighting for the Confederacy*, 402, 404.

31. Baltz, *Cold Harbor*, 130–32.

32. W. W. Blackford, *War Years with Jeb Stuart* (1945; rpt., Baton Rouge: Louisiana State University Press, 1993), 257.

33. E. M. Law, "From the Wilderness to Cold Harbor," in *Battles and Leaders*, 4:138–39.

34. Porter, *Campaigning with Grant*, 174–75.

35. Lyman to his parents, June 3, 1864, *Meade's Headquarters*, 143; Wilkeson, *Turned Inside Out*, 128.

36. John D. Billings, *History of the Tenth Massachusetts Battery of Light Artillery in the War of the Rebellion* (Boston: Arakelyon Press, 1909), 261–62.

37. Wilkinson, *Turned Inside Out*, 131.

38. Smith, "The Eighteenth Corps at Cold Harbor," 225.

39. Baltz, *Cold Harbor*, 137–40.

40. Billings, *History of the Tenth Massachusetts Battery*, 200.

41. A. DuBois, "Cold Harbor Salient," *SHSP* 30 (1902): 278.

42. Baltz, *Cold Harbor*, 137–44.

43. Qtd. in Baltz, *Cold Harbor*, 142.

44. Qtd. in Trudeau, *Bloody Roads South*, 286.

45. Asa W. Bartlett, *History of the Twelfth New Hampshire Volunteers in the War of the Rebellion* (Concord NH: Ira C. Evans, 1897), 206; qtd. in Trudeau, *Bloody Roads South*, 287.

46. Lyman to his parents, June 3, 1864, *Meade's Headquarters*, 143.

47. Baltz, *Cold Harbor*, 161–65.

48. *OR* 36, pt. 3, 525, 545, 526.

49. *OR* 36, pt. 3, 530.

50. *OR* 36, pt. 3, 544, 553, 531.

51. *OR* 36, pt. 3, 531.

52. Smith, "The Eighteenth Corps at Cold Harbor," 227; Martin T. McMahon, "Cold Harbor," in *Battles and Leaders*, 4:218.

53. Bartlett, *History of the Twelfth New Hampshire*, 206; McMahon, "Cold Harbor," 218; Swinton, *Campaigns of the Army of the Potomac* (1866; rpt., Secaucus NJ: Blue and Gray Press, 1988), 487.

54. Porter, *Campaigning with Grant*, 177; *OR* 36, pt. 3, 526.

55. *OR* 36, pt. 3, 528–29, 524.

56. Union and Confederate losses for June 3 have long been in dispute, because of the dearth of records on the Confederate side and the fact that Union casualty figures cover the entire period of operations at Cold Harbor (June 1–15). Most authorities estimate that the Army of Northern Virginia suffered 1,500 killed and

wounded on June 3, mostly on Early's front. See, e.g., Baltz, *Cold Harbor*, 207; E. B. Long, *The Civil War Day by Day: An Almanac, 1861–1865* (Garden City NY: Doubleday, 1971), 514. Union losses for the entire fifteen days total 12,738 (*OR* 36, pt. 1, 180). Traditionally it has been said that the assault cost the Army of the Potomac 7,000 casualties in twenty minutes. That is an extreme characterization, but certainly the majority of losses did occur during the first hour of the attack. A. A. Humphreys, *Virginia Campaign,* 191, notes that 4,517 Union wounded were received at the field hospitals on June 3–4. Applying the rule that about four men are wounded for each man killed, he estimates that at least 1,100 Federal soldiers perished in the attack, for a total of 5,617. Given the fact that many wounded remained between the lines for several days and died for lack of treatment, Humphreys's estimate of the Union dead is almost certainly too low. Thomas Livermore, *Numbers and Losses in the Civil War* (1900; rpt., Bloomington: Indiana University Press, 1957), 115n. 3, estimates the total Union loss at not over 7,000. This is as good an estimate as we are likely to get.

57. E. P. Alexander, *Military Memoirs of a Confederate,* 542, accepts a contemporary estimate of 1,500 Confederate casualties on June 3. Humphreys, *Virginia Campaign,* 192, dissents, saying that the actual Confederate loss was "probably much greater." Long, *The Civil War Day by Day,* 514, believes that Confederate losses were "probably under 1,500." Law, "From the Wilderness to Cold Harbor," 141; William C. Oates, *The War between the States and Its Lost Opportunities* (New York: Neale, 1905), 367; D. Augustus Dickert, *History of Kershaw's Brigade* (Newberry SC: E. A. Aull, 1899), 375.

58. John E. Cooke, *Wearing of the Gray* (New York: E. B. Treat, 1867), 406; Walter H. Taylor, *Four Years with General Lee,* 135.

59. John H. Reagan, *Memoirs with Special Reference to Secession and the Civil War* (New York: Neale, 1906), 192–93.

60. *OR* 36, pt. 3, 528–29, 534, 541, 546.

61. Baltz, *Cold Harbor,* 168–78; Bartlett, *History of the Twelfth New Hampshire,* 210. See also Trudeau, *Bloody Roads South,* 296.

62. Baltz, *Cold Harbor,* 183–93; Catton, *Grant Takes Command,* 271–72.

63. Wilkeson, *Turned Inside Out,* 139

8. THE CAMPAIGN'S SIGNIFICANCE

1. *OR* 36, pt. 3, 598–99.

2. Duncan, *Lee's Endangered Left,* 137–302.

3. For the length of the pontoon bridge across the James River estuary, see Maurice Matloff, ed., *American Military History* (Washington: GPO, 1969), 269. See also Brian Holden Reid, "Another Look at Grant's Crossing of the James, 1864," *Civil War History* 39, no. 4 (December 1993): 291–316. The siege of

Petersburg was technically a "quasi-siege," since Union forces never surrounded the town.

4. *OR* 36, pt. 1, 18; James M. McPherson, *Battle Cry of Freedom: The Civil War Era* (New York: Oxford University Press, 1988), 757, 771.

5. The most imaginative argued that Grant's record compared favorably with that of Lee, who had lost 45,000 men from June through October 1862, gained no signal advantage, and supposedly had nearly wrecked the morale of his own army. See the 1896 *Philadelphia Times* article reprinted as "A Parallel for Grant's Action," *SHSP* 24 (1896): 138–45.

6. John C. Ropes, "Grant's Campaign in Virginia in 1864," *PMHSM*, 4:404.

7. E. P. Alexander, *Fighting for the Confederacy*, 346; Jefferson Davis, *The Rise and Fall of the Confederate Government*, 2 vols. (1881; rpt., New York: Thomas Yoseloff, 1958), 2:526.

8. Dowdey, *Lee's Last Campaign*, 354; Bevin Alexander, *How Great Generals Win* (New York: Norton, 1993), 27.

9. Young, "Numbers and Losses," *North and South* 3, no. 3 (March 2000): 15–29.

10. *OR* 33, 904.

11. This passage follows the generally sympathetic treatment of Butler in Robertson, *Back Door to Richmond*, 246–50.

12. For the recommendation of Barnard and Meigs, see *OR* 36, pt. 3, 177–78.

13. John Gibbon, *Personal Recollections of the Civil War* (New York: Putnam, 1928), 239–40; Furgurson, *Not War but Murder*, 237–38.

14. *OR* 36, pt. 2, 695; Porter, *Campaigning with Grant*, 114–15.

15. Charles Francis Adams Jr. to Charles Francis Adams Sr., May 29, 1864, in *A Cycle of Adams Letters, 1861–1865*, 2 vols., ed. Worthington C. Ford (Boston: Houghton Mifflin, 1920), 2:133–34; Meade to his wife, May 19, 1864, *Life and Letters*, 2:197–98.

16. For the basic insight into "control" versus "coping," I am indebted to my colleague, Alan Beyerchen of Ohio State University.

17. Wilson, *Under the Old Flag*, 1:395–97.

18. Baltz, *Cold Harbor*, 97–98; Grant, *Memoirs*, 2:267–68.

19. *OR*, series 3, vol. 5, 293; *OR* 36, pt. 3, 246.

20. *OR* 36, pt. 3, 665; Charles Harvey Brewster to his brother, June 11, 1864, *When This Cruel War Is Over*, 316; Lyman to his parents, May 18, 1864, *Meade's Headquarters*, 102.

21. E. P. Alexander, *Military Memoirs of a Confederate*, 557–58. See also Lee's Farewell Order to his troops at Appomattox, which declared that "the Army of Northern Virginia has been compelled to yield to overwhelming numbers and resources." General Order No. 9, April 10, 1865, *Wartime Papers*, 934.

22. E. A. Pollard, *The Lost Cause* (New York: E. B. Treat, 1867), 510.

23. Qtd. in Eugene D. Genovese, *A Consuming Fire: The Fall of the Confederacy*

in the Mind of the White Christian South (Athens: University of Georgia Press, 1998), 33.

24. Taylor to his wife, May 15, 1864, *Lee's Adjutant,* 160.

25. Gordon, *Reminiscences of the Civil War,* 258.

26. C. S. Venable, "The Campaign from the Wilderness to Petersburg," SHSP 14 (1886): 534.

Further Reading

Although this is the first book-length work to examine the Virginia campaign of May and June 1864 as a unified whole, its component operations have received extensive coverage. Pride of place belongs to the Overland campaign: the duel between Grant and Lee from the Rapidan to the James, which Noah Andre Trudeau evokes in *Bloody Roads South: The Wilderness to Cold Harbor, May–June 1864* (Boston: Little, Brown, 1989). Clifford Dowdey supplies a Confederate perspective in *Lee's Last Campaign: The Story of Lee and His Men against Grant, 1864* (Boston: Little, Brown, 1960). Also useful is William A. Frassanito, *Grant and Lee: The Virginia Campaigns, 1864–1865* (New York: Charles Scribner's Sons, 1983), which briefly narrates the campaign and beyond, while shrewdly analyzing the photographs taken by the cameramen who accompanied the Union army. Old but useful nonetheless is Andrew A. Humphreys, *The Virginia Campaign of '64 and '65* (New York: Charles Scribner's Sons, 1883). Written by Meade's chief of staff, it has the authority of an eyewitness account and the critical detachment of a thorough military professional.

Gordon C. Rhea masterfully narrates the first great encounter of the campaign in *The Battle of the Wilderness, May 5–6, 1864* (Baton Rouge: Louisiana State University Press, 1994), the first of a projected five-volume work that will follow Grant's army to the banks of the James River. Also useful are Robert G. Scott, *Into the Wilderness with the Army of the Potomac* (Bloomington: Indiana University Press, 1985); and Edward Steere, *The Wilderness Campaign* (Harrisburg PA: Stackpole Books, 1960). Gary W. Gallagher, ed., *The Wilderness Campaign* (Chapel Hill: University of North Carolina Press, 1997), is a rewarding study of several specific facets of the battle, some famous, some unexpected.

William D. Matter, *If It Takes All Summer: The Battle of Spotsylvania* (Chapel Hill: University of North Carolina Press, 1988), is the only single-volume study of the operations of May 8–21. But Gordon C. Rhea, *The Battles for Spotsylvania Court House and the Road to Yellow Tavern, May 7–12, 1864* (Baton Rouge: Louisiana State University, 1997), is the most thorough account of the battle up through the fight for the Mule Shoe. Gary W. Gallagher, ed., *The Spotsylvania Campaign* (Chapel Hill: University of North Carolina Press, 1998), effectively reprises the formula of *The Wilderness Campaign* and includes excellent studies of the Bloody Angle and the Yellow Tavern Raid.

For many years the rest of the campaign received notably less treatment, but that is rapidly changing. For operations on the North Anna (as well as the final maneuvers at Spotsylvania), see Gordon C. Rhea, *To the North Anna River: Grant and Lee, May 13–25, 1864* (Baton Rouge: Louisiana State University Press, 2000); and J. Michael Miller's *"Even to Hell Itself": The North Anna Campaign, May 21–26, 1864,* 2d ed. (Lynchburg VA: H. E. Howard, 1989). Modern accounts of Cold Harbor include Ernest B. Furgurson, *Not War but Murder: Cold Harbor, 1864* (New York: Alfred A. Knopf, 2000), and Louis J. Baltz III, *The Battle of Cold Harbor, May 27–June 13, 1864,* 2d ed. (Lynchburg VA: H. E. Howard, 1994).

Although viewed as a separate campaign today, the Union offensive at Bermuda Hundred was an integral part of Grant's strategy for the Virginia campaign. This fact is fully comprehended by William Glenn Robertson in *Back Door to Richmond: The Bermuda Hundred Campaign, April–June 1864* (Baton Rouge: Louisiana State University Press, 1987), an excellent study that is surprisingly kind to Butler and surprisingly critical of Grant. A more traditional view of Butler is in Herbert M. Schiller, *The Bermuda Hundred Campaign* (Dayton OH: Morningside Press, 1988). Edward G. Longacre, *Army of Amateurs: General Benjamin F. Butler and the Army of the James, 1863–1865* (Harrisburg PA: Stackpole Books, 1997), devotes extensive coverage to both the Bermuda Hundred campaign and the XVIII Corps's involvement at Cold Harbor.

Operations in the Shenandoah Valley and southwest Virginia have received their due in Richard R. Duncan, *Lee's Endangered Left: The Civil War in Western Virginia, Spring of 1864* (Baton Rouge: Louisiana State University Press, 1998). Adopting a strategic perspective, Duncan covers the New Market campaign, the raids of Averell and Crook, as well as Hunter's raid up the Valley. For tactical coverage of specific engagements, see William C. Davis's fine book, *The Battle of New Market* (Garden City NY: Doubleday, 1975), and Howard Rollins McManus, *The Battle of Cloyd's Mountain: The Virginia and Tennessee Railroad Raid, April 29–May 19, 1864* (Lynchburg VA: H. E. Howard, 1989).

Biographies of the principal commanders are numerous and, for the most part, good. For the Union side, Brooks D. Simpson's *Ulysses S. Grant: Triumph over Adversity, 1822–1865* (New York: Houghton Mifflin, 2000), is a fine study of the Union general in chief. Also worthwhile is Bruce Catton, *Grant Takes Command* (Boston: Little, Brown, 1969). George G. Meade still awaits a first-class biography, but in the meantime we have Freeman Cleaves's *Meade of Gettysburg* (Norman: University of Oklahoma Press, 1960).

With the exception of Horatio G. Wright, Meade's corps commanders have been the subject of biographies, the best of which include William Marvel, *Burnside* (Chapel Hill: University of North Carolina Press, 1991); David M. Jordan, *Winfield Scott Hancock: A Soldier's Life* (Bloomington: Indiana University Press, 1988); Richard Elliott Winslow, *General John Sedgwick, the Story of a Union Corps Commander* (Novato CA: Presidio Press, 1982); Roy Morris Jr., *Sheridan: The Life and Wars of General Phil Sheridan* (New York: Crown, 1992); and David M. Jordan, *"Happiness Is Not My Companion": The Life of General G. K. Warren* (Bloomington: Indiana University Press, 2001).

Biographies for the Army of Northern Virginia's principal commanders are plentiful. Needless to say, Robert E. Lee has been the subject of numerous life studies, the most useful of which, from a military point of view, remains Douglas Southall Freeman's magnificent *R. E. Lee: A Biography*, 4 vols. (New York: Charles Scribner's Sons, 1934–35). Each of the five corps commanders who served under him during the campaign has received book-length treatment. Joseph Cantey Elliott's *Richard Heron Anderson: Lee's Noble Soldier* (Dayton, OH: Morningside Press, 1985), owing to the dearth of its subject's papers, is necessarily little more than a sketch, but the remaining works are more substantial: Charles C. Osborne, *Jubal: The Life and Times of General Jubal A. Early, CSA, Defender of the Lost Cause* (Baton Rouge: Louisiana State University Press, 1992); Donald C. Pfanz, *Richard S. Ewell: A Soldier's Life* (Chapel Hill: University of North Carolina Press, 1998); James I. Robertson Jr., *General A. P. Hill: The Story of a Confederate Warrior* (New York: Random House, 1987); Jeffry D. Wert, *General James Longstreet: The Confederacy's Most Controversial Soldier* (New York: Simon and Schuster, 1993); and Emory M. Thomas, *Bold Dragoon: The Life of J. E. B. Stuart* (New York: Random House, 1986).

Biographies of key generals in the campaign's subsidiary operations include T. Harry Williams, *P. G. T. Beauregard: Napoleon in Gray* (Baton Rouge: Louisiana State University Press, 1955); Hans L. Trefousse, *Ben Butler: The South Called Him BEAST!* (New York: Twayne, 1957); William C. Davis, *Breckinridge: Statesman, Soldier, Symbol* (Baton Rouge: Louisiana State University Press, 1974); and Stephen D. Engle, *Yankee Dutchman: The Life of Franz Sigel* (Fayetteville: University of Arkansas Press, 1993). William F. Smith merits a place in this company, but unfortunately he has no modern biography.

In a class by themselves are several works that examine senior leaders through the lens of command issues. Douglas Southall Freeman, *Lee's Lieutenants: A Study in Command*, vol. 3, *Gettysburg to Appomattox* (New York: Charles Scribner's Sons, 1944), chronicles the terrible attrition that the Overland campaign inflicted on the Army of Northern Virginia's leadership. Alfred H. Burne, *Lee, Grant, and Sherman: A Study of Leadership in the 1864–1865 Campaign* (1939; rpt., Lawrence: University Press of Kansas, 2000), offers a concise, incisive appraisal of the campaign, placing it in the context of overall Union strategy during the war's final year. J. F. C.

Fuller analyzes the campaign in two works, *Grant and Lee: A Study in Personality and Generalship* (Bloomington: Indiana University Press, 1957), and especially *The Generalship of Ulysses S. Grant* (Bloomington: Indiana University Press, 1958).

First-person accounts of the campaign are numerous and good, but a few stand out as classics. Theodore Lyman's *Meade's Headquarters, 1863–1865* (Boston: Atlantic Monthly Press, 1922), conveniently reprinted as *With Grant and Meade from the Wilderness to Appomattox* (Lincoln NE: University of Nebraska Press, 1994), is often and justly quoted for its unforgettable portraits of Grant, Meade, Hancock, and other Union notables. An outstanding view from a line officer's perspective is provided by Rufus R. Dawes in *Service with the Sixth Wisconsin Volunteers* (Madison: State Historical Society of Wisconsin, 1962), also available as *A Full Blown Yankee of the Iron Brigade* (Lincoln NE: University of Nebraska Press, 1999). For the view from the ranks, see Frank Wilkeson, *Recollections of a Private Soldier in the Army of the Potomac* (New York: G. P. Putnam's Sons, 1887), reprinted as *Turned Inside Out* (Lincoln NE: University of Nebraska Press, 1997).

One valuable Confederate memoir is Gary W. Gallagher, ed., *Fighting for the Confederacy: The Personal Recollections of General Edward Porter Alexander* (Chapel Hill: University of North Carolina Press, 1989), which offers not only a vivid description of the campaign but also clear, fearless judgments by one in a position to know. Robert Stiles, *Four Years under Marse Robert* (1903; rpt., Marietta GA: R. Bemis, 1995), and J. F. J. Caldwell, *The History of a Brigade of South Carolinians, Known First as "Gregg's" and Subsequently as "McGowan's" Brigade* (1866; rpt., Marietta GA: Continental, 1951), are two superior perspectives from the regiment and company level.

Finally, for those interested in the fate of the campaign's casualties, two works stand out. The plight of the wounded is vividly described in Stephen B. Oates's powerful and moving book, *A Woman of Valor: Clara Barton and the Civil War* (New York: Free Press, 1994). The fate of many of the Union soldiers captured in the campaign is unflinchingly told in William Marvel, *Andersonville: The Last Depot* (Chapel Hill: University of North Carolina Press, 1994).

Index

Index

In the Great Campaigns of the Civil War series

Six Armies in Tennessee
The Chickamauga and Chattanooga Campaigns
By Steven E. Woodworth

Fredericksburg and Chancellorsville
The Dare Mark Campaign
By Daniel E. Sutherland

Banners to the Breeze
The Kentucky Campaign, Corinth, and Stones River
By Earl J. Hess

The Chessboard of War
Sherman and Hood in the Autumn Campaigns of 1864
By Anne J. Bailey

Atlanta 1864
Last Chance for the Confederacy
By Richard M. McMurry

Struggle for the Heartland
The Campaigns from Fort Henry to Corinth
By Stephen D. Engle

And Keep Moving On
The Virginia Campaign, May–June 1864
By Mark Grimsley

Vicksburg Is the Key
The Struggle for the Mississippi River
By William L. Shea and Terrence J. Winschel

Now for the Contest
Coastal and Oceanic Naval Operations in the Civil War
By William H. Roberts

Counter-Thrust
From the Peninsula To the Antietam
By Benjamin Franklin Cooling

CPSIA information can be obtained
at www.ICGtesting.com
Printed in the USA
LVHW081352200722
723872LV00004BA/316